Global Environmental Governance
Reconsidered

Global Environmental Governance Reconsidered

edited by Frank Biermann and Philipp Pattberg

The MIT Press
Cambridge, Massachusetts
London, England

MIT Press books may be purchased at special quantity discounts for business or sales promotional use. For information, please email special_sales@mitpress.mit.edu or write to Special Sales Department, The MIT Press, 55 Hayward Street, Cambridge, MA 02142.

This book was set in Sabon by Toppan Best-set Premedia Limited. Printed and bound in the United States of America.

Library of Congress Cataloging-in-Publication Data

Global environmental governance reconsidered / edited by Frank Biermann and Philipp Pattberg.
    p.   cm. — (Earth system governance: a core research project of the international human dimensions programme on global environmental change)
Includes bibliographical references and index.
ISBN 978-0-262-01766-4 (hardcover : alk. paper) — ISBN 978-0-262-51770-6 (pbk. : alk. paper)
1. Environmental policy—International cooperation. 2. Environmental responsibility—International cooperation. 3. Global environmental changes. I. Biermann, Frank, 1967– II. Pattberg, Philipp H., 1975–
GE170.G5548   2012
304.2—dc23

                                                                      2011048964

10   9   8   7   6   5   4   3   2   1

Contents

Series Foreword

Humans now influence all biological and physical systems of the planet. Almost no species, no land area and no part of the oceans has remained unaffected by the expansion of the human species. Recent scientific findings suggest that the entire earth system now operates outside the normal state exhibited over the past 500,000 years. Yet at the same time, it is apparent that the institutions, organizations, and mechanisms by which humans govern their relationship with the natural environment and global biogeochemical systems are utterly insufficient— and poorly understood. More fundamental and applied research is needed.

Yet such research is no easy undertaking. It must span the entire globe because only integrated global solutions can ensure a sustainable coevolution of natural and socioeconomic systems. But it must also draw on local experiences and insights. Research on earth system governance must be about places in all their diversity, yet seek to integrate place-based research within a global understanding of the myriad human interactions with the earth system. Eventually, the task is to develop integrated systems of governance, from the local to the global level, that ensure the sustainable development of the coupled socio-ecological system that the Earth has become.

The series Earth System Governance is designed to address this research challenge. Books in this series will pursue this challenge from a variety of disciplinary perspectives, at different levels of governance, and with a plurality of methods. Yet all will further one common aim: analyzing current systems of earth system governance with a view to increased understanding and possible improvements and reform. Books in this series will be of interest to the academic community but will also inform practitioners and at times contribute to policy debates.

This series is related to the long-term international research effort "Earth System Governance Project," a core project of the International Human Dimensions Programme on Global Environmental Change.

Frank Biermann, *VU University Amsterdam and Lund University*
Oran R. Young, *University of California, Santa Barbara*
Earth System Governance Series Editors

Preface

This book brings together the core findings of a ten-year research program involving more than forty researchers at thirteen leading European research institutions: the Global Governance Project. The program was formally launched in 2001; this book brings together its major theoretical insights and key empirical findings.

When the Global Governance Project was started, the notion of global governance was still rather new. Today, dozens of leading universities have set up research centers on global governance, specialized university chairs have been created, and the notion of global governance is widely in use in academic research and political practice. Yet despite a growing body of literature, even the very meaning of the term remains disputed, and many of its elements are yet insufficiently understood. To contribute to academic and policy debates on global governance has thus been the aim of the Global Governance Project. Although we address the phenomenon of global governance in general, most of our research has focused on global environmental change and governance for sustainable development. Consequently, throughout its duration the Global Governance Project operated with the endorsement of the core project "Institutional Dimensions of Global Environmental Change" of the UN-affiliated International Human Dimensions Programme on Global Environmental Change (IHDP).

The science agenda of the Global Governance Project was built on an understanding of global governance that juxtaposed it with traditional notions of intergovernmental relations. The project conceptualized global governance as a new phenomenon of world politics characterized by three major trends. These trends were chosen to shape the research agenda of the project and to organize scholarly analysis in three research clusters. First, the project conceptualized global governance as characterized by increasing participation of actors other than states, ranging from multinational corporations and (networks of) scientists to intergovernmental bureaucracies. These new actors of global governance have been the focus of the research group MANUS (Managers of Global Change). Second, the project defined global governance through new mechanisms of public-private and private-private cooperation along with the traditional system of legal treaties negotiated by states. This has been the focus of the research group MECGLO (New Mechanisms of Global Governance). Third, the project conceptualized global governance as increasing segmentation of different layers and clusters of rule making and rule implementing, vertically among supranational, international, national, and subnational layers of authority and horizontally between different parallel rule-making systems maintained by different groups of actors. This fragmentation stood at the center of the research group MOSAIC (Multiple Options, Solutions, and Approaches: Institutional Interplay and Conflict).

To increase academic debate on global (environmental) governance, the Global Governance Project initiated an international conference series on the human dimensions of global environmental change in Berlin in 2001, which has evolved into a regular venue in this field, with the tenth event held in October 2010. More than two thousand scientists have participated in this international conference series since its inception, with broadly equal numbers of colleagues from the Americas, Europe, and Asia. Important conceptual developments have been triggered and supported at the conferences, for example, on the relationship of global environmental change and the nation state (2001 Berlin Conference), on the role of knowledge and scientific information in global environmental governance (2002 Berlin Conference), on the influence of international environmental organizations (2005 Berlin Conference), or on the role of equity and social issues in global environmental governance (2010 Berlin Conference).

The Global Governance Project has been the largest and longest-standing research network in this field in Europe. It involved core members of thirteen research institutions: the Institute for Environmental Studies of the VU University Amsterdam, the Netherlands; the Environmental Policy Research Centre of the Freie Universität Berlin, Germany; Sciences Po Bordeaux, France; Bremen University, Germany; the Institute for European Studies at the Vrije Universiteit Brussel, Belgium; The Fridtjof Nansen Institute, Norway; the German Development Institute, Germany; the Graduate Institute of International and Development Studies, Switzerland; the London School of Economics and Political

Science, United Kingdom; Lund University, Sweden; Oldenburg University, Germany; the Potsdam Institute for Climate Impact Research, Germany; and the Environmental Policy Group at Wageningen University, the Netherlands.

The project was directed by Frank Biermann, who initiated it in 2001 at the Potsdam Institute for Climate Impact Research and continued to lead the network from the Institute for Environmental Studies at the VU University Amsterdam, which he joined in 2003. The deputy director was first Bernd Siebenhüner at the University of Oldenburg, and since 2006 Philipp Pattberg at the VU University Amsterdam. About forty researchers have contributed to the program during its decade of existence. The lead faculty members included Steinar Andresen, Fridtjof Nansen Institute; Karin Bäckstrand, Lund University; Steffen Bauer, German Development Institute; Daniel Compagnon, Sciences Po Bordeaux; Klaus Dingwerth, University of Bremen; Robert Falkner, London School of Economics and Political Science; Aarti Gupta, Wageningen University; Joyeeta Gupta, VU University Amsterdam; Klaus Jacob, Freie Universität Berlin; Andreas Nölke, Goethe University Frankfurt am Main; Sebastian Oberthür, Vrije Universiteit Brussel; and Bernd Siebenhüner, Oldenburg University.

In addition, many researchers were involved in the project as research fellows at a postdoctoral or predoctoral level: Nathalie Berny, Sciences Po Bordeaux; Katja Biedenkopf, Vrije Universiteit Brussel; Ingrid Boas, University of Kent; Mairon Bastos Lima, VU University Amsterdam; Per-Olof Busch, Universität Potsdam; Sander Chan, VU University Amsterdam; Eleni Dellas, VU University Amsterdam; Thijs Etty, VU University Amsterdam; Nicolien van der Grijp, VU University Amsterdam; Lars Gulbrandsen, Fridtjof Nansen Institute; Constanze Haug, VU University Amsterdam; Harald Heubaum, University College London; Agni Kalfagianni, VU University Amsterdam; Jonas Meckling, Harvard University; Ayşem Mert, VU University Amsterdam; Amandine Orsini (née Bled), Université Libre de Bruxelles; Justyna Pozarowska, Vrije Universiteit Brussel; Claire Roche Kelly, Vrije Universiteit Brussel; Kirsten Selbmann, Potsdam Institute for Climate Impact Research; Mireia Tarradell, Freie Universität Berlin; Kyla Tienhaara, Australian National University; Harro van Asselt, University of Oxford; Fariborz Zelli, German Development Institute; and Ruben Zondervan, Lund University and International Project Office, Earth System Governance Project. Many more colleagues have been affiliated with the project in its initial years, including Sliman Abu Amara, Lilibeth Acosta-Michlik, Lydia Andler, Steffen Behrle, Rainer

Brohm, Sabine Campe, Ulrike Ehling, Sofia Frantzi, Kenneth Bergsli Hansen, Robert Marschinski, Anna Schreyögg, Kunihiko Shimada, Hans-Dieter Sohn, David Wabnitz, and Carolin Zerger.

In addition to its forty core members, many others have contributed to the success of the Global Governance Project. Important contributions from many colleagues outside the core network include notably Michele M. Betsill, Colorado State University; Harriet Bulkeley, University of Durham; Veronika Chobotová, Slovak Academy of Sciences; Carsten Helm, University of Oldenburg; Matthew J. Hoffmann, University of Toronto; Norichika Kanie, Tokyo Institute of Technology; Tatiana Kluvánková-Oravská, Slovak Academy of Sciences; Ronald B. Mitchell, University of Oregon; and Stacy D. VanDeveer, University of New Hampshire. We owe particular gratitude to Oran R. Young, who has been a close supporter of the project throughout its duration, not the least as chair of the core project "Institutional Dimensions of Global Environmental Change," and since 2006, as chair of the International Human Dimensions Programme on Global Environmental Change. Dozens of researchers have also participated in numerous workshops organized by the project, and many have contributed important insights in their presentations in the Global Governance Speakers Series. We are grateful to all these colleagues for their vital input.

For all its duration, the project has relied on a variety of public funding institutions, which generously supported the research of its members. Listing all funding institutions in the past ten years for all researchers is hardly possible. Especially important in the start-up phase has been a major grant by the Volkswagen Foundation, Germany. Many researchers, especially PhD researchers, have been supported by numerous dissertation grants, ranging from the king of Spain to national talented student programs in Germany, France, or the Netherlands. In the last years, several meetings—including for the compilation of this book—were financed by the European COST Action IS0802 "The Transformation of Global Environmental Governance: Risks and Opportunities." The Secretariat of the Global Governance Project has been hosted and financially supported by the Potsdam Institute for Climate Impact Research (2001–2003) and by the Institute for Environmental Studies of the VU University Amsterdam (2003–2011). We owe our gratitude to all public funding agencies that have made this ten-year program possible.

This book has benefited substantially from numerous comments, suggestions, and pieces of advice. In particular, we are grateful to the three reviewers who helped improve the manuscript by highly useful, constructive comments. Clay Morgan of MIT Press was as always very helpful and supportive in shepherding the manuscript through the submission and production phase and providing instant valuable feedback. We are also grateful to copy editor Susan Geraghty and senior manuscript editor Sandra Minkkinen for copyediting this multiauthored volume that was written almost exclusively by nonnative speakers. Special thanks go to management and editorial assistant Tineke Reus at the VU University Amsterdam, who invested endless days to put this manuscript together and bring all references into shape. The glossary has been compiled by our research assistants Svenja Fox and Andrea Brock, and the index by Kathrin Ludwig.

The Global Governance Project has not only been an academic endeavor. It has also been a lot of fun. We can all recall its many great moments: exquisite wine tasting in the south of France, dancing parties that ended when the day began, live recitations of the *Blues Brothers* movie, gorgeous palaces in the Swedish countryside, late-night strategic visioning in the Zapfhahn at Berlin Zoo, boating in Amsterdam's canals, writing retreats in remote forest inns that somebody thought was "central for all of us," Saarlandish schwenkbraten on warm summer evenings, rustic cellar restaurants near the Rhine, as well as many weddings and numerous lovely children who keep us from work by making us laugh and play.

Although the Global Governance Project, in its current form, is coming to an end with this book, its research agenda focusing on new actors in global environmental governance, the relevance of private and public-private mechanisms, and the causes and consequences of horizontal and vertical fragmentation remains important. Most researchers involved in the ten-year Global Governance Project have thus joined a new global research network in this field, the Earth System Governance Project, launched in 2009. This initiative is a new ten-year core project of the IHDP, and as such, it follows the former core project Institutional Dimensions of Global Environmental Change, which ended in 2007. The science and implementation plan of the Earth System Governance Project further develops several elements that have also been at the core of the Global Governance Project. The quest for understanding new actors in global governance is vital for the analytical problem of "agency in earth system governance" advanced by the Earth System Governance Project. The study of horizontal and vertical fragmentation and integration in global governance has become a major research question in the Earth System Governance Project under its notion of "architectures of earth system governance." And the role and relevance of new types of transnational governance are part and parcel of the study of agency and architecture in earth system governance. Other analytical problems advanced by the Earth System Governance Project have been pioneered by researchers of the Global Governance Project, for example, the conceptualization of democracy and legitimacy beyond the nation state.

Therefore, we are confident that the vibrant, dynamic, and ambitious research community that has been at the core of the Global Governance Project since 2001 will continue to collaborate in the future. Earth system transformation and global environmental change have become vital challenges for our generation, in scholarly and political senses. Governance mechanisms to deal with these challenges clearly lack effectiveness and often legitimacy, and the research challenge of understanding the governance of socioecological systems at local and global levels remains urgent. In this book, we thus look back to distill key insights from work done so far and look forward by outlining the most important research challenges for the future.

Frank Biermann and Philipp Pattberg
Amsterdam, August 2011

Acronyms

CBD	Convention on Biological Diversity
CDM	Clean Development Mechanism
CFC(s)	chlorofluorocarbon(s)
CSD	Commission on Sustainable Development
CTE	Committee on Trade and Environment of the World Trade Organization
EU	European Union
FSC	Forest Stewardship Council
GMO(s)	Genetically modified organism(s)
GRI	Global Reporting Initiative
HCFC(s)	Hydrochlorofluorocarbon(s)
HFC(s)	Hydrofluorocarbon(s)
IPCC	Intergovernmental Panel on Climate Change
ISO	International Organization for Standardization
IWC	International Whaling Commission
NAFTA	North American Free Trade Agreement
NEG-ECP	New England Governors and Eastern Canadian Premiers
NGO	nongovernmental organization
OECD	Organisation for Economic Co-operation and Development
PCB(s)	polychlorinated biphenyl(s)
REDD	Reduced emissions from deforestation and degradation
RGGI	Regional Greenhouse Gas Initiative
SPS	Sanitary and Phytosanitary Measures
UN	United Nations

UNCED	United Nations Conference on Environment and Development
UNCTAD	United Nations Conference on Trade and Development
UNEP	United Nations Environment Programme
UNESCO	United Nations Educational, Scientific, and Cultural Organization
WWF	World Wide Fund for Nature
WTO	World Trade Organization

1

Global Environmental Governance Revisited

Frank Biermann and Philipp Pattberg

Global governance has become a key term in academic and policy debates since the late 1990s. Whereas an Internet search in 1997 produced merely 3,418 references to *global governance,* and in January 2004 the same search turned up fewer than ninety thousand sources, in late 2010, more than twelve million websites mentioned the term. Global governance has become a rallying call for policy advocates who hail it as panacea for the evils of economic and ecological globalization, a global menace for opponents who fear it as the universal hegemony of the powerful few over the disenfranchised masses, and an analytical concept for new empirical phenomena of world politics that has given rise to much discussion among scholars. Yet despite a growing body of new literature, even the very meaning of the term *global governance* remains disputed, and many of its elements are as yet insufficiently understood.

This book contributes to resolving this research challenge. It provides in-depth conceptual and empirical analysis of three core elements of global governance that shows how it is different from traditional intergovernmental relations. First, this book describes and analyzes the emergence of new and often powerful actors beyond central governments that create an essentially new political context with new actor constellations and power relations. Second, this book studies the emergence of new mechanisms of transnational rule setting and rule implementation that go beyond the traditional realm of intergovernmental cooperation, including transnational regimes, public-private partnerships, and market-based arrangements. Third, this book scrutinizes new types of horizontal and vertical fragmentation and interlinkages in world politics that require a new understanding. This book argues that these three trends underscore the usefulness of the global governance concept as opposed to traditional interstate perspectives on world politics.

In analyzing these three trends in detail, the book focuses empirically on an area of global governance that we see as a prime illustration of these developments since the 1980s: global environmental governance. Here, actors beyond central governments have taken center stage in many policy processes. New types of transnational governance have become important components of the political process. Often, these novel arrangements are even heralded as highly effective alternatives to traditional intergovernmental cooperation, which some see as too slow and cumbersome to resolve complex problems of global environmental change. In addition, increasing fragmentation and interlinkages are core characteristics of global environmental governance, and many important studies on fragmented governance systems have used environmental politics as an empirical research area. Whether it is the influence of nongovernmental organizations on environmental policy making, the role of expert networks, or the increased relevance of transnational environmental institutions, global environmental governance generally serves as an overarching conceptual orientation. Yet what global environmental governance eventually means, and what the key elements of this recent concept are, often remains ill defined. This book thus revisits the discourse on global environmental governance. Our aim is conceptual advancement, explanatory progress, and policy reform.

The book results from a long-term research program that brought together more than forty scholars of thirteen leading European research institutions in close collaboration with colleagues in North America and other parts of the world. This research program—known as the Global Governance Project—began in 2001 and focused its science plan on the three core developments that we sketched previously and that we further elaborate in this chapter: the wide array of new actors, new mechanisms, and new types of fragmentation and interlinkages in global environmental governance. In this book, we present the synthesis of this multiyear international research program. All ten analytical chapters were written by core participants of the project, who collaborated over more than two years to bring together their findings from numerous long-term research efforts conducted under the overall umbrella of the Global Governance Project.[1]

This introductory chapter reports our theoretical and conceptual groundwork that also serves as the organizational structure for this book. We first situate the research program among different usages of the term *global governance*. We then highlight the three key characteristics of global environmental governance that make it different, in our view, from traditional international environmental politics. The three characteristics have also informed the core structure of this book in its three parts. Chapter 12 (Biermann and Pattberg) concludes this synthesis and presents an outlook of what we see as future study needs and core questions that may guide renewed research efforts in this field.

What Is Global Environmental Governance?

A research program on global environmental governance first requires a common understanding of this evolving concept. This section provides a conceptual outline of how global governance is understood in this book.

The notion of *governance* originated in national debates where it often describes new forms of regulation that differ from traditional hierarchical state activity (van Kersbergen and van Waarden 2004; Jordan 2008). At the national level, the governance concept generally implies some degree of self-regulation by societal actors, private-public cooperation in solving societal problems, and new forms of multilevel policy. Also in development studies, the governance concept has gained relevance throughout the 1990s, frequently with the contested qualifier "good governance" (de Alcántara 1998).

The notion of *global governance* is more recent. It builds on earlier debates among political scientists working on domestic issues and tries to capture similar developments at the international level. Clear definitions of global governance, however, have not yet been agreed on. Global governance means different things to different authors (Biermann 2006; Dingwerth and Pattberg 2006; Young 1997, 1999). Whereas earlier debates in the 1990s focused on global governance as a new framework for multilateralism and interstate cooperation (Young 1994, 1997, 1999), later debates in the early 2000s highlighted the transformative developments under way in contemporary world politics (Overbeek et al. 2010). It is the latter notion of global governance that informs our project and this book.

We differentiate between two broad usages of the term *global governance*. First the concept is used analytically as a description of current sociopolitical transformations. Second, the concept is used normatively as a description of a political program that copes with challenges of globalization.

In its analytical usage, the notion of global governance highlights distinct qualities of current world politics, such as nonhierarchical steering modes and the inclusion of private actors, both for-profit and nonprofit. Within this body of literature, studies generally differ according to the breadth of their definitional scope. Some writers restrict the global governance concept to problems of foreign policy and include more traditional forms of world politics. Oran R. Young, for example, sees global governance as "the combined efforts of international and transnational regimes" (Young 1999, 11). Lawrence Finkelstein defines the concept as "governing, without sovereign authority, relationships that transcend national frontiers" (Finkelstein 1995, 369). One challenge with these more restricted phenomenological understandings of global governance is the need to distinguish the novel concept from traditional notions of international relations.

Other writers address this problem by broadening the term to encompass an increasing number of social and political interactions. James Rosenau, for example, contends that "the sum of the world's formal and informal rules systems at all levels of community amount to what can properly be called global governance" (Rosenau 2002, 4). Such all-encompassing definitions, however, hardly leave room for anything that is not global governance. Given increasing international interdependence, few political rules will have no repercussions beyond the nation state. In this broad usage, the concept thus threatens to become synonymous with politics and therefore rather useless.

The normative understanding of global governance starts from a perceived inadequacy of political responses to globalization. From this perspective, global governance is first and foremost a political program to regain the necessary steering capacity for problem solving in the postmodern age. Writers who espouse this line call for the construction of new global governance architectures as a counterweight to the negative consequences of economic and ecological globalization. They often develop and promote new institutions, such as multilateral treaties and conventions, new and more effective international organizations, and new forms of financial mechanisms to account for the dependence of current international regimes on the goodwill of national governments. The United Nations (UN) Commission on Global Governance (Commission on Global Governance 1995), for example, elaborated on a plethora of reform proposals to deal with problems of globalization. Global governance is seen here as a solution, a tool that politicians need to develop and employ to solve the problems that globalization has brought about.

This use of the term is popular in continental Europe. A commission of inquiry of the German parliament, for example, defined global governance as the problem-adequate re-organization of the international institutional environment (Deutscher Bundestag 2002). French analyst Marie-Claude Smouts (Smouts 1998, 88) argued that global governance is not an "analytical reflection on the present international system [but a] standard-setting reflection for building a better world." Yet this understanding of global governance as a political program is not restricted to European discourses. Also some US academics, such as Leon Gordenker and Thomas G. Weiss (1996, 17), see global governance as "efforts to bring more orderly and reliable responses to social and political issues that go beyond capacities of states to address individually."

Some writers have adopted the programmatic definition of global governance, yet without its affirmative connotation. For example, some neoconservative writers see global governance as the attempt of the United Nations and other international organizations to limit the freedom of action of powerful states, in particular, the United States. Writers in the tradition of critical theory and neomarxism view global governance as a project of ruling elites to deal more effectively with economic and political crises that result from neoliberal socioeconomic transformations (Brand 2003, 10; Overbeek et al. 2010). Others again view global governance through the lens of North-South power conflicts. The Geneva-based South Centre, for example, cautioned in 1996 that in "an international community ridden with inequalities and injustice, institutionalizing 'global governance' without paying careful attention to the question of who wields power, and without adequate safeguards, is tantamount to sanctioning governance of the many weak by the powerful few" (South Centre 1996, 32).

There is no clear solution to this conceptual diversity. Yet the current coexistence of analytical and programmatic uses of the term is not a problem per se as long as authors retain clarity as to what definition they employ.

In this book, both broad usages are combined. Our main goal has been analytical: the identification and analysis of the three trends in current world politics that make the new system of global (environmental) governance different from earlier forms of intergovernmental cooperation. These trends are used to organize this book in its three parts and ten analytical chapters: first, the emergence of new types of agency and of actors beyond national governments, the traditional core actors in international environmental politics; second, the emergence of new mechanisms and institutions of global environmental governance that go beyond traditional forms of state-led, treaty-based regimes; and third, the increasing fragmentation and emerging interlinkages of the overall governance system across levels and functional spheres.

Yet despite its essentially analytical perspective and understanding of the concept of global governance, our project has also contributed to crucial policy debates and initiated, analyzed, and at times criticized reform proposals that intend to improve global governance especially in the area of global environmental change. This, too, is reflected in the analytical chapters of this book, many of which provide a synopsis of policy reform proposals that have been studied in, and advanced by, the project.

We now turn to elaborating in more detail the three core trends that stand at the center of this book.

The New Actors

First, this book maintains that the concept of global environmental governance describes world politics that are no longer confined to nation states but are characterized by increasing participation of actors that have so far been largely active at the subnational level. This transnational multiactor governance includes private actors such as networks of experts, environmentalists, and multinational corporations, and also new agencies set up by governments, including intergovernmental bureaucracies. The novelty is not simply the increase in numbers but also the ability of nonstate actors to take part in steering the political system. In our reading, agency—understood as the power of individual and collective actors to change the course of events or the outcome of processes—is increasingly located in sites beyond the central governments of nation states (Biermann, Betsill, et al. 2009; Pattberg, Betsill, and Dellas 2011). Many vital institutions of global environmental governance are today inclusive of, or even driven by, a wide array of nonstate actors. Nongovernmental organizations have joined governments to put international norms into practice, for example, as quasi-implementing agencies for development assistance programs administered by the World Bank or bilateral agencies. Private actors, both for-profit and nonprofit, also participate in global institutions to address environmental problems without being forced, persuaded, or funded by states and other public agencies, for example, in the area of forest and fisheries governance. This "agency beyond the state" sets global environmental governance apart from more traditional international environmental politics.

There are three elements to this new development. First, the number of actors and the degree of their participation in global environmental governance has increased substantially since the 1980s. Second, the variety of types of organizations has increased, too. Next to governments, intergovernmental bureaucracies, nongovernmental organizations, and business actors, novel forms of organizations have emerged, such as private rule-making organizations in issue areas ranging from forest management to biodiversity conservation. Third, established organizations have adapted new roles and responsibilities. For example, intergovernmental bureaucracies have become more autonomous from their principals, that is, the governments that created them (Bauer, Andresen, and Biermann, this book, chapter 2). Also nongovernmental organizations have taken a different role by more often directly engaging in agenda setting, policy formulation, and the establishment of rules and regulations (Pattberg, this book, chapter 5).

Of all nonstate actors that at present influence global environmental governance, environmentalist advocacy groups have been analyzed early and extensively (e.g., Conca 1995; Raustiala 1997; Wapner 1996). This research has shown that activist groups provide research and policy advice, monitor the commitments of states, inform governments and the public about the actions of their own diplomats and those of negotiation partners, and give diplomats at international meetings direct feedback (Keck and Sikkink 1998; Betsill and Corell 2001). Carefully orchestrated campaigns of environmentalists have proved to be able to change the foreign policy of powerful nation states—as shown in the campaign against the dumping of the Brent Spar oil rig. The influence of such nonstate lobbying groups has been acknowledged since the early 1990s; it has therefore been studied less in the Global Governance Project. Other types of actors that have been widely studied but not elaborated in this book are transnational coalitions of cities (see Bulkeley and Betsill 2003).

Instead, we focus on three other types of actors beyond central governments and the nation state: international bureaucracies, transnational business actors, and transnational science networks. These three types of actors are analyzed in detail in part I of this book.

First, Bauer, Andresen, and Biermann (this book, chapter 2) analyze the increasing influence of intergovernmental bureaucracies in global environmental governance. Regarding environmental policy, many international organizations today address environmental concerns in their activities and have specialized bureaucratic units in this field. In addition, more than two hundred international bureaucracies have been set up in the form of secretariats to the many international treaties concluded since the 1990s (for nonenvironmental fields, see for example, Barnett and

Finnemore 2004). A series of studies conducted by the Global Governance Project has highlighted the autonomous role of many of these international bureaucracies in creating and disseminating knowledge, framing the definition of problems and adequate solutions, influencing negotiations through ideas and expertise, and implementing solutions on the ground (Biermann and Siebenhüner 2009a). Cases extensively studied within the project include the environmental department of the International Bank for Reconstruction and Development (Marschinski and Behrle 2009), the environmental department within the secretariat of the International Maritime Organization (Campe 2009), the environment directorate of the Organisation for Economic Co-operation and Development (Busch 2009b), the secretariat of the United Nations Environment Programme (Andresen and Rosendal 2009; Bauer 2009c), and the secretariat of the Global Environment Facility (Andler 2009). We have also looked in detail at a number of treaty secretariats, including the secretariat of the Convention on Biological Diversity (Siebenhüner 2009), the secretariat of the 1985 Vienna Convention for the Protection of the Ozone Layer and its 1987 Montreal Protocol (Bauer 2009b), the secretariat of the United Nations Convention to Combat Desertification in Countries Experiencing Serious Drought and/or Desertification, Particularly in Africa (Bauer 2009a), and the secretariat of the United Nations Framework Convention on Climate Change (Busch 2009a). All of these studies have shown in detail the different degrees of the influence of international bureaucracies on the structures and processes of global environmental governance. One overarching finding is that the overall problem structure and internal factors of organizations such as leadership and staff composition can explain much variation in the influence of international bureaucracies (Andresen 2007; Andresen and Rosendal 2009; Biermann and Siebenhüner 2009b).

Second, as Tienhaara, Orsini, and Falkner (this book, chapter 3) analyze, transnational corporations have taken a more prominent role in international environmental decision making. Again, the influence of major companies on international affairs is not new, and in some social theories, such as Marxism, business actors have center stage. This "old" pressure by the corporate sector, however, was mainly indirect through its influence on national governments. Today, many corporations take a more visible, direct role in international negotiations as immediate partners of governments, for example, in the framework of the United Nations and of the Global Compact that major corporations have concluded with the world organization (Cutler, Haufler, and Porter 1999;

Higgot, Underhill, and Bieler 1999; Hall and Biersteker 2002). Recent research, including by members of the Global Governance Project, has thus scrutinized the power of business in global environmental governance and provided a nuanced assessment of corporate influence (Bled 2008, 2009; Clapp 2005, 2007; Falkner 2005, 2008; Levy and Newell 2005; Tienhaara 2009).

Transnational networks of scientists represent a third type of nonstate actor that has been extensively analyzed in our program. As Gupta et al. (this book, chapter 4) show, networks of scientists have assumed a new role in providing complex technical information that is indispensable for policy making on issues marked by analytic and normative uncertainty. Although the role of experts in world politics is evident in many policy areas, it is particularly prevalent in the field of global environmental policy. International networks of scientists and experts have emerged in a mix of self-organization and state sponsorship to provide scientific information on the kind of environmental problem at stake and the options available for decision makers to cope with it. Such scientific advice for political decision making is not new in world politics; negotiations on fishing quotas, for example, have long been assisted by the International Council for the Exploration of the Sea. These early examples, however, have significantly increased in number and impact, which is mirrored in the substantial academic interest in global scientific networks (e.g., Haas 1990, 2000; Mitchell et al. 2006). Gupta et al. (this book, chapter 4) report on the approaches and findings of our project in the area of transnational networks of scientists.

The New Mechanisms

The increased participation of nonstate actors has given rise to new forms of cooperation in addition to the traditional system of legally binding agreements negotiated by states. This is the main theme of the second part of this book.

In recent years, a growing number and variety of nonstate actors have become part of norm-setting and norm-implementing mechanisms in global governance, which denotes a shift from intergovernmental regimes to public-private ones and increases in private-private cooperation and policy making (Cutler, Haufler, and Porter 1999; Pattberg 2005). Private actors have become partners of governments in the implementation of international standards, for example, as quasi-implementing agencies for many programs of development assistance administered through the

World Bank or bilateral agencies. At times, private actors negotiate their own global standards, such as in the Forest Stewardship Council or the Marine Stewardship Council, two standard-setting bodies created by major corporations and environmental advocacy groups without direct involvement of governments (Gulbrandsen 2009; Pattberg 2006). Public-private cooperation has received even more impetus with the 2002 Johannesburg World Summit on Sustainable Development and its focus on partnerships of governments, nongovernmental organizations, and the private sector—the so-called Partnerships for Sustainable Development (Bäckstrand et al., this book, chapter 6). More than 330 such partnerships have been registered with the United Nations around or after the Johannesburg Summit (Glasbergen, Biermann, and Mol 2007).

A number of conceptual terms have been suggested to analyze these new institutions in global environmental governance. Whereas the term *transnational environmental regime* (Pattberg, this book, chapter 5) stresses the similarity to intergovernmental environmental regimes (with the difference that the norms, rules, and decision-making procedures derive largely from cooperation between nonstate actors), the terms *public-private partnership* (Bäckstrand et al., this book, chapter 6) and *global public policy network* (Reinicke 1998) are used to describe a more flexible and less institutionalized actor constellation. Despite these conceptual differences, the central analytical questions are similar.

The recent literature on the new mechanisms of global environmental governance—within and outside the Global Governance Project—has focused on several overarching research questions.

One line of research has studied the emergence of these novel institutional arrangements. Different theoretical approaches and single or comparative case studies offer a range of explanations for the formation of transnational institutions that address global environmental problems (Lober 1997; Cashore 2002; Bartley 2003). The problem seems to be, however, that most theoretical approaches are not specifically tailored to the new governance mechanisms. Empirical studies that address them tend to isolate causal factors or fail to specify their relationship and the causal pathways in institutional formation. One common assumption, for example, is that transnational institutions aiming to regulate business behavior have emerged as a reaction to increased capital flows across borders and declining regulatory capacities of states (Haufler 2003). To this end, the increasing institutionalization of nonstate environmental governance is analyzed predominantly in functionalist terms. Such demand-based explanations, however, become difficult when specifying whose "demand" for transnational regulation is sufficient for establishing new institutions. In addition, many studies fail to account for interactions of larger systemic transformations (i.e., change at the macro level such as discursive and ideological shifts) and the decisive conditions at the organizational level (i.e., change at the micro level such as new organizational capacities and strategies). Alternative explanations for the emergence of novel institutional arrangements have therefore highlighted the interconnectedness of macro and micro conditions (Pattberg 2005), the importance of resource-exchange processes for institution building (Nölke 2006), and the level of organizational fields as the appropriate level of analysis in studying the emergence and institutionalization of novel transnational mechanisms of global environmental governance (Dingwerth and Pattberg 2009).

A second line of research has analyzed the effectiveness and influence of such new mechanisms of global environmental governance. Researchers in this project have studied, for example, the regulatory, cognitive, and integrative functions of transnational environmental regimes in forest politics and corporate environmental management (Pattberg 2007). Other comparative studies suggest that differences in influence can be explained by the types of policies that are applied (e.g., market-based approaches such as forest certification or information-based approaches such as sustainability indicators), the regulatory environment of transnational regimes, and the support of civil society organizations (Dingwerth and Pattberg 2007).

A related line of research has studied whether novel governance mechanisms contribute to closing governance gaps left by the intergovernmental process, such as insufficient regulation, implementation, or participation (Bäckstrand 2006). Members of the Global Governance Project have studied this problem, for example, through a statistical analysis of more than three hundred public-private partnerships for sustainable development. This study revealed that at the aggregate level, partnerships for sustainable development hardly improve problems of participation, implementation, and regulation in global environmental governance, even though at the individual level, some partnerships may well be effective (Biermann et al. 2007; Pattberg et al. 2012).

Third, members of the Global Governance Project have addressed the democratic legitimacy and accountability of transnational environmental regimes and partnerships (Bäckstrand 2006; Chan and Pattberg 2008; Dingwerth 2005, 2007). With traditional intergovernmental policy making being more frequently replaced by novel institutions—which some see as being more efficient and transparent—serious questions of the legitimacy of nonstate standard setting arise. For example, the World Commission on Dams has been hailed as a new and effective mechanism that has quickly generated widely accepted standards, which had earlier been difficult to negotiate due to the persistent resistance of affected countries. Yet this very success of nonstate standard setting also gives rise to critical voices that point to inherent problems of legitimacy in nonstate policy making (Dingwerth 2005).

Part II of this book presents the core research of our project in this field. It is organized around three types of new mechanisms of global (environmental) governance: transnational regimes, transnational public-private partnerships, and transnational governance experiments, in particular market-based arrangements.

First, as Pattberg (this book, chapter 5) shows, many novel mechanisms of global environmental governance can be understood as transnational environmental regimes based on some similarities with intergovernmental systems of norms and rules known as regimes. A key difference is that in transnational regimes, norms, rules, and decision-making procedures derive largely from cooperation among nonstate actors. One finding of our study program is that transnational environmental regimes are important beyond simple measures of standard uptake and compliance. Instead, the mechanisms also influence the behavior of actors through cognitive and normative processes, and they may have a number of unintended side effects, positive and negative, that are often overlooked.

Second, Bäckstrand and colleagues (this book, chapter 6) offer a detailed assessment of transnational public-private partnerships for sustainable development with regard to their problem-solving capacity, their legitimacy and accountability, and their contribution to wider goals such as increased participation of marginalized stakeholders. Bäckstrand and colleagues find that transnational public-private partnerships perform well below frequently voiced expectations of increased efficiency, effectiveness, accountability, and legitimacy. There are, however, also a number of positive effects, such as the improved deliberative quality and inclusiveness of stakeholder participation in the UN "major groups" process, where civil society input is organized according to different interests, such as "youth" or "farmers." Whereas many academic debates around transnational public-private partnerships are polarized between a liberal functionalist and a critical perspective, Bäckstrand and colleagues offer a more balanced assessment of public-private partnerships, highlighting in particular the added value of an interpretive perspective.

Third, as Bulkeley and colleagues (this book, chapter 7) show, a growing array of more or less institutionalized forms of transnational governance is emerging outside private regimes or intergovernmental processes. One prominent feature of many of these initiatives is their foundation in market principles (e.g., of economic efficiency) and the use of market mechanisms (e.g., cap-and-trade schemes) as a means of governing the actions of private and public actors. Chapter 7 examines this growing experimentation with novel forms of transnational governance beyond private regimes and formal public-private partnerships. It focuses in particular on the issue of climate change.

The New Interlinkages and Fragmentations

Finally, this book argues that global environmental governance is characterized by an increasing segmentation of different layers and clusters of rule making and rule implementing, fragmented vertically among supranational, international, national, and subnational layers of authority (multilevel governance) and horizontally among different parallel rule-making systems maintained by different groups of actors (multipolar governance).

First, the increasing global institutionalization of environmental politics does not occur, and is indeed not conceivable, without continuing policy making at national and subnational levels. Global standards need to be implemented and put into practice locally, and global norm setting requires local decision making and implementation. This results in the coexistence of policy making at the subnational, national, regional, and global levels in more and more issue areas, with the potential of conflicts and synergies between different levels of regulatory activity. The international regulation of trade in genetically modified organisms is a prime example of such multilevel governance (Gupta 2000, 2004; Gupta and Falkner 2006).

Likewise, the increasing global institutionalization of environmental politics does not occur in a uniform manner across the international community. In the case of the 1987 Montreal Protocol on Substances that Deplete the Ozone Layer, for example, various amendments have provided for new standards and timetables that are not accepted by all parties from the original agreement in 1987. This leads to a substantial multiplicity of subregimes within the overall normative framework. The most prominent example of such horizontal fragmentation of policies is humankind's response to the global warming problem. Here, we observe the emergence of parallel policy approaches that may develop into divergent regulatory regimes in global climate governance (Biermann, Pattberg, et al. 2009).

Students of global environmental governance have highlighted the significant challenges that divergent policy approaches within such a horizontally and vertically segmented policy arena pose. First, lack of uniform policies may jeopardize the success of the policies adopted by individual groups of countries or at different levels of decision making. Regarding climate policy, for instance, the global emissions trading regime as envisioned by the 1997 Kyoto Protocol may create perverse incentives if the United States is not party to the mechanism. In addition, the possibly strong economic implications of stringent environmental policies adopted by one group of states may have severe ramifications for other policy arenas such as the world trade regime (Biermann and Brohm 2005). Likewise, fragmented governance may complicate positive linkages with other policy areas (Biermann, Pattberg, et al. 2009). It is also conceivable that business actors use regulatory fragmentation to choose among different levels of obligation, thereby starting a race to the bottom within and across industry sectors. An additional challenge is inconsistent decision making under different regimes. Power differentials are also crucial. As Benvenisti and Downs argue, fragmentation functions to maintain and even extend the disproportionate influence of a handful of powerful states—and the domestic interests that shape their foreign policies—on the international regulatory order (Benvenisti and Downs 2007). Powerful states thus have the flexibility to opt for a mechanism that best serves their interests and can create new agreements if the old ones do not fit their needs anymore (Hafner 2004).

However, fragmented governance architectures also may have advantages. Distinct institutions allow for the testing of innovative policy instruments in some nations or at some levels of decision making, with subsequent diffusion to other regions or levels (Vogel 1995; Busch and Jörgens 2005). Regulatory diversity might increase innovation. Fragmentation could enhance innovation at the level of the firm or public agency and increase innovation in the entire system of environmental governance. What is important is the notion of diffusion of innovation, including innovations of policies, technologies, procedures, and ideas.

Many of these issues are studied in detail in part III of this book. First, Zelli, Gupta, and van Asselt (chapter 8) analyze horizontal institutional interlinkages in global environmental governance, which they define as connections among policy processes, rules, norms, and principles of two or more institutions. They study how overarching global norms of environmental governance shape specific sets of institutional interlinkages. They focus on three interlinkages: between the UN climate regime and the World Trade Organization (WTO), between the UN climate regime and the biodiversity convention, and between the Cartagena Protocol on Biosafety under the biodiversity convention and the WTO. They argue that the nature and resolution of potential regime conflicts is explainable by the normative dominance in a global context of liberal environmentalism, even as this global norm remains contested by key actors.

Whereas Zelli, Gupta, and van Asselt focus on horizontal interlinkages, Busch, Gupta, and Falkner (chapter 9) concentrate on vertical interlinkages between international and domestic politics. In particular, they investigate whether multilevel policy linkages result in convergence or divergence of domestic policies across countries. Although their findings draw on a wide variety of in-depth empirical research projects, they illustrate their argument with the example of two policy areas: governance of genetically modified organisms in developing countries and renewable electricity policies in the European Union. They argue that the common dichotomy of whether convergence tends toward more stringent (race to the top) or less stringent (race to the bottom) levels of regulation is too simplistic and does not capture the complexity of international-domestic linkages. Instead, they show that contesting regulatory approaches at the international level can prevent a crossnational convergence of policies toward one or the other regulatory approach, even when strong pressures exist for convergence domestically and when relatively high regulatory convergence has already been achieved.

Kluvánková-Oravská and Chobotová (chapter 10) focus on regional multilevel governance and analyze the factors that influence convergence and divergence of subnational biodiversity policies with existing regional policy frameworks (here with a focus on European regional integration). Kluvánková-Oravská and Chobotová show convincingly how informal, long-standing institutions at the national and subnational levels play a decisive role in explaining policy convergence at the regional level. Chapter 10 consequently concludes that successful coevolution of new political and economic regional institutions with existing institutions for biodiversity protection is the key driving force behind policy convergence in the new European Union (EU) member states.

Interlinkages in and fragmentation of global governance, including the rise of complex systems of multilevel governance, raise fundamental questions relating to the changing role of the state. In terms of political analysis, this raises the point that the remaining agency of the central governments of nation states is likely to be diminishing—all findings of the Global Governance Project indicate this trend—yet that it is still present and undoubtedly important. In legal terms, this raises crucial questions of sovereignty and the emergence of legal systems where states are no longer the only actor. In terms of political theory, it appears vital to understand also the legitimization of new governance processes that lack formal approval and consent through traditional democratic representation. For these reasons, chapter 11 of the book focuses on the state (Compagnon, Chan, and Mert). On the one hand, this chapter considers the position of the three directly preceding chapters on horizontally and vertically fragmented governance. On the other hand, chapter 11 also serves as a reflection on the other chapters of this book. After the emergence of the new, nonstate actors and transnational mechanisms of global governance—in sum, after the rise of global governance as opposed to traditional intergovernmentalism—what role is left for the state when responding to global environmental challenges?

Structure of the Book

The book is organized around the three core trends in global environmental governance: part I studies the emergence of new actors of global governance, with a focus on international bureaucracies (Bauer, Andresen, and Biermann, chapter 2), global corporations (Tienhaara, Orsini, and Falkner, chapter 3), and science networks (Gupta et al., chapter 4). Part II then looks into the new mechanisms of global governance, with particular emphasis on transnational environmental regimes (Pattberg, chapter 5), transnational public-private partnerships (Bäckstrand et al., chapter 6), and transnational governance experiments (Bulkeley et al., chapter 7). Part III then investigates new interlinkages and fragmentation, with a focus on horizontal institutional fragmentation (Zelli, Gupta, and van Asselt, chapter 8), international-domestic linkages and policy convergence (Busch, Gupta, and Falkner, chapter 9), and regional governance arrangements (Kluvánková-Oravská and Chobotová, chapter 10). After that, Compagnon, Chan, and Mert (chapter 11) provide an overarching analysis of the changing role of the state within the overall context of multilevel governance. Chapter 12 (Biermann and Pattberg) concludes the book and outlines our suggestions for a future research agenda.

All chapters follow an identical structure. After a short introduction to the topic of the chapter, all authors first conceptualize the key trend they are analyzing. They then sketch the empirical development in their field of investigation and show in each case the central new developments that make global environmental governance different from traditional state-based cooperation. In most chapters, this section is based on a review of a large number of empirical studies that are, in general, all products of the Global Governance Project and its partner institutions. In some cases, chapter authors also have chosen to provide longer analyses of cases that emphasize and illustrate the novelty of the phenomenon under investigation. After these sections on experiences, all chapters turn to explanations. In this part, authors bring together the core findings in the issue area under investigation. Although these parts are based largely on insights from the Global Governance Project, other research has been reported when appropriate and in particular when it was found to be supportive of or in conflict with the core findings of our project. All ten analytical chapters end with a summary of main findings, a reflection on policy relevance and (when appropriate) reform, and a discussion of future research needs and agendas. Overall, this book offers a comprehensive overview of recent research on current transformations in global environmental governance.

Notes

1. Author workshops were held in Amsterdam (November 2008), Lund (June 2009), and Bonn (October 2009). We acknowledge financial support from the European Cooperation in Science and Technology (COST) Action IS0802, "The Transformation of Global Environmental Governance: Risks and Opportunities."

References

Andler, Lydia. 2009. The Secretariat of the Global Environment Facility: From Network to Bureaucracy. In *Managers of Global Change: The Influence of International Environmental Bureaucracies*, ed. Frank Biermann and Bernd Siebenhüner, 203–223. Cambridge, MA: MIT Press.

Andresen, Steinar. 2007. The Effectiveness of UN Environmental Institutions. *International Environmental Agreement: Politics, Law and Economics* 7:317–336.

Andresen, Steinar, and Kristin Rosendal. 2009. The Role of the United Nations Environment Programme in the Coordination of Multilateral Environmental

Agreements. In *International Organizations in Global Environmental Governance*, ed. Frank Biermann, Bernd Siebenhüner, and Anna Schreyögg, 133–150. London: Routledge.

Bäckstrand, Karin. 2006. Multi-stakeholder Partnerships for Sustainable Development: Rethinking Legitimacy, Accountability, and Effectiveness. *European Environment* 16 (5):290–306.

Barnett, Michael, and Martha Finnemore. 2004. *Rules for the World: International Organizations in Global Politics*. Ithaca, NY: Cornell University Press.

Bartley, Tim. 2003. Certifying Forests and Factories: States, Social Movements, and the Rise of Private Regulation in the Apparel and Forest Products Fields. *Politics & Society* 31:433–464.

Bauer, Steffen. 2009a. The Desertification Secretariat: A Castle Made of Sand. In *Managers of Global Change: The Influence of International Environmental Bureaucracies*, ed. Frank Biermann and Bernd Siebenhüner, 293–317. Cambridge, MA: MIT Press.

Bauer, Steffen. 2009b. The Ozone Secretariat: The Good Shepherd of Ozone Politics. In *Managers of Global Change: The Influence of International Environmental Bureaucracies*, ed. Frank Biermann and Bernd Siebenhüner, 225–244. Cambridge, MA: MIT Press.

Bauer, Steffen. 2009c. The Secretariat of the United Nations Environment Programme: Tangled Up in Blue. In *Managers of Global Change: The Influence of International Environmental Bureaucracies*, ed. Frank Biermann and Bernd Siebenhüner, 169–201. Cambridge, MA: MIT Press.

Benvenisti, Eyal, and George W. Downs. 2007. The Empire's New Clothes: Political Economy and the Fragmentation of International Law. *Stanford Law Review* 60:595–632.

Betsill, Michele M., and Elisabeth Corell. 2001. NGO Influence in International Environmental Negotiations: A Framework for Analysis. *Global Environmental Politics* 1:65–85.

Biermann, Frank. 2006. Global Governance and the Environment. In *International Environmental Politics*, ed. Michele M. Betsill, Kathryn Hochstetler, and Dimitris Stevis, 237–261. Basingstoke, UK: Palgrave Macmillan.

Biermann, Frank, Michele M. Betsill, Joyeeta Gupta, Norichika Kanie, Louis Lebel, Diana Liverman, Heike Schroeder, and Bernd Siebenhüner. with contributions from Ken Conca, Leila da Costa Ferreira, Bharat Desai, Simon Tay, and Ruben Zondervan. 2009. Earth System Governance: People, Places, and the Planet. Science and Implementation Plan of the Earth System Governance Project. *Earth System Governance Project 1, IHDP Report 20*. Bonn: The Earth System Governance Project.

Biermann, Frank, and Rainer Brohm. 2005. Implementing the Kyoto Protocol without the United States: The Strategic Role of Energy Tax Adjustments at the Border. *Climate Policy* 4:289–302.

Biermann, Frank, Sander Chan, Ayşem Mert, and Philipp Pattberg. 2007. Multi-stakeholder Partnerships for Sustainable Development: Does the Promise Hold?

In *Partnerships, Governance, and Sustainable Development: Reflections on Theory and Practice*, ed. Pieter Glasbergen, Frank Biermann, and Arthur P. J. Mol, 239–260. Cheltenham, UK: Edward Elgar.

Biermann, Frank, Philipp Pattberg, Harro van Asselt, and Fariborz Zelli. 2009. The Fragmentation of Global Governance Architectures: A Framework for Analysis. *Global Environmental Politics* 9:14–40.

Biermann, Frank, and Bernd Siebenhüner, eds. 2009a. *Managers of Global Change: The Influence of International Environmental Bureaucracies*. Cambridge, MA: MIT Press.

Biermann, Frank, and Bernd Siebenhüner. 2009b. The Influence of International Bureaucracies in World Politics: Findings from the MANUS Research Program. In *Managers of Global Change: The Influence of International Environmental Bureaucracies*, ed. Frank Biermann and Bernd Siebenhüner, 319–349. Cambridge, MA: MIT Press.

Bled, Amandine. 2008. Getting the Strongest Players Doesn't Make a Winning Team: Business and the Cartagena Protocol on Biosafety. In *Global Environmental Agreements: Insights and Implications*, ed. Asha Joshi, 189–206. Hyderabad, India: The Icfai University Press.

Bled, Amandine. 2009. Business to the Rescue: Private Sector Actors and Global Environmental Regimes' Legitimacy. *International Environmental Agreement: Politics, Law and Economics* 2:153–171.

Brand, Ulrich. 2003. Nach dem Fordismus: Global Governance als der Neue Hegemoniale Diskurs des Internationalen Politikverständnisses. [After Fordism: Global Governance as the New Hegemonic Discourse of the International Understanding of Politics] *Zeitschrift für Internationale Beziehungen* 10:143–165.

Bulkeley, Harriet, and Michele M. Betsill. 2003. *Cities and Climate Change: Urban Sustainability and Global Environmental Governance*. Oxford: Routledge.

Busch, Per-Olof. 2009a. The Climate Secretariat: Making a Living in a Straitjacket. In *Managers of Global Change: The Influence of International Environmental Bureaucracies*, ed. Frank Biermann and Bernd Siebenhüner, 245–264. Cambridge, MA: MIT Press.

Busch, Per-Olof. 2009b. The OECD Environment Directorate: The Art of Persuasion and Its Limitations. In *Managers of Global Change: The Influence of International Environmental Bureaucracies*, ed. Frank Biermann and Bernd Siebenhüner, 75–99. Cambridge, MA: MIT Press.

Busch, Per-Olof, and Helge Jörgens. 2005. International Patterns of Environmental Policy Change and Convergence. *European Environment* 15:80–101.

Campe, Sabine. 2009. The Secretariat of the International Maritime Organization: A Tanker for the Tankers. In *Managers of Global Change: The Influence of International Environmental Bureaucracies*, ed. Frank Biermann and Bernd Siebenhüner, 143–168. Cambridge, MA: MIT Press.

Cashore, Benjamin. 2002. Legitimacy and the Privatization of Environmental Governance: How Non-State Market-Driven (NSMD) Governance Systems Gain Rule-making Authority. *Governance* 15:503–529.

Chan, Sander, and Philipp Pattberg. 2008. Private Rule-Making and the Politics of Accountability: Analyzing Global Forest Governance. *Global Environmental Politics* 8 (3):103–121.

Clapp, Jennifer. 2005. Transnational Corporations and Global Environmental Governance. In *Handbook of Global Environmental Politics*, ed. Peter Dauvergne, 284–297. Cheltenham, UK: Edward Elgar.

Clapp, Jennifer. 2007. Transnational Corporate Interests in International Biosafety Negotiations. In *The International Politics of Genetically Modified Food*, ed. Robert Falkner, 34–47. Basingstoke, UK: Palgrave Macmillan.

Commission on Global Governance. 1995. *Our Global Neighbourhood: The Report of the Commission on Global Governance*. Oxford: Oxford University Press.

Conca, Ken. 1995. Greening the United Nations: Environmental Organizations and the UN System. *Third World Quarterly* 16:441–457.

Cutler, A. Claire, Virginia Haufler, and Tony Porter, eds. 1999. *Private Authority and International Affairs*. Albany: SUNY Press.

de Alcántara, Cynthia H. 1998. Uses and Abuses of the Concept of Governance. *International Social Science Journal* 155:105–113.

Deutscher Bundestag. 2002. *Schlussbericht der Enquete-Kommission Globalisierung der Weltwirtschaft*. [Final report of the Enquete Commission Globalization of the World Economy] Opladen, Germany: Leske and Budrich.

Dingwerth, Klaus. 2005. The Democratic Legitimacy of Public-Private Rule-Making: What Can We Learn from the World Commission on Dams? *Global Governance* 11:65–83.

Dingwerth, Klaus. 2007. *The New Transnationalism: Transnational Governance and Democratic Accountability*. Basingstoke, UK: Palgrave Macmillan.

Dingwerth, Klaus, and Philipp Pattberg. 2006. Global Governance as a Perspective on World Politics. *Global Governance* 12:185–203.

Dingwerth, Klaus, and Philipp Pattberg. 2007. Wirkungen transnationaler Umweltregime. *Politische Vierteljahresschrift* 39:133–156.

Dingwerth, Klaus, and Philipp Pattberg. 2009. World Politics and Organizational Fields: The Case of Sustainability Governance. *European Journal of International Relations* 15:707–743.

Falkner, Robert. 2005. The Business of Ozone Layer Protection: Corporate Power in Regime Evolution. In *The Business of Global Environmental Governance*, ed. David L. Levy and Peter Newell, 105–134. Cambridge, MA: MIT Press.

Falkner, Robert. 2008. *Business Power and Conflict in International Environmental Politics*. Basingstoke, UK: Palgrave Macmillan.

Finkelstein, Lawrence S. 1995. What Is Global Governance? *Global Governance* 1:367–372.

Glasbergen, Pieter, Frank Biermann, and Arthur P. J. Mol, eds. 2007. *Partnerships for Sustainable Development: Reflections on Theory and Practice*. Cheltenham, UK: Edward Elgar.

Gordenker, Leon, and Thomas G. Weiss. 1996. Pluralizing Global Governance: Analytical Approaches and Dimensions. In *NGOs, the UN, and Global Governance*, ed. Thomas G. Weiss and Leon Gordenker, 17–47. Boulder, CO: Lynne Rienner.

Gulbrandsen, Lars H. 2009. The Emergence and Effectiveness of the Marine Stewardship Council. *Marine Policy* 33 (4):654–660.

Gupta, Aarti. 2000. Governing Trade in Genetically Modified Organisms: The Cartagena Protocol on Biosafety. *Environment* 42:23–33.

Gupta, Aarti. 2004. When Global Is Local: Negotiating Safe Use of Biotechnology. In *Earthly Politics: Local and Global in Environmental Governance*, ed. Sheila Jasanoff and Marybeth L. Martello, 127–148. Cambridge, MA: MIT Press.

Gupta, Aarti, and Robert Falkner. 2006. The Influence of the Cartagena Protocol on Biosafety: Comparing Mexico, China, and South Africa. *Global Environmental Politics* 6:23–44.

Haas, Peter M. 1990. *Saving the Mediterranean: The Politics of International Environmental Cooperation*. New York: Columbia University Press.

Haas, Peter M. 2000. International Institutions and Social Learning in the Management of Global Environmental Risks. *Policy Studies Journal: The Journal of the Policy Studies Organization* 28:558–575.

Hafner, Gerhard. 2004. Pros and Cons Ensuing from Fragmentation of International Law. *Michigan Journal of International Law* 25:849–863.

Hall, Rodney B., and Thomas J. Biersteker, eds. 2002. *The Emergence of Private Authority in Global Governance*. Cambridge, UK: Cambridge University Press.

Haufler, Virginia. 2003. New Forms of Governance: Certification Regimes as Social Regulations of the Global Market. In *Social and Political Dimensions of Forest Certification*, ed. Errol E. Meidinger, Chris Elliott, and Gerhard Oesten, 237–247. Remagen, Germany: Verlag Kessel.

Higgot, Richard A., Geoffrey D. Underhill, and Andreas Bieler, eds. 1999. *Nonstate Actors and Authority in the Global System*. London: Routledge.

Jordan, Andrew J. 2008. The Governance of Sustainable Development: Taking Stock and Looking Forwards. *Environment and Planning C: Government and Policy* 26:17–33.

Keck, Margaret E., and Kathryn Sikkink. 1998. *Activists beyond Borders: Advocacy Networks in International Politics*. Ithaca, NY: Cornell University Press.

Levy, David L., and Peter J. Newell, eds. 2005. *The Business of Global Environmental Governance*. Cambridge, MA: MIT Press.

Lober, Doublas J. 1997. Explaining the Formation of Business-environmentalist Collaborations: Collaborative Windows and the Paper Task Force. *Policy Sciences* 30:1–24.

Marschinski, Robert, and Steffen Behrle. 2009. The World Bank: Making the Business Case for the Environment. In *Managers of Global Change: The*

Influence of International Environmental Bureaucracies, ed. Frank Biermann and Bernd Siebenhüner, 101–142. Cambridge, MA: MIT Press.

Mitchell, Ronald B., William C. Clark, David W. Cash, and Nancy M. Dickson, eds. 2006. *Global Environmental Assessments: Information and Influence.* Cambridge, MA: MIT Press.

Nölke, Andreas. 2006. Private Norms in the Global Political Economy. In *Global Norms in the Political Economy*, ed. Klaus-Gerd Giesen and Kees van der Pijl, 134–149. Cambridge, UK: Cambridge Scholar's Press.

Overbeek, Henk, Klaus Dingwerth, Philipp Pattberg, and Daniel Compagnon. 2010. Global Governance: Decline or Maturation of an Academic Concept? *International Studies Review* 12 (4):619–642.

Pattberg, Philipp. 2005. The Institutionalization of Private Governance: How Business and Non-profits Agree on Transnational Rules. *Governance: An International Journal of Policy, Administration, and Institutions* 18:589–610.

Pattberg, Philipp. 2006. The Influence of Global Business Regulation: Beyond Good Corporate Conduct. *Business and Society Review* 111:241–268.

Pattberg, Philipp. 2007. *Private Institutions and Global Governance: The New Politics of Environmental Sustainability.* Cheltenham, UK: Edward Elgar.

Pattberg, Philipp, Michele M. Betsill, and Eleni Dellas, eds. 2011. Agency in Earth System Governance. Special Issue of *International Environmental Agreements: Politics, Law, and Economics* 11 (1).

Pattberg, Philipp, Frank Biermann, Sander Chan, and Ayşem Mert, eds. 2012. *Public-Private Partnerships for Sustainable Development: Emergence, Impacts, and Legitimacy.* Cheltenham, UK: Edward Elgar.

Raustiala, Kal. 1997. States, NGOs, and International Environmental Institutions. *International Studies Quarterly* 42:719–740.

Reinicke, Wolfgang H. 1998. *Global Public Policy: Governing without Government?* Washington, DC: Brookings Institution.

Rosenau, James N. 2002. Globalization and Governance: Sustainability between Fragmentation and Integration. Paper presented at the Conference on Governance and Sustainability: New Challenges for the State, Business, and Civil Society, Berlin, 30 September.

Siebenhüner, Bernd. 2009. The Biodiversity Secretariat: Lean Shark in Troubled Waters. In *Managers of Global Change: The Influence of International Environmental Bureaucracies*, ed. Frank Biermann and Bernd Siebenhüner, 265–291. Cambridge, MA: MIT Press.

Smouts, Marie-Claude. 1998. The Proper Use of Governance in International Relations. *International Social Science Journal* 155:81–89.

South Centre. 1996. *For a Strong and Democratic United Nations: A South Perspective on UN Reform.* Geneva: South Centre.

Tienhaara, Kyla. 2009. *The Expropriation of Environmental Governance: Protecting Foreign Investors at the Expense of Public Policy.* Cambridge, UK: Cambridge University Press.

van Kersbergen, Kees, and Frans van Waarden. 2004. "Governance" as a Bridge between Disciplines: Cross-disciplinary Inspiration Regarding Shifts in Governance and Problems of Governability, Accountability and Legitimacy. *European Journal of Political Research* 43:143–171.

Vogel, David. 1995. *Trading Up: Consumer and Environmental Regulation in a Global Economy*. Cambridge, MA: Harvard University Press.

Wapner, Paul. 1996. *Environmental Activism and World Civic Politics*. Albany: SUNY Press.

Young, Oran R. 1994. *International Governance: Protecting the Environment in a Stateless Society*. Ithaca, NY: Cornell University Press.

Young, Oran R., ed. 1997. *Global Governance: Drawing Insights from the Environmental Experience*. Cambridge, MA: MIT Press.

Young, Oran R. 1999. *Governance in World Affairs*. Ithaca, NY: Cornell University Press.

I

The New Actors

2

International Bureaucracies

Steffen Bauer, Steinar Andresen, and Frank Biermann

Research on international relations is marked today by a resurgence of interest in the role and relevance of international bureaucracies and international organizations after a long period of academic neglect since the late 1970s (overview in Bauer et al. 2009). This chapter makes a threefold contribution to this thriving field of research. First, we add to current research by conceptualizing international bureaucracies as a distinct category of actors within international organizations and international relations. This helps to relate them to other types of nonstate actors that have been emphasized in recent research on global governance, such as multinational corporations (Tienhaara, Orsini, and Falkner, this book, chapter 3) or transnational networks of scientists (Gupta et al., this book, chapter 4). Second, this chapter sheds light on the role of international bureaucracies as distinct stakeholders within new types of governance mechanisms, such as transnational environmental regimes (Pattberg, this book, chapter 5), transnational public-private partnerships (Bäckstrand et al., this book, chapter 6), and transnational governance experiments (Bulkeley et al., this book, chapter 7). Third, we assess and explain the influence of international bureaucracies within an overarching institutional architecture that is marked by increasing segmentation of different layers and clusters of rule making and rule implementing (see part III, this book).

Although the insights advanced in this chapter apply to global governance in a broader sense, empirical manifestations of key developments are particularly prominent in the realm of environmental policy, which has long been a fertile ground for institutional innovation in international cooperation (Zürn 1998; Mitchell 2002; Young 2008). The Global Governance Project early on focused its research on the role and relevance of international bureaucracies, involving six partner institutions in three countries. This chapter presents the core findings from these diverse research efforts and places them in the wider context of global governance research (for more extensive treatments, see Andresen and Skjærseth 1999; Andresen 2001, 2002, 2007; Bauer 2006a; Bauer, Busch, and Siebenhüner 2009; Biermann, Siebenhüner, and Schreyögg 2009a,b; Biermann and Siebenhüner 2009a).

Conceptualization

We conceptualize international bureaucracies in our work as agencies that have been created by governments or other public actors with some degree of permanence and coherence and beyond formal direct control of single national governments, and that act in the international arena to pursue a policy. The capacity of a bureaucracy to act is vested in an administrative apparatus with a hierarchically organized group of international civil servants that have an externally defined mandate and resources, explicit organizational boundaries, and a set of formal rules of procedures within their policy area (Biermann, Siebenhüner et al. 2009; see also Biermann and Bauer 2004).

This notion of international bureaucracy is more comprehensive than the narrower concepts of international organizations in international law that focus on the legal status of an entity regardless of functions, actual role, or effectiveness. However, our notion is more specific than the broader concepts that are prevalent in organizational studies. What's important is that our definition allows differentiating between international *organizations* and international *bureaucracies*. An international organization is, in our use of the term, an institutional arrangement that combines three elements: a normative framework, a group of member states, and a bureaucracy as administrative core. For instance, the International Maritime Organization agrees through decision of its general assembly and subsequent ratification by member states on the creation of new international principles and rules in its area of activity. States can join the organization and they can participate in rule making, with the expectation that they accept and implement the collectively agreed rules. In addition, the International Maritime Organization comprises a hierarchically organized group of civil servants that acts within the mandate of the organization and within the decisions of the assembly of member states. This is what we call the *international bureaucracy*. This conceptualization thus allows helping "to keep analytically apart the international bureaucracies as actors and the collectivity of member states of an international organization, both of which are referred to as international organizations in much writing in the mainstream international relations literature" (Biermann, Siebenhüner, et al. 2009, 40). Consequently, we also distinguish between bureaucracies and institutions, which we see purely as sets of principles and rules.

Research on international bureaucracies, as defined, contributes to two developments in the study of international organization and global governance. These developments make international bureaucracies, even though some have been established decades ago, a very timely and increasingly important subject of study.

First, the community of international bureaucracies has significantly grown in mandates, numbers, and visibility. This is prevalent for the many specialized agencies of the United Nations system, such as the World Health Organization or the UN Food and Agriculture Organization. Many new organizations with new mandates have been created, such as the World Trade Organization, the World Intellectual Property Organization, or the International Criminal Court. All comprise a considerable technical staff of international civil servants to pursue their political agendas and to implement policies agreed by member states. Particularly in global environmental governance, international bureaucracies have mushroomed in the form of treaty secretariats to the several hundred multilateral environmental agreements that have been negotiated and entered into force in recent decades (Bauer, Busch, and Siebenhüner 2009; Biermann and Siebenhüner 2009b).

Second, and partially as a consequence, numerous researchers have refocused their research on international organizations. For a long time, international organizations and especially their bureaucracies had been perceived as less relevant by mainstream scholarship on international relations. This has now changed especially with the emergence of a distinct social constructivist agenda. The work of Michael Barnett and Martha Finnemore (1999) and many others brought new momentum to debates about the bureaucratic character of international organizations. International organizations have thus gained prominence again. Scholars revisit older approaches of the 1970s (Cox and Jacobson 1973; Weiss 1975) and enrich it with new ideas—including from neighboring disciplines such as sociology, management studies, and organizational theories—and new empirical evidence gained from a host of innovative case studies across different policy arenas of global governance.

This renaissance of international bureaucracies and of organizational research was overdue for a discipline that was long rather state centric and narrowly focused on international regimes. It is also a logical step inasmuch as the discipline shifted from viewing world politics as "politics among nations" to emergent systems of global governance with a multiplicity of actors. The explicit distinction between international bureaucracies and international organizations is hence an important contribution to recent scholarship, even as pertinent empirical, methodological, and theoretical questions remain unanswered.

Two characteristics of international bureaucracies have been particularly important in recent research: the autonomy and the authority of international bureaucracies.

Scholarly research on the autonomy of international bureaucracies vis-à-vis member states applies insights from principal-agent analysis to the study of international organization (e.g., Abbott and Snidal 1998; Reinalda and Verbeek 1998, 2004b; Haftel and Thompson 2006; Hawkins et al. 2006b). This strand of research is driven by two related questions. First, why do states delegate authoritative tasks and responsibilities to international agents as opposed to taking unilateral action or cooperating directly? Second, how do they maintain control over agent behavior once authority has been delegated (Hawkins et al. 2006a)? The autonomy that results from delegation grants international bureaucracies agency in global governance even as this autonomy remains in the end conditional and revocable. Research on the autonomy of international bureaucracies scrutinizes the extent to which member states can control the autonomy of international bureaucracies, the limits of control that governments experience, and the political implications of the autonomy of bureaucracies.

This research rests on the assumption that states accept some autonomy of bureaucracies as a trade-off for their efficiency and effectiveness, but they also try to confine autonomy to a necessary minimum. In short, this research builds on the notion that the aim of principals is to delegate authority without surrendering it (Reinalda and Verbeek 2004a). Empirical studies of organizational autonomy and principal-agent relations flourished in particular in European Union studies, with its many thickly institutionalized relationships of delegation (see, for instance, Pollack 1997, 2003; Thatcher and Stone Sweet 2002; Kerremans 2004). Indeed, the quasi-domestic policy context of the European Union and the large bureaucratic apparatus of the European Commission are well suited for the application of principal-agent approaches to the study of international organization. Shortcomings of autonomy-centered approaches are revealed, however, when it comes to explaining the behavior of agents, not principals. It shows that the concept of autonomy is insufficient to explain whether and when agents take advantage of the autonomy that they potentially enjoy (Gould 2006). In sum, the concept of autonomy is key to establishing the influence of international bureaucracies, but it is inadequate to explain specific consequences of autonomous behavior as the internal dynamics of international bureaucracies remain a black box (Bauer et al. 2009).

Recent approaches that focus on the authority of international bureaucracies, often informed by sociological research, help to look inside this black box (Bauer 2006a). Instead of examining the autonomy of international bureaucracies vis-à-vis their principals, bureaucracies are conceptualized as autonomous actors from the outset. The specific authority that they muster is employed to explain the type and reach of their influence, including unintended consequences of their autonomous behavior. In international bureaucracies, such authority entails responsibilities that have been delegated by principals but that comprise more than just delegated authority (Barnett and Finnemore 2004). Based on a social constructivist critique of utilitarian approaches to international organization, authority-centered concepts allow examining the actorness of international bureaucracies as such, not just in relation to their principals. These approaches can thus be applied to the analysis of what international bureaucracies actually do, why they do it, and how (Bauer et al. 2009). In short, the notion of authority is instrumental to understanding the behavior of international bureaucracies and to opening the black boxes that they have represented so far. Consequently, sociological approaches offer useful complements to the empirical analysis of international bureaucracies and their specific influences even as they remain ontologically inconsistent with rationalist approaches that revolve around questions about the autonomy of agents (Bauer et al. 2009; Biermann and Siebenhüner 2009a).

This is also supported by recent advances in the literature on bureaucracies as formal organizations and the application of organizational learning approaches to the study of international organization (Drori, Meyer, and Hwang 2006; Siebenhüner 2008; Vetterlein and Park 2010). Few studies have applied concepts of organizational learning and change to international bureaucracies. Exceptions are E. B. Haas (1990), who studied different learning modes of international bureaucracies and distinguished between adaptation and learning as crucial forms of learning; P. M. Haas (2000) and P. M. Haas and McCabe (2001), who analyzed societal learning and the role of international bureaucracies as facilitators; and Barnett and Coleman (2005), who found organizational change (in the case of Interpol) to be rooted not in learning but in strategic choices in response to context conditions. Although most of these studies looked at the external conditions within which international bureaucracies act, more recent work also begins to bridge internal and external dynamics in learning and change processes of international bureaucracies (Nielson, Tierney, and Weaver 2006). This research supports an integrative view of international bureaucracies that considers their external relations vis-à-vis principals as well as the internal dynamics of organizational structures and personalities. Accordingly, international bureaucracies can be analyzed in their full capacity to act as largely independent collective actors.

Conceptualizing international bureaucracies as actors in global governance has profound normative implications. Among other things, it changes the paradigmatic lens of analysts to judge the accountability of intergovernmental organizations and the legitimacy of their policies. If international bureaucracies are not merely instrumental and may indeed act autonomously, they bear political responsibility for their actions even if these are formally sanctioned by the corresponding intergovernmental bodies. Indeed, as historian Paul Kennedy noted in his evolutionary appraisal of the United Nations, a diplomat who would have been time traveling from the year 1900 to our present days "would be astonished at the role that international bodies play on behalf of global society" (Kennedy 2006, xi).

Experiences

Following this reasoning, research in the Global Governance Project focused on the behavior of international bureaucracies as autonomous actors of global governance and on the effects of their activities on global policy processes and outcomes. Hundreds of international bureaucracies are active in world politics, from regional to global levels and from all-encompassing agencies to highly issue-specific treaty secretariats. The variety of international bureaucracies is particularly prevalent in the environmental field.

Within the Global Governance Project, we studied among others the environmental departments and divisions of the World Bank (Marschinski and Behrle 2009), the Organisation for Economic Co-operation and Development (Busch 2009b), and the International Maritime Organization (Campe 2009); the secretariats of the United Nations Environment Programme (Andresen and Rosendal 2009; Bauer 2009c) and of the

Global Environment Facility (Andler 2009; Rosendal and Andresen 2009); as well as detailed comparative studies of environmental treaty secretariats, including the secretariats of the United Nations Framework Convention on Climate Change, of the most important conventions on biodiversity, of the United Nations Convention to Combat Desertification, of the Vienna Convention for the Protection of the Ozone Layer and its Montreal Protocol, and of the three main conventions on chemicals (Bauer, Busch, and Siebenhüner 2009; Busch 2009a; Siebenhüner 2009; Bauer 2009a, 2009b; Andresen and Rosendal 2009).

Building on extensive field research, including interviews with some hundred international civil servants and external experts, our research indicates that most international bureaucracies have a sizeable influence on political processes. Our case studies illustrated in much detail the various types and degree of influence that international bureaucracies have in global environmental governance. Yet, we also found considerable variation regarding the extent of their influence.

We found the influence of international bureaucracies to be particularly prevalent in three areas (Biermann, Siebenhüner, et al. 2009 with further details):

First, our research showed that international bureaucracies have a sizeable cognitive influence by shaping global agendas in the environmental realm through synthesizing scientific findings and distributing knowledge and information to all kinds of stakeholders, from national and local governments to scientists, citizens, environmental advocates, and the business sector. For instance, the United Nations Environment Programme (UNEP) was designed by governments in 1972 explicitly as a "small secretariat." Nonetheless, this bureaucracy provides a striking illustration of the considerable agenda-setting power that international bureaucracies can have (Bauer 2009c). In fact, policy-relevant knowledge about the global environment and the institutional dimensions of environmental policy making became over time a trademark of this agency. In spite of its rather marginal status within the United Nations system and its peripheral location in Nairobi, UNEP has developed the capacity to act as the foremost knowledge broker of environmental governance at the international level.

Building on the technical expertise and institutional memory vested in its staff, the secretariat's ability to capitalize on specific issues that are generally covered by a broad general mandate provides an important asset to influence international environmental agendas. In a number of cases, this particular capacity was skillfully maximized by its leadership.

The UNEP secretariat has thus often played a catalytic role in the advancement of governmental responses to specific environmental issues (Bauer 2009c). Other bureaucracies, too, have cognitive influence on the agenda of global environmental politics. Environmental experts of the World Bank and the OECD, for instance, shape environmental discourses between policy makers by a wealth of applied research (Marschinski and Behrle 2009; Busch 2009b). These bureaucracies are thus directly involved in generating, synthesizing, and disseminating policy-relevant knowledge.

Second, our research demonstrated normative influence of international bureaucracies. International bureaucracies shape global cooperation through facilitating issue-specific institutionalization. They influence intergovernmental negotiations at various stages of international and transnational policy making. For instance, some bureaucracies initiate international conferences that lead to negotiations or intervene with processes pertaining to the implementation, revision, adaptation, or renegotiation of existent institutions. As well, the UNEP secretariat has shown its ability to facilitate international environmental negotiations. Although UNEP's more recent normative influence may seem less spectacular than the groundbreaking international environmental processes it triggered in the 1970s and 1980s, its officers continue to shape multilateral environmental agreements by participating in negotiations that tend to become ever more specific, detailed, and complex. One example is the significant role of UNEP in administering the Convention on Biological Diversity (Andresen and Rosendal 2009; Rosendal and Andresen 2004; Siebenhüner 2009) or the Montreal Protocol on Substances That Deplete the Ozone Layer (Bauer 2009b). Another example is the development and codification of international environmental law, where the UNEP secretariat musters considerable in-house expertise. In addition to such technical matters, the secretariat is also seen to further incremental political reforms in international environmental governance, wherein the prospects of the UNEP itself are at stake (Bauer 2009c).

Yet although our empirical analyses underscore the key role played by UNEP officers in the initial stages of institution building, they also reveal limits in its ability to follow up in subsequent policy processes (Andresen 2007). These are most visible in UNEP's often-lamented inability to better coordinate international environmental governance, despite its explicit coordinative mandate. This, along with other limitations, is rooted especially in the problem structure in which UNEP

operates (Andresen and Rosendal 2009; Bauer 2009c). This overall variation in normative influence is considerable, ranging from the all but
negligible autonomous policy influence on negotiations in the case of the
climate secretariat (Busch 2009a) to the sizeable policy influence mus-
tered by the biodiversity secretariat in negotiations (Siebenhüner 2009;
Andresen and Rosendal 2009) to the deliberately influential, even rather
advocacy-like, stance observed in the case of the desertification secretariat (Bauer 2006b, 2009a). Besides, multi-issue bureaucracies that
address environmental policy from an economic governance background,
such as the World Bank or the OECD Environment Directorate, have
demonstrated potential for normative influence by promoting specific
economic frameworks (Busch 2009b; Marschinski and Behrle 2009).

Third, our research showed that international bureaucracies have
significant autonomous executive influence in global environmental
governance. This is most visible in capacity-building initiatives that are
executed by major agencies such as the World Bank, the United Nations
Industrial Development Organization, or the United Nations Development Programme (Biermann and Siebenhüner 2009a). In those cases, it
is common for the bureaucracies to not merely implement technical
provisions of donor governments, but also to develop and implement
their own capacity-building policies with considerable autonomy. Many
of the environmental capacity-building programs of the World Bank
or the OECD fall in this category (Marschinski and Behrle 2009;
Busch 2009b). These findings are also in line with earlier research on
policy diffusion (e.g., Busch and Jörgens 2005) or on the influence of
the United Nations Educational, Scientific, and Cultural Organization
(UNESCO) on domestic capacities in schooling and education (Finnemore
1993; for a broader perspective on autonomous policy implementation
through international organizations see Joachim, Reinalda, and Verbeek
2008).

Moreover, many international bureaucracies also stretch their mandate
to executive functions even when they formally lack an operative
mandate. UNEP for example has built joint programs with other
UN agencies and participates in public-private partnerships. The UNEP
secretariat also supports capacity development in the area of environmental law, notably in developing countries (Bauer 2009c). There
even seems to be a general tendency for international bureaucracies to
develop operational activities and capacities even when their original
mandate and function do not provide for it (Biermann and Siebenhüner
2009a, 326).

Explanations

Notwithstanding significant degrees of differentiation between types of influence across international bureaucracies, one overarching finding of our research is that the overall problem structure and internal factors of organizations such as leadership and staff composition explain much of the variation in the influence of international bureaucracies (Andresen 2007; Andresen and Rosendal 2009; Biermann and Siebenhüner 2009a; Bauer and Andresen 2010). Conversely, the institutional design of environmental bureaucracies is less relevant for explaining variation in the behavior and influence of bureaucracies. Given the prominence attributed to questions of institutional design in much of the literature on international environmental regimes, this is rather surprising.

This is not to say that aspects of institutional design are completely irrelevant. The bureaucracies of major international agencies with far-reaching executive mandates and corresponding financial and technical resources will always muster more absolute influence than small treaty secretariats with a narrowly defined scope and limited capacities. Once such institutional components of a bureaucracy become more comparable, however, they will be much less relevant for explaining variation (Biermann and Siebenhüner 2009a).

The analysis of internal factors especially yields new insights into the behavior of international bureaucracies. Organizational expertise, organizational culture, organizational structure, and organizational leadership help explain variation in the authority and influence of these actors (Biermann and Siebenhüner 2009a). Organizational expertise is a key asset for bureaucratic influence in the cognitive and normative dimensions of international environmental policy, especially if it builds on a broad and well-balanced knowledge base. Organizational leadership, too, is a potentially strong source of influence as it shapes the internal dynamics of international bureaucracies and how their specific assets are employed vis-à-vis their external environment (Bauer and Andresen 2010). It is also apparent that for international bureaucracies to be perceived as authoritative actors, the appearance of neutrality is important. Although bureaucratic authority as such may draw on a variety of sources, organizational culture and leadership are key to developing and maintaining this delicate property over time (Bauer 2006a).

Rationalist-institutionalists have long neglected these factors partially due to their statist ontology, which tended to overlook intergovernmental actors in the first place. Recent research on international bureaucracies showed that this is insufficient. It indicated that the people and procedures of international bureaucracies are important to explain the behavior of international organizations and the outcomes of their actions. Indeed, these internal factors led scholars to reconsider the role of international bureaucracies in world politics. More specifically, they are key in explaining to a large part variation in the degree and type of influences that are empirically observable (Biermann and Siebenhüner 2009a).

A second important factor is the problem structure. In particular, we found that the more governments seek to limit the autonomy of international bureaucracies, the higher they consider the costs of regulation and the salience of the problem (Andresen 2007; also Miles et al. 2001). The significance of problem structure is particularly evident in the comparative analysis of environmental treaty secretariats, which are largely identical in terms of institutional design (Andresen and Skjærseth 1999; Bauer, Busch, and Siebenhüner 2009). The example of the UNEP secretariat's failure to coordinate policy processes in international environmental governance also demonstrates these structural issues. As each multilateral environmental agreement maintains its own specific jurisdiction, responsible treaty secretariats turn to the corresponding conferences of the parties for policy guidance. The parties in turn retain control over the policy issues governed under the treaty in question, but at the same time call on UNEP to coordinate treaty processes. The UNEP secretariat thus finds itself between a rock and a hard place and without the means to autonomously alter this structural disposition (Andresen 2001; Andresen and Rosendal 2009; Bauer 2009c).

In sum, the structure of a problem largely determines the scope of autonomous activity by international bureaucracies. We found less explanatory value in the role of the institutional design as far as the actual behavior of international bureaucracies is concerned. Authoritative behavior and autonomous influences of international bureaucracies largely depend on internal organizational factors such as expertise, culture, and leadership. This is also confirmed by recent research on nonenvironmental bureaucracies, even in the "high politics" realm of international security (Barnett and Finnemore 2004; Weinlich 2012).

Conclusions and Outlook

The research synthesized in this chapter gives ample evidence for the high relevance of international bureaucracies in global governance. It thus also supports the current renaissance of organizational research in the study of international relations. Our research contributes, in particular, by conceptualizing international bureaucracies as autonomous actors that need to be analytically distinguished from international organizations. Reflecting the autonomy and the authority of these actors, our work traces empirical manifestations of their influence, which can be found in cognitive, normative, and executive dimensions of global governance. We also provide explanations for the influences as well as the variation in influence across divergent types of international bureaucracies. Pertinent findings highlight the significance of internal factors such as organizational culture, expertise and leadership, as well as the problem structure within which a bureaucracy operates. By contrast, institutional design factors bear limited explanatory power regarding the influence of international bureaucracies.

This all notwithstanding, the state of knowledge on international bureaucracies is hardly sufficient. For instance, although many of our case studies highlight the importance of leadership and other internal factors in explaining organizational behavior, the causal relationship between the actions of the executive top and the external influence of international bureaucracies remains poorly understood (Bauer and Andresen 2010). Drawing largely from anecdotal evidence, scholars still struggle to conceptualize their insights in an adequately systematic manner that would allow for robust comparative research across time and cases.

More comparative studies would also help to test further hypotheses about the general conditions of bureaucratic influence. There remains a demand for systematic comparison of international bureaucracies from different policy areas as well as over time and in relation to other actors (Biermann and Siebenhüner 2009a; Bauer and Weinlich 2011).

Further promising avenues for research relate to a conceptual cross-fertilization of international relations theories and organizational studies, notably regarding organizational learning and change (LaPalombara 2001; Siebenhüner 2008; Vetterlein and Park 2010). Such efforts might not only enhance the conceptual toolbox for the study of international bureaucracies, but also help to build common ground between rationalist and sociological strands in international relations research. Established concepts to understand the effectiveness and legitimacy of international institutions could then also be adjusted to scrutinize the effectiveness and legitimacy of international bureaucracies (Biermann and Bauer 2004; Dingwerth 2007; Biermann and Siebenhüner 2009a).

Accordingly, further research on international bureaucracies has been identified as a key component in the global research program Earth

System Governance Project, the new global research initiative under the International Human Dimensions Programme on Global Environmental Change (Biermann 2007, 2008; Biermann, Betsill, et al. 2009). In its research plan, international bureaucracies are seen as constituting elements of the overarching institutional architecture of earth system governance and as arenas in which policy agendas are shaped and legitimized.

Finally, the research synthesized in this chapter is likely to enrich recurring debates on reforming international environmental governance in the United Nations system. These debates are gaining momentum yet again as governments prepare for the major United Nations Conference on Sustainable Development to be held in Rio de Janeiro in June 2012. The current reform debates on international environmental governance may now draw on fresh insights that were not available in previous iterations of United Nations reform when the role and relevance of international bureaucracies was often underestimated or neglected. The now better understanding of international bureaucracies as global actors will prove to be important for meaningful political discussions, and eventually, well-informed decision making, for example, regarding the upgrading of UNEP to a world environment organization (Biermann 2002; Biermann and Bauer 2005). Ultimately, the quest for legitimate and effective global governance will need to come to terms with the roles assigned to international bureaucracies.

Acknowledgments

This chapter is based on research undertaken from 2000 to 2009 by fifteen researchers at the following institutions: Environmental Policy Research Centre, Freie Universität Berlin, Germany; Fridtjof Nansen Institute, Oslo, Norway; Institute for Environmental Studies, VU University Amsterdam, the Netherlands; Potsdam Institute for Climate Impact Research, Germany; and the Carl von Ossietzky University, Oldenburg, Germany. The authors are grateful to Silke Weinlich and Bernd Siebenhüner for helpful comments on earlier versions of this chapter.

References

Abbott, Kenneth, and Duncan Snidal. 1998. Why States Act through Formal International Organizations. *Journal of Conflict Resolution* 42 (1):3–32.

Andler, Lydia. 2009. The Secretariat of the Global Environment Facility: From Network to Bureaucracy. In *Managers of Global Change: The Influence of*

International Environmental Bureaucracies, ed. Frank Biermann and Bernd Siebenhüner, 203–223. Cambridge, MA: MIT Press.

Andresen, Steinar. 2001. Global Environmental Governance: UN Fragmentation and Co-ordination. In *Yearbook of International Co-operation on Environment and Development 2001/2002*, ed. Olav Schram Stokke and Øystein B. Thommessen, 19–26. London: Earthscan Publications.

Andresen, Steinar. 2002. Leadership Change in the World Health Organization: Potential for Increased Effectiveness? FNI-rapport 08/2002. Lysaker: The Fridtjof Nansen Institute.

Andresen, Steinar. 2007. The Effectiveness of UN Environmental Institutions. *International Environmental Agreements: Politics, Law and Economics* 7 (4): 317–336.

Andresen, Steinar, and Kristin Rosendal. 2009. The Role of the United Nations Environment Programme in the Coordination of Multilateral Environmental Agreements. In *International Organizations in Global Environmental Governance*, ed. Frank Biermann, Bernd Siebenhüner, and Anna Schreyögg, 133–150. London: Routledge.

Andresen, Steinar, and Jon Birger Skjærseth. 1999. Can International Environmental Secretariats Promote Effective Co-operation? Paper read at United Nations University's International Conference on Synergies and Coordination between Multilateral Environmental Agreements, Tokyo, 14–16 July.

Barnett, Michael N., and Liv Coleman. 2005. Designing Police: Interpol and the Study of Change in International Organizations. *International Studies Quarterly* 49:593–619.

Barnett, Michael N., and Martha Finnemore. 1999. The Politics, Power, and Pathologies of International Organizations. *International Organization* 53 (4):699–732.

Barnett, Michael N., and Martha Finnemore. 2004. *Rules for the World: International Organizations in Global Politics*. Ithaca, NY: Cornell University Press.

Bauer, Steffen. 2006a. Does Bureaucracy Really Matter? The Authority of Intergovernmental Treaty Secretariats in Global Environmental Politics. *Global Environmental Politics* 6 (1):23–49.

Bauer, Steffen. 2006b. The United Nations and the Fight against Desertification: What Role for the UNCCD Secretariat? In *Governing Global Desertification: Linking Environmental Degradation, Poverty, and Participation*, ed. Pierre M. Johnson, Karel Mayrand, and Marc Paquin, 73–88. Aldershot, UK: Ashgate.

Bauer, Steffen. 2009a. The Desertification Secretariat: A Castle Made of Sand. In *Managers of Global Change: The Influence of International Environmental Bureaucracies*, ed. Frank Biermann and Bernd Siebenhüner, 293–317. Cambridge, MA: MIT Press.

Bauer, Steffen. 2009b. The Ozone Secretariat: The Good Shepherd of Ozone Politics. In *Managers of Global Change: The Influence of International Environmental Bureaucracies*, ed. Frank Biermann and Bernd Siebenhüner, 225–244. Cambridge, MA: MIT Press.

Bauer, Steffen. 2009c. The Secretariat of the United Nations Environment Programme: Tangled Up in Blue. In *Managers of Global Change: The Influence of International Environmental Bureaucracies*, ed. Frank Biermann and Bernd Siebenhüner, 169–201. Cambridge, MA: MIT Press.

Bauer, Steffen, and Steinar Andresen. 2010. Bureaucratic Leadership: The Missing Link to Understanding IO Influence? Paper read at 51st Annual Convention of the International Studies Association, New Orleans. 17–20 February.

Bauer, Steffen, Frank Biermann, Klaus Dingwerth, and Bernd Siebenhüner. 2009. Understanding International Bureaucracies: Taking Stock. In *Managers of Global Change: The Influence of International Environmental Bureaucracies*, ed. Frank Biermann and Bernd Siebenhüner, 15–36. Cambridge, MA: MIT Press.

Bauer, Steffen, Per-Olof Busch, and Bernd Siebenhüner. 2009. Treaty Secretariats in Global Environmental Governance. In *International Organizations in Global Environmental Governance*, ed. Frank Biermann, Bernd Siebenhüner, and Anna Schreyögg, 174–191. London: Routledge.

Bauer, Steffen, and Silke Weinlich. 2011. International Bureaucracies: Organizing World Politics. In *The Ashgate Research Companion to Non-state Actors*, ed. Bob Reinalda, 251–262. Aldershot, UK: Ashgate.

Biermann, Frank. 2002. Strengthening Green Global Governance in a Disparate World Society: Would a World Environment Organization Benefit the South? *International Environmental Agreements: Politics, Law and Economics* 2:297–315.

Biermann, Frank. 2007. "Earth System Governance" as a Crosscutting Theme of Global Change Research. *Global Environmental Change: Human and Policy Dimensions* 17:326–337.

Biermann, Frank. 2008. Earth System Governance: A Research Agenda. In *Institutions and Environmental Change: Principal Findings, Applications, and Research Frontiers*, ed. Oran R. Young, Leslie A. King, and Heike Schroeder, 277–301. Cambridge, MA: MIT Press.

Biermann, Frank, and Steffen Bauer. 2004. Assessing the Effectiveness of Intergovernmental Organisations in International Environmental Politics. *Global Environmental Change: Human and Policy Dimensions* 14 (2):189–193.

Biermann, Frank, and Steffen Bauer, eds. 2005. *A World Environment Organization: Solution or Threat for Effective International Environmental Governance?* Aldershot, UK: Ashgate.

Biermann, Frank, Michele M. Betsill, Joyeeta Gupta, Norichika Kanie, Louis Lebel, Diana Liverman, Heike Schroeder, and Bernd Siebenhüner. with contributions from Ken Conca, Leila da Costa Ferreira, Bharat Desai, Simon Tay, and Ruben Zondervan. 2009. Earth System Governance: People, Places, and the Planet. Science and Implementation Plan of the Earth System Governance Project. *Earth System Governance Project 1, IHDP Report 20*. Bonn: The Earth System Governance Project.

Biermann, Frank, and Bernd Siebenhüner. 2009a. The Influence of International Bureaucracies in World Politics: Findings from the MANUS Research Program.

In *Managers of Global Change: The Influence of International Environmental Bureaucracies*, ed. Frank Biermann and Bernd Siebenhüner, 319–349. Cambridge, MA: MIT Press.

Biermann, Frank, and Bernd Siebenhüner. 2009b. The Role and Relevance of International Bureaucracies: Setting the Stage. In *Managers of Global Change: The Influence of International Environmental Bureaucracies*, ed. Frank Biermann and Bernd Siebenhüner, 1–14. Cambridge, MA: MIT Press.

Biermann, Frank, Bernd Siebenhüner, Steffen Bauer, Per-Olof Busch, Sabine Campe, Klaus Dingwerth, Torsten Grothmann, Robert Marschinski, and Mireia Tarradell. 2009. Studying the Influence of International Bureaucracies: A Conceptual Framework. In *Managers of Global Change: The Influence of International Environmental Bureaucracies*, ed. Frank Biermann and Bernd Siebenhüner, 37–74. Cambridge, MA: MIT Press.

Biermann, Frank, Bernd Siebenhüner, and Anna Schreyögg. 2009. Global Environmental Governance and International Organizations: Setting the Stage. In *International Organizations in Global Environmental Governance*, ed. Frank Biermann, Bernd Siebenhüner, and Anna Schreyögg, 1–16. London: Routledge.

Busch, Per-Olof. 2009a. The Climate Secretariat: Making a Living in a Straitjacket. In *Managers of Global Change: The Influence of International Environmental Bureaucracies*, ed. Frank Biermann and Bernd Siebenhüner, 245–264. Cambridge, MA: MIT Press.

Busch, Per-Olof. 2009b. The OECD Environment Directorate: The Art of Persuasion and Its Limitations. In *Managers of Global Change: The Influence of International Environmental Bureaucracies*, ed. Frank Biermann and Bernd Siebenhüner, 75–99. Cambridge, MA: MIT Press.

Busch, Per-Olof, and Helge Jörgens. 2005. International Patterns of Environmental Policy Change and Convergence. *European Environment* 15 (2):80–101.

Campe, Sabine. 2009. The Secretariat of the International Maritime Organization: A Tanker for Tankers. In *Managers of Global Change: The Influence of International Environmental Bureaucracies*, ed. Frank Biermann and Bernd Siebenhüner, 143–168. Cambridge, MA: MIT Press.

Cox, Robert W., and Harold K. Jacobson, eds. 1973. *The Anatomy of Influence: Decision-Making in International Organization*. New Haven, CT: Yale University Press.

Dingwerth, Klaus. 2007. *The New Transnationalism: Transnational Governance and Democratic Legitimacy*. Basingstoke, UK: Palgrave.

Drori, Gili S., John W. Meyer, and Hokyu Hwang, eds. 2006. *Globalization and Organization: World Society and Organizational Change*. Oxford: Oxford University Press.

Finnemore, Martha. 1993. International Organizations as Teachers of Norms: The United Nations Educational, Scientific, and Cultural Organization and Science Policy. *International Organization* 47 (4):565–598.

Gould, Erica R. 2006. Delegating IMF Conditionality: Understanding Variations in Control and Conformity. In *Delegation and Agency in International Organizations*, ed. Darren G. Hawkins, David. A. Lake, Daniel L. Nielson, and Michael J. Tierney, 281–311. Cambridge, UK: Cambridge University Press.

Haas, Ernst B. 1990. *When Knowledge Is Power: Three Models of Change in International Organizations.* Berkeley: University of California Press.

Haas, Peter M. 2000. International Institutions and Social Learning in the Management of Global Environmental Risks. *Policy Studies Journal: The Journal of the Policy Studies Organization* 28 (3):558–575.

Haas, Peter M., and David McCabe. 2001. Amplifiers or Dampeners: International Institutions and Social Learning in the Management of Global Environmental Risks. In *Learning to Manage Global Environmental Risks: A Comparative History of Social Responses to Climate Change, Ozone Depletion, and Acid Rain,* ed. The Social Learning Group, 323–348. Cambridge, MA: MIT Press.

Haftel, Yoram Z., and Alexander Thompson. 2006. The Independence of International Organizations. *Journal of Conflict Resolution* 50 (2):253–275.

Hawkins, Darren G., David A. Lake, Daniel L. Nielson, and Michael J. Tierney. 2006a. Delegation under Anarchy: States, International Organizations, and Principal-Agent Theory. In *Delegation and Agency in International Organizations,* ed. Darren G. Hawkins, David A. Lake, Daniel L. Nielson, and Michael J. Tierney, 3–38. Cambridge, MA: Cambridge University Press.

Hawkins, Darren G., David A. Lake, Daniel L. Nielson, and Michael J. Tierney, eds. 2006b. *Delegation and Agency in International Organizations.* Cambridge, MA: Cambridge University Press.

Joachim, Jutta, Bob Reinalda, and Bertjan Verbeek, eds. 2008. *International Organizations and Implementation: Enforcers, Managers, Authorities?* London: Routledge.

Kennedy, Paul. 2006. *The Parliament of Man: The Past, Present, and Future of the United Nations.* London: Allen Lane.

Kerremans, Bart. 2004. The European Commission and the EU Member States as Actors in the WTO Negotiating Process. Decision Making between Scylla and Charibdis? In *Decision Making within International Organizations,* ed. Bob Reinalda and Bertjan Verbeek, 45–58. London: Routledge.

LaPalombara, Joseph. 2001. The Underestimated Contributions of Political Science to Organizational Learning. In *Handbook of Organizational Learning and Knowledge,* ed. Meinolf Dierkes, Ariane Berthoin Antal, John Child, and Ikujiro Nonaka, 137–161. Oxford, UK: Oxford University Press.

Marschinski, Robert, and Steffen Behrle. 2009. The World Bank: Making the Business Case for the Environment. In *Managers of Global Change: The Influence of International Environmental Bureaucracies,* ed. Frank Biermann and Bernd Siebenhüner, 101–142. Cambridge, MA: MIT Press.

Miles, Edward L., Arild Underdal, Steinar Andresen, Jørgen Wettestad, Jon Birger Skjærseth, and Elaine M. Carlin, eds. 2001. *Environmental Regime Effectiveness: Confronting Theory with Evidence.* Cambridge, MA: MIT Press.

Mitchell, Ronald B. 2002. International Environment. In *Handbook of International Relations,* ed. Walter Carlsnaes, Thomas Risse, and Beth A. Simmons, 500–516. London: Sage.

Nielson, Daniel L., Michael J. Tierney, and Catherine E. Weaver. 2006. Bridging the Rationalist-Constructivist Divide: Re-engineering the Culture of the World Bank. *Journal of International Relations and Development* 9 (2):107–139.

Pollack, Mark A. 1997. Delegation, Agency, and Agenda-Setting in the European Community. *International Organization* 51 (1):99–134.

Pollack, Mark A. 2003. *The Engines of European Integration: Delegation, Agency and Agenda Setting in the EU.* Oxford: Oxford University Press.

Reinalda, Bob, and Bertjan Verbeek, eds. 1998. *Autonomous Policy Making by International Organizations.* London: Routledge.

Reinalda, Bob, and Bertjan Verbeek. 2004a. The Issue of Decision Making within International Organizations. In *Decision Making within International Organizations,* ed. Bob Reinalda and Bertjan Verbeek, 9–41. London: Routledge.

Reinalda, Bob, and Bertjan Verbeek, eds. 2004b. *Decision Making within International Organizations.* London: Routledge.

Rosendal, Kristin, and Steinar Andresen. 2004. UNEP's Role in Enhancing Problem-Solving Capacity in Multilateral Environmental Agreements: Co-ordination and Assistance in the Biodiversity Conservation Cluster. *FNI Report 10/2003.* Lysaker: Fridtjof Nansen Institute.

Rosendal, Kristin, and Steinar Andresen. 2009. The Global Environment Facility: Merits and Shortcoming of a Decentralized Approach to International Environmental Governance. Paper read at 50th Annual Convention of the International Studies Association, New York, 15–18 February.

Siebenhüner, Bernd. 2008. Learning in International Organizations in Global Environmental Governance. *Global Environmental Politics* 8 (4):92–116.

Siebenhüner, Bernd. 2009. The Biodiversity Secretariat: Lean Shark in Troubled Waters. In *Managers of Global Change: The Influence of International Environmental Bureaucracies,* ed. Frank Biermann and Bernd Siebenhüner, 265–291. Cambridge, MA: MIT Press.

Thatcher, Mark, and Alec Stone Sweet. 2002. Theory and Practice of Delegation to Non-majoritarian Institutions. *West European Politics* 25 (1):1–22.

Vetterlein, Antje, and Susan Park. 2010. Teacher's Pet? IO Learning, Norms and Change. Paper read at 51st Annual Meeting of the International Studies Association, New Orleans, 17–20 February.

Weinlich, Silke. 2012. *Shaping Peace Operations: The Influence of the UN Secretariat.* Basingstoke, UK: Macmillan.

Weiss, Thomas G., ed. 1975. *International Bureaucracy.* Lexington, MA: Lexington Books.

Young, Oran R. 2008. Institutions and Environmental Change: The Scientific Legacy of a Decade of IDGEC Research. In *Institutions and Environmental Change: Principal Findings, Applications, and Research Frontiers,* ed. Oran R. Young, Leslie A. King, and Heike Schroeder, 3–46. Cambridge, MA: MIT Press.

Zürn, Michael. 1998. The Rise of International Environmental Politics: A Review of Current Research. *World Politics* 50 (4):617–649.

3

Global Corporations

Kyla Tienhaara, Amandine Orsini, and Robert Falkner

Global corporations have been key players in the development of global environmental governance. The significance of these actors has not always been acknowledged in the academic literature but recent scholarship has produced a wealth of studies on the theoretical and empirical dimensions of business involvement in international environmental politics (for overviews of this literature, see Levy and Newell 2005b; Falkner 2008). This shift in the literature is partly a reflection of the rapid proliferation and growth of global corporations. At the dawn of the global environmental movement in the early 1970s, there were a mere seven thousand parent enterprises (Clapp 2005). By 2005 there were estimated to be more than ten times that number (United Nations Conference on Trade and Development [UNCTAD] 2006, annex table A.I.6), and recent waves of mergers and acquisitions have led to the creation of ever larger transnational corporate conglomerates. Moreover, and more important, scholars have recognized that global corporations have also become more actively engaged in global environmental governance since the 1970s. They not only seek to shape international diplomatic efforts to create global environmental treaties but have also become sources of authority and providers of environmental governance functions in their own right. As in other areas of global governance, business has become a "pivotal political actor" (Fuchs 2007, 4) in the environmental arena.

This chapter aims to summarize the main findings of recent work on global corporations carried out by researchers in the Global Governance Project. The next section conceptualizes and introduces the topic. Following this, three specific examples of how global corporations have engaged in the negotiation and implementation of international environmental regimes are presented. The fourth section draws on these experiences in a discussion about the different dimensions, as well as the limitations, of corporate power. The chapter concludes with recommendations for future research.

Conceptualization

In the realm of global environmental governance, corporations can be thought of as having multiple identities. On the one hand, they can be seen as creators of environmental problems. Corporations are responsible for a significant percentage of global energy usage, for the depletion of much of the planet's stocks of natural resources, and for a large portion of annual releases of toxic chemicals and emissions into the environment (Elliott 1998). Furthermore, global corporations are relentless promoters of (over)consumption, which is increasingly recognized as a root cause of many (if not all) environmental problems (Dauvergne 2008). On the other hand, the actions of corporations are often critical to the success of environmental protection efforts. Global corporations have substantial capacity to conduct research and are key drivers of the social and technological change that is required to address environmental problems (Levy and Newell 2005a).

In the not-so-distant past, the majority of global corporations could have been expected to react to environmental measures in much the same way. Responses typically fell within a limited range from the skeptical and dismissive through to the outright hostile. The accepted ideology among corporate actors pitted environmental protection against economic success. Today, corporations are generally much more nuanced and diverse in their approach to environmental issues (Falkner 2008). This is not to say that one no longer finds individual corporations using old adversarial tactics. Exxon's continued funding of initiatives devoted to undermining the scientific evidence on climate change is a prime example (Adam 2009). In addition, corporations do still play the jobs-versus-environment card, which can be particularly effective in an economic crisis. For the most part, however, the modern global corporation is likely to agree that some action on environmental issues at the global level is necessary. Additionally, it may even acknowledge that "win-win" solutions to environmental problems are possible and that acting as a leader on environmental issues can be beneficial from an economic perspective, the so-called business case for environmentally responsible behavior. According to Braithwaite and Drahos (2000, 268), "the change in business leaders' attitudes on this issue is unmistakable. Many more now believe that green is lean and profitable." Nevertheless, as

Gunningham (2009, 221) points out, it remains unclear how much of this change in attitudes reflects empty rhetoric and to what extent corporations are actually "walking the talk."

How can one explain the shift in posture adopted by global corporations? To a large extent, it is purely strategic. It soon became obvious to corporate actors that taking a hostile stance on environmental issues was ineffective; the environmental movement grew substantially in size and influence in spite of continual attempts to undercut the emerging environmental agenda. Furthermore, despite fears (and corporate threats) of industrial flight to pollution havens, leading industrialized countries have steadily strengthened and expanded environmental regulation since the 1970s (Neumayer 2001).

The role of nongovernmental organizations (NGOs) must also be recognized. Organized boycotts of specific corporations and products have fundamentally altered the playing field. As Shell learned in the conflict over the disposal of its oil platform Brent Spar, the ability of NGOs to mobilize the public on environmental issues can result in serious damage to brand identity and a company's bottom line. Campaign groups have developed sophisticated strategies to cajole or pressure global corporations into more environmentally friendly behavior, giving rise to a new form of "world civic politics" (Wapner 1996) or "civil regulation" of business (Newell 2001).

In addition to being confronted with the need to at least appear to be concerned about the environment in order to maintain a favorable image in the eyes of conscientious consumers and ever-vigilant activists, corporations have also been inundated with accounts from academics, consultants, and other business experts of how (at least some) environmental practices can produce cost savings, reduce risk, and open up new green markets (see, e.g., Esty and Winston 2006). When leading corporate actors take up these practices, it creates pressure for others to follow suit (Gunningham 2009).

Finally, corporations have undoubtedly been appeased by government movements away from command-and-control style regulation at the domestic level and the lack of corporate accountability mechanisms at the global level (see Hajer 1995 for a discussion of this in the context of the broader shift to "ecological modernization" as the dominant discourse in environmental politics). As Utting (2002, 1) explains:

The confrontational politics of earlier decades, which had pitted a pro-regulation and redistributive lobby against [transnational corporations], lost momentum as governments, business and multilateral organizations alike, as well as an increasing number of NGOs, embraced ideas of "partnership" and "co-regulation" in which different actors or "stakeholders" would work together to find ways of minimizing the environmental cost of economic growth and modernization. The hands-on regulatory role of the state ceded ground to "corporate self-regulation" and "voluntary initiatives" as the best approach for promoting the adoption of instruments and processes associated with corporate environmental responsibility.

In other words, although global corporations have changed their behavior, to some extent, as a result of being pushed (e.g., through boycotts) and pulled (e.g., by green markets), this is not the whole story. Other actors have also changed their expectations for corporations and have altered the way that they approach and interact with them. This has made it easier for corporations to engage in environmental governance. Although some observers would view this finding of common ground as laudable, others decry the cooptation or marketization of the environmental agenda (Newell 2008).

Regardless of the position that one takes on this issue, it is clear that the new role, or more aptly new roles, adopted by global corporations in global environmental governance are significant and deserve attention from scholars. It is worth briefly outlining the key roles played by corporations that have been identified to date (see, for example, Falkner 2008; Fuchs 2007; Clapp 2005).

The most commonly accepted and extensively studied role is that of *lobbyist*. Although there is nothing new in itself about corporations lobbying domestically and even in some cases gaining official representation in government delegations to international meetings, it has been observed that, increasingly, corporate actors are also looking for their own seat at the international table (Elliott 1998; Clapp 2005). At intergovernmental meetings, they participate as observers, organize side events, and meet in the corridors with other key players. Corporations have also learned to coordinate their efforts at the global level and are now often represented by larger bodies such as the World Business Council for Sustainable Development or International Chamber of Commerce at negotiations (Orsini 2011). As is the case with intergovernmental bureaucracies, such bodies can have significant influence in governance outcomes (Bauer, Andresen, and Biermann, this book, chapter 2).

Once a multilateral environmental agreement has been signed and ratified, governments will take steps to implement it in their jurisdiction. In this process, global corporations may be subjected to new regulations. How global corporations respond to the implementation of multilateral environmental agreements—whether they take on the role of *supporter, acceptor,* or *challenger*—will have a strong impact on the effectiveness of global environmental governance. Technology may also be crucial to the implementation of a multilateral environmental agreement, and global corporations have tremendous resources to devote to research and development. Thus, global corporations can also take on the important role of *innovator,* using their technological prowess to shape the direction and effectiveness of environmental governance (Falkner 2005).

Another role adopted by global corporations that influences the development and the implementation of environmental measures is that of *communicator.* By influencing the language used in official documents and framing debates in the public sphere, corporations help to shape norms and ideas that in turn affect the direction of policy. According to Fuchs (2007, 154) "discursive power appears to be a particularly strong source of potential influence for business."

A final role that global corporations have recently assumed is that of *regulator.* Instead of simply passively accepting or trying to influence regulations by governments, global corporations are actively developing standards for themselves or cooperating with other private actors (e.g., NGOs) to do so. Examples of this form of private governance include reporting schemes (e.g., the Global Reporting Initiative), certification and labeling schemes (e.g., the Forest Stewardship Council), and sets of voluntary principles (e.g., the International Chamber of Commerce Business Charter for Sustainable Development) (Cutler, Haufler, and Porter 1999; Hall and Biersteker 2002; Falkner 2003; Pattberg 2007 and this book, chapter 5). These private initiatives are not only relevant in terms of how they affect corporate behavior with respect to the environment, but also in terms of how they influence the way in which environmental issues are dealt with in more traditional state-led forums.

Experiences

In this section, we employ three examples to illustrate how corporations shape the development of multilateral environmental agreements through lobbying and how they affect the implementation of multilateral environmental agreements once they have been ratified. This limited focus is taken due to considerations of space and is not reflective of our views on the importance of other dimensions of corporate agency and power, including discursive power (a topic that has been of increasing interest to scholars; see Fuchs 2007) or private governance, a subject that is more fully explored in part II of this book.

Influencing Regime Creation, Shaping Regime Evolution: Global Business in Ozone Politics

The international regime to combat stratospheric ozone-layer depletion is widely considered the greatest success in the history of international environmental policy making. It is also seen by many analysts as a clear example of the pervasive influence that global corporations have on environmental negotiations. A number of scholars have provided detailed accounts of the efforts by leading chemical firms to influence the creation of the 1987 Montreal Protocol (Levy 1997; Litfin 1994; Oye and Maxwell 1995). More recently, the focus has shifted to the role that business has played in shaping the evolution of the ozone regime after 1987, with greater attention being paid to other industrial sectors—from aerosol manufacturers to refrigeration and air-conditioning industries—and how they have helped to advance or hinder the international effort to phase out ozone-depleting substances such as chlorofluorocarbons (CFCs) (Falkner 2005).

The different roles played by corporations in international environmental governance have been evident in ozone politics. From the beginning of the ozone crisis in the mid-1970s, global corporations were actively involved as lobbyists of governments in an effort to influence the creation of national and international regulations to combat ozone-layer depletion. Initially, the business community was united in its opposition to any regulatory action. Led by the producers of CFCs and other ozone-depleting substances, business representatives in Europe and North America questioned the science that implicated CFCs in ozone depletion and argued that restricting their use would cause economic havoc. The small group of chemical firms (DuPont, Allied Chemical, ICI, Atochem, and Hoechst) that controlled the global market for CFC production provided the main impetus for the business community's lobbying campaign against the internationalization of ozone politics.

The first divisions within the business community emerged when certain CFC-using industries came under pressure by activist groups and regulators to reduce their reliance on ozone-depleting substances. The aerosol industry in the United States was the first to react to the growing controversy surrounding CFCs. By the late 1970s, US manufacturers of aerosol products had completely phased out the use of what was once described as a "miracle chemical." Their European competitors were also making efforts to reduce reliance on CFCs, but faced with much weaker public and regulatory pressure in Europe, they were able to continue using the controversial chemicals well into the late 1980s (Falkner 2008).

Growing business conflict—between CFC producers and users, and between US and European industries—was to play an important role in subsequent international negotiations. DuPont was the first chemical company in 1986 to advocate global restrictions on the production of ozone-depleting chemicals. It had closely followed the scientific debate on ozone depletion and recognized that new scientific discoveries were gradually strengthening the link between CFC emissions and ozone depletion. The company was also concerned about the growing imbalance between different national CFC restrictions, with European competitors enjoying a competitive advantage due to weaker regulations in Europe. The fact that the world's largest CFC producer was now backing an international regime undermined the anti-regulatory business front and boosted the chances of reaching an international accord in 1987. For a second time in 1988, DuPont broke rank with the rest of the chemical industry and announced its support for the eventual elimination of all CFC production and replacement with environmentally friendly substitute chemicals, provided this would apply to all major economies worldwide (Glas 1988; Falkner 2008).

Business conflict thus weakened the anti-regulatory business lobby and created political space for negotiators to agree on the Montreal Protocol. Divisions between and within industrial sectors also helped to shape the implementing and renegotiating of the ozone regime. After 1987, some CFC-using industries (e.g., aerosols and electronics) moved faster than others (e.g., air conditioning and refrigeration) in replacing ozone-depleting substances with safer alternatives. Although most user industries had been hostile toward any CFC restrictions until well after the Montreal Protocol was signed, rapid technological breakthroughs allowed some of them to move ahead of the internationally agreed CFC phase-out schedule. This in turn enabled negotiators to tighten the Montreal Protocol in several rounds of treaty revisions and bring forward deadlines for the phase-out of the various ozone-depleting substances.

In their role as innovators, certain CFC producers and users came to shape regime evolution and helped to speed up the phase-out of ozone-depleting substances. At the same time, other industrial sectors were either unable or unwilling to engage in radical product and process changes to replace CFCs. The air-conditioning and refrigeration industries, for example, adopted substitute chemicals that either were classified as transitional substances (hydrochlorofluorocarbons [HCFCs]) or had negative side effects due to their substantial contribution to global warming (hydrofluorocarbons [HFCs]). Together with the chemical industry that had backed hydrochlorofluorocarbons and hydrofluorocarbons solutions, the air-conditioning and refrigeration sectors fought to retain the right to use these substitute chemicals, rejecting calls by scientists and environmentalists for their early phase-out. The compromises reached in the post-1987 ozone negotiations largely reflected the innovation and investment decisions taken by different CFC-using industries (Falkner 2008).

The importance of the innovator role of business to the functioning of the ozone regime underlined the technological power of major corporations in global environmental governance. Leading industrial experts from a wide range of sectors were invited to join the Montreal Protocol's influential technology assessment panels, thus helping to direct the emerging discourse on the feasibility of CFC-replacement strategies and phase-out schedules. Business decisions on technological innovation and investment, by CFC producers and users alike, set important parameters for what other actors perceived as technologically feasible regulations. In this sense, corporations used their technological power to frame the knowledge structure within which the ozone regime evolved (Falkner 2005).

To be sure, corporations did not control, in a strict sense of the word, the process of technological change, nor did they determine the outcome of the international negotiation. Corporate power often found its match in the agency and power of other actors. States and environmental campaign groups created pressures and incentives for the CFC industries to address the ozone-depletion problem. They also exploited competitive dynamics between individual firms and benefited from the potential for business conflict to divide the initially united business front that had delayed regulatory action in the early days of the ozone controversy. To understand, therefore, the role and influence of global corporations in environmental governance, we need to focus not only on the sources of corporate power but also on the potential for disunity and conflict within the business community. The next section delves further into this topic in the area of biodiversity politics.

Coalitions, Conflicts, and the Limits of Lobbying Power: Global Business in Biodiversity Politics

The history of corporate engagement in the biodiversity regime holds important lessons for our understanding of the role of global corporations as lobbyists. Since its adoption in 1992, the Convention on Biological Diversity has been the framework for one of the most dynamic, though not necessarily most effective, regimes in the environmental field. Global corporations have actively engaged in negotiations taking place within the regime, in particular on biosafety and access and benefit sharing.

In 2000, the parties to the biodiversity convention adopted the Cartagena Protocol on Biosafety to regulate the transboundary movements of genetically modified organisms (GMOs), which are crops created by biotechnological manipulation (see Gupta et al., this book, chapter 4; Busch, Gupta, and Falkner, this book, chapter 9). The protocol regulates the international trade in GMOs by establishing the rules for importer decision making based on the precautionary principle. The Cartagena Protocol has had an appreciable impact on biotechnology companies, grain traders, and food retailers worldwide because it forces these private actors to follow precise procedures regarding GMO transport and handling (Andrée 2005; Falkner 2008).

In 2002, the parties to the biodiversity convention adopted international guidelines that regulate the conditions of access to natural genetic resources (known as the access and benefit-sharing objective). These genetic resources are used for innovative purposes by a broad range of corporations particularly in the pharmaceutical, biotech, and cosmetics sectors. Moreover, in October 2010 the parties to the biodiversity negotiations adopted a binding international agreement to improve the transparency of genetic resources supply chains, known as the Nagoya Protocol.

Global corporations were involved in the negotiations of the Cartagena Protocol and the Nagoya Protocol, and the importance of their lobbying activities has been emphasized in the literature to date (Andrée 2005; Clapp 2007; Tully 2003). This section, conversely, draws attention to the limits of corporate power in these negotiations. One indication of such limits is the constant adaptation of corporate lobbying strategies.

In terms of the negotiations for the Cartagena Protocol, the most active biotechnology companies were initially focused on trying to influence the process through their alliance with the US delegation. As the United States is not party to the biodiversity convention, however, it soon became a priority for these firms to shift their focus to other delegations with a direct role in the negotiations (Bled 2008). In pursuit of wider influence, these biotechnology firms created a new business lobbying coalition in 1998—the Global Industry Coalition—that lobbied forcefully in favor of nonbinding international regulations of biotechnology applications.

Despite its dynamism, the Global Industry Coalition suffered a major setback when the binding Cartagena Protocol was adopted in 2000. At the time, the coalition was facing internal as well as external difficulties. Internally, the Global Industry Coalition was far from unified (Falkner 2008; Orsini 2011). In particular, divisions emerged between pharmaceutical companies and agricultural biotechnology firms because agricultural products were meant to be released into the wider environment whereas pharmaceuticals were used in confined laboratories and were consequently supposed to have less impact on biodiversity. Divisions also evolved between biotechnology developers and grain traders in response to European consumers' request for GMO labeling. Moreover, the coalition developed a very obstructionist stance that gave the impression that the biotechnology companies wanted to dictate international decisions on GMOs. As a result, the Global Industry Coalition was excluded from coordination meetings organized by the European Union and developing countries (Bled 2008).

As a consequence of the Global Industry Coalition's failure to prevent the adoption of the Cartagena Protocol, corporate lobbying activities evolved in two directions. On the one hand, the Global Industry Coalition lost some of its allies when pharmaceutical companies left the negotiations after obtaining the elimination of pharmaceuticals from the scope of the protocol and when the grain traders decided to create a competing lobbying group—the International Grain Trade Coalition— that was less adverse to the adoption of rules on GMOs. On the other hand, the biotechnology firms decided to establish a steering committee for the Global Industry Coalition, charged with controlling internal decisions (Orsini 2011). In order to improve their reputation, these biotechnology firms also created CropLife International, a business NGO, enlisted with the task of communicating to society the benefits of biotechnology, and developed strong links with a transnational scientific organization, the Public Research and Regulation Initiative, to reinforce their expertise on biotechnology applications. Despite all of these efforts, recent developments in the negotiations reveal that the main biotechnology firms continue to face difficulties in their attempts to shape biodiversity governance (Bled 2010). In 2006, the parties to the Cartagena Protocol adopted mandatory rules on the documentation of GMO shipments, despite strong opposition to such labeling expressed by the Global Industry Coalition.

As in the Cartagena negotiations, global corporations involved in the access and benefit-sharing negotiations initially focused on exerting pressure on governments through their participation in national coordination meetings and national delegations. In particular, pharmaceutical companies developed strong links with the Swiss and German governments. In this instance, global corporations have had measured success in their lobbying efforts because voluntary international guidelines on access and benefit sharing were adopted in 2002. The guidelines were soon challenged, however, by several governments, mainly countries rich in biodiversity as well as Sweden. These governments asked for the negotiation of a mandatory regime on access and benefit sharing to be completed by 2010 (Bled 2010).

When the negotiations of this mandatory agreement began, corporations involved in the process adopted two different lobbying stances. On the one hand, the biggest pharmaceutical companies, which had been active in networking with governments during the negotiation of the voluntary guidelines, continued their efforts to influence the process. These efforts remained focused on lobbying national delegations, although they additionally increased their efforts to network with other private-sector actors under the auspices of the International Chamber of Commerce (Orsini 2011). On the other hand, several nationally based corporations such as the Brazilian company Natura took a proactive position on access to genetic resources and created strong links with their governments. Although the first category of business actors has had a limited influence on the process, mainly because of its obstructionist stance, the second has been successful in advocating a binding international regime on access and benefit sharing (Bled 2009).

The Cartagena Protocol and Nagoya Protocol negotiations indicate that there are limits to corporate influence in the biodiversity regime. As in the ozone regime, global corporations have been successful in certain instances—for example, initially restricting progress on access and benefit sharing to only voluntary measures—but overall they have been plagued by a lack of unity within specific coalitions and more generally between different sectors. Corporations have been forced to change tactics repeatedly in order to respond to these conflicts and the evolving dynamics of the negotiations. Additionally, when coalitions have fallen apart, energy has been expended to form new lobbying organizations and to restructure old ones. In sum, business conflict and corporate obstructionism have undermined the ability of global corporations to maintain a pervasive influence on the Cartagena Protocol and the Nagoya Protocol.

Challenging the Implementation of Environmental Regimes: Global Business and Investment Arbitration

The previous two sections have focused on how global corporations can shape the development of international environmental regimes. Empirical work in this area is critical to understanding the broader influence of corporations in global environmental governance. The story does not end there, however. As noted previously, global corporations can also play an important role in supporting, accepting, or challenging the implementation of environmental regimes at the domestic level. Global corporations have significant resources at their disposal and access to new technologies; their acceptance of or support for a regime can therefore be crucial to its success. Conversely, if global corporations oppose a particular regime it can become politically and financially costly for a government to implement it. This section looks at one instance in which a global corporation acted as a challenger to the implementation of a multilateral environmental agreement and examines the mechanism—investment arbitration—that it employed to facilitate its challenge.

The corporation in question is S. D. Myers—an international waste treatment company headquartered in Ohio—which had sought to import polychlorinated biphenyls (PCBs) and PCB wastes from Canada for processing in the United States in the early 1990s. The firm was (temporarily) thwarted by a 1995 Canadian government ban on the movement of these substances across the Canada–United States border. PCBs are highly toxic substances that have been the subject of increasingly strict regulation in Canada and the United States since the 1970s, including restrictions on imports and exports. Furthermore, Canada had ratified in 1992 the Basel Convention on the Transboundary Movement of Hazardous Wastes, a multilateral environmental agreement that prohibits the export and import of hazardous wastes (including PCBs) to and from nonparties (such as the United States) unless an agreement exists between the party and nonparty that is as stringent as the convention (article 11). Although there is a bilateral agreement (the 1986 Agreement Concerning the Transboundary Movement of Hazardous Waste) between Canada and the United States, it was unclear to the Canadian government at the time that it implemented the ban whether this agreement actually covered PCBs (which were not classified by the United States as hazardous waste) and met the requirements of article 11 of the Basel convention.

Because of its status as a foreign investor, S. D. Myers could use an arbitration clause in chapter 11 of the North American Free Trade Agreement (NAFTA) to initiate a special legal proceeding against the Canadian government challenging the ban. International investment arbitration is a rapidly growing field. Arbitration clauses are found in investor-state contracts, bilateral investment treaties (now at over 2,600; see UNCTAD 2009), and trade agreements like NAFTA. At least 390 cases of treaty-based, investor-state disputes had reached arbitration by the end of 2010 (UNCTAD 2011). An increasing number of these cases concern environmental regulation (for summaries of recent cases see Tienhaara 2011a).

In the S. D. Myers case, the arbitral tribunal determined that Canada had, in imposing the ban on the transborder movement of PCBs, breached some of the provisions of NAFTA chapter 11 and should pay S. D. Myers nearly Can$7 million dollars in damages and costs (Tribunal 2002a, 2002b). With regard to the Basel convention, the tribunal determined that article 11 clearly permitted crossborder movement of hazardous waste under the terms of the bilateral transboundary agreement. It also noted, however, "Even if the Basel convention were to have been ratified by NAFTA Parties, *it should not be presumed that Canada would have been able to use it to justify the breach of a specific NAFTA provision*" (Tribunal 2000, paragraph 215, emphasis added). The tribunal concluded that "where a state can achieve its chosen level of environmental protection through a variety of equally effective and reasonable means, it is obliged to adopt the alternative that is *most consistent with open trade*" (Tribunal 2000, paragraph 221, emphasis added).

Regardless of what one makes of the particular facts of this case, the tribunal has sent regulators a disturbing message that the commitments they have made to protect global corporations (vague and ill-defined as they are) trump those that they have made in multilateral environmental agreements. This gives global corporations a powerful tool to challenge the implementation of environmental agreements. Although arbitrators typically award only compensation to investors, rather than requiring the state to overturn a regulatory measure, there is understandable concern that arbitration or the threat of arbitration may cause "regulatory chill" (Mann 2001; Neumayer 2001; Tienhaara 2011b). In other words, governments may maintain the status quo in environmental regulation and even fail to implement multilateral environmental agreements (which generally lack strong enforcement mechanisms) because they fear the costs of breaching investment agreements. Moreover, even when governments do not refrain entirely from regulating, they are likely to employ those regulatory tools that are least likely to be challenged, rather than those that are most likely to be effective.

Although most investor-state disputes resolved to date have not con-cerned measures taken to implement multilateral agreements, there is a concern that global corporations will increasingly turn to arbitration as international environmental obligations become more onerous. A dispute that emerged in 2009 between the Swedish energy company Vattenfall and the government of Germany appears to give credence to this fear as well as to concerns about regulatory chill. Using the investment chapter of the Energy Charter Treaty, the firm, which invested in a proposed multibillion-Euro coal-fired power plant, challenged measures that the German government claimed were taken by state officials in order to comply with the requirements of the European Union's Water Frame-work Directive. Given that Vattenfall's investment was in the energy sector, this case also raised questions about the potential for disputes to arise over the implementation of state commitments in a future climate regime. As Bernasconi (2009, 6) noted, "With future measures on climate change soon to be agreed at the international level, one must wonder if this is a prelude to the arbitration of measures not just in Germany but any state that takes the measures necessary to implement new global standards and targets." In August 2010, the parties in the Vattenfall dispute reached a negotiated settlement. Although no details of the settle-ment have been released, media reports have suggested that local water-use restrictions, which would have prevented the completed plant from operating at full capacity, may have been eased to placate the company (Peterson 2010).

Finally, it is worth noting that although the S. D. Myers and Vattenfall cases both concern environmental measures adopted in developed coun-tries, the potential for global corporations to use investment arbitration in developing countries is actually much greater. The majority of inter-national investment agreements are signed between a developed and developing country. Although these agreements are reciprocal, global investment flows are currently highly asymmetrical (many investors from the North operate in the South, but less so the reverse) and thus in most instances only the developing country party faces significant exposure to arbitration claims. Furthermore, developing countries often lack the resources and expertise to mount an effective defense in arbitral proceed-ings as well as the funds to pay investors compensation (which can reach the range of several hundred million US dollars) and are therefore more likely to capitulate to corporate demands in order to avoid arbitration (Tienhaara 2009). From a global environmental governance perspective, this is a serious problem, especially when one considers that developing countries are likely to be expected to take on more binding targets in international environmental treaties in the near future.

Explanations

As these three examples have shown, it is unquestionable that global corporations are increasingly involved in global environmental governance. The influence of firms is felt at the stages of regime formation and implementation. Although the overall picture of business participation is clear, these experiences also point to the fact that the consequences of corporate engagement are varied. Greater involvement of global corporations cannot be considered either unequivocally positive or negative in terms of creating effective global environmental governance. Even within a specific issue area, corporations behave in obstructive and constructive ways. As a group, corporations are diverse; individually, they can be mercurial. It is therefore inadvisable to generalize about their impact on global environmental governance. Nevertheless, some specific findings can be drawn out from our research.

One finding is that although it is important to acknowledge that multiple interest groups endeavor to influence global environmental politics, it must be recognized that global corporations occupy a privileged position in the international hierarchy. Although this argument has been made by others, the focus has often been on the structural economic power that global corporations wield (see references for Clapp 2005 and Fuchs 2007, chapter 5). That is to say that because global corporations are a major provider of employment, contribute significantly to economic growth, and can credibly threaten to exit a given jurisdiction, national governments are more sensitive to their concerns than to those, for example, of NGOs. Our research and the cases discussed in this chapter, however, highlight some additional sources of power that can be drawn on by global corporations.

One, illustrated in the discussion of the ozone regime, is technological power. As a result of their predominant role in research and development, global corporations are able not only to provide solutions to environmental problems, but also to define the boundaries of what policy options are considered technologically and economically feasible (Falkner 2005; see also Beck 2002). Many global environmental problems require societies to make fundamental changes to industrial and technological systems, for example, with regard to the use of energy and natural resources or the production and disposal of toxic substances. In this regard, global corporations play a critical role. They shape the direction and speed of processes of technological change. Their investments in industrial infrastructure and technological innovation give them a powerful and indeed privileged position in global debates on how to bring about change toward greater environmental sustainability.

A second source, particularly evident in the biodiversity regime, is organizational power. Firms have the financial and material capacities to establish and maintain diverse alliances inside the business community (in international lobbying coalitions and business NGOs) as well as externally (with governments and environmental NGOs). With regard to the Cartagena Protocol on Biosafety, the Global Industry Coalition has been very successful in networking with the main grain-exporting states, which have decided not to ratify the final agreement. In the access and benefit-sharing negotiations, several pharmaceutical companies have been very active in advising the Swiss and German governments for the elaboration of international voluntary guidelines on the issue. The Brazilian company Natura has also developed strong links with the Brazilian government to push for the adoption of the Nagoya Protocol. Although the need to continually change tactics indicates that there are limits to corporate power, the capacity of firms to adapt their strategies in order to achieve greater influence is noteworthy (Bled 2008; Levy and Newell 2005a).

A third source, exemplified in the use of investment arbitration by global corporations, is institutional power. The landscape of global governance is of course not populated solely by environmentally focused institutions; global corporations have been actively involved in lobbying for and shaping the development of what Levy and Egan (1998) call "enabling institutions," designed to facilitate economic processes such as trade and investment. Although often (legally) isolated from one another at the international level, regulatory and enabling institutions can overlap and come into conflict at the stage of implementation. These types of conflicts have been extensively studied in the context of the trade-environment debate (Esty 1994; O'Neill and Burns 2005). Investment agreements, however, have been given less attention by scholars even though they allow for a more active role for global corporations. These agreements provide global corporations with leverage in national and international politics that other actors cannot attain. As access to investment arbitration is exclusive to foreign investors, only global corporations and not domestic firms (let alone nonbusiness actors) can use this mechanism to challenge environmental regulation. Thus, international investment agreements in effect elevate global corporations to a level of recognition in international law not usually afforded to nonstate actors. Sornarajah (2006) points out that, ironically, although international investment agreements give foreign investors standinzg in international law, efforts to create responsibilities on the part of global corporations have been resisted on the grounds of the absence of international legal personality.

Although we argue that global corporations, as a broad group, occupy a privileged position in global politics, clearly the extent to which individual firms can draw on technological, organizational, and institutional power will vary. As the experiences discussed in the previous section indicate, there is in fact a wide array of views and strategies that global corporations adopt in response to global environmental governance. It is perhaps unsurprising that corporations do not collectively comprise a monolithic entity that speaks with a single voice on environmental issues. It is after all well recognized that environmental regulation creates winners and losers. The level of dissonance among corporate actors, however, appears to surpass that which would occur if only this basic win-lose dichotomy was in operation. Even within a group of purported winners or losers, there may be rifts and renegades, and such divisions are of eminent political significance in international processes of regime building and implementation.

Essentially, the diversity of corporate responses to global environmental governance reflects the inherent diversity of the business community. As noted, corporations vary in terms of the strength of their technological, organizational, and institutional power. It is also the case that incentives to act will vary (Gunningham 2009). Certain business sectors and individual corporations are more susceptible to negative media exposure and NGO campaigns and are therefore more likely to want at least to appear to be playing a positive role in global environmental governance (Lock 2006). Whether a corporation is owned publicly or privately may also affect its willingness (and ability) to adopt approaches that are less focused on short-term profit maximization. Corporations are also differentiated by the location of their headquarters. Strong home state regulation may trigger a global corporation's involvement in the establishment of an international regime, particularly if it is highly exposed to competition in foreign markets (Falkner 2008). Additionally, the stage at which a corporation becomes involved in the negotiation and implementation of a multilateral environmental agreement will affect how invested it will be in the outcome of that process and how well it understands the underlying issues. A corporation that has been active since the emergence of a regime would possibly be more in tune with what points various actors are likely to compromise on and might also better predict when the tide is about to turn against its position. Corporations that are completely uninvolved with the negotiation of a multilateral environmental agreement may be more likely to challenge its implementation, for example, through investment arbitration.

The reasons for heterogeneity will obviously vary from case to case. What is common across different areas of global environmental governance, however, is the fact that divisions that emerge within coalitions of business actors are a significant factor in limiting corporate influence. As was clearly illustrated in the discussion of the ozone and biodiversity regimes, business conflict can severely impede efforts on the part of global corporations to prevent the creation of environmental regimes or to shape their development. Given the increasing complexity of environmental issues and the increasing number of businesses with divergent interests being affected by global environmental governance, it seems unlikely that global corporate unity will emerge in the near future.

Another significant factor limiting corporate influence is the existence of countervailing forces. NGOs can play an especially important role in this respect. In the case of biotechnology applications, NGOs have had a strong impact on governments as well as on industries (demonstrated by the position adopted by the grain traders during negotiations) (Arts and Mack 2003). On access and benefit-sharing issues, NGOs have continually sought more proactive participation from corporations in access and benefit-sharing legislation, with some degree of success (Miller 2006). Even in the area of investment arbitration, NGOs can influence corporate behavior (e.g., convincing them to drop an investor-state dispute) through negative media campaigns and can additionally influence arbitrators through the submission of *amicus curiae* (friend of the court) briefs (Tienhaara 2007, 2009).

In sum, corporations are increasingly involved in global environmental governance in a variety of ways. Outcomes that are favorable to business and detrimental to environmental progress, however, are only intermittent. Although global corporations have significant power advantages relative to other interest groups, such as technological power, organizational power, and access to enabling institutions, they also face limitations. In order to achieve greater influence in global environmental governance, global corporations will first have to overcome the obstacles to reaching greater consensus within the business community.

Conclusions and Outlook

Although many authors, particularly in the popular literature, have portrayed global corporations as a one-dimensional and homogenous group, we have argued in this chapter that in reality, these actors are complex and their relationships with each other are often contentious. Global corporations do not have one role to play in global environmental governance, but many. As lobbyists, communicators, and regulators they can be either obstructive or constructive in the development of international environmental regimes. Subsequently, as innovators, supporters, acceptors, or challengers they can facilitate or impede the implementation of these regimes.

Global corporations have received greater attention from environmental scholars in recent years but significant gaps in our knowledge remain. Whereas a considerable amount of work has been done on the role that global corporations have played in the climate regime (e.g., Levy and Egan 2003; Falkner 2010; Vormedal 2008), there are other areas that have not been studied sufficiently, such as the emerging regimes on persistent organic pollutants and nanotechnology. Another worthwhile endeavor would be to examine more closely the determinants of corporate positions on specific environmental issues. Falkner (2008) has developed an analytical framework to explain corporate behavior (using parameters such as firm size, supply chain position, and technological capacity) that could be used in future research. There is also room for further inquiry on issues that we have only briefly touched on here, such as the discursive power of business. On this and other issues, it could be helpful to look outside the field of environmental policy to other areas of global governance (e.g., labor, human rights, trade, and security) for comparison. Finally, it is important to remember that global environmental governance is not insulated from major developments in other areas of global politics. For example, the financial crisis that erupted in 2008 and the global economic downturn that ensued have likely had a significant impact on the way that global corporations and states respond to demands for environmental protection. It would be interesting to investigate in future research whether the crisis has also had an impact on the influence of business in global environmental governance.

References

Adam, David. 2009. ExxonMobil continuing to fund climate sceptic groups, records show. *The Guardian*, July 1. http://www.guardian.co.uk/environment/2009/jul/01/exxon-mobil-climate-change-sceptics-funding.

Andrée, Peter. 2005. The Genetic Engineering Revolution in Agriculture and Food: Strategies of the Biotech Bloc. In *The Business of Global Environmental Governance*, ed. David Levy and Peter Newell, 135–166. Cambridge, MA: MIT Press.

Arts, Bas, and Sandra Mack. 2003. Environmental NGO's and the Biosafety Protocol: A Case Study on Political Influence. *European Environment* 13:19–33.

Beck, Ulrich. 2002. *Power in the Global Age*. Cambridge, UK: Polity Press.

Bernasconi, Nathalie. 2009. *Background Paper on Vattenfall v. Germany Arbitration*. Winnipeg, Canada: International Institute for Sustainable Development.

Bled, Amandine. 2008. Getting the Strongest Players Doesn't Make a Winning Team: Business and the Cartagena Protocol on Biosafety. In *Global Environmental Agreements: Insights and Implications*, ed. Asha Joshi, 189–206. Hyderabad, India: The Icfai University Press.

Bled, Amandine. 2009. Business to the Rescue: Private Sector Actors and Global Environmental Regimes' Legitimacy. *International Environmental Agreement: Politics, Law and Economics* 2:153–171.

Bled, Amandine. 2010. Technological Choices in International Environmental Negotiations: An Actor-Network Analysis. *Business & Society* 49 (4):570–590.

Braithwaite, John, and Peter Drahos. 2000. *Global Business Regulation*. Cambridge, UK: Cambridge University Press.

Clapp, Jennifer. 2005. Transnational Corporations and Global Environmental Governance. In *Handbook of Global Environmental Politics*, ed. Peter Dauvergne, 284–297. Cheltenham, UK: Edward Elgar.

Clapp, Jennifer. 2007. Transnational Corporate Interests in International Biosafety Negotiations. In *The International Politics of Genetically Modified Food*, ed. Robert Falkner, 34–47. Basingstoke, UK: Palgrave Macmillan.

Cutler, A. Claire, Virginia Haufler, and Tony Porter. 1999. Private Authority and International Affairs. In *Private Authority in International Affairs*, ed. A. Claire Cutler, Virginia Haufler, and Tony Porter, 1–28. Albany: SUNY Press.

Dauvergne, Peter. 2008. *The Shadows of Consumption: Consequences for the Global Environment*. Cambridge, MA: MIT Press.

Elliott, Lorraine. 1998. *The Global Politics of the Environment*. New York: New York University Press.

Esty, Daniel C. 1994. *Greening the GATT: Trade, Environment, and the Future*. Washington, DC: Institute for International Economics.

Esty, Daniel C., and Andrew S. Winston. 2006. *Green to Gold: How Smart Companies Use Environmental Strategy to Innovate, Create Value, and Build Competitive Advantage*. New Haven, CT: Yale University Press.

Falkner, Robert. 2003. Private Environmental Governance and International Relations: Exploring the Links. *Global Environmental Politics* 3 (2):72–87.

Falkner, Robert. 2005. The Business of Ozone Layer Protection: Corporate Power in Regime Evolution. In *The Business of Global Environmental Governance*, ed. David L. Levy and Peter Newell, 105–134. Cambridge, MA: MIT Press.

Falkner, Robert. 2008. *Business Power and Conflict in International Environmental Politics*. Basingstoke, UK: Palgrave Macmillan.

Falkner, Robert. 2010. Business and Global Climate Governance: A Neo-pluralist Perspective. In *Business and Global Governance*, ed. Morten Ougaard and Anna Leander, 99–117. London: Routledge.

Fuchs, Doris. 2007. *Business Power in Global Governance*. London: Lynne Rienner.

Glas, Joseph. 1988. DuPont's Position on CFCs. *Forum for Applied Research and Public Policy* 3 (3):71–72.

Gunningham, Neil. 2009. Shaping Corporate Environmental Performance: A Review. *Environmental Policy and Governance* 19:215–231.

Hajer, Maarten A. 1995. *The Politics of Environmental Discourse: Ecological Modernization and the Policy Process*. Oxford: Clarendon Press.

Hall, Rodney Bruce, and Thomas J. Biersteker. 2002. The Emergence of Private Authority in the International System. In *The Emergence of Private Authority in Global Governance*, ed. Rodney Bruce Hall and Thomas J. Biersteker, 3–22. Cambridge, UK: Cambridge University Press.

Levy, David L. 1997. Business and International Environmental Treaties: Ozone Depletion and Climate Change. *California Management Review* 39 (3): 54–71.

Levy, David L., and Daniel Egan. 1998. Capital Contests: National and Transnational Channels of Corporate Influence on the Climate Change Negotiations. *Politics & Society* 26 (3):337–361.

Levy, David L., and Daniel Egan. 2003. A Neo-Gramscian Approach to Corporate Political Strategy: Conflict and Accommodation in the Climate Change Negotiations. *Journal of Management Studies* 40 (4):803–829.

Levy, David L., and Peter Newell. 2005a. Introduction: The Business of Global Environmental Governance. In *The Business of Global Environmental Governance*, ed. David L. Levy and Peter Newell, 1–17. Cambridge, MA: MIT Press.

Levy, David L., and Peter Newell, eds. 2005b. *The Business of Global Environmental Governance*. Cambridge, MA: MIT Press.

Litfin, Karen. 1994. *Ozone Discourses: Science and Politics in Global Environmental Cooperation*. New York: Columbia University Press.

Lock, Ineke C. 2006. Corporate Social Responsibility and Codes of Conduct. In *Nature's Revenge: Reclaiming Sustainability in the Age of Corporate Globalization*, ed. Josée Johnston, Michael Gismondi, and James Goodman, 117–133. New York: Broadview Press.

Mann, Howard. 2001. *Private Rights, Public Problems: A Guide to NAFTA's Controversial Chapter on Investor Rights.* Winnipeg, Canada: International Institute for Sustainable Development.

Miller, Michael J. 2006. Biodiversity Policy Making in Costa Rica: Pursuing Indigenous and Peasant Rights. *Journal of Environment & Development* 15 (4):359–381.

Neumayer, Eric. 2001. *Greening Trade and Investment: Environmental Protection without Protectionism.* London: Earthscan.

Newell, Peter. 2001. Managing Multinationals: The Governance of Investment for the Environment. *Journal of International Development* 13:907–919.

Newell, Peter. 2008. The Marketization of Global Environmental Governance: Manifestations and Implications. In *The Crisis of Global Environmental Governance: Towards a New Political Economy of Sustainability*, ed. Jacob Park, Ken Conca, and Matthias Finger, 77–95. London: Routledge.

O'Neill, Kate, and William C. G. Burns. 2005. Trade Liberalization and Global Environmental Governance: The Potential for Conflict. In *Handbook of Global Environmental Politics*, ed. Peter Dauvergne, 319–333. Cheltenham, UK: Edward Elgar.

Orsini, Amandine. 2011. Thinking Transnationally, Acting Individually: Business Lobby Coalitions in International Environmental Negotiations. *Global Society* 25 (3):311–329.

Oye, Kenneth A., and James H. Maxwell. 1995. Self-Interest and Environmental Management. In *Local Commons and Global Interdependence: Heterogeneity and Cooperation in Two Domains*, ed. Robert O. Keohane and Elinor Ostrom, 191–222. Newbury Park, CA: Sage.

Pattberg, Philipp. 2007. *Private Institutions and Global Governance: The New Politics of Environmental Sustainability.* Northampton, UK: Edward Elgar.

Peterson, Luke Eric. 2010. Parties Announce Settlement of Dispute over German Power Plant. *Investment Arbitration Reporter*, 28 August.

Sornarajah, Muthucumaraswamy. 2006. Power and Justice: Third World Resistance in International Law. *Singapore Year Book of International Law* 10:19–57.

Tienhaara, Kyla. 2007. Third Party Participation in Investment-Environment Disputes: Recent Developments. *Review of European Community & International Environmental Law* 16 (2):230–242.

Tienhaara, Kyla. 2009. *The Expropriation of Environmental Governance: Protecting Foreign Investors at the Expense of Public Policy.* Cambridge, UK: Cambridge University Press.

Tienhaara, Kyla. 2011a. International Investment Developments. *Yearbook of International Environmental Law* 20:465–480.

Tienhaara, Kyla. 2011b. Regulatory Chill and the Threat of Arbitration: A View from Political Science. In *Evolution in Investment Treaty Law and Arbitration*, ed. Chester Brown and Kate Miles, 606–627. Cambridge, UK: Cambridge University Press.

Tribunal. 2000. *S. D. Myers, Inc. v. Government of Canada*. Partial Award, 13 November 2000.

Tribunal. 2002a. *S. D. Myers, Inc. v. Government of Canada*. Second Partial Award, 21 October 2002.

Tribunal. 2002b. *S. D. Myers, Inc. v. Government of Canada*. Final Award, 30 December 2002.

Tully, Stephen. 2003. The Bonn Guidelines on Access to Genetic Resources and Benefit Sharing. *Review of European Community & International Environmental Law* 12 (1):84–98.

UNCTAD (United Nations Conference on Trade and Development). 2006. FDI from Developing and Transition Economies: Implications for Development. World Investment Report 2006. Geneva: United Nations.

UNCTAD. 2009. Recent Developments in International Investment Agreements (2008–June 2009). IIA MONITOR No. 3, UNCTAD/WEB/DIAE/IA/2009/8. Geneva: United Nations.

UNCTAD. 2011. Latest Developments in Investor-State Dispute Settlement. IIA ISSUES NOTE No. 1, UNCTAD/WEB/DIAE/IA/2011/3. Geneva: United Nations.

Utting, Peter. 2002. Towards Corporate Environmental Responsibility. In *The Greening of Business in Developing Countries: Rhetoric, Reality and Prospects*, ed. Peter Utting, 1–13. London: Zed Books.

Vormedal, Irja. 2008. The Influence of Business and Industry NGOs in the Negotiation of the Kyoto Mechanisms: The Case of Carbon Capture and Storage in the CDM. *Global Environmental Politics* 8 (4):36–65.

Wapner, Paul. 1996. *Environmental Activism and World Civic Politics*. Albany, NY: SUNY Press.

4

Science Networks

Aarti Gupta, Steinar Andresen, Bernd Siebenhüner,
and Frank Biermann

Within debates about global environmental governance, voices from science are often heard and referred to. Be it in the media, official negotiation documents, activist campaigns, or public speeches, scientific findings are regularly quoted and interpreted. Although the climate regime is the most visible case in point, other policy arenas such as biodiversity governance, transboundary air pollution, or ozone depletion are no exceptions. Whether this signals increased scientific influence in the governance of crucial global environmental challenges remains, however, a matter of scrutiny.

The role of science in global environmental governance has changed since the 1980s in the direction of greater institutionalization of scientific input into global policy fora, often through globally organized assessments or scientific advisory bodies. Given this greater institutionalization of science, is its influence growing as a result? A diverse set of scholarly writings in international relations, global environmental politics, risk analysis, and science and technology studies have analyzed this question in recent years (see, for instance, Gibbons, Limoges, and Nowotny 1995; Biermann 2001, 2002; Gallopin et al. 2001; Jasanoff 2004; Haas 2005; Mitchell et al. 2006; Andresen and Skjærseth 2007). As members of the Global Governance Project, we have drawn on and extended this body of work through participating in broad-ranging and empirically diverse projects on the role of science in global environmental governance.[1]

In this contribution, we bring together insights from the broader literature as well as our own work in reconsidering the influence of science in governance. We proceed by distilling two sets of theoretical claims—each with different analytical roots—about factors that shape the influence of science in global policy making, and assess whether these claims hold in a number of highly contested problem areas of global environmental governance (so-called malign problems; see Andresen et al. 2000). The two sets of theoretical propositions are as follows. First, much science-policy writing emphasizes that the influence of science depends at least partly on whether it has been produced through a participatory and inclusive process (Renn, Webler, and Wiedemann 1995; Forrester 1999; Kasemir et al. 2003; Joss and Bellucci 2002; Siebenhüner 2004). This literature argues that a science that is more inclusive is likely to be more legitimate and hence more influential, particularly in normatively contested areas.

Second, a long-discussed aspect of the influence of science turns on the extent to which it is removed from, or embedded in, political processes. A dominant but contested assumption is that an objective, value-free (consensual) science separated from politics is the most likely to exercise influence, especially in normatively contested issue areas.

A central concern of this chapter is to reassess these two claims by analyzing the role of science in three highly contested global governance challenges: climate change, whaling, and trade in GMOs. We analyze the participatory processes through which policy-relevant science is being generated in these areas of global environmental governance and the kind of science that such processes yield. We also analyze whether policy-relevant science in such normatively contested areas is characterized by a lack of consensus and whether this translates into a lack of influence. When there is scientific agreement, we discuss whether this signals the triumph of objective, value-free science over contested politics or rather implies a negotiated science that reflects, and leaves undisturbed, underlying normative conflicts.

By addressing such questions in a variety of scientifically complex and normatively contested global environmental issue areas, we seek to evaluate and extend theoretical and empirical insights about influence of science in global environmental politics.

Conceptualization

In this section, we elaborate on the two sets of factors noted previously as central to the influence of science: participatory processes of generating policy-relevant science and the perceived objective or negotiated nature of scientific input into policy processes.

Understanding Scientific Influence: Participatory and Inclusive Processes

A long-established set of writings within risk analysis and ecological economics offers a process-oriented perspective on what constitutes influential science in global environmental governance. These writings argue for an explicitly participatory "postnormal science" that is geared toward the inherent uncertainty surrounding current global environmental and risk challenges (Funtowicz and Ravetz 1991, 1992, 1993). A postnormal science is characterized, first, by extended peer review, that is, by calls for expert and lay perspectives to join in the production of relevant knowledge. This also includes new ways of communicating between scientists and nonscientists and their institutions.

In line with this now almost two-decade-old call for a more participatory postnormal science, recent writings emphasize the need for a broadened and more inclusive approach to scientific knowledge generation, deployment, and use. This lies at the heart of more recent writings about sustainability science. Sustainability science analysts see the need for novel forms of research and science-policy interaction through stakeholder participation and the integration of diverse forms of (context-specific) expertise in knowledge production. Sustainability science has been defined as a "new field . . . that seeks to understand the fundamental character of interactions between nature and society. Such an understanding must encompass the interaction of global processes with the ecological and social characteristics of particular places and sectors" (Kates et al. 2001, 641). The challenge is to render knowledge usable within science and society.

To address this, sustainability science scholars call for the integration of societal stakeholders such as the private sector and the broader public as well as diverse scientific disciplines within scientific assessments. The aim is to develop knowledge in an embedded way together with societal stakeholders and policy makers (Clark 2001), with the underlying assumption that doing so will enhance the influence of science in policy. Such a perspective highlights that a "new paradigm" of scientific work can no longer call for objectivity but has to accept a normative and political element in any research effort—also to be politically influential.

Understanding Scientific Influence: Objective versus Negotiated Science
Even (or especially) in normatively contested areas, a dominant strand of literature within international relations has long argued that consensual technical input provided by scientific "epistemic communities" can assist in reaching politically difficult compromises as a result of its authoritativeness, value neutrality, and distance from politics (Haas 1992). The call is for an objective, value-free science with the moral authority to "speak

truth to power." An early critique of this perspective was offered by Karen Litfin in her analysis of the global ozone regime, where she argued that scientific discourses tended, in many instances, to "articulate or rationalize existing interests and conflicts" (Litfin 1994, 197). Mitchell et al. (2006) have sought to take this discussion further by arguing that the influence of science, particularly in contested areas, will depend not only on its perceived scientific credibility (its soundness), but also on its perceived political legitimacy (fairness in considering diverse aspects of a problem) and perceived salience (relevance) for multiple stakeholders. The key claim here is that only a science perceived as salient and legitimate, in addition to credible, can exercise influence. In our own contributions to this 2006 study, we also drew attention to the inseparability of such attributes of influence, arguing that perceptions of legitimacy and salience cannot be separated from credibility (Gupta 2006; Biermann 2006).

Peter Haas (2004) has offered another version of credible, salient, and legitimate science in his concept of "usable knowledge" as a form of consensually agreed knowledge that is legitimate because of how it is generated and because of its relevance for decision making. Others writing in the same vein have emphasized the need to strike a balance between scientific integrity and political involvement (Underdal 2000). Notwithstanding these elaborations, a key claim in much environmental governance science–policy writing remains that a science that is consensual, credible through its distance from politics, and promoted by a scientific epistemic community is likely to be influential.

In contrast to this view, an alternative perspective is advanced by scholars of science and technology studies and constructivist writings within international relations, which have long contested the dominant portrayal of policy-relevant science as a universally valid, value-neutral, and objective language through which to mediate normative conflict (Jasanoff 1998, 2004; Herrick and Sarewitz 2000; Gupta 2004). Writings in this vein note that a claim to objectivity and value neutrality implies that science can be set apart from political considerations, that is, it implies the possibility of boundary drawing between science and politics. Such boundary making is critiqued, however, as an explicitly political legitimization strategy (Jasanoff 1987; Gieryn 1995). As Gieryn suggests, "Social construction of the science/policy boundary is a crucial strategy through which distinctive interests of diverse players are advanced or thwarted . . . boundary-work occurs as people contend for, legitimate, or challenge the cognitive authority of science" (Gieryn 1995, 436, 405, quoted in Gupta 2004).

From this perspective, the interesting question then becomes where these boundaries are sought to be drawn and why, and what the impact of doing so is on the cognitive authority of science. In an influential early analysis of such questions, Shackley and Wynne introduced the notion of "boundary-ordering devices" as "contextual discursive attempts to reconcile authority with uncertainty in science" (Shackley and Wynne 1996, 275). The key distinguishing feature of such discursive devices (for instance, the notion of "uncertainty" in climate change) is that they allow flexible interpretations of their meaning, thus maintaining the cognitive authority of science even as they allow cooperation and policy dialogue to continue (Shackley and Wynne 1996).

In sum, writings from this latter perspective differ fundamentally from a view of scientific influence that sees an objective and value-neutral science removed from politics as the most likely to be influential. They highlight, instead, that negotiated and deliberately ambiguous science that requires context-based re-interpretation (also through relying on boundary-ordering devices) is likely to be influential in contested global governance areas.

Taken together, these strands of literature suggest a set of (sometimes contradictory) assertions about when and how science is likely to be relevant and hence influential in global environmental decision making. In what follows, we take two sets of assertions as our points of departure for further analysis. First, we assess the claim that in an era of contested global environmental challenges, only a postnormal science generated through inclusion of expert and lay views, broadly defined, can be influential. Second, we assess whether a consensual science promoted by scientific epistemic communities is influential because of its perceived objectivity, value neutrality, and distance from politics or whether the influence of science in normatively contested areas depends on its being negotiated, deliberately ambiguous, and explicitly linked to political imperatives.

In the next sections, we analyze the growing institutionalization of scientific input into policy making (and the increasingly participatory and inclusive processes of generating policy-relevant science) in a number of key issue areas, its perceived objective or negotiated nature, and the prospects for such science to be influential.

Experiences

This section documents the growing institutionalization of scientific input in global governance of climate change, whaling, and trade in

GMOs. This includes the diverse processes by which scientific input into the policy process is being generated, and the nature of the science being produced. The following section then considers the nature and limits of scientific influence in these normatively contested areas of environmental governance.

Institutionalized Science for Policy: Participatory and Inclusive Processes?

Institutionalized scientific input into policy making is evident in an ever-expanding range of global environmental governance challenges. With an increasing institutionalization of scientific input into policy, diverse mechanisms for generating and sharing scientific findings have evolved. A key challenge in this institutionalization has been how to be more inclusive of diverse views and maintain the cognitive authority of science. A quintessential example of this is offered by the Intergovernmental Panel on Climate Change (IPCC).

The IPCC was established in 1988 as an intergovernmental (scientific) organization that involves governmental participation in approval of scientific conclusions. Its purpose is to provide scientific knowledge for international climate negotiations through producing a series of state-of-the-art assessment reports. Since its formation, the IPCC has undergone several changes with regard to its internal structures and procedures (Bolin 2007). With its innovative and unique governmental-approval mechanism, the IPCC has pioneered a new scientific assessment technique that has been consistently refined in its various assessment reports after 1988. According to this mechanism, the official interaction between scientists and policy makers is restricted to well-defined stages of the assessment. Scientists of the IPCC bureau first develop an outline of an IPCC report and identify topics of the working groups and the division of labor. They suggest this to national governments and select the authors and reviewers based on their scientific expertise and issues of geographical representation. The subsequent redrafting of chapters and the first round of peer review is undertaken by scientists. Governments enter the process once again in the second round of the review process, when their comments on revised assessment drafts are solicited. Finally, they have a crucial role in the approval of the summary for policy makers and the synthesis report. The rules of procedure for this have evolved significantly over the four assessments conducted by the IPCC from 1988 to 2007, with the process becoming more formal with stricter quality control after controversies alleging political interference with the assessment (Edwards and Schneider 2001; Siebenhüner 2004; Girod et al. 2009).

Since 2009, however, the credibility of IPCC has arguably been reduced. It started with the so-called climate-gate incident that involved the leakage of e-mails of researchers at the University of East Anglia. At about the same time, some errors were reported in the 2007 IPCC report, for example, the incorrect prediction that the Himalayas could lose their glaciers within a few decades. Because of such incidents, a series of reviews of the content and process of generating IPCC reports have been conducted. They have all concluded that the main substantive conclusions of the IPCC remain valid but that the transparency and accountability of the knowledge-synthesis process could be improved (Andresen and Skodvin 2011).

Another area where scientific input into policy making is marked by a growing institutionalization and a broadening of participatory processes is in global governance of whaling. The International Whaling Commission (IWC) was set up in 1948 based on the 1946 International Whaling Convention. From its very start, science has been assigned a key role in the IWC, with the dictum that management "shall be based on scientific findings" (article V.2.b of the 1946 International Whaling Convention). A scientific committee was set up but initial participation in it was very limited, and in the first phase "the scientific institutional structure was both immature and weak" (Andresen 2000, 43). In the 1970s, however, the scientific agenda and input from the scientific committee expanded considerably as a result of increasing pressure from antiwhaling forces. Since then, the committee has continually evolved in its modes of functioning and links to the political negotiations.

The history of the IWC itself is one of transformation, with four key phases identifiable in its development (Andresen 2008). In its first phase, it started out as a "whalers club," with all large whale species depleted by the early 1960s. In a second phase until the end of the 1970s, management became stricter and whaling quotas were reduced. This resulted in a protectionist third phase, which lasted until the mid-1990s, when commercial whaling was prohibited through a moratorium effective from around 1985. By the end of the 1980s, commercial whaling had been halted.

During this third phase, there was a strong influx of new members in the IWC with a large majority being antiwhaling, making possible the adoption of the moratorium by the necessary three-fourths majority. The third phase, however, was also characterized by intense hostility between pro- and antiwhaling nations (DeSombre 2001). Although the moratorium still stands, a fourth phase is now discernible from the mid-1990s onwards, since which time the prowhaling forces have been on the rise. As of 2011, pro- and antiwhaling perspectives are now more evenly divided among the IWC's eighty-eight members. Furthermore, the catch of whales is increasing again, with Norway and Iceland having resumed commercial whaling, Japan invoking a special permit for scientific whaling, and the United States, Russia, and Denmark (for Greenland) asserting their rights as aboriginal whaling countries.

The work of the IWC scientific committee was in its earlier years done by whaling nations because all IWC members were initially whaling states. As membership grew, states opposed to whaling also joined the organization. As a result, various innovations in processes of scientific knowledge generation and interactions between science and policy have resulted. An important turning point in the science-policy nexus was reliance on external and independent scientists in the IWC's scientific committee from 1977 onwards.

Over time, the scientific committee has become a much more open, representative, and larger forum. In 1974, for example, there were only twenty-four scientists attending. In the 1990s, attendance increased to approximately one hundred scientists. The workload and breadth of research expanded because of the elaboration of new and more complex models to estimate size of whaling stocks. The IWC scientific committee has continued to grow in terms of scope and participation in recent years, with more than two hundred scientists now involved. The independent participants are now the largest group, numbering fifty, and fewer than half the members send scientific representatives. Those represented usually send a few scientists, and the two main contenders, the United States and Japan, are represented by some twenty-five scientists each.

Topics for scientific research have also expanded. They include a revised management procedure to govern commercial whaling, an aboriginal subsistence management procedure, as well as other research areas such as stock assessments, environmental concerns (including effects of climate change), whale watching, scientific permits, estimation of bycatch and other human-induced mortality, ecosystem modeling, and whale sanctuaries. In short, the IWC's scientific committee has come a long way in institutionalizing various mechanisms for generating policy-relevant science for the governance of whaling over the years and in becoming more inclusive of diverse perspectives.

Scientific input has also become more institutionalized, if not necessarily more participatory, in the third issue area we examine here: global governance of safe trade and use of GMOs. Unlike the case of climate governance, there is no globally organized large-scale biosafety assessment to feed policy-relevant science into global GMO governance. Nonetheless, risk assessments relating to GMOs are central to the evolving global biosafety governance architecture (Gupta 2006). Underpinning this architecture, however, are fundamental political disagreements about whether and to what extent GMOs pose risks, which influence the design and scope of biosafety assessments, the criteria for policy decisions, and perceptions of whose science is sound.

The international institutional fora most relevant for governing global GMO flows are the World Trade Organization and its agreement on the Application of Sanitary and Phytosanitary Measures (WTO-SPS agreement); the Codex Alimentarius Commission (mandated to develop global food safety standards, including safety standards for foods obtained from modern biotechnology); and the Cartagena Protocol on Biosafety under the Convention on Biological Diversity (which regulates safe transboundary transfers of GMOs). In each of these settings, guidelines and participatory processes by which to generate policy-relevant science are becoming institutionalized.

Scientific assessments as a basis for policy choices are, for example, at the heart of the Cartagena Protocol on Biosafety. The biosafety protocol requires sharing of national-level safety assessments between GMO-exporting and GMO-importing countries as a way to facilitate importer decisions about whether to accept potentially risky GMOs. It also requires importing countries to undertake their own context-specific national biosafety assessments prior to making GMO trade (restrictive) decisions. Scientific assessments of risk and the exchange of information between countries are thus central elements of this global biosafety governance regime (Gupta 2002, 2010).

A concern with science-based domestic health and safety regulations (including those for GMOs) is also at the heart of the WTO-SPS agreement, which seeks to ensure that such regulations are not unnecessarily trade restrictive. This is to be achieved either through harmonization of domestic regulatory standards by adoption of international standards, such as those of the Codex Alimentarius Commission, or by basing domestic regulatory decisions on "sound" science. In this latter case, the WTO-SPS agreement requires that health and safety standards be "based on scientific principles and . . . not maintained without sufficient scientific evidence" (WTO-SPS agreement 1994, article 4). Thus, at the heart of the WTO-SPS agreement is a requirement that national sanitary and phytosanitary standards, including GMO regulations, have a clear scientific justification.

Where there is scientific uncertainty about adverse effects, a much-debated obligation of the WTO-SPS agreement permits trade restrictive precautionary action for a provisional period, even as members are called on to "obtain the additional information necessary for a more objective assessment of risk and review the sanitary or phytosanitary measure accordingly within a reasonable period of time" (WTO-SPS agreement 1994, article 5.7). Excluded from the WTO-SPS agreement rules are socioeconomic considerations that cannot be directly related to sanitary or phytosanitary harm, such as public acceptability or consumer opposition, even though these factors are often key to GMO policy choices. It is also noteworthy that the Cartagena Protocol, negotiated with the explicit purpose to allow (more) choice to GMO importers to restrict trade than previously available, does not necessarily conflict with the WTO-SPS agreement on key provisions relating to precaution and socioeconomic dimensions of the global GMO trade, although this is open to interpretation (for detailed analysis, see Gupta 2001, 2008; Young et al. 2008).

This discussion implies, then, a strong potential influence of science on GMO policy choices. Scientific input is an increasingly institutionalized aspect of global biosafety governance. The overall push from global regimes is for domestic GMO trade decisions to be based on narrowly circumscribed, expert-driven, and scientifically assessable notions of risk and safety, even as this push to "technicalize" biosafety decisions remains contested (Gupta 2002; 2011). This has implications for the nature and influence of policy-relevant science in this realm, as discussed in the following section.

Institutionalized Science for Policy: Objective or Negotiated Science?

Given the growing institutionalization of scientific input into policy, an important question becomes whether the science being produced is perceived to be consensual, objective, and removed from politics or negotiated and inextricably linked to political processes and considerations.

With regard to climate change, it can be persuasively argued that the scientific message has become more consensual as well as more "alarmist" over time. The very creation of the IPCC suggests that the need for scientific input into the policy process was widely acknowledged. Its design, however, acknowledges the political and in parts explicitly negotiated nature of scientific knowledge in the field of climate change. With regard to its perceived consensual nature, the science dealing with the description and causes of climate change has become less contested over time. Although former US president George W. Bush contested some IPCC conclusions in 2001, he also commissioned a study by the United States National Academy of Sciences that largely confirmed IPCC findings. This resulted in even the Bush administration accepting overall IPCC scientific messages, viewing not so much the IPCC as the Kyoto Protocol as flawed. IPCC assessments of the policy options to combat climate change, however, remain highly debated and have not found broad agreement.

More generally, however, IPCC science has played a crucial role in creating greater public awareness about the climate governance challenge. This role was made easier by close cooperation with green NGOs as well as by demand for green policies from a concerned public (at least in OECD countries) in the late 1980s and early 1990s. Thus, in the climate case, in addition to increasingly participatory and inclusive processes of generating scientific knowledge, the science being generated is acknowledged to be scientifically undisputed in its broadest parameters, the climate-gate controversies of 2009 notwithstanding.

Turning next to the role of science in whaling policy, a diverse picture emerges. In the early 1960s, most of the few scientists who attended the IWC scientific committee meetings recommended that whaling quotas should be reduced but their advice was not followed, and quotas remained high throughout the period. This gradually changed by the late 1960s because quotas were reduced in line with the scientific recommendations of the time (although, as explained further in the next section, factors other than scientific input also accounted for this development). This newly emerging alignment between scientific advice and political decisions was, however, disrupted during the third, more protectionist, phase of the IWC, when a moratorium on whaling was imposed in the mid-1980s. The vast majority of scientists in the scientific committee preferred a more selective approach rather than a blanket moratorium on whaling, although a small but vocal minority among scientists with close links to environmental groups argued in favor of a moratorium. The moratorium was thus seen, particularly by prowhaling nations, as driven by politics rather than science (Andresen 2000).

Because the moratorium was adopted by a large majority, however, it implied that the IWC was moving from a concern with sustainable management of whales to a more antiwhaling stance. The moratorium still stands currently, notwithstanding a massive scientific effort undertaken by whaling nations in the 1990s to demonstrate that a modest catch of whales could be taken without harm to the relevant species. Although this has not been sufficient to lift the moratorium, it has arguably contributed to undermining the antiwhaling stance in the IWC.

Interestingly, the whaling case shows that political decisions to restrict whaling through a moratorium are contrary to the dominant scientific input currently being provided into the policy process, which calls for a loosening of such constraints. This is in clear contrast to the climate change case, where there is a broad-based scientific consensus emerging that increasingly stringent political action is needed to mitigate and adapt to climate change. Whether such differences in the thrust of scientific advice (that is, in calling for more or less stringent environmental responses) are related not only to differences in problem structure, but also to more or less inclusive processes of generating scientific input is considered further in the next section.

Turning to our third case—scientific input into GMO governance— much scholarly analyses suggest that, rather than being consensual, the scientific criteria to underpin GMO policy choices remain in the eye of the political storm in all global fora where they are debated, including the WTO, the Codex Alimentarius Commission, and the Cartagena Protocol on Biosafety (Young et al. 2008; Gupta 2008; Zurek 2007). The WTO-SPS agreement's call for science-based decision making has not resulted in political conflicts being resolved based on science. This is evident from the series of disputes brought before the WTO over domestic sanitary and phytosanitary measures and their scientific justifications (for a comprehensive overview, see Christoforou 2000).

This includes the case brought by the United States against the European Union's moratorium on GMO imports, alleging that it was not scientifically based and hence violated the WTO-SPS agreement. The United States argued that trade restrictions on GMOs need to be based on "sound scientific" risk assessments, and the European Union argued for a precautionary approach as the only legitimate scientific principle that can guide GMO policy. Aside from not resolving whose science was sound, this dispute left aside whether socially precautionary decisions are also permitted, even if it did not result in an overall change in the EU's approach to GMO governance (Zurek 2007). From the perspective of this chapter, this case reveals that what constitutes credible science remains contested *and* that reliance on science alone (as per the WTO-SPS agreement) is untenable as the sole basis for GMO policy choices.

Similar lessons are also discernible from conflicts under way over what is to be considered credible scientific input into policy decisions within the Codex Alimentarius, where the extent to which science-based versus "other legitimate factors" to guide GMO policy remains a matter of conflict (Codex Alimentarius Commission 2003; Gupta 2008). A Codex "statement of principle regarding the role of science in the Codex decision-making process and the extent to which other factors are taken into account" is striking in its attempt to spell out what constitutes science-based decisions in this realm and the role that other legitimate factors should play, even as it leaves vague what these factors are (Codex Alimentarius Commission n.d).

Some light can be shed on this from examining a previous contested science-policy issue addressed by the Codex Alimentarius: that of safety standards for hormone-treated beef, where again a high-profile transatlantic dispute was fought out in the arena of disputed scientific claims. In this case, Codex safety standards existed for five hormones used by the United States to treat beef exported to the European Union. These standards were, however, not adopted by consensus (the normal method of functioning in Codex) but by a narrow margin of victory in a secret ballot requested by the United States, with thirty-three governments approving the standards, twenty-nine opposing them, and seven abstaining (Kastner and Pawsey 2002). With the European Union subsequently restricting imports of US hormone-treated beef, the United States initiated a WTO dispute settlement process, arguing that the European Union's restrictions were not in line with Codex safety standards. The European Union argued, however, that these standards were not based on consensus and hence the safety assessment contained therein was contested. This argument was dismissed as irrelevant by the WTO dispute-settlement panel because the WTO-SPS agreement does not require that international standards be adopted by consensus.

This example has clear implications for the dominant (and similar) call for science-based GMO governance in these global fora. Ongoing controversial debates within the Codex Alimentarius over threshold levels and safety assessment procedures for genetically modified foods guarantee a lack of consensus here as well. This suggests that, instead of global (food) safety standards providing an objective means by which to reduce political conflict, negotiation of such standards will remain inextricably tied to such conflicts.

Similar conclusions can be reached in considering the nature of scientific input into crucial elements of the Cartagena Protocol on Biosafety's rules and obligations. The objective of this global agreement is to "contribute to ensuring an adequate level of protection in the field of the safe transfer, handling and use of living modified organisms resulting from modern biotechnology" (Cartagena Protocol 2000, Article 1). In order to operationalize this objective, a scientific and technical expert group was mandated during negotiation of the protocol to develop consensual definitions of key scientific concepts such as living modified organism and modern biotechnology (UNEP 2000). The expert group consisted of members of government delegations who were scientists; hence, they participated in the group both as representatives of their countries and in their capacity as technical experts. Detailed analysis of this group's deliberations, however, show that shared scientific agreements over how to define ostensibly technical concepts could only be reached among this multiculturally diverse group of scientists by explicitly allowing for deliberate ambiguity and negotiation, as well local reinterpretation of globally negotiated understandings rather than through objectivity or technical precision (for a detailed analysis, see Gupta 2004).

Taken together, these observations reveal, first, that a growing institutionalization of scientific input into policy making is discernible in all of the three governance realms examined here. Even so, participation in the generation of scientific input remains largely limited to selected scientific experts, with environmental NGOs, indigenous communities, or critical think tanks remaining largely outside official processes. Second, discussion of the three cases suggests that negotiated scientific input into policy processes is discernible in all three issue areas. We turn next to explaining further these dynamics of scientific knowledge generation and outcomes and their relevance for the influence that science may have in global environmental governance.

Explanations

In this section, we draw on the previous discussion to consider when and under what conditions policy-relevant science influences global environmental governance. In doing so, we focus on two explanatory factors, namely, process design and the need for negotiation.

Influence of Science: The Importance of Process

Although ever-broader participation in scientific knowledge generation is becoming the norm in global governance of climate change, and to some extent in whaling, the case of global GMO governance is somewhat distinct insofar as no single global scientific assessment body is mandated to provide scientific input for policy making. What lessons about the importance of broadly participatory processes do these three cases suggest?

As seen in the previous section, although the IPCC has become increasingly inclusive of diverse scientific and other forms of knowledge, societal actors such as NGOs or business associations are, however, not given access to its deliberations unless their members are included as scientific experts. Thus, it is not (yet) representative of models of postnormal or sustainability science, as conceptualized in diverse writings. Whether and how this specific sort of participatory deficit reduces its relevance and hence influence remains an important question. This notwithstanding, in being awarded the Nobel Peace Prize in 2007, the IPCC was honored for bringing the problem of climate change to greater public attention and thus spurring international, domestic, and local political action (Grundmann 2007). In that sense, it has clearly been influential despite many critical voices. This is also partly because of the constant evolution in its modes of inclusion of diverse disciplines, geographical representation, and breadth of topics to be assessed within the broad rubric of climate change causes and effects.

Despite the undisputed merits of the IPCC and the impact of its assessments on the broader public debate, however, such assessments have not resulted in major policy change. Greenhouse gas emissions continue to increase. The Kyoto Protocol, for all its political and institutional merits, will have little effect on mitigating and adapting to climate change. Considering that the IPCC called in 1990 for a 60 percent reduction in greenhouse gas emissions in order to bring the climate system into balance, crafters of the global climate regime have paid little attention to IPCC advice. Even when acknowledging the enormously challenging problem structure (Miles et al. 2001) of climate governance, scientific input has had an insufficient impact on policy. Furthermore, as one of us has recently argued elsewhere, public interest in the issue of climate change may even be declining, with one reason posited to be perceived reduced legitimacy of the IPCC because of climate-gate controversies (Andresen and Skodvin 2011).

In the case of whaling, the lack of influence of science in the earlier phases of IWC negotiations is attributable mainly to the fact that there was huge uncertainty as well as a lack of consensus in the scientific committee. The scientists were not able to produce specific recommendations and the IWC was completely dominated by the short-term economic interests of the main whaling nations (Andresen 2000). This changed as more specific and more consensual advice was given by a more broadly participatory scientific committee in the 1970s. The main reason, however, was depletion of the stocks of large whales because whaling nations were no longer able to fulfill the quotas adopted. This made it exceedingly important to accept reduced quotas. The fact that the moratorium was adopted by the mid-1980s against the advice of most scientists illustrates that science is simply neglected when strong political interests point in another direction (Andresen 2000).

As noted previously, scientific efforts in the 1990s have now focused increasingly on the question of whether sustainable whaling is possible. Experiments with broader participation in the scientific committee, and the consequences for the influence of scientific findings, is perhaps best seen from deliberations over a revised management procedure for whaling, where this question was central. In 1990, an innovative approach to agree on the contents of a revised management procedure was established within the scientific committee, whereby five competing teams were set up. Due to strong polarization over the issue, some teams were composed of scientists from whaling nations and others came from countries and groups with close connections to the antiwhaling movement. According to Schweder (2001, 29), "The process of mutual learning and competition has turned out to be productive (and) the five candidate procedures ended up with broadly similar performance." The resultant revised management procedure was, according to the IWC secretary, "very conservative compared with anything that has gone before, and also by comparison with management regimes for other wildlife and fisheries resources" (Gambell 1995, 701).

What is striking, however, is that the IWC was reluctant to adopt the revised management procedure, with its implications that cautious whaling could be conducted. This resulted in the chair of the scientific committee resigning in protest in 1993, alleging a deliberate strategy of neglecting scientific advice (Andresen 2000). In 1994, the IWC did adopt the revised management procedure, even as the majority of IWC members continued to oppose commercial whaling. This is evident from the fact that the moratorium still stands, although the implications of the revised management procedure and stock estimates by the scientific committee are that cautious catch may be resumed.

Thus, as with climate change, seemingly consensual scientific assertions do not necessarily enhance scientific influence, particularly in normatively contested areas such as whaling. Nonetheless, as with the IPCC, there have been certain important effects of the policy-relevant science generated by the IWC's scientific committee, especially regarding newer issues such as bycatches and environmental matters. Furthermore, the largely consensual scientific message that cautious whaling may resume has also contributed to weakening the previously strong antiwhaling norm within the IWC (Andresen 2008). This has paved the way for present discussions over a possible political compromise.

Turning next to processes of scientific knowledge generation for global GMO governance, the previous brief discussion suggests that process and participation (or lack thereof) is important in this case as well, as revealed in the example of the Codex Alimentarius Commission's development of global food (and GMO) safety standards. Codex standards are often alleged to be OECD- and industry-dominated and developed in relatively nontransparent processes. This was strikingly evident in the process by which agreement was reached on safety standards for hormones in beef, for which the unprecedented use of a secret ballot was required, given the fundamental political conflicts underpinning science and safety assessments (Kastner and Pawsey 2002).

The importance of including multiculturally diverse perspectives in generating policy-relevant science is also revealed in the Cartagena Protocol's scientific expert group's attempts to develop shared technical definitions of key protocol terminology. Analysis of how agreement was finally reached in this specific negotiating forum reveals that the acceptability and hence influence of science is enhanced when it is multilaterally negotiated, inclusive of diverse political priorities, and explicitly linked to, rather than separated from, a political process. This was evident from the process by which agreement was reached on "technical" definitions of living modified organisms (where the key notion of novelty was left deliberately undefined) and modern biotechnology (where agreement on whether cell fusion should be part of the definition was explicitly linked to outcomes of the broader political negotiation rather than on scientific arguments voiced within the expert group) (Gupta 2004). The negotiated nature of such scientific input is discussed in the following section.

Influence of Science: The Need for Negotiation

Questions of consensual, negotiated, or objective science stand at the heart of the IPCC enterprise. Despite many critical voices, the IPCC's model has proved to be operational in seeking to provide consensus-based, state-of-the-art knowledge on the dimensions, the causes, the effects, and the potential counterstrategies of climate change

(Siebenhüner 2003). Yet its explicit rules for scientific consensus during knowledge generation may paradoxically limit its influence. To neglect the diversity of perspectives on the climate problem by emphasizing the need for consensus among scientists can result in scientific assertions that are less-than-emphatic and hence less relevant in shaping policy outcomes.

More important from our perspective, the IPCC's model of political negotiation of its summaries for policy makers has also been implicated in its lack of influence. Haas (2004), for example, sees the influence of the IPCC as minimal and maintains that the IPCC is highly dominated by northern political interests, and its setup as an intergovernmental process has kept the scientific process on a tight leash of governments. In particular, he and others argue that the IPCC is not supposed to be policy prescriptive and therefore merely publishes policy options, an outcome that is seen as a severe limitation to greater political influence of the reports (Simonis 2009).

This implies, however, that greater integration and closeness to the political process might actually enhance the influence of science, as we also claim previously for the GMO governance case. The most important innovation of the IPCC, in this latter line of thinking, lies in how it has sought to ensure scientific independence in its core work and political involvement in agreeing on overall scientific messages. Such political negotiation is needed to secure not only the legitimacy of the message but also its (scientific) credibility. This is particularly so in global issues such as climate change with pronounced North-South conflicts (Biermann 2001, 2002, 2006; Skodvin 2000). Thus, we disagree with Haas (2004) on this point. Instead of a weakness in the IPCC's mechanisms of producing policy-relevant science, the political negotiation of its key scientific messages is, in our view, central to its relevance and legitimacy, and hence potential influence.

Turning to the case of whaling, detailed empirical research on the evolution of the influence of science in the whaling regime suggests that political conflicts between pro- and antiwhaling forces have gradually reduced in intensity, after heated debates in the 1980s and 1990s (Andresen 2008). It also appears, however, that the sobering scientific message about depleting whale stocks has influenced the IWC's deliberations. This suggests that growing scientific consensus about the nature of the problem is contributing to reducing normative conflict, as many scholars and practitioners calling for an objective science to "speak truth to power" hope.

However, in a comparative study of the role of science within five environmental regimes, the IWC stands out as a conspicuous outlier. It showed a declining influence of science in the very phases of policy making (the later phases), when the science itself is becoming increasingly sophisticated and more widely accepted (Andresen et al. 2000). The explanation for this appears to lie in the fact that global governance of whaling is still shaped by conflicts over basic values. Scientific research on the state of a whale stock and sustainable levels of harvest cannot resolve the issue of whether it is morally right or wrong to use a particular species for consumptive purposes. This illustrates as well that there are few universal truths that global governance of whaling can rely on for legitimization.

In the case of scientific influence in GMO governance, detailed analyses of the deliberations of the Cartagena Protocol's multiculturally diverse scientific expert group reveal that technical imprecision and even political compromise—in a word, negotiation—characterizes scientific agreements reached in this global forum. In this case, scientific agreements on key biosafety concepts function as boundary-ordering devices, allowing for multiple interpretations. This highlights that although scientific input is critical to governance of technological and environmental change, it cannot be the definitive and neutral mediator of political conflict. As long pointed out in risk analysis and science studies writings, an attempt to separate science from politics in decision making or to designate certain deliberations as solely technical can result in the exclusion of diverse lay perspectives from problem framing and governance processes (Press 1994; Rose-Ackerman 1995; Jasanoff 1998; Gupta 2010). In a global context, such exclusions can prevent developing countries from fully articulating their concerns within "technical" debates on global environmental and risk governance (Biermann 2002) or force them to voice social concerns in the language of technically assessable harm, as has been evident in GMO governance at multiple levels. This can result in a problematic "technicalization" of politics (Gupta 2002, 2011), a phenomenon meriting at least as much attention as the more oft-noted scholarly concern with a "politicization" of science.

Conclusions and Outlook

As Ulrich Beck noted in 1992, the paradox facing global governance of contested environmental challenges is that scientific input is most ardently sought in precisely those areas characterized by the most severe scientific and institutional uncertainty and lack of trust, where consensual science is hardest to achieve (Beck 1992; see also Beck 2002). In concurring with this, critics of an epistemic community perspective note that scientific consensus is more likely to follow after, rather than facilitate, resolution of political conflicts in such issue areas (Sarewitz 1996, 2000; Jasanoff 1998).

In line with this, our analysis suggests that objective scientific input that is separable from political considerations is neither attainable nor essential for the influence of policy-relevant science. Going beyond this, it emphasizes that science is only one ingredient in effective, legitimate, and democratic global environmental governance. As the examples here indicate, the global politics of whaling, climate change, or GMOs transcend scientifically assessable concerns over human health, ecological risks, depleted resource stocks, or adaptive capacity. They are characterized by a wide range of moral, social, political, and economic conflicts and priorities.

Our analysis suggests, therefore, that the influence of science in such areas will depend on the evolution of global institutions and processes that can confer legitimacy on the generation and content of policy-relevant science for decision making (see also Jasanoff 2004). Such a goal is partly furthered by the participatory turn in scientific assessments and institutions. Ultimately, however, "good" (or credible) science for policy making requires good politics, that is, representative, accountable, and a more democratic politics. How to harness such good politics remains a frontier research question, linking analysis of scientific influence to broader questions of the appropriate normative and institutional foundations for a more democratic and accountable global environmental governance.

Note

1. We are referring to the Global Environmental Assessment project at Harvard University's Belfer Center for Science and International Affairs, with which Biermann, Gupta, and Siebenhüner were affiliated; and various projects at the Fridtjof Nansen Institute in which Andresen participated.

References

Andresen, Steinar. 2000. The Whaling Regime. In *Science and Politics in International Environmental Regimes: Between Integrity and Involvement,* ed. Steinar Andresen, Tora Skodvin, Arild Underdal, and Jørgen Wettestad, 35–68. Manchester, UK: Manchester University Press.

Andresen, Steinar. 2008. The Volatile Nature of the International Whaling Commission: Power, Institutions, and Norms. In *International Governance of Fisheries Ecosystems: Learning from the Past, Finding Solutions for the Future*, ed. Michael Schechter, Nancy Leonard, and William Taylor, 173–189. Betheseda, MD: American Fisheries Society.

Andresen, Steinar, and Jon Birger Skjærseth. 2007. Science and Technology: From Agenda Setting to Implementation. In *The Oxford Handbook of International Environmental Law*, ed. Daniel Bodansky, Jutta Brunnée, and Ellen Hey, 182–202. Oxford: Oxford University Press.

Andresen, Steinar, and Tora Skodvin. 2011. The Climate Regime: Achievements and Challenges. In *The World Ocean in Globalization: Challenges and Responses*, ed. Vidas Davor and Peter Johan Schei, 165–186. Boston: Brill.

Andresen, Steinar, Tora Skodvin, Arild Underdal, and Jørgen Wettestad, eds. 2000. *Science and Politics in International Environmental Regimes: Between Integrity and Involvement*. Manchester, UK: Manchester University Press.

Beck, Ulrich. 1992. *Risk Society: Towards a New Modernity*. London: Sage.

Beck, Ulrich. 2002. *Ecological Politics in an Age of Risk*. Cambridge, UK: Polity Press.

Biermann, Frank. 2001. Big Science, Small Impacts—in the South? The Influence of Global Environmental Assessments on Expert Communities in India. *Global Environmental Change: Human and Policy Dimensions* 11 (4):297–309.

Biermann, Frank. 2002. Institutions for Scientific Advice: Global Environmental Assessments and Their Influence in Developing Countries. *Global Governance* 8 (2):195–219.

Biermann, Frank. 2006. Whose Experts? The Role of Geographic Representation in Global Environmental Assessments. In *Global Environmental Assessments: Information and Influence*, ed. Ronald B. Mitchell, William C. Clark, David W. Cash, and Nancy M. Dickson, 87–112. Cambridge, MA: MIT Press.

Bolin, Bert. 2007. *A History of the Science and Policy of Climate Change: The Role of the Intergovernmental Panel on Climate Change*. Cambridge, UK: Cambridge University Press.

Cartagena Protocol. 2000. *Cartagena Protocol on Biosafety to the Convention on Biological Diversity: Text and Annexes*. Montreal: Secretariat of the Convention on Biological Diversity.

Christoforou, Theofanis. 2000. Settlement of Science-based Trade Disputes in the WTO: A Critical Review of the Developing Case Law in the Face of Scientific Uncertainty. *New York University Environmental Law Journal* 8:622–648.

Clark, William C. 2001. Research Systems for a Transition toward Sustainability. In *Challenges of a Changing Earth*, ed. Will Steffen, Jill Jäger, David J. Carson, and Clare Bradshaw, 197–199. Berlin: Springer.

Codex Alimentarius Commission. 2003. Report of the Fourth Session of the Codex Ad Hoc Intergovernmental Task Force on Foods Derived from Biotechnology. Yokohama, Japan, 11–14 March.

Codex Alimentarius Commission. n.d. Statement of Principle Regarding the Role of Science in the Codex Decision-making Process and the Extent to Which Other Factors are Taken into Account. In *Codex Alimentarius Commission Procedural Manual 14th Edition.* Appendix: General Decisions of the Commission.

DeSombre, Elizabeth R. 2001. Distorting Global Governance: Membership, Voting and the IWC. In *Towards a Sustainable Whaling Regime,* ed. Robert L. Friedheim, 183–200. Seattle: University of Washington Press.

Edwards, Paul N., and Stephan H. Schneider. 2001. Self-governance and Peer Review in Science-for-Policy: The Case of the IPCC Second Assessment Report. In *Changing the Atmosphere: Expert Knowledge and Environmental Governance,* ed. Clark Miller and Paul N. Edwards, 219–246. Cambridge, MA: MIT Press.

Forrester, John. 1999. The Logistics of Public Participation in Environmental Assessments. *International Journal of Environment and Pollution* 11:316–330.

Funtowicz, Silvio O., and Jerome R. Ravetz. 1991. A New Scientific Methodology for Global Environmental Issues. In *Ecological Economics: The Science and Management of Sustainability,* ed. Robert Costanza, 137–152. New York: Columbia University Press.

Funtowicz, Silvio O., and Jerome R. Ravetz. 1992. The Good, the True and the Post-modern. *Futures* 24 (10):963–976.

Funtowicz, Silvio O., and Jerome R. Ravetz. 1993. Science for the Post-normal Age. *Futures* 27 (9):739–755.

Gallopin, Gilberto C., Silvio O. Funtowicz, Martin O'Connor, and Jerry O. Ravetz. 2001. Science for the 21st Century: From Social Contract to the Scientific Core. *International Social Science Journal* 53:219–229.

Gambell, Ray. 1995. Management of Whaling in Coastal Communities. In *Whales, Seals, Fish, and Man,* ed. Arnoldus S. Blix, Lars Walløe, and Øyvind Ulltang, 699–708. Amsterdam: Elsevier Science.

Gibbons, Michael, Camille Limoges, and Helga Nowotny. 1995. *The New Production of Knowledge: The Dynamics of Science and Research in Contemporary Societies.* London: Sage.

Gieryn, Thomas. 1995. Boundaries of Science. In *Handbook of Science and Technology Studies,* ed. Sheila Jasanoff, Gerald E. Markle, James C. Peterson, and Trevor J. Pinch, 393–443. Thousand Oaks, CA: Sage.

Girod, Bastien, Arnim Wiek, Harald Mieg, and Mike Hulme. 2009. The Evolution of the IPCC's Emissions Scenarios. *Environmental Science & Policy* 12 (2):103–118.

Grundmann, Reiner. 2007. Climate Change and Knowledge Politics. *Environmental Politics* 16 (3):414–432.

Gupta, Aarti. 2001. Advance Informed Agreement: A Shared Basis to Govern Trade in Genetically Modified Organisms? *Indiana Journal of Global Legal Studies* 91 (1):265–281.

Gupta, Aarti. 2002. Ensuring "Safe Use" of Biotechnology: Key Challenges. *Economic and Political Weekly*, July 6:2762–2769.

Gupta, Aarti. 2004. When Global Is Local: Negotiating Safe Use of Biotechnology. In *Earthly Politics: Local and Global in Environmental Governance*, ed. Sheila Jasanoff and Marybeth Long-Martello, 127–148. Cambridge, MA: MIT Press.

Gupta, Aarti. 2006. Problem Framing in Assessment Processes: The Case of Biosafety. In *Global Environmental Assessments: Information and Influence*, ed. Ronald B. Mitchell, William C. Clark, David W. Cash, and Nancy M. Dickson, 57–86. Cambridge, MA: MIT Press.

Gupta, Aarti. 2008. Global Biosafety Governance: Emergence and Evolution. In *Institutional Interplay: Biosafety and Trade*, ed. Oran R. Young, W. Bradnee Chambers, Joy A. Kim, and Claudia ten Have, 19–46. Tokyo: United Nations University Press.

Gupta, Aarti. 2010. Transparency as Contested Political Terrain: Who Knows What about the Global GMO Trade and Why Does It Matter? *Global Environmental Politics* 10 (3):32–52.

Gupta, Aarti. 2011. An Evolving Science-Society Contract in India: The Search for Legitimacy in Anticipatory Risk Governance. *Food Policy* 36:736–741.

Haas, Peter M. 1992. Epistemic Communities and International Policy Coordination. *International Organization* 46 (1):1–35.

Haas, Peter M. 2004. When Does Power Listen to Truth? A Constructivist Approach to the Policy Process. *Journal of European Public Policy* 11 (4):569–592.

Haas, Peter M. 2005. Science and International Environmental Governance. In *Handbook of Global Environmental Politics*, ed. Peter Dauvergne, 383–401. Cheltenham, UK: Edward Elgar.

Herrick, Charles, and Daniel Sarewitz. 2000. Ex-post Evaluation: A More Effective Role for Scientific Assessments in Environmental Policy. *Science, Technology & Human Values* 25 (3):309–331.

Jasanoff, Sheila. 1987. Contested Boundaries in Policy-Relevant Science. *Social Studies of Science* 17 (2):195–230.

Jasanoff, Sheila. 1998. Contingent Knowledge: Implications for Implementation and Compliance. In *Engaging Countries: Strengthening Compliance with International Environmental Accords*, ed. Edith Brown Weiss and Harold K. Jacobson, 63–87. Cambridge, MA: MIT Press.

Jasanoff, Sheila. 2004. *States of Knowledge: The Co-production of Science and Social Order*. London: Routledge.

Joss, Simon, and Sergio Bellucci, eds. 2002. *Participatory Technology Assessment: European Perspectives*. London: Center for the Study of Democracy.

Kasemir, Bernd, Jill Jäger, Carlo C. Jaeger, and M. T. Gardner, eds. 2003. *Public Participation in Sustainability Science*. Cambridge, UK: Cambridge University Press.

Kastner, Justine, and Rosa K. Pawsey. 2002. Harmonizing Sanitary Measures and Resolving Trade Disputes through the WTO-SPS Framework. Part I: A Case Study of the US-EU Hormone-treated Beef Dispute. *Food Control* 13:49–55.

Kates, Robert W., William C. Clark, Robert Corell, J. Michael Hall, Carlo C. Jaeger, Ian Lowe, James J. McCarthy, et al. 2001. Sustainability Science. *Science* 292 (5517):641–642.

Litfin, Karen T. 1994. *Ozone Discourses: Science and Politics in Global Environmental Cooperation.* New York: Columbia University Press.

Miles, Edward L., Arild Underdal, Steinar Andresen, Jørgen Wettestad, Jon Birger Skjærseth, and Elaine M. Carlin, eds. 2001. *Environmental Regime Effectiveness: Confronting Theory with Evidence.* Cambridge, MA: MIT Press.

Mitchell, Ronald B., William C. Clark, David W. Cash, and Nancy M. Dickson, eds. 2006. *Global Environmental Assessments: Information and Influence.* Cambridge, MA: MIT Press.

Press, Daniel. 1994. *Democratic Dilemmas in the Age of Ecology: Trees and Toxics in the American West.* Durham, NC: Duke University Press.

Renn, Ortwin, Thomas Webler, and Peter M. Wiedemann. 1995. *Fairness and Competence in Citizen Participation.* Dordrecht: Kluwer.

Rose-Ackerman, Susan. 1995. *Controlling Environmental Policy: The Limits of Public Law in Germany and the United States.* New Haven, CT: Yale University Press.

Sarewitz, Daniel. 1996. *Frontiers of Illusion: Science, Technology, and the Politics of Progress.* Philadelphia: Temple University Press.

Sarewitz, Daniel. 2000. Science and Environmental Policy: An Excess of Objectivity. In *Earth Matters: The Earth Sciences, Philosophy, and the Claims of Community,* ed. Robert Frodemen, 49–98. Upper Saddle River, NJ: Prentice Hall.

Schweder, Tore. 2001. Protecting Whales by Distorting Uncertainty: Non-precautionary Mismanagement? *Fisheries Research* 52:217–225.

Shackley, Simon, and Brian Wynne. 1996. Representing Uncertainty in Global Climate Science and Policy: Boundary-Ordering Devices and Authority. *Science, Technology & Human Values* 21 (3):275–302.

Siebenhüner, Bernd. 2003. The Changing Role of Nation States in International Environmental Assessments: The Case of the IPCC. *Global Environmental Change: Human and Policy Dimensions* 13:113–123.

Siebenhüner, Bernd. 2004. Social Learning and Sustainability Science: Which Role Can Stakeholder Participation Play? *International Journal of Sustainable Development* 7:146–163.

Simonis, Udo E. 2009. The IPCC and Climate Politics: Small Potatoes. *Environmentalist* 29 (3):330–332.

Skodvin, Tora. 2000. The Intergovernmental Panel on Climate Change. In *Science and Politics in International Environmental Regimes: Between Integrity and Involvement,* ed. Steinar Andresen, Tora Skodvin, Arild Underdal, and Jørgen Wettestad, 146–181. Manchester, UK: Manchester University Press.

Underdal, Arild. 2000. Comparative Conclusions. In *Science and Politics in International Environmental Regimes: Between Integrity and Involvement*, ed. Steinar Andresen, Tora Skodvin, Arild Underdal, and Jørgen Wettestad, 181–202. Manchester, UK: Manchester University Press.

UNEP [United Nations Environment Programme] 2000. Report on the Extraordinary Meeting of the Conference of the Parties to the Convention on Biological Diversity for Adoption of the Protocol on Biosafety. UNEP/CBD/ExCOP/1/3.

WTO [World Trade Organization].-SPS Agreement. 1994. Agreement on the Application of Sanitary and Phytosanitary Measures. Annex IA to the Final Act Embodying the Results of the Uruguay Round of Multilateral Trade Negotiations. Marrakesh, 15 April.

Young, Oran R., W. Bradnee Chambers, Joy A. Kim, and Claudia ten Have. 2008. *Institutional Interplay: Biosafety and Trade*. Tokyo: United Nations University Press.

Zurek, Laylah. 2007. The European Communities Biotech Dispute: How the WTO Fails to Consider Cultural Factors in the Genetically Modified Food Debate. *Texas International Law Journal* 42:345–368.

II

The New Mechanisms

5

Transnational Environmental Regimes

Philipp Pattberg

It is a widely held understanding among scholars of international relations that increased participation of nonstate actors has given rise to new forms of governance beyond the state that transcend the traditional system of legally binding agreements negotiated by governments. In addition to classical intergovernmental—that is, state-based—regimes like the ozone regime, the climate regime, or the regime for the conservation of biodiversity, a broad range of nongovernmental transboundary regimes have emerged and proliferated since the early 1990s. Examples include the accounting standards developed by the International Accounting Standards Board (Nölke 2006), the credit-rating standards developed by a small number of private companies (Kerwer 2002), the labor standards of the Fair Labor Association (Marx 2008), the certification system for diamonds developed within the Kimberly Process (Beffert and Benner 2004; Kantz 2006), the generic accountability standard AA 1000 developed by the Institute for Social and Ethical Accountability (Beschorner and Müller 2007; Reynolds and Yuthas 2008), and the numerous transnational environmental regimes that are the focus of this chapter (for an overview, see Espach 2009).

In general, these transnational institutions resemble international regimes. The core difference is that nongovernmental actors, not states, generate the "principles, norms, rules, and decision-making procedures around which the expectations of actors converge in a given issue area" (Krasner 1983, 2). Another major difference is that the norms and rules of transnational regimes are not legally binding. The fact that addressees are not legally bound to implement the rules that emerge from transnational regimes raises a number of questions about their effectiveness: do "voluntary" transnational norms and rules matter? And if so, when, why, and how do they make a difference?

To answer these questions, the chapter is organized as follows: in the next section, I sketch the state of research on transnational environmental regulation. Subsequently, I provide an overview of a number of concrete experiences that serve as empirical illustrations of the nature and consequences of transnational environmental regimes. The following section provides (preliminary) explanations for two central questions: first, why do transnational regimes emerge? Second, what measurable and significant effects do they have? I then conclude with the lessons learned and suggest future avenues of research.

Conceptualization

Within the discipline of international relations, the literature on global governance has brought about a rather fundamental shift in perspectives (Dingwerth and Pattberg 2006). Starting from the observation that state-centric conceptions of world politics face increasing difficulties in their attempts to account for the empirical realities we observe, it seeks to broaden the scope through reconceptualizing world politics as "the sum of myriad—literally millions of—control mechanisms driven by different histories, goals, structures, and processes" (Rosenau 1995, 16). The political landscape of world politics is characterized by a bifurcation in which the state-centric world is increasingly complemented by a multicentric world that had some links to, but operated largely independently of, interstate politics (Rosenau 1990). In other words, an

increasingly pertinent feature of the global public order in and beyond environmental protection and sustainability is the dynamic mixing of the public and the private, with state-based public power being exercised by state institutions alongside and along with the exercise of private power by market and civil society institutions and other actors committed to the public interest and public weal (Thynne 2008, 329).

Similar interpretations of a transformation of world politics are expressed in the English School's interest in the shift from international to world society (Buzan 2005), in the literature on a legalization of world politics in its international and transnational dimensions (Zangl and Zürn 2004), in John Ruggie's account of the emergence of a "global public domain" (2004), in Paul Wapner's identification of "politics beyond the state" (1995), and in the literature on private authority in world affairs (Cutler, Haufler, and Porter 1999; Hall and Biersteker 2002).

For the regime literature in international relations research, this shift implies that the focus on international regimes needs to be complemented by a focus on transnational regimes. Accordingly, Oran R. Young (1999, 11) defines global governance as "the combined efforts of international and transnational regimes." Transnational regimes are thus conceptualized as the societal, private, or nongovernmental equivalent of intergovernmental regimes like the international regime to protect the ozone layer or the world trade regime. They thus can be defined as sets of norms, rules, and decision-making procedures that are made and implemented across borders predominantly through the activities of nonstate actors (also Espach 2009). Prominent examples beyond the environmental realm include the transboundary governance of commercial contracts, sports, or the Internet (Zangl and Zürn 2004) but also public-private standards regimes such as those developed within the International Organization for Standardization (ISO) (Clapp 1998; Haufler 2000).

Research on transnational regimes has largely followed the succession of questions and puzzles that already structured the debate about intergovernmental regimes, including questions about their relevance and independence from prevailing power structures, the causes for their emergence and persistence, as well as questions about their effects and effectiveness. In line with this array of interests, research on transnational regimes has paid considerable attention to their emergence (e.g., Bartley 2003; Gulbrandsen 2009; Pattberg 2005c). A major puzzle to solve is the observation that a number of transnational regimes have been institutionalized between actors that, according to standard accounts of behavioral logic, follow different motivations for action (profit versus not-for-profit motives). Although a number of studies focus on the systemic level (e.g., the influence of broad discursive formations such as neoliberal globalization), more explanatory leverage seems to be in accounts that theorize the issue-specific process of resource exchange and additional field-level explanations (Nölke 2006; Dingwerth and Pattberg 2009).

A second fundamental question with regard to emerging phenomena is, Do they matter? This question is relevant because it directs our attention to problems of measurement and to the corresponding functional pathways of "mattering." With regard to transnational environmental regimes, a superficial answer to this question seems to be "no" or "very little" because the question of effects is predominantly equated with assessing the actual implementation and compliance with transnational rules and norms (Mattli and Büthe 2003; Hertin et al. 2004; Kollman and Prakash 2001; Sasser et al. 2004). As a result, analyses focusing on the rate of standard uptake and rule compliance run the risk of concluding that transnational rules and norms are epiphenomena and can largely be neglected in accounts of world politics (e.g., Doane 2005). This chapter argues, however, that transnational environmental regimes have considerable effects that reach beyond direct regulation through rules and standards.

In line with core assumptions of the international regimes literature on effectiveness and compliance (Bernauer 1995; Chayes and Chayes 1995; Miles et al. 2001), assessing the effects of transnational environmental regimes by targeting rule implementation and rule following seems to be a justified and straightforward approach (also Bauer, Andresen, and Biermann, chapter 2, this book). This strategy, however, may not be sufficient for several reasons. First, the focus on direct effects of transnational environmental regimes potentially obscures substantial effects that go significantly beyond rule implementation and compliance. Second, as a result, scholars may systematically underestimate the importance of transnational environmental regimes in world politics. A counterargument has been made for example by Daniel Drezner (2004), who contends that states have consciously delegated problem-solving authority to nonstate actors rather than being weakened by globalization in general (see also Raustiala 1997). Finally, as a consequence, the question of variation in effects has largely been confined to the question of firm-level choices in accounting for different standard uptakes and growth rates (e.g., Kollman and Prakash 2001). To overcome this state of affairs, this chapter employs a wider understanding of effects and possible ways of assessing them.

An attempt to understand the effects of transnational environmental regimes, and thereby their overall relevance, will benefit from a review of the literature on international soft law, which has a longer tradition in analyzing the effects of voluntary rule systems. Research in this field shows that voluntary rule systems can have effects to the extent that material incentives can be attached to them or that norms and rules can be framed as an expression of "appropriate" behavior for actors (Kirton and Trebilcock 2004; Shelton 2000).

For the description of these effects, I distinguish three categories: (1) *Normative and regulatory effects* refer to changes in the expectations for appropriate behavior for actors and encompass changes in the norms, rules, and standards at different levels of the political system. They include the adjustment of national legislation and the adoption of transnational norms and rules by national administrations, by intergovernmental agencies, or in international treaties. (2) *Discursive effects* are changes of the perceptions and descriptions of a policy problem and of the meaning of basic normative conceptions such as sustainability or corporate environmental responsibility. (3) *Material and structural effects* include changes in access to specific markets or market segments, changes of market shares, changes in the cost structure of different products or producers, or changes in the institutional environment of a transnational regime. Based on such distinction, the effects of transnational environmental regimes can be measured and compared.

Experiences

Transnational environmental regimes operate in a number of distinct issue areas. These range from coffee (Bitzer, Francken, and Glasbergen 2008; Kolk 2005; Neilson and Pritchard 2007; Muradian and Pelupessy 2005; Rice 2001) to fair trade (Bacon 2010; Courville 2003), organic farming (Luttikholt 2007), sustainability reporting (Hedberg and von Malmborg 2003; Hussey, Kirsop, and Meissen 2001; Willis 2003), marine governance (Constance and Bonanno 2000; Gulbrandsen 2009; Oosterveer 2008; Shuman, Hodgson, and Ambrose 2004; Thrane, Ziegler, and Sonesson 2009) to mining (Danielson 2006; Whitmore 2006), sustainable tourism (Jamal, Borges, and Stronza 2006), and freshwater governance (Dingwerth 2005; Dubash 2009).

One issue that has received much attention in recent years is global forest governance (Auld, Gulbrandsen, and McDermott 2008; Gulbrandsen 2005, 2008; Overdevest 2010; Pattberg 2005a, 2005b, 2005c, 2006; Schepers 2010; Visseren-Hamakers and Glasbergen 2007). Forest governance has been a prime site of experimenting with novel instruments for and approaches toward halting environmental degradation (see Bulkeley et al., this book, chapter 7). In particular, certification has been frequently invoked as an example of nonstate market-driven governance (Cashore 2002). This section therefore provides a more detailed account of the formation as well as the measurable effects of the Forest Stewardship Council, which is regarded as the global benchmark, or gold standard, in sustainable forest management and certification.

The Forest Stewardship Council (FSC) is a private nonprofit organization with a heterogeneous membership of environmental and social NGOs, corporations in the forestry sector, scientific institutions, and individuals from more than sixty countries. The FSC administers a self-elaborated third-party certification system on wood and timber products that tries to verify whether products originate from sustainable forestry.

The basis of the certification scheme is the FSC's international standard principles and criteria for forest stewardship (Forest Stewardship Council 2002). Organized into ten principles and fifty-six criteria, these general rules are transformed into national standards, which serve as a basis for the on-ground certification of forest management units. Among other things, the global rules demand compliance with all applicable national and international regulations; a clear definition and documentation of long-term ownerships and rights of using land and forest resources; the preservation of the social and economical well-being of employees and the local population as well as of biodiversity, water resources, soils, ecosystems, and landscapes; and the exemption of high-conservation-value forests and forests converted into plantations from certification.

To date more than 330 million hectares of forests have been certified by certification programs, roughly 8 percent of the global forest cover. Whereas Africa, Latin America, Asia, and Oceania together have only 6 percent of their forest under certification, North America has certified 38 percent, and western European countries reached a remarkable 53 percent in 2009. The estimated potential global industrial roundwood supply from certified forests amounts to 411 million cubic meters annually, which equals 26 percent of the total industrial roundwood supply (for the period from May 2008 to May 2009, see UNECE and FAO 2009). The FSC's contribution to these figures is substantial. Until early 2010, more than 127 million hectares of forests have been certified in accordance with the FSC standard, approximating 5 percent of the world's productive forests. The FSC-certified forest area per region stands at 46.6 percent for Europe, 36.5 percent for North America, and more than 16 percent for Latin America, Africa, Asia, and Oceania, as compared to 6 percent for all certification schemes (Forest Stewardship Council 2010).

Emergence of a Transnational Regime Regulating Global Forestry

The Forest Stewardship Council dates back more than twenty years. In March 1991, a group of timber users, traders, and representatives of social and environmental organizations convened in California to discuss the need for a credible system for identifying well-managed forests as a trustworthy source for forest products (on the history of the FSC see in more detail Pattberg 2007; Conroy 2007, 61–79). One year later, the World Wide Fund for Nature (WWF) had teamed up with major retailers in the United Kingdom to form the UK Forest and Trade Network. In addition, after eighteen months of consultations in ten countries—

including the United States, Canada, Sweden, and Peru—in October 1993, the FSC held its first general assembly in Canada. Among the approximately 120 participants from twenty-four countries were dedicated individuals and representatives from a wide range of organizations, including environmental NGOs, retailers, trade unions, and indigenous interest groups. Although consultations among the different stakeholder groups had been going on since the early 1990s, it was not until 1994 that the founding members of the FSC agreed on the "FSC Standards and Principles," the substantive basis of the FSC's work on the definition and operationalization of sustainable forest management.

This unusual development has to be placed within the context of four distinct features that characterized the problem structure within the forest issue area at that time:

1. By the late 1980s, buying mahogany furniture had become contentious among northern consumers. Extensive media coverage on tropical deforestation and related social issues such as the Amazonian rubber tappers' protest against illegal logging and the subsequent investment in cattle had quickly turned the term *tropical timber* into a negative synonym for environmental degradation and human exploitation.

2. Faced with environmental NGOs organizing boycotts against tropical timber retailers and some governments discussing the possibility of banning timber imports, companies were looking for ways to protect their profits. Major business players realized that they could not account for the origin (and thus social and environmental quality) of their raw materials, which in turn made them vulnerable to civil society protests, and as a result, created a need for transparent product labels (which were nonexistent at that time). In addition, some NGOs were unsatisfied with the practice of timber boycott as the main campaigning tool, which especially the moderate WWF saw as too radical and counterproductive. Around this time, WWF UK conducted a seminar on pressing challenges within the forestry sector, entitled "Forests Are Your Business." This led to the creation of the "WWF 95 Group," in which ten major do-it-yourself and furniture companies agreed to phase out, by 1995, the purchase and sale of nonsustainable timber and timber products (Murphy and Bendell 2000).

3. The conflicting interests of the major stakeholders became evident at that point in time. An increasingly competitive global market for timber products put large multinational corporations under pressure, and at the same time brand reputation became a major concern. Small forest owners

demanded their share of the market but also sought to maintain their independence, communities relied on forests to finance community infrastructure, indigenous people demanded the recognition of fundamental rights, and workers sought to secure employment and the application of fundamental labor standards. Environmental organizations focused on protecting and preserving the integrity of the forest ecosystems within the discursive context of biodiversity conservation and sustainability.

4. By 1992, the negotiations about an international agreement on the world's forest had raised expectations among NGOs, corporations, and the wider public for a credible solution to the global forest crisis. With the 1983 International Tropical Timber Agreement focusing on trade in tropical timber, the international community had already agreed on the first international treaty to regulate some aspects of the forest crisis. Yet it was not until the late 1980s that the governments reached a consensus on the necessity of a global approach to forest degradation and deforestation. In the end, the failure of the intergovernmental process gave an additional boost to the idea of establishing a transnational environmental regime. Remarking on the United Nations Conference on Environment and Development (UNCED), FSC's first executive director Timothy Synnott concluded that "[a] clear impulse for the formation of FSC in 1993 came out of the failure of the Rio conference in 1992 and its failure to produce a legally binding forestry element" (quoted in FSC and WWF Germany 2002, 8). Other experts involved in the early days of the FSC also highlight that in the face of the international stalemate, taking action among business and civil society seemed the appropriate way forward (Pattberg 2007).

Although the 1992 UNCED could not deliver a binding agreement to protect the world's forests, it nevertheless provided important input to the FSC's formation. The concept of sustainable development took center stage at the conference. Based on the 1987 Brundtland Report, UNCED agreed on the Agenda 21 as the blueprint for sustainability in the twenty-first century. The document calls on governments to identify appropriate national strategies for the sustainable use of forest resources, acknowledging the crucial contribution of nongovernmental actors and business interests. Observers called the FSC the "archetype of the participatory process envisioned by Agenda 21" (FSC and WWF Germany 2002, 3). The idea of participation and equal representation based on the general assumption of the sustainability discourse that environmental, social, and economic interests are at equal footing has been an important prerequisite for cooperation between stakeholders that hold quite conflicting interests. Especially the unique tripartite governance structure, ensuring equal representation of all interests, has served as an early point of reference and a common ground for further cooperation.

The Effects of a Transnational Regime Regulating Global Forestry

Normative and Regulatory Effects

I now turn to the question of measurable effects. As some scholars have claimed, "[T]here is a general view that certification has had a positive impact on policy development and institutions" (Nussbaum and Simula 2004, 27). A number of countries have adopted national legislation that resembles FSC rules, prescribes FSC certification in exchange for long-term concessions of state-owned forests, or exempts holders of FSC certificates from particular forms of public control (Domask 2003). For instance, Bolivian forest legislation introduced in 1996 stipulates that independent certification can replace public monitoring of national forest management standards (Bass et al. 2001; Conroy 2007). The South African government ties the privatization of state-owned forests to FSC certification, and legislation in Mexico and Guatemala is also partially linked or adapted to FSC standards (Segura 2004; Pattberg 2006).

At the international level, the World Wildlife Fund and the World Bank initiated a so-called Forest Alliance in 1998. In this alliance, both organizations committed themselves to have 200 million hectares of forests independently certified as sustainably managed by the year 2005. Although this target was missed by a wide margin (in 2005, the official result was 32 million hectares of certified forests outside of protected areas in countries eligible for World Bank lending), the 2005 annual report (WWF and World Bank 2005, 5) noted that the

Alliance's support for national certification working groups, through funding and technical support, has enabled certification to gain ground in many countries and regions where WWF and the Bank work.

Because the WWF only accepts FSC certification as truly independent, the commitment is effectively tied to the principles and criteria set by the FSC (Auld, Gulbrandsen, and McDermott 2008). In the words of Renström (2007, 2):

Thus, while WWF acknowledges that several schemes may contribute to improve forest management, the organization will continue to focus its active efforts on improving the FSC system, on adapting FSC certification to different scales and national contexts, and on promoting the FSC logo as an internationally recognized hallmark of responsible forest management.

The Forest Alliance (WWF 2010) has broadened its target for the period 2006–2010 to having 300 million hectares of forest outside of protected areas under improved forest management, to be achieved through a combination of independent forest certification, approaches to improved forest governance and management, community-based forest management, and restoration of degraded forest lands.

Finally, normative effects also result from the link of FSC principles to other international norms like the core labor standards of the International Labour Organization. That the FSC requires compliance with these international standards means that internationally binding but often weakly implemented norms become effective through certification according to the FSC's principles and criteria. As Poschen (2003, 85) summarizes,

Social and labor aspects need to be brought into focus to balance the current bias towards ecological and sometimes economic functions. It is encouraging that the FSC and to some extent the PEFC [Program for the Endorsement of Forest Certification] are incorporating the above suggestions into their schemes. All avenues should be pursued to promote good social and labor practices in forestry.

Social norms that are widely accepted across national borders are thus strengthened in spheres that are formally part of national territories, but are functionally regulated beyond the state. A study on the effects of FSC certification in six European countries thus concludes (WWF Europe 2005, 2) the following:

Certification has improved the social conditions for forest workers. The employment of local people has been favoured, formal job training has increased and it also led to better compliance with social and legal requirements. It has evaded the erosion of social contributions and ensured that employment rights are complied with.

In sum, normative and regulatory effects are clearly visible as a result of the FSC's activities.

Similar observations can be made with regard to other transnational environmental regimes, although to varying degrees. Consider for example the Global Reporting Initiative (GRI; see Dingwerth and Pattberg 2007; Brown, de Jong, and Lessidrenska 2009). The organization claims that sustainability reporting has become mandatory in an increasing number of countries and that several national initiatives are directly influenced by the GRI. Yet the European Commission is very clear in stressing the voluntary character of the GRI's guidelines (Commission of the European Communities 2002). Even though EU reports recommend the GRI, and some European pension funds require their members to issue GRI reports, it seems quite optimistic to expect the GRI guidelines to become the right thing to do for companies doing business in Europe any time soon (Dingwerth 2008, 616).

Discursive Effects

A range of discursive effects can be identified for the FSC. In the words of a participant in the early formation process (Mankin, cited in Viana et al. 1996, 185–187),

The rapid emergence over the past years of independent third-party forest certification programs, and of the Forest Stewardship Council (FSC), has changed the nature of the entire international forest policy debate. . . . In practical terms, it can be said that the FSC is writing the world's definition of sustainable forest management. While it is true that other organizations are writing theirs as well, the FSC is clearly setting the pace at the international level. . . . I am absolutely convinced that few other entities have changed the political debate over the world's forests—for the better—as much as has the FSC.

That the discursive shifts initiated by the FSC have had an effect is, for instance, illustrated by the observation that "even firms that denounce the FSC for one reason or another are taking precautionary steps in order to keep from falling too far behind in their operations" (Domask 2003, 178). In addition, announcements of business and governmental representatives to amend procurement policies in favor of "FSC or equivalent" certificates indicate that the FSC is seen as the most appropriate benchmark. The German Ministry for Food, Agriculture, and Consumer Protection (BMELV 2010), for example, stipulates that

proof may be provided by presenting a credible certificate of sustainable forest management or an individual specification. First of all, the certificates of FSC and PEFC [Program for the Endorsement of Forest Certification], which are common in Germany, will be accepted. Wood products with a different certificate or without a certificate may be accepted if the bidder is able to satisfactorily prove in their bid that these were produced in compliance with the FSC or PEFC standards applicable for the respective country of origin.

The fact that governmental actors identify the FSC as a benchmark is particularly remarkable given the exclusion of governments from the FSC process and the continuing efforts of regional intergovernmental processes to identify criteria and indicators for sustainable forest management. In addition, through promoting the idea of nonstate multistakeholder processes as an appropriate alternative to intergovernmental negotiations, the FSC also lends support to more general discourses about the democratic quality of global decision making (Dingwerth 2007; Steffek 2009). At the practical level, the principles and criteria have successfully introduced new concepts such as "high conservation value forests" to global forest policy discourses.

In relation to discourses about the world's forests, the FSC is, however, only one actor among many. Its activities are situated in a rhetorical struggle in which many developing countries see forests as an integral part of their national sovereignty over the natural resources within their national territories, and representatives of environmental nongovernmental organizations from industrialized countries tend to invoke a "common concern" or even a "common heritage of humankind." Given this context, the FSC's attempt to define what counts as "responsible forest management" remains contested.

In contrast to other transnational environmental regimes such as the World Commission on Dams or the Global Reporting Initiative, the FSC is thus not as much involved in bringing about paradigmatic change in the area of its main activities. Rather, it lends support to discourses about what constitutes sound and sustainable forest management. Because of this embeddedness into broader societal discourses, the independent discursive effects of the FSC are difficult to measure.

Material and Structural Effects

With regard to material and structural effects, the Forest Stewardship Council is facing a sustained criticism from the South because the largest part of certified timber originates in North America and Europe (also Klooster 2005). In this way, certification gives advantage to producers from countries whose legal requirements are already in line with the FSC standards. By contrast, the situation for developing countries is different. Whereas industrialized countries have to make relatively few changes to existing forestry practices because of already high standards, developing nations have to make substantial investments to the certification requirements, often resulting in a comparative disadvantage vis-à-vis competitors in the North. Ebeling and Yasué (2008, 1151) draw a similar conclusion in their comparative study of forest certification in Bolivia and Ecuador when they conclude, "forest certification currently does not appear to be a universally applicable, effective international conservation tool."

Similar to the GRI and the ISO 14000 processes (Clapp 1998), stake-holders in the developing countries express the concern that the FSC standards mainly reflect the interests of campaigners from the North, and that the effects of the FSC might primarily consist in reducing development perspectives in the South. On this account, FSC certification is compared by some authors to the tropical timber boycotts of the 1980s (Smouts 2002, 13–14):

So far, the main result has been to boost the comparative advantages of temperate forests on the timber marketplace. . . . Over 90 percent of the FSC certified forests are temperate and boreal forests. Conclusion: if you feel you must have FSC certified timber, buy Scandinavian, Eastern European and North American wood, not tropical wood. If that is not a boycott, it bears a close resemblance.

This criticism is underscored by the fact that over four-fifths of the FSC-certificated wood still comes from Europe and North America. Overall, Canadian, Swedish, or Polish producers benefit from the success of the FSC much more than producers in Malaysia and Indonesia. It corresponds to the development of the global timber trade since the establishment of the FSC in 1993. Although the value of wood export from developing countries increased in reference periods 1993–1997 and 2000–2004 by about 4 percent, the value of wood export from industrialized countries in the same period increased triplefold (approximately 13 percent). Canada, Sweden, and Poland recorded a growth of 71.1, 5.2, and 116.5 percent in the reference period, whereas Malaysia and Indonesia had a decrease of 33.3 and 3.9 percent (Dingwerth and Pattberg 2007; based on data from World Resources Institute 2006).

In other words, wood imports to industrialized countries increasingly originate from other industrialized countries. The causes for that are manifold but they include the demand for certificated wood in industrialized countries, which has been strongly increasing in the same period. In short, timber producers from developing countries have difficulties in gaining significant access to premium markets in the OECD region (Gullison 2003, 158). In addition, looking at the roundwood production from certified sources per region, the neglect of certain geographic areas becomes painstakingly visible: zero percent of global certified roundwood supply came from Africa between 2007 and 2009 (UNECE and FAO 2009). Generalizations about the North-South dimension of transnational environmental regimes, however, are hard to make because the judgment will depend on the specific issue. For example, although sustainable forest governance seems to be biased in favor of northern producers and consumers, the issue area of fair trade (e.g., the Fair Labeling Organization) is by nature of its goals much more open to southern interests.

Further to influencing markets, the FSC has induced substantial unintended side effects that can be subsumed under structural effects: the creation of numerous alternative and competing certification schemes in the forestry sector. In the words of Auld, Gulbrandsen, and McDermott (2008, 200), "[P]robably the most significant unintended outcome of the creation of the FSC was how producers around the world responded by creating their own national certification schemes." Evaluations of this outcome are mixed. Although additional certification programs have increased the overall coverage of sustainable forest management around the globe, competing claims and alternative standards have allowed companies to benefit from the general positive connotation of forest certification without making substantive changes to their operations. Given the various competing labels in the marketplace, it becomes increasingly difficult for consumers to assess the claims made on behalf of the various certification programs.

In sum, the material and structural effects of forest certification are not only clearly visible, but also go beyond those of other transnational environmental regimes. Although the material effects of, for example, the Global Reporting Initiative or the World Commission on Dams have so far been rather theoretically assumed than empirically verified (and consequently, more comparative research is urgently needed), the FSC's effect on market structures in the global forestry business cannot be denied. As Conroy (2007, 95) concludes, the FSC is "the most important example of increasingly successful certification systems that are transforming major industries around the world."

Explanations

Explanations for the emergence of transnational environmental regimes have focused on the broader discursive and material environment of neoliberalism as a major cause for the shift from public intergovernmental regimes to often semiprivate regimes (Barteley 2003). This structural account provides, however, an incomplete picture at best. It cannot convincingly explain why some environmental problems have been subjected to transnational regulation and others have not (e.g., forest governance versus biodiversity) or why some problems have been addressed by private regulation while they are already addressed by a host of inter-governmental regimes (e.g., marine governance).

One approach to overcome the inflexibility of structural arguments is to combine conditions at the macro level with concrete explanations at the micro level (Pattberg 2005c). What is interesting to observe is that in the initial institutionalization of the FSC, organizational resources played a greater role than strategic reduction of transaction costs. Although companies were able to decrease costs, for example by elimi-nating intermediate traders based on information they obtained through the cooperation with local NGOs or by enhancing a positive brand repu-tation, this has been an unintended consequence rather than a clear strategic vision on parts of the companies. More decisive was that NGOs were perceived as legitimate actors by the public and thus could deliver the much-needed credibility to contested forest certification systems (Pattberg 2005c). Furthermore, NGOs provided expert knowledge on many complex issues related to the technical aspects of certification. Retailers for their part could exercise pressure on timber producers by demanding certified raw materials and products, inducing change in the supply chain. Forest managers perceived the chance to increase their profits by positioning themselves on the newly emerging market for sustainable timber. In sum, by early 1994, the FSC had emerged as the first credible transnational environmental regime for sustainable forestry at the global scale, inspiring a host of other processes to follow suit.

A second explanation with regard to the overall question of emergence of transnational regimes has focused on the influence of an organiza-tional field of transnational nonstate rule making on the diffusion and concrete organizational forms of transnational environmental regulation (Dingwerth and Pattberg 2009). This argument is based on a sociological reading of transnational regimes because it focuses on the organizational actors, that is, the secretariats administering the transnational environ-mental regimes (Bauer, Andresen, and Biermann, this book, chapter 2). As Dingwerth and Pattberg (2009) show, social interaction and the norms that follow from it are central explanatory factors. In particular, Dingwerth and Pattberg (2009) hold that microlevel dynamics are crucial to making sense of private authority beyond the state. In more detail, they argue that in the early 1990s, an organizational field of transna-tional rule making gradually developed in global sustainability politics. Responding to a broader social discourse about appropriate means of global governance that stressed a need for innovative forms of coop-eration among different societal sectors, this field quickly gained in legitimacy and strength. Rather than interest-based calculations of gains or power-based behavior, it was the sustained and gradually intensifying interaction among a small number of transnational organizations that spurred the formation of an organizational field of transnational rule making.

Similar to the study of intergovernmental environmental regimes, after initial attempts to theorize the emergence of transnational regimes, the interest has quickly shifted to the question of effectiveness. Hence, the central research question is, Do transnational environmental regimes matter? And if yes, why and how? Concerning the effects of transnational environmental regimes, a number of studies have measured concrete and issue-specific effects such as the area of certified forests (Auld, Gulbrandsen, and McDermott 2008). This rather narrow focus, however, obscures the wider effects of transnational environmental regimes. The central puzzle in this regard has been why the measured effects differ quite substantially across the different types of effects (that is, normative, discursive, and material) and between different transnational environmental regimes (such as the Forest Stewardship Council and the Global Reporting Initiative).

A preliminary explanation for the observed variation can be found in different strategies to induce intended effects (Dingwerth and Pattberg 2007, 2008): first, steering by incentives, that is, through linking desired outcomes to (economic) costs or benefits. Second, steering by norms, that is, through linking desired outcomes to expectations about the appropriate behavior of actors in a particular situation. The performance of transnational regimes then depends on the extent to which they manage to make use of these two strategies—either to change the costs structures of particular activities or to change the way society evaluates particular activities. Regime activities that follow the logic of appropriateness are primarily targeted at inducing discursive and normative effects. In contrast, regime activities that build on a logic of expected consequences are geared toward material and structural effects.

In sum, transnational environmental regimes have a range of significant effects beyond instigating compliance with their standards. In contrast to accounts of transnational governance that measure relevance in terms of "hard" effects, the current analytical perspective should be broadened to include normative, discursive, and structural effects. A preliminary conclusion with regard to explaining variation in regime effects can also be drawn: the regime type influences what kind of effect a transnational environmental regime is likely to have. Although information-based regimes tend to have stronger normative and discursive effects, market-based regimes are more likely to show regulatory and material effects. Finally, the overall effects of transnational environmental regimes appear to be less dependent on the latter's cooperation with governmental and intergovernmental institutions than is often assumed in the literature.

Conclusions and Outlook

At first sight, it might seem as if the implications of transnational environmental regimes such as those examined in this chapter could be easily assessed. Analysis could for instance focus on the area of certified forests, the number of companies that regularly publish sustainability reports, or the number of governments that link their public procurement policies to global certification programs. Such an assessment, however, would misread the nature of transnational environmental regimes. In some sense, it would amount to assessing the relevance of a nongovernmental organization such as Greenpeace based on the number of its members. In both cases, it is of course possible to infer the acceptance of the institution from the change over time (certified area, members, and so forth). Yet it would tell us very little about the structural implications and indirect effects on societal norms and the larger discourses these norms are embedded in. As I argue in this chapter, these additional effects of transnational environmental regimes are particularly noteworthy because they connect to important questions of equity, fairness, and accountability. In particular, the observation that transnational environmental regimes have measurable effects on stakeholders in the South is a central conclusion of this chapter (also Dingwerth 2008). Unfortunately, comparative data on the North-South dimension of all transnational environmental regimes is largely absent. Consequently, future research should focus on comparative analyses among transnational regimes, within and beyond the environmental arena. In addition, three more specific questions could guide research on transnational regimes in the years to come.

First, we know relatively little about the influence of institutional design and organizational structures on the effectiveness of transnational environmental regimes. Although some studies have theorized the relationship between legitimacy and effectiveness (e.g., Beisheim and Dingwerth 2008), no overall assessment exists that compares transnational environmental regimes according to variations in institutional design. Yet it seems obvious that variation of performance in a similar issue area (e.g., between the FSC and the industry-based Program for the Endorsement of Forest Certification) could be explained by differences in the internal organizational setup, decision-making procedures, and monitoring and compliance mechanisms employed. This line of inquiry could build on the rich theoretical knowledge created by international regimes research (Miles et al. 2001).

Second, we are in need of better theoretical arguments about the limits of transnational environmental regimes. Often based on market mechanisms (such as certification) and the demand of well-educated and affluent consumers in the North, many transnational environmental regimes seem to be limited in their ability to change underlying patterns of environmental degradation. What is needed is a critical discussion of those limits and how the success of transnational governance might be linked to dominating worldviews such as neoliberalism and free trade.

Finally, interlinkages, overlaps, and potential synergies with international and public governance have emerged as key questions of theoretical and practical relevance. Whereas the first generation of scholarship on transnational environmental governance was right in highlighting the distinct nature of emerging private institutions for sustainability, painting a more nuanced picture of how public and private sources of authority co-produce positive and negative governance outcomes should now be the focus of future research in the field of global environmental governance.

Acknowledgments

Although this chapter is single authored (and any error that might have gone unnoticed is the responsibility of the author), the research presented here is the result of many fruitful interactions with my colleague Klaus Dingwerth, to whom I am intellectually indebted. Research assistance by Eleni Dellas and Emily Kilham is gratefully acknowledged.

References

Auld, Graeme, Lars Gulbrandsen, and Constance McDermott. 2008. Certification Schemes and the Impacts on Forests and Forestry. *Annual Review of Environment and Resources* 33:187–211.

Bacon, Christopher M. 2010. Who Decides What Is Fair in Fair Trade? The Agri-environmental Governance of Standards, Access, and Price. *Journal of Peasant Studies* 37 (1):111–147.

Bartley, Tim. 2003. Certifying Forests and Factories: States, Social Movements, and the Rise of Private Regulation in the Apparel and Forest Products Fields. *Politics & Society* 31 (3):433–464.

Bass, Stephen, Kirsti Thornber, Matthew Markopoulos, Sarah Roberts, and Maryanne Grieg-Gran. 2001. *Certification's Impacts on Forests, Stakeholders, and Supply Chains*. London: IIED.

Beffert, David, and Thorsten Benner. 2004. *Stemming the Tide of Conflict: The Kimberley Process. Hertie School of Governance Teaching Case 2/2005. Part A/B/C.* Berlin: Global Public Policy Institute.

Beisheim, Marianne, and Klaus Dingwerth. 2008. Procedural Legitimacy and Private Transnational Governance. Are the Good Ones Doing Better? SFB 700 Working Paper. Berlin: Freie Universität.

Bernauer, Thomas. 1995. The Effect of International Environmental Institutions: How We Might Learn More. *International Organization* 49 (2):351–377.

Beschorner, Thomas, and Martin Müller. 2007. Social Standards: Toward an Active Ethical Involvement of Businesses in Developing Countries. *Journal of Business Ethics* 73 (1):11–20.

Bitzer, Verena, Mara Francken, and Pieter Glasbergen. 2008. Intersectoral Partnerships for a Sustainable Coffee Chain: Really Addressing Sustainability or Just Picking (Coffee) Cherries? *Global Environmental Change: Human and Policy Dimensions* 8 (2):271–284.

BMELV. 2010. Explanatory Notes Regarding the Procurement of Wood Products. Retrieved from http://www.pefc.at/download/2007_german_procurement_policy.pdf.

Brown, Halina Szejnwald, Martin de Jong, and Teodorina Lessidrenska. 2009. The Rise of the Global Reporting Initiative: A Case of Institutional Entrepreneurship. *Environmental Politics* 18 (2):182–200.

Buzan, Barry. 2005. *From International to World Society*. Cambridge, UK: Cambridge University Press.

Cashore, Benjamin. 2002. Legitimacy and the Privatization of Environmental Governance: How Non-state Market-Driven (NSMD) Governance Systems Gain Rule-making Authority. *Governance: An International Journal of Policy and Administration* 15 (4):503–529.

Chayes, Abram, and Antonia Handler Chayes. 1995. *The New Sovereignty: Compliance with International Regulatory Agreements*. Cambridge, MA: Harvard University Press.

Clapp, Jennifer. 1998. The Privatization of Global Environmental Governance: ISO 14000 and the Developing World. *Global Governance. A Review of Multilateralism and International Organizations* 4 (3):295–316.

Commission of the European Communities. 2002. *Communication from the Commission Concerning Corporate Social Responsibility: A Business Contribution to Sustainable Development*. [COM(2002) 347, 2 July 2002] Brussels: Commission of the European Communities.

Conroy, Michael E. 2007. *Branded: How the Certification Revolution Is Transforming Global Corporations*. Gabriola Island, British Columbia, Canada: New Society Publishers.

Constance, Douglas H., and Alessandro Bonanno. 2000. Regulating the Global Fisheries: The World Wildlife Fund, Unilever, and the Marine Stewardship Council. *Agriculture and Human Values* 17 (2):125–139.

Courville, Sascha. 2003. Social Accountability Audits: Challenging or Defending Democratic Governance? *Law & Policy* 25 (3):269–297.

Cutler, A. Claire, Virginia Haufler, and Tony Porter. 1999. Private Authority and International Affairs. In *Private Authority and International Affairs*, ed. A. Claire Cutler, Virginia Haufler, and Tony Porter, 3–28. Albany: SUNY Press.

Danielson, Luke. 2006. *Architecture for Change: An Account of the Mining, Minerals, and Sustainable Development Project History*. Berlin: Global Public Policy Institute.

Dingwerth, Klaus. 2005. The Democratic Legitimacy of Public-Private Rule-making: What Can We Learn from the World Commission on Dams? *Global Governance* 11 (1):65–83.

Dingwerth, Klaus. 2007. *The New Transnationalism: Transnational Governance and Democratic Accountability*. Basingstoke, UK: Palgrave Macmillan.

Dingwerth, Klaus. 2008. Private Transnational Governance and the Developing World: A Comparative Perspective. *International Studies Quarterly* 52 (3): 607–634.

Dingwerth, Klaus, and Philipp Pattberg. 2006. Global Governance as a Perspective on World Politics. *Global Governance: A Review of Multilateralism and International Organizations* 12 (2): 185–203.

Dingwerth, Klaus, and Philipp Pattberg. 2007. Wirkungen transnationaler Umweltregime. *Politische Vierteljahresschrift* 39:133–156.

Dingwerth, Klaus, and Philipp Pattberg. 2008. The New Politics of Environmental Sustainability: Assessing the Effects of Transnational Environmental Regimes. Unpublished manuscript. On file with author.

Dingwerth, Klaus, and Philipp Pattberg. 2009. World Politics and Organizational Fields: The Case of Sustainability Governance. *European Journal of International Relations* 15 (4):707–743.

Doane, Deborah. 2005. *The Myth of CSR*. Stanford, CA: Stanford Graduate School of Business.

Domask, John. 2003. From Boycotts to Global Partnership: NGOs, the Private Sector, and the Struggle to Protect the World's Forests. In *Globalization and NGOs: Transforming Business, Government, and Society*, ed. Jonathan Doh and Hildey Teegen, 157–185. Westport, CT: Praeger.

Drezner, Daniel W. 2004. The Global Governance of the Internet: Bringing the State Back. *Political Science Quarterly* 119 (3):477–498.

Dubash, Navroz. 2009. Global Norms through Global Deliberation? Reflections on the World Commission on Dams. *Global Governance* 15 (2):219–238.

Ebeling, Johannes, and Mai Yasué. 2008. The Effectiveness of Market-based Conservation in the Tropics: Forest Certification in Ecuador and Bolivia. *Journal of Environmental Management* 90:1145–1153.

Espach, Ralph H. 2009. *Private Environmental Regimes in Developing Countries: Globally Sown, Locally Grown*. New York: Palgrave Macmillan.

Forest Stewardship Council. 2002. *FSC International Standard: FSC Principles and Criteria for Forest Stewardship* (Version 4–0, last amended 2002). Bonn: FSC International.

Forest Stewardship Council [FSC] and WWF Germany. 2002. *Forest Stewardship Council: Political Instrument, Implementation and Concrete Results for Sustainability since 1993*. Frankfurt: FSC and WWF Germany.

Forest Stewardship Council. 2010. Global FSC Certificates: Type and Distribution, January. Retrieved from http://www.fsc.org/fileadmin/web-data/public/document_center/powerpoints_graphs/facts_figures/Global-FSC-Certificates-2010-01-15-EN.pdf.

Gulbrandsen, Lars. 2005. Explaining Different Approaches to Voluntary Standards: A Study of Forest Certification Choices in Norway and Sweden. *Journal of Environmental Policy and Planning* 7 (1):43–59.

Gulbrandsen, Lars. 2008. Accountability Arrangements in Non-state Standards Organizations: Instrumental Design and Imitation. *Organisation* 15 (4):563–583.

Gulbrandsen, Lars. 2009. The Emergence and Effectiveness of the Marine Stewardship Council. *Marine Policy* 33 (4):654–660.

Gullison, Robert E. 2003. Does Forest Certification Conserve Biodiversity? Oryx 37 (2): 153–165.

Hall, Rodney Bruce, and Thomas J. Biersteker, eds. 2002. *The Emergence of Private Authority in Global Governance*. Cambridge, UK: Cambridge University Press.

Haufler, Virginia. 2000. Private Sector International Regimes. In *Non-state Actors and Authority in the Global System*, ed. Richard A. Higgott, Geoffrey R.D. Underhill, and Andreas Bieler, 121–137. London: Routledge.

Hedberg, Carl-Johan, and Fredrik von Malmborg. 2003. The Global Reporting Initiative and Corporate Sustainability Reporting in Swedish Companies. *Corporate Social Responsibility and Environmental Management* 10 (3):153–164.

Hertin, Julia, Frans Berkhout, Marcus Wagner, and Daniel Tyteca. 2004. Assessing the Link between Environmental Management Systems and the Environmental Performance of Companies: An Eco-efficiency Approach. In *Governance for Industrial Transformation: Proceedings of the 2003 Berlin Conference on the Human Dimensions of Global Environmental Change*, ed. Klaus Jacob, Martin Binder, and Anna Wieczorek, 459–478. Berlin: Forschungsstelle für Umweltpolitik.

Hussey, Dennis M., Patrick L. Kirsop, and Ronald E. Meissen. 2001. Global Reporting Initiative Guidelines: An Evaluation of Sustainable Development Metrics for Industry. *Environmental Quality Management* II:143–162.

Jamal, Tazim, Marcos Borges, and Amanda Stronza. 2006. The Institutionalisation of Ecotourism: Certification, Cultural Equity and Praxis. *Journal of Ecotourism* 51 (3):145–175.

Kantz, Carola. 2006. Public-Private Partnerships and the South: The Case of the Kimberley Process. Paper presented at the 47th Meeting of the International Studies Association, "The North-South Divide and International Studies," San Diego, 22–25 March.

Kerwer, Dieter. 2002. Standardizing as Governance: The Case of Credit Rating Agencies. In *Common Goods: Reinventing European and International Governance*, ed. Adrienne Heritier, 293–316. Lanham, MD: Rowman and Littlefield.

Kirton, John, and Michael J. Trebilcock, eds. 2004. *Hard Choices, Soft Law: Voluntary Standards in Global Trade, Environment, and Social Governance*. Aldershot, UK: Ashgate.

Klooster, Daniel. 2005. Environmental Certification of Forests: The Evolution of Environmental Governance in a Commodity Network. *Journal of Rural Studies* 21:403–417.

Kolk, Ans. 2005. Corporate Social Responsibility in the Coffee Sector: The Dynamics of MNC Responses and Code Development. *European Management Journal* 23 (2):228–236.

Kollman, Kelly, and Aseem Prakash. 2001. Green by Choice? Cross-national Variations in Firms' Responses to EMS-based Environmental Regimes. *World Politics* 53 (3):399–430.

Krasner, Stephen D. 1983. Structural Causes and Regime Consequences: Regimes as Intervening Variables. In *International Regimes*, ed. Stephen D. Krasner, 1–21. Ithaca, NY: Cornell University Press.

Levi-Faur, David, and Jacint Jordana, eds. 2005. *The Rise of Regulatory Capitalism*. London: Sage.

Luttikholt, Louise. 2007. Principles of Organic Agriculture as Formulated by the International Federation of Organic Agriculture Movements. *NJAS-Wageningen Journal of Life Sciences* 54 (4):347–360.

Marx, Axel. 2008. Limits to Non-state Market Regulation: A Qualitative Comparative Analysis of the International Sport Footwear Industry and the Fair Labor Association. *Regulation and Governance* 2 (2):253–273.

Mattli, Walter, and Tim Büthe. 2003. Setting International Standards: Technological Rationality or Primacy of Power? *World Politics* 56:1–42.

Miles, Edward L., Arild Underdal, Steinar Andresen, Jørgen Wettestad, Jon Birger Skjærseth, and Elaine M. Carlin, eds. 2001. *Environmental Regime Effectiveness: Confronting Theory with Evidence*. Cambridge, MA: MIT Press.

Muradian, Roldan, and Wim Pelupessy. 2005. Governing the Coffee Chain: The Role of Voluntary Regulatory Systems. *World Development* 33 (12): 2029–2044.

Murphy, David F., and Jem Bendell. 2000. Planting the Seeds of Change: Business-NGO Relations and Tropical Deforestation. In *Terms for Endearment:*

Business, NGOs and Sustainable Development, ed. Jem Bendell, 65–78. Sheffield, UK: Greenleaf Publishing.

Neilson, Jeffrey, and Bill Pritchard. 2007. Green Coffee? The Contradictions of Global Sustainability Initiatives from an Indian Perspective. *Development Policy Review* 25 (3):311–331.

Nölke, Andreas. 2006. The Transnational Politics of Global Accounting Standard Harmonization. Paper presented at GARNET Congress, Amsterdam, September.

Nussbaum, Ruth, and Markku Simula. 2004. *Forest Certification: A Review of Impacts and Assessment Frameworks*. New Haven, CT: Yale University School of Forestry and Environmental Studies.

Oosterveer, Peter. 2008. Governing Global Fish Provisioning: Ownership and Management of Marine Resources. *Ocean and Coastal Management* 51 (12): 797–805.

Overdevest, Christine. 2010. Comparing Forest Certification Schemes: The Case of Ratcheting Standards in the Forest Sector. *Socio-economic Review* 8 (1):47–76.

Pattberg, Philipp. 2005a. The Forest Stewardship Council: Risk and Potential of Private Forest Governance. *Journal of Environment & Development* 14 (3): 356–374.

Pattberg, Philipp. 2005b. What Role for Private Rule-making in Global Environmental Governance? Analyzing the Forest Stewardship Council (FSC). *International Environmental Agreement: Politics, Law and Economics* 5 (2):175–189.

Pattberg, Philipp. 2005c. The Institutionalization of Private Governance: How Business and Non-profit Organizations Agree on Transnational Rules. *Governance: An International Journal of Policy, Administration, and Institutions* 18 (4):589–610.

Pattberg, Philipp. 2006. Private Governance and the South: Lessons from Global Forest Politics. *Third World Quarterly* 27 (4):579–593.

Pattberg, Philipp. 2007. *Private Institutions and Global Governance: The New Politics of Environmental Sustainability*. Cheltenham, UK: Edward Elgar.

Poschen, Peter. 2003. Economic and Social Justice. In *Social and Political Dimensions of Forest Certification*, ed. Errol Meidinger, Chris Elliott, and Gerhard Oesten, 83–104. Remagen-Oberwinter, Germany: Dr. Kessel.

Raustiala, Kal. 1997. States, NGOs, and International Environmental Institutions. *International Studies Quarterly* 41 (4):719–740.

Renström, Margaret. 2007. WWF Position Paper on Forest. Retrieved from http://assets.panda.org/downloads/wwf_forest_certification_pp_oct07.pdf.

Reynolds, MaryAnn, and Kristi Yuthas. 2008. Moral Discourse and Corporate Social Responsibility Reporting. *Journal of Business Ethics* 78 (1–2): 47–64.

Rice, Robert A. 2001. Noble Goals and a Challenging Terrain: Organic and Fair Trade Coffee Movements in the Global Marketplace. *Journal of Agricultural & Environmental Ethics* 14 (1):39–66.

Rosenau, James N. 1990. *Turbulence in World Politics: A Theory of Change and Continuity*. Princeton, NJ: Princeton University Press.

Rosenau, James N. 1995. Governance in the Twenty-First Century. *Global Governance* 1 (1):13–43.

Ruggie, John G. 2004. Reconstructing the Global Public Domain: Issues, Actors, and Practices. *European Journal of International Relations* 10 (4):499–531.

Sasser, Erika N., Benjamin Cashore, Aseem Prakash, and Graeme Auld. 2004. Competition Among Non-governmental Regimes: Direct Targeting by ENGOs and Its Impact on Firm-level Choice in the U.S. Forest Products Sector. Paper read at 45th Annual International Studies Association Convention, Montreal, March 17–20.

Schepers, Donald H. 2010. Challenges to Legitimacy at the Forest Stewardship Council. *Journal of Business Ethics* 92:279–290.

Segura, Gerardo. 2004. *Forest Certification and Governments: The Real and Potential Influence on Regulatory Frameworks and Forest Policies*. Washington, DC: Forest Trends.

Shelton, Dinah H., ed. 2000. *Commitment and Compliance: The Role of Non-binding Norms in the International Legal System*. Oxford: Oxford University Press.

Shuman, Craig S., Gregor Hodgson, and Richard F. Ambrose. 2004. Managing the Marine Aquarium Trade: Is Eco-certification the Answer? *Environmental Conservation* 31 (4):339–348.

Smouts, Marie-Claude. 2002. Forest Certification and Timber Labelling: The Hidden Agenda. Paper presented at 43rd Meeting of the International Studies Association, New Orleans, 24–27 March.

Steffek, Jens. 2009. Discursive Legitimation in Environmental Governance. *Forest Policy and Economics* 11 (4–5):313–318.

Thrane, Mikkel, Friederike Ziegler, and Ulf Sonesson. 2009. Eco-labelling of Wild-caught Seafood Products. *Journal of Cleaner Production* 17 (3):416–423.

Thynne, Ian. 2008. Climate Change, Governance, and Environmental Services: Institutional Perspectives, Issues, and Challenges. *Public Administration and Development* 28 (5):327–339.

UNECE and FAO. 2009. Forest Products Annual Market Review, 2008-2009. Retrieved from http://timber.unece.org/fileadmin/DAM/publications/Final _FPAMR2009.pdf.

Viana, Virgilio M., Jamison Ervin, Richard Z. Donovan, Chris Elliott, and Henry Gholz, eds. 1996. *Certification of Forest Products: Issues and Perspectives*. Washington, DC: Island Press.

Visseren-Hamakers, Ingrid J., and Pieter Glasbergen. 2007. Partnerships in Forest Governance. *Global Environmental Change: Human and Policy Dimensions* 17 (3–4):408–419.

Wapner, Paul. 1995. Politics beyond the State: Environmental Activism and World Civic Politics. *World Politics* 47 (3):311–340.

Whitmore, Andy. 2006. The Emperor's New Clothes: Sustainable Mining? *Journal of Cleaner Production* 14 (3–4):309–314.

Willis, Alan. 2003. The Role of the Global Reporting Initiative's Sustainability Reporting Guidelines in the Social Screening of Investments. *Journal of Business Ethics* 43 (3):233–237.

World Resources Institute. 2006. EarthTrends: The Environmental Information Portal. Washington DC: World Resources Institute. Retrieved from http://earthtrends.wri.org.

WWF Europe. 2005. The Effects of FSC Certification in Estonia, Germany, Latvia, Russia, Sweden and the UK. An Analysis of Corrective Action Requests. Summary Report. Retrieved from http://www.panda.org/europe/forests.

WWF and World Bank. 2005. Global Forest Alliance Annual Report 2005. Retrieved from http://www.worldwildlife.org/what/globalmarkets/forests/WWFBinaryitem7334.pdf.

WWF and World Bank. 2010. Forest Alliance. Targets 2010. Retrieved from http://www.worldwildlife.org/what/globalmarkets/forests/worldbankalliancetargets.html.

Young, Oran R. 1999. *Governance in World Affairs*. Ithaca, NY: Cornell University Press.

Zangl, Bernhard, and Michael Zürn. 2004. Make Law, Not War: Internationale Verrechtlichung als Baustein für Global Governance. In *Verrechtlichung: Baustein für Global Governance?* ed. Bernhard Zangl and Michael Zürn, 12–45. Bonn: Dietz.

6

Transnational Public-Private Partnerships

Karin Bäckstrand, Sabine Campe, Sander Chan, Ayşem Mert, and Marco Schäferhoff

Transnational public-private partnerships for sustainable development are frequently advanced as policy innovations to reduce implementation and legitimacy deficits in global governance (Haas 2004). Partnerships are conceived as more adequate and effective governance instruments compared to traditional regulatory mechanisms. They are often framed as win-win solutions that increase the democratic credentials of global governance while simultaneously strengthening its environmental performance (Benner, Streck, and Witte 2003; Streck 2004). The Global Governance Project has systematically conducted a series of quantitative studies, in-depth and comparative case studies, as well as interpretive policy and text analyses on transnational partnerships for sustainable development. This chapter critically synthesizes the outcomes of these studies, supplemented by a literature review examining the emergence, legitimacy, and effectiveness of public-private partnerships for sustainable development.

Our focus is the more than three hundred partnerships that were adopted around the 2002 World Summit on Sustainable Development and/or have been registered with the Commission on Sustainable Development (CSD). We take stock of our previous assessments of the performance and legitimacy of these "Johannesburg partnerships"[1] and highlight individual partnerships, such as the Water and Sanitation for the Urban Poor Partnership and the Global Water Partnership.

We structure our argument around three questions that reflect the expanding scholarship on transnational public-private partnerships. First, how and why did the partnerships emerge? Second, are they effective in solving environmental problems? Third, are they legitimate governance mechanisms, that is, inclusive, accountable, and transparent?

The many studies on public-private partnerships reach different conclusions on these questions, partially because different research appraisals of partnerships do not always share the same ontological, epistemological, and normative assumptions on the nature and effects of public-private partnerships. Also in the Global Governance Project, we approached questions of emergence, effectiveness, and legitimacy from different theoretical and methodological angles. Questions of emergence were studied primarily with an interpretive perspective. Functionalist and critical perspectives have been used to understand effectiveness and legitimacy. We used these different approaches because their explanatory potentials for each of the analytical problems are complementary. For instance, effectiveness in a liberal-functionalist analysis primarily concerns the role of partnerships in fulfilling certain governance gaps, whether they reach their proclaimed goals and whether they are more effective than alternative instruments. However, the question of effectiveness is less relevant, or differently interpreted, from a critical perspective (Mert 2009; Miraftab 2004; Ottoway 2001). For example, "goal attainment" has been criticized for being a rather apolitical frame that obscures the question of whose interests are served or (re)instated by partnerships. In addition, critical approaches have addressed the sources of legitimacy for partnerships.

The following section conceptualizes transnational public-private partnerships as multisectoral network governance instruments and contrasts the liberal-functionalist, critical, and interpretive approaches to the study of transnational partnerships. The second section summarizes the context for the Johannesburg partnerships. The third section focuses on how different theoretical approaches have explained (or critically examined) the emergence, effectiveness, and legitimacy of partnerships. In the conclusions, we revisit the effectiveness and legitimacy of transnational public-private partnerships by summarizing the cumulated research insights on partnership performance, participation, and accountability emanating from the research synthesized in this chapter.

Conceptualization

Public-private partnerships are not a new phenomenon: they emerged as governance instruments in domestic politics already in the 1980s. The tenacious privatization policies of the Thatcher and Reagan administrations promoted the ideas of new public management, based on the assumptions that the private sector provides public goods and services more efficiently than the public sector, and that consequently the public sector should be downsized by outsourcing governance functions.

Building partnerships with the private sector, governments could promote the provision of public services without undertaking them. For the private sector, partnerships were a means to expand their activities to previously restricted areas. As a result, corporations enjoyed a number of public relations benefits from building partnerships with governments and communities. Although new public management was often criticized, national and local partnerships had become an accepted and legitimate governance tool in many industrialized countries in the 1980s.

The move toward public-private partnerships has been replicated at the international level. Since the 1990s, the United Nations have promoted partnerships ranging from the UN Global Compact to the Johannesburg partnerships as a way to restore the legitimacy of the United Nations in the context of a weakened multilateral system (Bull and McNeill 2007; Martens 2007).

Nevertheless, these global partnerships differ from national and local governance contexts. First, they lack a centralized accountability and monitoring mechanism by a public body. This relates to the general claim that "new" transnational public-private partnerships have replaced "old" traditional state-based regulation. This claim is misleading, however, because both mechanisms at best complement each other. Scholars have also pointed to the continuing relevance of the "shadow of hierarchy," that is, the prevalent influence of states and intergovernmental organizations in global environmental governance (Bauer, Andresen, and Biermann, this book, chapter 2; Compagnon, Chan, and Mert, this book, chapter 11; Beisheim, Campe, and Schäferhoff 2010; Börzel and Risse 2005). A second difference between the domestic and the global level is the lack of a coherent *demos* for transnational partnerships. Although in a national context, the failure of a policy (that is, partnerships) would be the responsibility of an elected body, in the transnational context this is not the case.

Given these differences between public-private partnerships in the domestic and in the transnational context, how can partnerships be defined? In scholarly work, mechanisms such as public-private partnerships are often analyzed as a form of network governance (Andonova, Betsill, and Bulkeley 2009; Biermann et al. 2007; Benne, Reinicke, and Witte 2005; Bäckstrand 2008; Pattberg 2010; Pattberg et al. 2012). The notion of partnerships, for its part, is often used as an all-inclusive term that encompasses everything from informal cooperation between two actors to multilateral organizations. Martens (2007, 4) argues that the term *partnerships* "now covers virtually every interaction between state and nonstate actors, particularly between [the] UN and the business sector." There is often a positive connotation to partnerships in academic and policy circles. They are frequently seen as tools to facilitate win-win situations and engage multilateral organizations, companies, and nonprofit actors in mutual and symmetric cooperation in the pursuit of global common goods (Benner, Reinicke, and Witte 2005). We see it as problematic, however, to define partnerships and their activities as a priori positive because this impedes any further analysis on their effectiveness (Schäferhoff, Campe, and Kaan 2009). Public-private partnerships can indeed reconfigure authority from state toward nonstate actors, yet this does not necessarily constitute win-win or even desirable situations.

Accordingly, we define transnational public-private partnerships as multisectoral networks that bring together governments, business, and civil society, that is, as institutionalized transboundary interactions between public and private actors, which aim at the provision of collective goods (Schäferhoff, Campe, and Kaan 2009). This definition is open enough to take into account the variety among transnational partners; the diverse functions including agenda setting, rule making, advocacy, implementation, and service provision; and the different policy areas (Bull and McNeill 2007; Martens 2007).

This chapter focuses on sustainable development, but partnerships also appear in sectors such as human rights, health, development, security, and finance (Broadwater and Kaul 2005). Moreover, the degree of institutionalization is another variable that varies because the institutional designs of partnerships range from loose cooperations to highly formalized initiatives. Partnerships also have different geographical scopes from the local, national, and regional to the global levels. Public-private partnerships thus epitomize multilevel governance structures because they cross the local-global divide, jurisdictions, and sectors (Zelli, Gupta, and van Asselt, this book, chapter 8; Busch, Gupta, and Falkner, this book, chapter 9; Beisheim, Campe, and Schäferhoff 2010).

These diverse definitions already point to some of the contestations related to the emergence of transnational partnerships. The academic definitions vary between more critical or more mainstream scholarship, mainly because of the political contestations over the definition and workings of partnerships in the UN system. Our relatively open conceptualization of partnerships as institutionalized transboundary interaction between private and public actors for the provisions of public goods allows for the use of several theoretical perspectives. The liberal-functionalist, the critical, and the interpretive perspectives represent distinct theoretical accounts to understand and explain the rise of transnational partnerships.

First, the interpretive perspective asks a new set of questions regarding partnerships by shedding light on the various meanings of partnerships and institutions, also in a historical perspective. Different actor constellations define and understand the concept of partnership in radically different ways. The interpretive approach problematizes competing interpretations in the emergence of partnerships.

Second, liberal functionalists view public-private partnerships as a response to market and state failure, shaped by the functional need to supply better governance (Liese and Beisheim 2011; Schäferhoff, Campe, and Kaan 2009). Functionalists explain the emergence of partnerships through the beneficial consequences that they have for the current global governance system. Partnerships can decrease the implementation, governance, and legitimacy deficits. The emergence of public-private partnerships is also a response to the inadequacies of interstate bargaining. Principal-agent theories suggest that international organizations act as policy entrepreneurs to initiate and broker transnational public-private partnerships (Andonova 2010). Governance functions such as agenda setting, monitoring, verification, enforcement, and service provision can be outsourced to public-private partnerships by governments and multilateral agencies. Public-private partnerships can generate effective collective problem solving and increased participation by nonstate actors through pooling together the skills, expertise, and resources from for-profit, nonprofit and public sectors. Liberal-functionalist accounts primarily focus on the performance of partnerships.

Third, the critical perspective analyzes public-private partnerships primarily as neoliberal instruments that pave the way for a power shift from multilateral institutions to the corporate sector, thereby reinforcing market environmentalism (Tienhaara, Orsini, and Falkner, this book, chapter 3). Accordingly, the turn to partnerships may pave the way to marketization, privatization, and commodification of global governance, leading to market multilateralism (Matthews and Paterson 2005; Miraftab 2004). Partnerships, in this regard, reflect trends of new public management, the hollowing out of the state, rise of the corporate sector, fragmentation of global governance, and the retreat of state in environmental politics. Critical perspectives, however, also focus on the legitimacy and accountability of partnerships as an important value in itself, thereby drawing on normative democratic theory (Bexell and Mörth 2010; Meadowcroft 2007). These theories range from liberal theories of democracy to radical theories of participatory and discursive democracy. Hence, critical perspectives focus on the legitimacy of partnerships.

The most significant difference among the three perspectives is the prioritization of agency and structure. Although scholars of critical governance and international political economy mostly focus on structure, the liberal functionalists primarily focus on the rationality of agency. The interpretive perspective employs interchangeably agency and structure, depending on which of these are highlighted through the orders of meaning under scrutiny. Scholars from the different perspectives have also highlighted different questions. For instance, the question of emergence has been studied—although not exclusively—from critical and interpretative perspectives, and the question of effectiveness has primarily been a concern within the liberal-functionalist perspective. Finally, the question of how legitimacy has been approached from liberal-functionalist and critical theories.

Experiences

The Johannesburg partnerships have been advanced as innovations in global sustainability governance (United Nations 2008). One interpretation is that the failure of the 2002 Johannesburg Summit to deliver binding intergovernmental agreements paved the way for transnational partnerships (Mert 2009; Andonova and Levy 2003). There are four characteristics of the Johannesburg partnerships.

First, these partnerships are multilaterally sanctioned under the auspices of the United Nations Commission on Sustainable Development. As of 2011, 348 partnerships are registered and reviewed by the CSD under its annual sessions as core elements in the implementation of Agenda 21 and the Johannesburg Plan of Implementation.

Second, the Johannesburg partnerships are multistakeholder instruments. They generally involve a diverse set of actors, such as intergovernmental organizations, governments, NGOs, and business. These partnerships involve participation from the UN's nine major groups: business, NGOs, youth, farmers, scientific communities, women, indigenous people, local governments, and trade unions.[2] As we discuss in the following, the Johannesburg partnerships fall short of ensuring participation of all sectors or social groups because participation has been limited to established actors such as NGOs and multinational corporations, as well as scientific and technological communities and local governments. The most vulnerable and the least articulate of the UN's major groups are in most cases not partners. Women, indigenous peoples, youth and children, and farmers groups are much less represented in partnerships, but they are influenced heavily by the decisions. However, business actors, even when they focus on rather controversial technologies (e.g., nuclear energy and biotechnologies), can fund and use partnerships as a public relations tool.

Third, the primary function of the Johannesburg partnerships is implementation, in particular of multilateral targets and provisions of the Johannesburg Plan of Implementation. The UN Commission on Sustainable Development defines partnerships for sustainable development as "voluntary multi-stakeholder initiatives, which contribute to the implementation of intergovernmental commitments" (United Nations 2008, 1). This 2002 definition differs in emphasis from the earlier Agenda 21 from 1992, which stated, "Achieving sustainable development would require broad-based participation and partnerships with non-governmental actors" (United Nations 1992, paragraph 23.1); in other words, while the focus in 1992 was on participation, in 2002 it shifted to implementation. There are two reasons for this change toward implementation: one reason is that in the United Nations system, participation by nonstate actors is contested by some authoritarian governments. To balance this, multi-stakeholder partnerships have been constructed as implementation mechanisms (Chan 2009). Nonstate actors are here invited to participate, yet this participation is restricted to the implementation of agreements negotiated by governments. Another reason is that in contrast to the 1992 Rio Summit, the overall focus of 2002 Johannesburg Summit was on implementation. This implementation focus of the Johannesburg Summit thus became dominant also in the meaning of the then-negotiated partnerships.

Fourth, the Johannesburg partnerships are voluntary. There are no strong sanctioning mechanisms for noncompliance. There is no legal enforcement of their rules. Most partnerships operate with only vaguely defined goals and less stringent modes of operation than many other governance instruments. Partnerships are not required to report on any specific set of criteria. Some do not even take off and are operational. Their loose description in UN documents allows each partnership to choose voluntarily a country of implementation and issue area, which results in geographical and thematic imbalances. Because no single UN agency undertakes the role of organizing partnerships and channeling them into areas with greater implementation deficits, no party is responsible for the risks of noncompliance with partnership goals.

Explanations

This section synthesizes our research on why partnerships emerged, how and why they were effective, and how we can evaluate their legitimacy. The first subsection explains the emergence of the Johannesburg partnerships. Then we move on to examine the performance and legitimacy of the Johannesburg partnerships.

Emergence of Transnational Public-Private Partnerships

Why did transnational public-private partnerships for sustainable development emerge in the first place? Liberal perspectives explain the emergence of transnational partnerships in the wake of the "crisis of multilateralism" in the 1990s as a means for intergovernmental organizations to reinvent their mission and regain their legitimacy by outsourcing key governance functions to hybrid public-private partnerships (Benner, Streck, and Witte 2003). Accordingly, a principal-agent perspective highlights the role of international organizations as policy entrepreneurs for initiating hybrid collaboration between nonstate and state actors because environmental governance becomes increasingly complex and fragmented (Andonova 2010). Critical perspectives, however, argue that the rise of transnational partnerships can be explained by processes of deregulation, privatization, and marketization, where the state has retreated from key governance functions, including providing environmental protection (Ottaway 2001). In this perspective, the ideological context of new public management and neoliberal globalization reinforces the partnership trend (Miraftab 2004).

Why and how did the Johannesburg partnerships emerge in this particular way? Partnerships for sustainable development do not only represent a "microcosm of competing and overlapping discourses," which reflect debates in the study of international environmental relations at large (Bäckstrand and Lövbrand 2006, 50–51), but also generate conflicts and contestations in global environmental politics. These conflicts are sometimes replicated in the official texts that define partnerships. Yet more often, they are left out in these texts. This again results in ambiguities and gaps that may limit the success of partnerships or cause failures in implementation or participation. Interpretive perspectives are particularly powerful at problematizing the ambiguities in meaning, resulting from the competition, contestation, and overlap of several discourses.

To explain, partnerships embody endless prospects and have been regarded by Andersen (2008, 3) as "machines of possibility." The negative side of this fundamental openness is that although they are described "in almost completely positive terms, they often fail" because the numerous ambiguities also make partnerships open to collapsing into indifference or becoming dissolved conflicts. However, the same flexibility and openness make partnerships a favorable policy instrument. The partnership discourse unites the political left and right as well as the public sector, voluntary organizations, and private companies, especially by overcoming the dilemma between competition and cooperation and through their highly flexible definition (Andersen 2008; Liese and Beisheim 2011). Although the former results in a consensus among public and private actors to form partnerships, the latter gives them plasticity: partnerships never assume a fixed form but remain a process. Even if actors from different sectors (or even partners within the same partnership) understand and define the concept differently, partnerships link these agents not based on a specific exchange relationship but rather "in a project-based obligation towards an imagined future" (Andersen 2008, 1).

The concept of partnership is ambiguous in three respects: first, the term *partnership* is tied historically and linguistically to business contracts and modern forms of business ownership. Most definitions either regard legal contracts as the condition for partnerships or require a resemblance between the two. However, no contracts among partners within a partnership or between the partnership and the United Nations lay down the ground rules. Ninety-five of the Johannesburg partnerships indicate no protocol, contract, or even a nonbinding memorandum of understanding between partners (Mert 2012; Pattberg et al. 2012). The CSD does not sign a contract as the partnerships register, and the two official documents on partnerships, the Bali Guidelines for the Johannesburg partnerships and the Millennium Development Goals, are nonbinding texts.

A second ambiguity concerns the question of to what extent the goals of actors are identical. There is a lack of consensus as to whether business and UN interests are similar or at times conflicting (Zammit 2003). Cooperating with corporations on issues resulting from their activities has been criticized within the United Nations not only by the South Centre headed by Boutros Boutros-Ghali, but also by the more marginalized major groups within the CSD (Mert 2009). Moreover, as powerful groups form many more partnerships than the less powerful, partnerships can reproduce power asymmetries if the United Nations assumes identical goals among partners.

Third, Johannesburg partnerships rest on the conflicting aims of environmental conservation and economic development. Until the 1980s, *sustainability* was a concept that was successfully launched by ecological and environmental movements. Most famously advocated by the Club of Rome report *Limits to Growth* (Meadows et al. 1972), the term drew attention to the ecological limits of industrial development and population growth, suggesting a change in rationale based on ecological sustainability. The term *sustainable development* was coined because "development and conservation are equally important for our survival" (IUCN 1980, 1). It became paradigmatic through its endorsement in the 1987 Brundtland Report *Our Common Future*, which has defined *sustainable development* as "development which meets the needs of the present without compromising the ability of future generations to meet their own needs" (World Commission on Environment and Development 1987, 8). Not only was the term *environment* excluded from the definition, but what was to sustain has also changed: "Humanity has the ability to make *development* sustainable" headed the Brundtland definition of sustainable development (World Commission on Environment and Development 1987, 8, emphasis added). In *Limits to Growth*, population and economic growth were understood as the reasons for environmental degradation. Sustainable development altered this causality as *Our Common Future* postulated that growth as such can be limitless and that "economic development can be consolidated with environmental protection" (World Commission on Environment and Development 1987, 40). Not development but underdevelopment caused environmental degradation. This change in meaning resulted in the (re)prioritization of developmental issues over environmental problems, forming a new paradigm that guided the UN institutions and texts throughout the 1990s. This is explicit in the eight Millennium Development Goals, only one of which refers to environmental sustainability, and in the 2002 Johannesburg Declaration, which adopted the universal aim "to banish underdevelopment forever" in the name of "human dignity" through technology transfer and opening of markets (United Nations 2002, paragraph 18). In this sense, partnerships can be seen as instrumental in legitimizing technologies that are often regarded as problematic in other UN contexts and that promote "a corporate vocabulary"[3] while excluding vulnerable groups from decisions.

Effectiveness of Transnational Public-Private Partnerships

The question of effectiveness has been addressed in our research in two different ways. First, we have conducted statistical large-*n* studies of the entire universe of partnerships, accumulating data of over 348 partnerships registered with the UN Commission on Sustainable Development. These large-*n* study efforts (Biermann et al. 2007; Pattberg et al. 2012) provided inroads into the theoretical discussion of partnerships as a phenomenon at the level of international sustainability governance. In an important way, our large-*n* analyses supported the critical argument that partnerships consolidate vested corporate interests rather than facilitate broader participation (Biermann et al. 2007). In addition, we conducted a series of case studies to analyze performance in a more functional understanding, with a focus on goal attainment of individual partnerships. For instance, researchers at the Berlin-based Research Center came out with "Governance in Areas of Limited Statehood," which assessed the effectiveness of transnational partnerships that implement the Millennium Development Goals in twenty-one in-depth case studies. In the following, we summarize the findings of the large-*n* studies and case study research.

Quantitative studies of effectiveness and partnerships are difficult to compare because scholars tend to hold different standards for effectiveness. There seems to be agreement that an effectiveness evaluation in terms of biophysical and ecological terms, usually known as *impact,* is difficult. Rather, research focuses on outputs and outcomes. Output refers to "regulations, programs, and organizational arrangements that actors establish to operationalize the provisions of regimes" (Young 1999, 111) and outcome refers to changes in the behavior of the norm targets or to changes at the population level. Even when a common understanding of effectiveness is agreed on, the evaluation of effectiveness of partnerships for sustainable development remains demanding because they aim at different functions. Some concentrate on research and knowledge exchange, others focus on standard setting and implementation, and still others provide services such as water supply and try to create new markets (Reinicke and Deng 2000; Bull and McNeill 2007). Due to this great diversity of functions that public-private partnerships fulfill, the effectiveness of a public-private partnership can be assessed against its aims and functions (Schäferhoff, Campe, and Kaan 2009). In this sense, large-*n* analysis has employed a functionalist approach to assess the effectiveness of partnership regimes, in particular the partnerships regime that emanated from the 2002 World Summit on Sustainable Development.

The overall rationale for the summit was that the implementation gap could be reduced by result-based and outcome-oriented partnerships. Several studies, however, have demonstrated that the Johannesburg partnerships lack implementation (Bäckstrand 2006; Biermann et al. 2007; Pattberg et al. 2012). Our research has shown that partnerships are more frequent in areas that are heavily institutionalized and regulated, and that they are on average less concerned with implementation than with further institution building (Biermann et al. 2007, 259). Partnerships lack capacity; most are unfunded and seek financial support. The Johannesburg Summit failed to mobilize new and additional resources in terms of official development assistance. Due to the bias of northern countries as lead and implementing states, there are fewer partnerships in the least developed regions in the world. Fewer than a third of Johannesburg partnerships focus on direct environmental effects. Many partnerships only aim at building more partnerships or at further institutionalization with very little direct environmental impact, despite their claimed goal of implementation of sustainable development goals (OECD 2006). This is particularly significant because the Johannesburg partnerships were expected to implement sustainable development goals and the Millennium Development Goals are clearly defined with explicit deadlines. Instead, most partnerships are process oriented and focus on building capacity, increasing awareness, and strengthening means of implementation. In sum, the Johannesburg partnerships have no clear quantifiable goals that can be used as a yardstick to measure their performance. The weak implementation review and institutional machinery for reporting, monitoring, and control precludes an analysis of the environmental impact and effectiveness of Johannesburg partnerships. In sum, our large-*n* analyses have shown that effectiveness of partnerships in terms of value added is limited. The partnership system is self-repetitive by not aiming at impact but at the creation of new partnerships.

The rather poor achievements of the entire group of partnerships, however, do not rule out the effectiveness of an individual partnership, as shown by the case study–based research at the Berlin-based Research Center, "Governance in Areas of Limited Statehood" (Beisheim, Liese, and Ulbert 2007, 2008; Beisheim, Campe, and Schäferhoff 2010). These case studies evaluate the effectiveness of twenty-one transnational partnerships in terms of output, outcome, and impact. Moreover, the project has investigated which factors determine the effectiveness of transnational partnerships. The case selection speaks to the large-*n* study discussed previously, because five of the twenty-one transnational partnerships—which all aim at implementing the Millennium Development Goals—are also registered with the CSD. The Water and Sanitation for the Urban Poor Partnership, the Renewable Energy and Energy Efficiency Partnership, the Global Water Partnership, the Global Network on Energy for Sustainable Development, and the Global Village Energy Partnership also registered within the Johannesburg process. Therefore, the large-*n* study and the case-study approach complement each other because the two samples overlap.

In the case study research, we distinguished among three types of partnerships: partnerships that focus on service provision, on standard setting, and on knowledge exchange. Generally, our findings underscore that the level of institutionalization matters: when partnerships have precise and binding norms that are strictly monitored and enforced, they are more effective than others. This holds especially for transnational public-private partnerships that provide services or set standards, whereas knowledge partnerships do not require a high level of institutionalization to perform effectively. Knowledge partnerships rather need a good communication and process management to be effective.

For example, Water and Sanitation for the Urban Poor has been evaluated as effective in terms of output and outcome. Here, precise and binding rules in combination with close monitoring have arguably led to successful performance. The partnership's degree of institutionalization is comparatively high. First, many of its rules are binding. For instance, members have to pay a membership fee and make a commitment for three years. When they do not pay membership fees, they may lose their voting rights and can be expelled.[4] At the project level, legally binding contracts are signed and the obligation of the commitments has supported the quick pace at which the partnership has been able to demonstrate results. The cooperation among the partners is also regulated through precise terms of reference and, as the interviewees report, these clear responsibilities have fostered the successful implementation of the partnership's projects.[5] Second, the precision of the rules is also relatively high with regard to its overall activities as well as to the individual projects. For instance, there is detailed regulation under what conditions members may become active in the partnership, for example, regarding the fees they charge for their contributions; and the partnership has a service level agreement with each member.[6] Finally, a project is monitored right from the start, which has improved compliance and goal attainment. The project's internal monitoring is not public but it is centrally enforced by the partnership. Projects have to report regularly to the project director, who is appointed by the partnership board, and to the secretariat. When a project fails to live up to its business plans, decisions on how to proceed are taken and enforced by the partnership. This example illustrates that a high level of institutionalization promotes the successful performance of a public-private partnership (Liese and Beisheim 2011; Campe and Beisheim 2008).

To give another example, the Global Water Partnership, whose main task is to foster the implementation of an "integrated water resource management" approach, is a knowledge partnership. It is generally regarded as rather ineffective. Although this partnership could advocate integrated water resource management as blueprint for water policy and raise greater awareness in some Asian countries (PARC 2003), strong criticism persists. For instance, the Global Water Partnership has not succeeded in furthering the successful implementation of integrated water resource management policies at the country level. One reason is that the Global Water Partnership "puts too much energy on awareness-raising of IWRM [integrated water resource management], and insufficient energy on local capacity-building" (PARC 2003, 5). Even in terms of awareness raising and capacity building, its success is debatable. For instance, a specially developed toolbox on integrated water resource management in the form of a CD-ROM with case studies on integrated water resource management and road maps for planning was criticized for being too academic, even though it has been used more widely recently also by policy makers (PARC 2003, 2008). The partnership has not been able to "translate vision into practical management."[7] Moreover, the partnership did not change the fact that integrated water resource management remains a highly controversial concept, featuring an institutionalized site of normative struggle (Conca 2006; Dombrowsky 2008; Wouters 2008).

An important reason for the partnership's poor performance lies in the institutional setup, which is enough for providing some output but inadequate to bring about change in the behavior of target countries. The partnership's operations are governed by nonbinding recommendations, and the precision of the rules that govern its activities is low. This hampered the implementation of integrated water resource management: because the Global Water Partnership "seems to have no clear action plans and projects" (Allouche and Finger 2007, 46), practical results are scarce. Monitoring is relatively weak and the regional and country–level water partnerships only undergo a self-reporting process (Global Water Partnership 2002, 2006). Only selected partnerships at the regional and country levels are evaluated as part of the external evaluations of the entire Global Water Partnership, which take place every five years (PARC 2003, 2008). This case shows that despite its low level of institutionalization, the partnership could facilitate knowledge exchange on integrated water resource management, yet lacked capacity to further the implementation.

In sum, our overall research results show that the effectiveness of transnational public-private partnerships is mixed. Our large-*n* research suggests that the effectiveness of the overall partnerships regime is limited, especially if one observes how partnerships focus on institutional entrenching through the creation of new partnerships rather than focusing on impact. Yet some positive achievements of individual partnerships have also been found. Case study research points to different determinants of effectiveness, of which the degree of institutionalization is most important. This also links back to the global partnerships regime. Although there is to some degree synchronization of global partnerships in the Johannesburg process, the process itself is poorly defined and offers little guidance to the goal formulation, coordination, and monitoring of partnerships.

Legitimacy of Transnational Partnerships

Legitimacy is a central and essentially contested concept in social science and political philosophy. Transnational partnerships are increasingly examined from critical perspectives inspired by normative democratic theory (Bexell and Mörth 2010). Yet democratic legitimacy is only one source of legitimacy, which is closely associated with domestic models of electoral democracy (Grant and Keohane 2005). Arguably, democratic state-centered legitimacy is less suitable for evaluating nonelectoral, nonterritorial governance arrangements, such as partnerships. More recently, attention has turned to the legitimacy of new modes of public-private environmental governance, such as transnational partnerships for environment and sustainable development (Bäckstrand 2006; Schäferhoff, Campe, and Kaan 2009). Partnerships can be evaluated to what extent they conform to norms of procedural legitimacy and provide problem-solving capacity and effectiveness. Several studies of transnational public-private partnerships have employed Scharpf's (1999, 2006) twofold notion of legitimacy: output legitimacy and input legitimacy.

Output legitimacy is simply about whether norms and institutions lead to collective problem solving and overall effectiveness. In the last section, we summarized our research in the Global Governance Project on the influence and effectiveness of partnerships, and hence on their output legitimacy.

Input, or procedural, legitimacy asks whether policies and norms have been developed in a transparent, fair, inclusive, and accountable manner. Procedural legitimacy is derived from norms, values, and principles of liberal democracy, such as accountability, transparency, inclusion, and deliberation. In this perspective, an institution, governance system, or political order is legitimate if it is based on values such as transparency, rule of law, accountability, or participation.

The following analysis follows a threefold notion of input legitimacy developed by Dingwerth (2007), which focuses on participation and inclusion, democratic control and accountability, and deliberative quality.

Participation and Inclusion

Participation by individuals and societal groups is a core element of democratic theory and practice. It asks to what extent those subject to a decision are represented in policy making. To what extent are the relevant stakeholders affected by the rule making and represented in the policy process (Dingwerth 2007)? Are there equal opportunities to participate? In what phases of the policy process are actors (agenda setting, policy making, implementation) participating and is participation symbolic or real? In an electoral democracy within the bounds of the state, individual citizens are key constituencies. In transnational public-private partnerships, nonelectoral and group-based participation is central. When transnational constituencies are affected by decisions, the model of stakeholder democracy has been institutionalized, which entails representation, deliberation, and participation of nonstate actors, such as NGOs and business (Bäckstrand 2006; Nanz and Steffek 2004). What are the patterns of representation and inclusion and exclusion of different types of actors in the Johannesburg partnerships?

First, our research showed that the Johannesburg partnerships demonstrate a geographical imbalance in which northern actors predominate. Around 60 percent of the registered partnerships have an industrialized countries partner, whereas only 17 percent are led by a developing country (Biermann et al. 2007). Seventy percent of the partnerships led by an industrialized country are implemented in another OECD country. This indicates that relatively few partnerships are directed to neglected regions with high poverty rates and environmental pressures. Large developing countries, such as South Africa and Indonesia, which hosted the preparatory meetings and the Johannesburg Summit, are more frequent as partners. In this vein, the Johannesburg partnerships represent a "coalition of willing" between industrialized countries and a few large developing countries (Andonova and Levy 2003).

Second, scholars in the Global Governance Project conclude that public actors dominate the Johannesburg partnerships whereas NGOs and business actors have a more marginal presence. Governments or international agencies often are the lead partner and take part in most partnerships: 83 percent of partnerships involve governments, 62 percent UN organizations, and 61 percent other intergovernmental organizations. Only 8 percent of the partnerships are led by NGOs, whereas business actors lead only 3 percent. Private-sector involvement is lower than expected because business actors choose their own partnerships with their own reporting mechanisms; the financing of partnerships by private sectors has been minimal (Mert 2009).

Third, there is minimal participation of those UN major groups that are perceived as marginalized. Only 1 percent of the partnerships involve women's groups, youth, indigenous people, and farmers. The more established major groups, however, are better represented. Thirty percent of the partnerships have NGO involvement, 38 percent have business, 18 percent science and technology communities, and 8 percent local authorities (United Nations 2008). This pattern reveals that partnerships involve well-established nonstate actors such as large NGOs, the scientific community, and business from primarily the northern hemisphere. Local actors, least developed countries, southern grassroots movements, indigenous people, and women are less represented.

Democratic Control and Accountability

Accountability is the second dimension of legitimacy. It means that those who govern are subject to control and held accountable, hence, those in positions of influence should be responsive to the interests of their constituencies. Accountability is about the relation between an agent and a principal and means "to answer" or to be liable, to be called into account. Accountability "implies that some actors have the right to hold other actors accountable to a set of standards, to judge whether they have fulfilled their responsibilities in light of these standards, and to impose sanctions if they determine that these responsibilities have not been met" (Grant and Keohane 2005, 29). Accountability depends on if there are sanctions available when actions or decisions are incompatible with the values and preferences of principals. The ultimate sanction is if an agent is removed from its position because of a failure to comply, deliver promises, or implement goals. Transparency and access to information is a precondition of accountability.

Our research has shown here that transparency and accountability are closely linked because accountability depends on access to information about the performance of partnerships. The Johannesburg partnerships lack formal mechanisms for accountability. The absence of any single principal or agent in these partnerships raises the question to whom the partnerships should be accountable. There is no centralized agency overseeing goal attainment in the Johannesburg partnerships and no formalized monitoring and implementation review of partnerships, which stems from the soft law nature of these partnerships. The Bali guidelines, which were an outcome of preparatory meetings a few months before the 2002 Johannesburg Summit, did not grant the CSD secretariat, which is the responsible body, power to enforce reviewing and reporting of partnerships activities (Mert 2009). Although the CSD was designated as the relevant organ of the United Nations for partnerships for sustainable development, it was not given power to enforce reviewing (or even reporting) of partnership activities. The "Partnerships Team" (which employs two full-time staff and one intern as of 2007) can only "screen" partnerships that would like to register with the UN, and invite them to partnership fairs that are held every year, in which partnerships can hold side events to actual policy meetings. They keep a record of partnerships on the online UN Partnerships Database, but have little power to ensure the updating of partnership information. Due to this lack of formal accountability, transparency has been emphasized in the partnership initiative. Three principal mechanisms of transparency have been identified for the Johannesburg partnerships: a website, a reporting system, and a monitoring mechanism (Hale and Mauzerall 2004). A website comprising data for all partnerships was set up by the CSD secretariat in 2004, which has subsequently been updated and amended in 2006 and 2007 (United Nations 2008). Less than a third of the partnerships fulfill the threefold criteria of transparency, and less than 50 percent have a mechanism for monitoring effectiveness and progress of partnerships in place (Hale and Mauzerall 2004). Monitoring is based on voluntary reports of partnerships themselves and the lack of systematic monitoring of the progress of partnerships remains a challenge (United Nations 2008). There is not a known example of Johannesburg partnerships that has been removed from the registry because of insufficient performance.

The weak accountability mechanisms of the Johannesburg partnerships stems from unclear guidelines and a lack of mandatory reporting requirements. The guidelines for the reporting and monitoring of the partnerships were unspecified and vague. Of the registered partnerships, only 20 percent have submitted progress updates. These voluntary progress reports concern organizational activities, coordination activities, and implementation activities.

Deliberative Quality

Deliberative quality concerns whether public-private partnerships rest on "deliberative rationality" such as inclusiveness, unconstrained dialog, and free and public reason among equal individuals. What is the quality of the deliberation and does it allow for "arguing" rather than "bargaining" (Risse 2004)? Such questions concern the deliberative quality in public-private partnerships. Dingwerth (2007) proposes several criteria for assessing deliberative quality: if the deliberation is limited to negotiations between a narrow set of elites, it will compromise the deliberative quality. Coercion and power asymmetries between actors are believed to distort communication and rational discourse. A key question is to what extent the deliberative process remains open to competing discourses and arguments from citizens as well as elites. Deliberative theorists suggest that reciprocity ensures that arguments of different participants are included and treated in an impartial and respectful manner.

To what extent, if any, do the Johannesburg partnerships live up to ideals of deliberative democracy such as communicative rationality, unconstrained dialog, and free and public reason? First, whether or not public-private partnerships promote a venue for deliberation largely depends on the function partnerships perform. The primary function of the Johannesburg partnerships is rule implementation, which limits deliberative processes compared to rule making, agenda setting, or service provision partnership. Deliberative processes tend to be cosmetic and symbolic because they are added on or serve to legitimize decisions already made.

Second, the deliberative quality also depends on the context of deliberation. We need to distinguish between deliberation about partnerships by various public and private actors at the annual sessions of the UN Commission on Sustainable Development and deliberation within public-private partnerships. The Johannesburg partnerships clearly have an institutionalized model for deliberation about partnerships through partnerships fairs and multistakeholder deliberations among the nine major groups (Bäckstrand 2006).

Third, the quality of deliberation is adversely affected by barriers to participation such as power asymmetries between partners and lack of competing and alternative discourses from citizens and marginalized actors. The bias of representation and participation in the Johannesburg partnerships toward northern states, large developing countries, professional NGOs, and multilateral bureaucracies at the expense of poor countries, local grass root movements, women, and indigenous peoples limits free and authentic discursive contest.

Conclusions and Outlook

To sum up, the Johannesburg partnerships are largely supply driven rather than demand driven; northern actors or large developing countries with relatively more resources and capacity reap the benefits of partnerships rather than actors with the largest needs, such as least developed countries. Partnerships institutionalize rather than transform patterns of power, inclusion, and exclusion between North and South, public and private authority, and professional NGOs and local grass root movements.

Does the emergence of transnational public-private partnerships for sustainable development pave the way for more effective and legitimate global environmental governance? The debate on the promises and pitfalls of public-private partnerships is polarized between the liberal-functionalist perspective that analyzes whether partnerships can be win-win instruments that can decrease the implementation, governance, and legitimacy deficit, and critical perspectives arguing that partnerships reinforce market environmentalism and lack democratic legitimacy. Beyond this contestation, there is a need for a comparative empirical research agenda to assess the performance and legitimacy of public-private partnerships across different sectors and in different multilateral settings. Scholarship within the Global Governance Project has systematically studied the emergence, effectiveness, and legitimacy of partnerships.

Cumulated research insights have demonstrated that the legitimacy and effectiveness record of Johannesburg partnerships are modest at best. On the positive side, the Johannesburg partnerships have paved the way for deliberative quality and inclusion because the CSD has institutionalized stakeholder participation and dialog among the UN major groups. The Johannesburg partnerships, however, have virtually no mechanisms for accountability and a weak transparency record. The effectiveness of public-private partnerships is difficult to ascertain, partially due to persisting methodological challenges. A key contribution from the Global Governance Project is the finding that institutional mechanisms for compliance, monitoring, and implementation are decisive. It is, however, nearly impossible to evaluate the environmental effectiveness of the Johannesburg partnerships given the absence of quantitative goals and monitoring. There are no benchmarks for goal attainment and environmental impact or performance. One reason is that these partnerships rely on voluntary action: the CSD has no mandate to review, monitor, supervise, or enforce implementation. Another key observation is that the Johannesburg partnerships do not necessarily reflect trends of privatization and free-market environmentalism. By contrast, they signify the continued power of intergovernmental organizations that have found new tasks in being facilitators and administrators of voluntary multi-stakeholder partnerships. The separation between "new" instruments of public-private partnerships and "old" modes of regulation and command and control is problematic. Public-private partnerships operate in the shadow of the hierarchy with background conditions of state authority, intervention, steering, and control.

Notes

1. The partnerships adopted at the World Summit on Sustainable Development are referred to as the *Johannesburg partnerships*; see http://webapps01.un.org/dsd/partnerships/public/welcome.do.

2. Since the establishment of the UN Commission on Sustainable Development in 1992, nonstate actor civil society organizations have been represented in negotiations and deliberations through nine major groups; see http://www.un.org/esa/dsd/dsd_aofw_mg/mg_index.shtml.

3. Interviews with workers and trade unions representatives to the Commission on Sustainable Development.

4. Water and Sanitation for the Urban Poor 2005. Articles of Association of Water and Sanitation for the Urban Poor—interpretation, paragraph 37 and 10.2.

5. Interview with the chief executive officer of Water and Sanitation for the Urban Poor, London, May 2008, and telephone interview with member of Water and Sanitation for the Urban Poor's board, May 2008.

6. Interview with the chief executive officer of Water and Sanitation for the Urban Poor, London, May 2008.

7. Interview with the chair of Global Water Partnership's Technical Committee, the Palisades, New York, November 2007.

References

Allouche, Jeremy, and Matthias Finger. 2007. Public-Private Partnerships (PPPs) and Global Environmental Governance: The Water Sector as a Paradigmatic Case and Empirical Field of Study. Paper presented at the 48th Annual Convention of the International Studies Association, Chicago, February 28–March 3.

Andersen, Niels Åkerstrøm. 2008. *Partnerships: Machines of Possibility*. Bristol, UK: Policy Press.

Andonova, Liliana B. 2010. Public-Private Partnerships for the Earth: Politics and Patterns of Hybrid Authority in the Multilateral System. *Global Environmental Politics* 10 (2):25–53.

Andonova, Liliana B., Michele M. Betsill, and Harriet Bulkeley. 2009. Transnational Climate Governance. *Global Environmental Politics* 9 (2):52–73.

Andonova, Liliana, and Marc Levy. 2003. Franchising Global Governance: Making Sense of the Johannesburg Type II Partnerships. In *Yearbook of International Cooperation on Environment and Development 2003/04*, ed. Olav Schram Stocke and Øystein B. Thomessen, 19–31. London: Earthscan.

Bäckstrand, Karin. 2006. Multi-stakeholder Partnerships for Sustainable Development: Rethinking Legitimacy, Accountability, and Effectiveness. *European Environment* 16:290–306.

Bäckstrand, Karin. 2008. Accountability of Networked Climate Governance: The Rise of Transnational Climate Partnerships. *Global Environmental Politics* 8 (3):74–104.

Bäckstrand, Karin, and Eva Lövbrand. 2006. Planting Trees to Mitigate Climate Change: Contested Discourses of Ecological Modernization, Green Governmentality, and Civic Environmentalism. *Global Environmental Politics* 6 (1):51–71.

Beisheim, Marianne, Sabine Campe, and Marco Schäferhoff. 2010. Global Governance through Public-Private Partnerships. In *Handbook on Multi-level Governance*, ed. Henrik Enderlein, Sonja Wälti, and Michael Zürn, 370–382. Cheltenham, UK: Edward Elgar.

Beisheim, Marianne, Andrea Liese, and Cornelia Ulbert. 2007. Erfolgsbedingungen transnationaler Partnerschaften: Hypothesen und erste Ergebnisse. In *Regieren ohne Staat? Governance in Räumen begrenzter Staatlichkeit*, ed. Thomas Risse and Ursula Lehmkuhl, 247-271. Baden-Baden: Nomos.

Beisheim, Marianne, Andrea Liese, and Cornelia Ulbert. 2008. Transnationale öffentlich-private Partnerschaften: Bestimmungsfaktoren für die Effektivität ihrer Governance-Leistungen. In *Governance in einer sich wandelnden Welt*, ed. Gunnar Folke Schuppert and Michael Zürn, 452–474. Wiesbaden: VS-Verlag.

Benner, Thorsten, Charlotte Streck, and Jan-Martin Witte, eds. 2003. *Progress and Perils, Networks and Partnerships in Global Environmental Governance: The Post-Johannesburg Agenda*. Berlin: The Global Public Policy Institute.

Benner, Thorsten, Wolfgang H. Reinicke, and Jan Martin Witte. 2005. Multisectoral Networks in Global Governance: Towards a Pluralistic System of Global Governance. In *Global Governance and Public Accountability*, ed. David Held and Mathias Koenig-Archbugi, 67–86. Malden, MA: Blackwell Publishing.

Bexell, Magdalena, and Ulrika Mörth, eds. 2010. *Democracy and Public-Private Partnerships in Global Governance*. Houndmills, UK: Palgrave Macmillan.

Biermann, Frank, Chan Man-san, Ayşem Mert, and Philipp Pattberg. 2007. Multi-stakeholder Partnerships for Sustainable Development: Does the Promise Hold? In *Partnerships, Governance and Sustainable Development: Reflections on Theory and Practice*, ed. Pieter Glasbergen, Frank Biermann, and Arthur P. J. Mol, 239–260. Cheltenham, UK: Edward Elgar.

Börzel, Tanja, and Thomas Risse. 2005. Public-Private Partnerships: Effective and Legitimate Tools of International Governance? In *Reconstituting Political Authority: Complex Sovereignty and the Foundations of Global Governance*, ed. Edgar Grande and Louis W. Pauly, 195–216. Toronto: Toronto University Press.

Broadwater, Ian, and Inge Kaul. 2005. *Global Public-Private Partnerships: The Current Landscape*. Study Outline (UNDP/ODS Background Paper). New York.

Bull, Benedicte, and Desmond McNeill. 2007. *Development Issues in Global Governance: Public Private Partnerships and Market Multilateralism*. London: Routledge.

Campe, Sabine, and Marianne Beisheim. 2008. Transnational Water Public-Private Partnerships: Explaining their Success and Failure. Paper presented at the Annual Meeting of the American Political Science Association, Boston, 28–31 August.

Chan, Sander. 2009. Partnerships for Sustainable Development in China: Adaptation of a Global Governance Instrument. *European Journal of East Asian Studies* 8 (1):121–134.

Conca, Ken. 2006. *Governing Water: Contentious Transnational Politics and Global Institution Building*. Cambridge, MA: MIT Press.

Dingwerth, Klaus. 2007. *The New Transnationalism: Transnational Governance and Democratic Legitimacy*. Houndmills, UK: Palgrave Macmillan.

Dombrowsky, Ines. 2008. Integration in the Management of International Waters: Economic Perspectives on a Global Policy Discourse. *Global Governance* 14:455–477.

Global Water Partnership. 2002. *Statutes for the Global Water Partnership Network and the Global Water Partnership Organization*. Stockholm: Global Water Partnership.

Global Water Partnership. 2006. Setting the Stage for Change. Second Informal Survey by the Global Water Partnership Network Giving the Status of the 2005 WSSD Target on National Integrated Water Resources Management and Water Efficiency Plans. Stockholm.

Grant, Ruth, and Robert O. Keohane. 2005. Accountability and Abuses of Power in World Politics. *American Political Science Review* 99 (1):29–43.

Haas, Peter M. 2004. Addressing the Global Governance Deficit. *Global Environmental Politics* 4 (4):1–15.

Hale, Thomas, and Denise Mauzerall. 2004. Thinking Globally and Acting Locally: Can the Johannesburg Partnerships Coordinate Action on Sustainable Development? *Journal of Environment & Development* 13 (3):220–239.

IUCN (International Union for Conservation of Nature and Natural Resources). 1980. *World Conservation Strategy: Living Resource Conservation for Sustainable Development.* Switzerland: Gland.

Liese, Andrea, and Marianne Beisheim. 2011. Transnational Public-Private Partnerships and the Provision of Collective Goods in Developing Countries. In *Governance without a State: Policies and Politics in Areas of Limited Statehood,* ed. Thomas Risse, 115–143. New York: Columbia University Press.

Martens, Jens. 2007. Multistakeholder Partnerships. Future Models of Multilateralism? Friedrich Ebert Stiftung Occasional Paper "Dialogue on Globalization." No. 29.

Matthews, Karina, and Matthew Paterson. 2005. Boom or Bust? The Economic Engine behind the Drive for Climate Change Policy. *Global Change, Peace & Security* 17 (1):59–75.

Meadowcroft, James. 2007. Democracy and Accountability. The Challenge for Cross-sectoral Partnerships. In *Partnerships, Governance and Sustainable Development: Reflections on Theory and Practice,* ed. Pieter Glasbergen, Frank Biermann, and Arthur P. J. Mol, 194–213. Cheltenham, UK: Edward Elgar.

Meadows, Donella H., Dennis L. Meadows, Jørgen Randers, and William W. Behrens. 1972. *The Limits to Growth: A Report for the Club of Rome's Project on the Predicament of Mankind.* New York: Universe.

Mert, Ayşem. 2009. Partnerships for Sustainable Development as Discursive Practice: Shifts in Discourses on Environment and Democracy. *Forest Policy and Economics* 11 (2):109–122.

Mert, Ayşem. 2012. Partnerships and the Privatisation of Environmental Governance: On Myths, Forces of Nature and Other Inevitabilities. *Environmental Values* 21 (4).

Miraftab, Faranak. 2004. Public-Private Partnerships: The Trojan Horse of Neoliberal Development? *Journal of Planning and Environmental Research* 24: 89–101.

Nanz, Patricia, and Jens Steffek. 2004. Global Governance, Participation, and the Public Sphere. *Government and Opposition* 39 (2):314–334.

OECD (Organisation for Economic Co-operation and Development). 2006. *Evaluating the Effectiveness and Efficiency of Partnerships.* Paris: OECD.

Ottaway, Marina. 2001. Corporatism Goes Global: International Organizations, Nongovernmental Organization Networks, and Transnational Business. *Global Governance* 7:265–292.

PARC (Performance Assessment Resource Centre). 2003. *External Review of the Global Water Partnership. Final Report.* Birmingham, UK: PARC.

PARC (Performance Assessment Resource Centre). 2008. *Global Water Partnership. Joint Donor External Evaluation. Final Report.* Sheffield, UK: PARC.

Pattberg. Philipp. 2010. Public-Private Partnerships in Global Climate Governance. *Wiley Interdisciplinary Reviews: Climate Change* 1 (2): 279–287.

Pattberg, Philipp, Frank Biermann, Sander Chan, and Ayşem Mert, eds. 2012. *Public-Private Partnerships for Sustainable Development: Emergence, Impacts, and Legitimacy.* Cheltenham, UK: Edward Elgar.

Reinicke, Wolfgang H., and Francis Deng. 2000. *Critical Choices: The United Nations Networks, and the Future of Global Governance.* Ottawa: IDRC.

Risse, Tomas. 2004. Global Governance and Communicative Action. *Government and Opposition* 39:288–313.

Schäferhoff, Marco, Sabine Campe, and Christopher Kaan. 2009. Transnational Public-Private Partnerships in International Relations—Making Sense of Concepts, Research Frameworks and Results. *International Studies Review* 11 (3):451–474.

Scharpf, Fritz W. 1999. *Governing in Europe: Effective and Democratic?* Oxford: Oxford University Press.

Scharpf, Fritz W. 2006. *Problem Solving Effectiveness and Democratic Accountability in the European Union.* Vienna: Institute for Advanced Studies.

Streck, Charlotte. 2004. New Partnerships in Global Environmental Policy: The Clean Development Mechanism. *Journal of Environment & Development* 13:295–322.

United Nations. 1992. *Earth Summit Agenda 21: The United Nations Programme of Action from Rio.* New York: United Nations.

United Nations. 2002. *Johannesburg Plan of Implementation.* Johannesburg, South Africa: World Summit on Sustainable Development.

United Nations. 2008. Partnerships for Sustainable Development—Report of the Secretary General. E/CN.17/2008/1. Commission on Sustainable Development. Sixteenth Session, 5–16 May. New York: Department of Economic and Social Affairs.

World Commission on Environment and Development. 1987. *Our Common Future.* Oxford: Oxford University Press.

Wouters, Patricia. 2008. Global Water Governance through Many Lenses. *Global Governance* 14:523–534.

Young, Oran R. 1999. *Governance in World Affairs.* Ithaca, NY: Cornell University Press.

Zammit, Ann. 2003. *Development at Risk: Rethinking UN-Business Partnerships.* Geneva: The South Centre and UNRISD. Retrieved from http://globalpolicy.org/images/pdfs/risk.pdf.

7

Transnational Governance Experiments

Harriet Bulkeley, Matthew J. Hoffmann, Stacy D. VanDeveer, and
Victoria Milledge

In this chapter, we develop an account of transnational governance that
moves beyond specific forms of private regimes (Pattberg, this book,
chapter 5) and public-private partnerships (Bäckstrand et al., this book,
chapter 6) to encompass what we term *transnational governance experiments*. Empirically, it is clear that a growing array of more or less institutionalized forms of transnational governance are emerging that are not
captured within these frameworks, and that they are contributing to the
growing diversity and fragmentation of the global governance landscape.
Actors that used to orient themselves toward traditional multilateral
governance mechanisms are now experimenting with new arrangements.
Yet in the midst of experimentation, a prominent feature of many of
these initiatives is their basis in established market principles (e.g., of
economic efficiency) and the use of market mechanisms (e.g., cap-and-
trade schemes) as a means of governing the actions of private and public
actors.

This chapter examines this phenomenon of growing transnational
governance experimentation through markets (Hoffmann 2007, 2011),
focusing in particular on the issue of climate change. First, we consider
how such experiments might be conceptualized. The following section
examines transnational governance experiments in the climate change
arena, focusing in particular on the Regional Greenhouse Gas Initiative
(RGGI), the New England Governors and Eastern Canadian Premiers
Climate Change Action Plan, and initiatives that are being established in
order to foster the emergence of the voluntary offset carbon market.
Then, the chapter explains the emergence of climate change governance
experiments before the final section outlines some implications of such
experiments and some possible directions for continuing research in
this area.

Conceptualization

The notion of transnational governance experiments and experimentation emerges from advances in the broader transnational governance literature chronicled in chapters 1 and 5 of this book. This recent and growing area of study outlines what counts as transnational governance—who participates and what modes of governance constitute this phenomenon. In this chapter, we focus on another aspect of this phenomenon: its experimental character.

Why speak of emergent "transnational governance experiments"? One of the reasons for the diversity of approaches that have been developed to conceptualize transnational governance (Pattberg, this book, chapter 5; Bäckstrand et al., this book, chapter 6) can be found in the sheer variety of initiatives taking place and in the multiple factors that have influenced their emergence. Given the amount of analytical attention that has been paid to transnational environmental governance, especially in the area of climate change, it is fair to inquire as to the value added in defining and examining experimentation as a significant aspect of transnational environmental governance. Not all transnational governance processes are experimental. So which are, and why does it matter?

The notion of experimentation highlights two facets of some transnational governance arrangements. First, governance experiments implicitly or explicitly give a sense of a process of trial and error going on in environmental governance: the actors and modes of governance discussed previously are combining in innovative ways in an attempt to govern environmental problems. This may be implicit in that actors are not consciously setting out to experiment but rather merely to try to find practical solutions to problems (environmental, political, economic, or organizational) that they face. From the vantage point of an external observer, however, such actions can appear experimental. Experimentation can also be explicit. Some actors, having come to the conclusion that traditional governance mechanisms (transnational or otherwise) cannot provide the institutional setting they desire, consciously experiment with new ones. The US Mayors' Climate Protection Agreement, along with various US state and Canadian province climate initiatives, are illustrative of this tendency.

Second, and perhaps more important analytically, transnational governance experiments are constructed in an institutional vacuum. For some, transnational governance in all its forms emerges in the political spaces created by the absence of international regimes and nation states. For example, Visseren-Hamakers and Glasbergen (2007, 409) argue that such initiatives "fill in what governments are not (yet) willing or able to regulate, sometimes to outplay them and to prevent the governments from taking action, and sometimes to show alternatives for public governance or to challenge it to take up more thorough public action." For others, it is not the lack of governance by other means but rather issues of governance failure or implementation deficit that transnational initiatives seek to address (Kolk and Pinkse 2008; Biermann, Mol, and Glasbergen 2007; Bäckstrand 2008), suggesting a more complex relationship between "new" forms of transnational governance and government practice. Such analysis suggests that rather than taking place in the political spaces in between states, transnational governance may be leading to "the negotiation and redefinition of political authority in geographically complex ways" (Agnew 2005, 438). Such analyses suggest that forms of transnational (environmental) governance may challenge conventional accounts of the boundaries of public and private authority (Pattberg and Stripple 2008) and of the geographies of political power.

We suggest that the transnational governance initiatives that are truly experimental embody and encompass what Hajer (2003) has described as policy making without a polity. In other words, transnational governance experiments are taking place in and actively creating new political spaces that do not have an established infrastructure for governing. There is simply no set of established institutional rules that determine how cities can cooperate across jurisdictional boundaries or how US states and Canadian provinces can forge an agreement on governing carbon emissions trading. In fact, in the latter case, the supremacy clause of the US constitution may even call into question the legal validity of such endeavors. This feature of policy making without a polity is even more striking when the development of carbon markets is considered. Carbon markets are of course varied, including project markets like the Clean Development Mechanism (CDM), offset markets, and allowance markets such as emissions trading. Some are being developed by traditional authorities (e.g., the EU Emissions Trading System); however, other markets are entirely experimental including the aforementioned state-provincial trading systems.

A focus on transnational governance experiments is justifiable in that the experiments represent a significant and understudied phenomenon within the broad contours of transnational governance. Neither structured by the complex interactions of private regimes nor necessarily taking the form of public-private partnerships, experiments are diverse in their constitution and reach. Of course, individual transnational environmental governance experiments—specific instances in which actors work to propose and implement rules to govern behavior in environmental issue areas—are diverse in their scope, membership, focus, resources, and approaches. The label *transnational environmental governance experiment* captures disparate governance activities not immediately discernible as sharing common characteristics.[1] For instance, beyond a mutual focus on climate change, it is difficult to determine how the Carbon Disclosure Project—an experiment that coordinates the behavior of institutional investors controlling US$57 trillion in assets (www.cdproject.net)—has much in common with Carbon Rationing Action Groups, in which small, linked groups of individuals in three countries have organized themselves to reduce their individual carbon footprints (www.carbonrationing.org.uk).

Yet among the heterogeneity that exists in the population of transnational governance experiments, there is a larger phenomenon of experimentation that provides some coherence as to what appears to be the chaotic emergence of a multitude of initiatives. First, although there is a bubbling of innovation among transnational governance initiatives, experimentation is not random. On the contrary, transnational governance experiments draw on established tropes and functions. Perhaps most significantly, transnational governance experiments tend to embody market liberal principles, following what Bernstein (2001) has called the compromise of liberal environmentalism (Hoffmann 2011). The brief examples in the following sections hint at how this commitment to market liberal ideas brings coherence to what is a diverse set of initiatives. Second, because experiments exist outside traditional institutional frameworks, very few have authority to command actors to participate. Instead, experiments tend to be voluntary associations of like-minded actors. At the same time, such initiatives are voluntary in the sense that very few have obvious accountability measures (in terms of monitoring or enforcement). We can theorize a process of experimentation that serves to set an analytic agenda— research on the general process whereby experiments emerge along with the prospects for their having a significant impact on environmental governance. Diverse experiments can be corralled within a generic analytic framework. This task is briefly begun in the subsequent section.

Experiences

Experimentation in climate governance seems the most evident and has received significant attention in the literature (e.g., Paterson 2001; Betsill and Bulkeley 2004; Rabe 2004, 2008; Moser 2007; Lindseth 2006; Selin and VanDeveer 2005, 2009a), even when initiatives are not explicitly labeled as experiments. First, in keeping with the general phenomenon of governance experimentation, climate change experiments tend to be based in liberal environmentalism. An established starting point for experimenting seems to be acceptance of market liberal principles. Just as one example, a major serial publication for the Climate Group (an initiative that brings together corporate actors and subnational governments) is titled "Profits Up, Carbon Down" (http://www.theclimategroup.org/about/publications). As we explore in more detail in the following, a significant number of climate governance experiments are involved in developing carbon markets (emission trading venues), working on efficient development and deployment of new technology, actively incorporating climate change into investment and insurance strategies, or laying the foundation for future carbon markets (registries). Second, emerging outside of formal governance arenas, climate governance experiments are also voluntary in nature. US state and Canadian provincial emissions trading venues such as RGGI (discussed in the following) are exceptions to this general rule because although they are voluntary associations, the actors involved do have the political authority to force other actors (that is, corporations, electric utilities, citizens) to participate. From this common foundation, diverse experiments have been developed with very different ideas as to how climate change should be governed. In order to provide some more detail about this phenomenon and to investigate what it means in practice, we turn now to consider two examples in more depth: RGGI and the development of the voluntary carbon market. In examining these case studies, we consider the reasons for their emergence, the actors involved, the functions that they perform, and their effects and implications.

Regional Greenhouse Gas Initiative

A growing number of states, provinces, municipalities, firms, and civil society organizations across North America are at the forefront of expanding climate change policy action and greenhouse gas–reduction efforts (Selin and VanDeveer 2007, 2009a). These actors are deeply embedded in complex networks that connect actors within each type of actor group—such as state and provincial civil servants—and connect actors from different sectors. In other words, actors seeking increased public awareness of climate change and policy-making efforts in the public and private sectors tend to belong to multiple, overlapping, institutionalized climate action networks that link public, private, and civil society individuals and organizations in climate change advocacy and action.

A regionally based example can be found in the US Northeast, with the 2001 New England Governors and Eastern Canadian Premiers (NEG-ECP) Climate Change Action Plan created by six New England state governments and a host of engaged environmental NGOs and the 2009 establishment of a regional carbon dioxide cap-and-trade scheme, the RGGI. These two regional initiatives are foci of regional climate action networks and they are used by such actors to pressure individual state governments, municipalities, firms, universities, and other organizations to "do their part" and enact climate action measures. The first initiative is embedded in an institution whose primary goals are to facilitate trade and economic development among the member states and provinces, whereas the second was launched by participating US states to seek efficient greenhouse gas reductions and demonstrate the need for similarly designed US federal action.

Under the 2001 NEG-ECP Climate Change Action Plan (NEG-ECP 2006), the states and provinces commit to reduce greenhouse gas emissions to 1990 levels by 2010 and to achieve a 10 percent reduction below 1990 levels by 2020. It outlines nine general actions and goals pursuant to these emissions reduction targets and a host of more specific policy recommendations.[2] Since 2001, state and provincial officials have worked to develop and implement state and provincial level policies and programs and develop institutions in support of this action plan (Selin and VanDeveer 2005, 2006). Accomplishments to date, in terms of actual greenhouse gas mitigation, are generally modest, varying significantly between states and provinces (New England Climate Coalition 2006, 2008; Stoddard and Murrow 2006; David Suzuki Foundation 2006). In conjunction with the plan's goals, state civil servants often work with local government personnel and national, state, and locally focused NGOs to launch relatively small-scale abatement programs (most often focused on energy efficiency and public awareness). Civil society actors often try to use the plan to push for additional mitigation actions from state, provincial, and local governments, including legal and regulatory changes to encourage renewable energy production and energy efficiency investments, changes in public programs or purchasing policies, and so on. The Pew Center for Global Climate Change tracks state-level climate change and energy-related policies and programs among US states. By 2008, the six New England states averaged 16.5 initiatives out of the 20 tracked by the Pew Center—far more than the average US state.

As a second major multi-jurisdictional governance initiative, northeastern states are building new collective institutions for carbon dioxide emissions trading under RGGI. This effort connects the six New England states with four other states in the Northeast not included in NEG-ECP cooperation: New York, New Jersey, Maryland, and Delaware (Canadian provinces are not part of RGGI). The RGGI trading scheme, negotiated and implemented between 2003 and 2008 and fully operational in 2009, is the first public sector carbon dioxide emissions trading scheme in North America. This effort draws on US experiences with earlier trading schemes for emissions of sulphur oxide and nitrogen oxide, which were originally launched by northeastern states and later became part of federal policy (Aulisi et al. 2005) and on the design and experience of the EU trading scheme (Schreurs, Selin, and VanDeveer 2009).

Through the development and implementation of RGGI, leader states in the Northeast are setting important technical and political precedents for North American climate change policy making. The RGGI process also aided in building regional coalitions for policy change and emission reductions among key stakeholders across public, private, and civil society sectors. RGGI is intended to help its member states to reduce their greenhouse gas emissions and set and meet state mitigation goals more efficiently. It is also explicitly intended to set precedents for, and to influence the establishment of, additional state and national mitigation efforts in the United States. In other words, RGGI participants try to steer their own policies and investments toward greater energy efficiency and renewable energy production (to mitigate their own greenhouse gas emissions) and to shape the political action and decisions of public, private, and civil society actors in the United States as a whole. Many other US states or regional groupings of states, provinces, and civil society actors are closely following RGGI as they explore possibilities for creating other regional trading schemes. This includes those engaged in the West Coast Governors Association and some officials and advocates around the North American Great Lakes and officials in California and Florida and several Canadian provinces. Furthermore, many of the Northeast region's public, private, and civil society actors have worked to upload aspects of RGGI to national climate policy making in the

United States and Canada (Selin and VanDeveer 2009a, 2009b). In this way, the RGGI experiment was designed to produce lessons for larger scale mitigation efforts, and it seems to be doing so.

Voluntary Carbon Offset Markets

The development of the voluntary offset market is experimental at two levels.[3] First, addressing climate change through the creation of carbon markets is a grand experiment in and of itself. There are clearly major questions about the effectiveness and even morality of carbon markets as well as debates over how markets should be designed and function (Newell and Paterson 2010). The carbon market experiment involves the construction of a brand new commodity and market from scratch, and a cluster of (strictly defined) climate governance experiments have emerged to participate in this building and the exchange of commodities that result. Second, transnational governance experiments—more concrete initiatives—are key participants in the construction of the market.

The notion of carbon offsetting emerged in the Kyoto Protocol in the form of the Clean Development Mechanism. This formal compliance market is an aspect of traditional multilateral climate governance in that CDM credits can be used to fulfill mandated emissions reduction commitments (for instance in the European Union emissions trading system). Yet a voluntary offset market has emerged alongside the CDM, catering to nonregulated entities. This has been especially important in North America because the United States' withdrawal from the Kyoto Protocol removed a huge potential source of demand for CDM credits. Developing credits—specified quantities of avoided emissions that consumers would like to obtain in order to offset their own emissions of greenhouse gases—that can serve as a reliable commodity is not a simple matter. Those providing the commodity are essentially promising not to emit that specified amount of greenhouse gases so that the buyer can consume the commodity by emitting that specified amount of greenhouse gases. Making this work requires devoting significant energy to measuring, verifying, and tracking credits to ensure that the exchange of credits has integrity in economic (avoiding fraud and double-counting of credits) and environmental (ensuring that emissions are actually reduced) ways. Measurement, verification, and reporting of emissions and emissions reductions are also a key challenge in these cap-and-trade systems. There must hence be systems in place to ensure the integrity of credits. This means accounting for the additionality (credit is only granted for emissions reductions that would not have occurred in business-as-usual circumstances) and permanence of the emissions reductions. In addition, it is necessary to establish clear ownership of credits and to ensure that they are only "consumed" once.

In the CDM, these tasks fall to the executive board of the CDM, which was created and is backstopped by the multilateral treaty-making process and the secretariat of the UN Framework Convention on Climate Change. It is more complicated in the voluntary sector because there is no single legal authority to make and oversee the rules.

Carbon credit markets do not begin with a tangible commodity. What has developed is a set of interactions, relationships, and standards oriented toward monetizing promises to not emit and reduce greenhouse gas emissions. The role of climate governance experiments in the development and functioning of offset markets has been explicit and varied. Experiments that initiate emissions trading such as the Chicago Climate Exchange serve as a source of demand for carbon credits (over two million metric tons of carbon dioxide equivalent credits were bilaterally traded just from September to December 2009 on the Chicago Climate Exchange) (Chicago Climate Exchange 2009). The Climate Registry provides the infrastructure for measuring the carbon footprints that complements demand sources to produce actual consumption. Yet it is clear that climate governance experiments have been most prominent in a particular role in the voluntary credit market: setting standards for offset credits. Such experiments, in that they induce behavior and knowledge changes in participating and some observing actors, are likely to influence a broad set of actors.

The voluntary credit market is an experiment inspired by opportunities and perceived voids in the multilateral process and the carbon markets being developed within it. Climate governance experiments are a keystone in this market, providing the methods and information that creates the very commodity being exchanged. They are certainly not alone in providing this infrastructural service—experimental standard setters draw on the CDM experience and more generalized standard-setting guidelines provided by the ISO[4]—but they have become a focal point around which the market is emerging.

Three prominent standard-setting experiments are the Voluntary Carbon Standard, the Climate Action Reserve, and the American Carbon Registry.[5] Each provides a stamp of approval on offset projects and serial numbers for carbon credits that turn the projects (efforts to reduce greenhouse gas emissions) into a source of commodities (specific credits in terms of metric tons of avoided or reduced emissions). They have each evolved slightly different approaches to standard setting—similar functional roles have produced diverse standard-setting procedures and methods. It is relatively simple to begin an offset project. The hard part is turning the project into a product—commercializing efforts at reducing emissions. The explosion of offset providers in the early 2000s generated a great deal of concern about the integrity of the markets because offsets were being developed and sold with little in the way of oversight over what was being purchased. This was a major concern in the retail market but caused even more significant worries among those committed to the development of carbon markets as a key component of the global response to climate change. Without being able to identify what counted as a ton of greenhouse gases and what counted as a ton of avoided emissions, the whole carbon market (voluntary or regulatory) would collapse (taking any hope of achieving emissions reductions through this mechanism with it). Taking a cue from the Kyoto process, which developed standards within the CDM program, experimental transnational governance initiatives—standard setters—began to emerge in the voluntary offsetting markets as well in order to "bring order to the wilderness."[6] These processes, like the development of certification regimes, also involve a struggle for legitimacy and credibility (Cashore, Auld, and Newsom 2004).

The key to the credit market is producing promises to not emit and reduce greenhouse gases that are verifiable, permanent (no emissions that will resume in subsequent years), additional (not something one would do anyway or something that one is required to do), and clearly owned. In other words, the credit market depends on knowing that an identifiable ton of greenhouse gas is not going into the atmosphere (but otherwise would have), that the seller of that ton has a right to sell it, and that it only gets "consumed" (retired or turned in to meet requirements) once. Standard setters (e.g., American Carbon Registry, Climate Action Reserve, Voluntary Carbon Standard, and Gold Standard) have developed or approved a number of specific methodologies for projects to ensure that they meet these more general criteria.

Akin to the global experience with cap-and-trade mechanisms, carbon credit markets have expanded beyond the original vision embedded in the Kyoto Protocol. Tons of carbon credits are being produced around the world to varying standards as a way to commodify greenhouse gas emissions and to provide opportunities for those seeking to manage their own emissions to do so cheaply and without necessarily fundamentally altering their own activities. The idea of carbon offset markets are experimental in and of themselves, and making these credit markets function has been a key area of activity for climate governance experiments.

Explanations

From our discussion so far, it is clear that transnational governance experiments can be conceptualized as a distinct form of governance, and one that is being experienced predominantly in the climate change arena. Here we consider the basis for the emergence of this form of experimentation and its potential significance—what role do and will transnational governance experiments play in the overall governance response to climate change and other global environmental issues?

Emergence of Experimentation
From the 1960s through the 1980s, when the international community awoke to the existence of environmental problems that flowed across multiple borders, the governance response that developed was one of mega-multilateralism (Hoffmann 2007).[7] Large-scale multilateral conferences (Stockholm 1972, Rio de Janeiro 1992, and Johannesburg 2002) and (near) universal state-centric agreements (Montreal Protocol, UN Framework Convention on Climate Change, Convention on Biological Diversity, UN Convention on Desertification, Kyoto Protocol) defined and were coincident with the notion of global environmental governance. There was a stable governance model—a set of ideas about which actors are responsible for governing and how—that prescribed states as the authoritative actors and multilateral processes as the appropriate means of governance. The environmental governance experiments we observe today contribute to and are made possible by the erosion of the dominance of this mega-multilateral governance model (Hoffmann 2011).

There are drivers of this erosion that are largely exogenous to (though not independent from) environmental politics. In general, we appear to be in the midst of a global shift toward the fragmentation of governing authority. Observers from multiple perspectives invoke such terms as globalization, global governance, private authority, or neo-medievalism to convey the sense that the authority of the state, and consequently that of interstate institutions (like mega-multilateral treaty making), is eroding or diffusing to other levels of politics (Rosenau 1990, 1997; Haufler 2001; Hall and Biersteker 2002; Ba and Hoffmann 2005; Biermann et al. 2009). This tendency has been observed across multiple issues and it provides a condition of possibility for actors to begin conceiving new governance models. The growth of privatization and devolution of state authority and the subsequent growth in private authority are particularly important drivers of the erosion of the dominance of multilateral governance models.

In essence, processes of privatization and devolution have served to hollow out the state, a dynamic that has been accompanied by and in some cases driven the rise of private authority across such diverse areas as security, economics, and the environment (Hewson and Sinclair 1997; Hall and Biersteker 2002; Haufler 2003). This literature suggests that (for good or ill) private actors, especially corporations, have begun to seize governing authority based on resources or expertise. More critically, Vandana Shiva argues that carbon markets are essentially privatizing the atmospheric commons and taking their governance further from democratic authority (Shiva 2008). For example, certification schemes have arisen in multiple environmental issue areas (e.g., Cashore, Auld, and Newsom 2004 on forestry), and corporate social responsibility initiatives in the security and environmental realms (Haufler 2003; Clapp and Dauvergne 2005) are becoming commonplace. These kinds of private authority mechanisms seek, in some sense, to head off or parallel governmental regulation by providing for self-governance initiatives among corporations (Prakash and Potoski 2006). They are also a testament to the growing pressure on corporate actors to address the increasing demands placed on them by citizens, nongovernmental actors, and government entities with respect to issues such as human rights and the environment as their authority to govern in these arenas increases. These broad structural dynamics are part of what Rosenau (1997, 2005) has identified as "fragmegration" in the ebb and flow of global political authority. He identifies linked patterns of integration and fragmentation that have increased the number of actors that generate authority. The proliferation of "spheres of authority" has changed the landscape of global politics by multiplying the avenues by which individuals can pursue their interests and goals and changing the nature of relationships between states and nonstate actors. The erosion or shift in the authority of states and state-centric governance models entailed by privatization and devolution and the rise of private authority provides a condition of possibility for actors to begin conceiving new environmental governance models even as globalized understandings of environmental problems produced the mega-multilateral responses that have become so familiar. The tension that Rosenau identifies between integrating and fragmenting tendencies within globalization has played out in global environmental governance first with the rise of mega-multilateral approaches and then more recently with multilevel governance challenges and experiments.

These exogenous structural dynamics create a global potential for fragmentation of governing authority to emerge in response to or in conjunction with large-scale multilateral approaches in global environmental governance, but that potential has to be realized through agency in particular contexts. Although in the last decade the potential to experiment has been evident, actors are not required to experiment and new conceptions of governance models emerge from adaptive actors that operationalize that potential. Political actors are adaptive in the sense that they interpret and evaluate the outcomes of their actions as well as their understandings of what counts as governance in deciding on courses of action. Further, the erosion of the dominance of the mega-multilateral governance model is a co-evolutionary process whereby structural and agential factors shape one another over time (O'Neill, Balsiger, and VanDeveer 2004; Hoffmann 2005).

When the broad context of governance provides for the potential for experimentation and actors perceive the dominant governance model to be failing, actors may work to realize the potential and experiment with governance. Evaluations of the multilateral process in a context where mega-multilateralism is no longer the unquestioned governance model can weaken the motivation to reenact this model of governance and make actors more likely to assert their own conceptions of how to address issues of environmental governance. For instance in the area of commodities production, Bitzer, Francken, and Glasbergen (2008, 281) suggest that the collapse "of the International Coffee Agreement in 1989 led to a reduction in governmental intervention, unstable commodity prices and a lack of global regulations." The evaluation of the dominant governance model led to reframing the discourses concerning the basis on which commodities should be regulated, with nongovernmental actors being particularly important in the process (Bitzer, Francken, and Glasbergen 2008). Climate change is perhaps the quintessential example of the process whereby negative evaluations of the mega-multilateral process (e.g., Depledge 2006) have combined with a structural potential for experimentation to produce a dizzying array of initiatives (e.g., Paterson 2001; Betsill and Bulkeley 2004; Rabe 2004, 2008; Moser 2007; Lindseth 2006; Selin and VanDeveer 2005). Adaptation by multiple actors at multiple levels has led to what Bulkeley (2005) and Lindseth (2004) deem a reframing of climate change and ultimately a seizing of authority over responses to climate change by multiple actors (Hoffmann 2011).

The motivations that drive adaptive actors to realize the potential to experiment are diverse but they are all variations of dissatisfaction with the dominant governance approach. Classes of motivation are discussed in the following sections.[8]

Profit
Carbon offsetting organizations, for instance, implicitly promote a governance model based on individual responsibility for climate change. This model is profitable for those who are selling offsets. Indeed, the business of environmental governance is increasingly lucrative with the development of carbon markets, public-private partnerships to exploit genetic resources, and certification measures that provide certain products with visibility and a green stamp of approval.

Urgency
A more standard explanation given for the motivation to innovate is that some actors desire to move quickly on environmental problems and are concerned about the slow pace of multilateral processes. In the climate issue, this explanation is often given for citizen groups and subnational governments, especially in those states like the United States and Australia, where federal authorities have been recalcitrant (Betsill and Bulkeley 2004).

Expansion of Authority and Claims on Resources
We should be cautious about ascribing only altruistic motives to those entities that want to move quickly on environmental problems. Although cities may be genuinely motivated by urgency in pushing for quicker action than is available multilaterally, it is crucial that they are pushing for municipal action. At a 2009 event at the University of Toronto that brought together two very climate-progressive mayors (Livingston of London and Miller of Toronto), it was not surprising to hear them simultaneously argue for the importance of cities in addressing climate change and call for more resources to come to cities from other levels of government. Similarly, at the 2007 Bali conference of the parties to the climate convention, at side event after side event, different actors (provinces, cities, corporations) stridently claimed the mantle of "the most important actor" for dealing with climate change.[9] Actors may experiment with governance as a way to enhance their own authority and resources in relation to other levels of political organization (state or nonstate).

Ideological Expression

On the one hand, the recent age of neoliberalism has brought a greater number of actors into governance experiments who believe, as a matter of course, that markets and private organizations are more effective and more efficient in the provisions of governance functions. On the other hand, hosts of other civil society arguments articulate the view that NGOs and other nonstate actors (and processes such as "stakeholder" engagement and management) bring needed aspects of representation and legitimacy to transjurisdictional governance that more traditional state-dominated governance models lack.

In seeking to explain the basis for the emergence of experimentation transnationally, we can therefore suggest that it arises as the coevolutionary product of structural and agential factors. Broad structural openings provide for the possibility of thinking differently about what models of governance are appropriate. Adaptive actors work with this opening and when they are dissatisfied with dominant governance models (for a variety of reasons), they innovate, accelerating the structural change that made experimentation possible originally. Across diverse arenas of environmental governance, but most specifically in relation to climate change, we can see this dynamic playing out in the increasing number of experiments seeking to govern beyond the traditional arenas of multilateral agreements.

Significance of Experimentation

The structural and agential reasons for the emergence of environmental governance experiments provide us with a means of explaining the growing visibility of this phenomenon. Yet it does not provide us with significant insight into the importance of experimentation. The discussion about the impacts and implications of transnational governance experiments has centered primarily on two debates regarding their roles in addressing governance deficits and accountability deficits. Turning first to the issue of governance deficits, one argument that emerges from the literature is that transnational governance experiments have successfully been able to address issues where government action has been slow or nonexistent. For example, Visseren-Hamakers and Glasbergen (2007, 417) suggest that "the most valuable contribution of partnerships for forest biodiversity conservation has been filling the gap when governments were not willing and/or able to regulate," including bringing issues of sustainable logging, the problems of illegal logging, and land conversion from forest to other uses to the table. In fact, it is often claimed that certification-based governance experiments fulfill sets of functions states and other actors have been unwilling or unable to engage—related to the trade in commodities as diverse as diamonds, cut flowers, bananas, and palm oil or sets of practices such as forestry, chemicals production and use, cotton and clothing production, or mining. As Bäckstrand (2008, 78) explains, transnational governance experiments can address governance deficits by "connecting local practice and global rules in a flexible and decentralized manner" and by complementing "multilateral treaties by providing voluntary standards and self-regulation." Such positive evaluations, however, are tempered with a great deal of caution. Transnational governance initiatives are found to be wanting in terms of the strength of regulations imposed, the extent of their impacts, the development of alternative markets, and their single-issue focus (Bitze, Francken, and Glasbergen 2008; Visseren-Hamakers and Glasbergen 2007). More significantly, some authors find that "new forms of global environmental governance, and their newly incorporated players, can be viewed simply as reflecting existing distributions of power rather than having changed anything fundamental" (Lemos and Agrawal 2006, 312).

In terms of accountability, it can be argued that transnational governance experiments "decrease the legitimacy and accountability deficits by including a diverse set of private and public actors" (Bäckstrand 2008, 78). Greater levels of involvement by a range of public and private actors in the sharing of information, the setting of norms and rules, and indirect forms of intervention with respect to global environmental issues could be regarded as a means of enhancing the legitimacy and accountability of global environmental governance, particularly given the somewhat distant and impenetrable nature of many intergovernmental processes. Yet there are also significant questions raised as to whether this is, in fact, the case. Do market-based experiments add to democratic accountability or are they likely to empower better-resourced economic actors? Bäckstrand (2008, 78) suggests that such experiments may instead lead to "increased business influence, power inequalities and skewed representation of stakeholders, fragmentation of global governance, reinforcement of elite multilateralism and the retreat of state responsibility in the production of public goods," which in turn may contribute to reducing the legitimacy of decision making and the scope for accountability. Likewise, in the case of Madagascar, Duffy (2006, 745–746) finds that the emergence of a "governance state" orchestrated through new forms of transnational environmental governance has led to the "co-option of local and global/southern and northern environmental NGOs," which means that "they can be effectively neutralized in terms of their resistance to external forms of governance," in turn reducing the scope for alternative forms of accountability.

In terms of the ability of transnational governance experiments to address widely perceived governance failures and deficits of implementation, legitimacy, and accountability within the global environmental arena, it seems that the jury is still firmly out. At the same time, research has provided little evidence of the environmental effects of such experiments and indeed their consequences for broader issues of sustainability and social justice.

Conclusions and Outlook

This chapter highlights the growing body of research examining the emergence and nature of transnational governance experiments, a distinct field of transnational initiatives based predominantly in market logics and taking place alongside transnational regimes and public-private partnerships. We suggest that experiments in this arena represent implicit or explicit attempts to produce novel governance arrangements within institutional voids. We have argued that the experience of such experiments is particularly predominant in the climate change arena because of structural conditions and agent interest and engagement. Case studies suggest some tensions or differences between those experiments designed primarily to govern in their own right and those explicitly aiming to shape the ways in which others act. RGGI seeks to govern carbon mitigation among its members and within its territory but most participants want these mechanisms to be overseen by national and international structures eventually. Here, RGGI is regarded as a means for shaping what those governance institutions will look like as policies and private-sector actions develop across the United States and the North American continent. However, those initiatives developed in relation to the carbon market do not seek to govern directly as much as to enhance the capacity of other actors (member cities) to govern. More broadly, the pace and variety of transnational environmental governance experimentation in the climate change arena shows no evidence of slowing. Indeed, at present it appears that experimentation is now a key feature of the transnational governance landscape and one that scholars will need to engage with in more depth in the future.

Experimentation appears to occur in response to broad exogenous factors (that is, ramifications of globalization) and specific factors endogenous to environmental politics, such as actors' sense of urgency and stalemate in multilateral processes and actor frustrations with this outcome. At the moment, it seems that such transnational governance experimentation remains primarily confined to OECD societies. Yet given that the structural issues of globalization have affected countries inside and outside of the OECD and that concerns surrounding climate change continue to grow in the global South, we may expect to see changes in the motivations of agents and the growing use of governance experiments beyond their OECD origins (see also Compagnon, Chan, and Mert, this book, chapter 11). Furthermore, the emergence of particular forms of experimentation, particularly those based on the development and extension of carbon markets, might be expected to lead to the emergence of constituencies with a stake in their continuation. A key research question is therefore whether the proliferation of experiments is creating new cohorts of actors whose interests and identities are dependent on (or connected to) individual experiments and their outcomes and successes. So, for example, public officials developing carbon trading schemes at multiple levels of governing authority may thus develop shared interests with private-sector firms engaged in carbon trading and its related functions. Such actors may seek to further expand trading or to create new schemes, further perpetuating the development and growth of transnational governance experiments.

At the same time that the diversity and reach of transnational governance experiments might be expected to grow, there are significant questions concerning their effectiveness and implications. On the one hand, such experiments and the market-based logics they espouse could be regarded as competing with more traditional forms of state-based regulation and multilateral negotiations, potentially deflecting attention from other more tried and tested forms of governance authority. On the other hand, we know little about how such forms of experimentation might interact with local, national, and international forms of environmental governance and what the sum of these parts might add up to. A research agenda in this field will therefore be to move beyond detailed cases of such experiments in isolation and to conduct a comparative analysis between experiments and other forms of environmental governance, a task that the Leverhulme Network on Transnational Climate Governance is undertaking. Finally, it is clear that despite their recent explosive growth, the impact of transnational experiments in terms of addressing global environmental problems has to date been negligible, and they remain peripheral to the vast machinery associated with the multilateral environmental governance process. A key task for future research will be to evaluate the collective implications of transnational experiments for how other forms of environmental governance evolve and in terms of their future effectiveness in reducing the burdens of environmental problems.

Acknowledgments

This chapter is based on research collaboration undertaken within the Transnational Climate Governance project, which was funded by the United Kingdom's Leverhulme Trust (2008–2010).

Notes

1. Hoffmann (2011) has compiled a database with fifty-seven experiments that span multiple levels of political organization and modes of governing, and the Leverhulme Network on Transnational Climate Governance (of which the authors are members) has identified sixty-five experimental initiatives in its work as well. These climate experiments include familiar initiatives such as ICLEI Local Governments for Sustainability's Cities for Climate Protection program and The Climate Group's cities, states, and regions program, capacity-building innovations like the Climate Registry, and investor-led groups like the Investor Network on Climate Risk.

2. (1) Establish a regional standardized greenhouse gas emissions inventory; (2) establish a plan for reducing greenhouse gas emissions and conserving energy; (3) promote public awareness; (4) state and provincial governments to lead by example; (5) reduce greenhouse gas emissions from the electricity sector; (6) reduce total energy demand through conservation; (7) reduce and/or adapt to negative social, economic, and environmental effects; (8) decrease the transportation sector's growth in greenhouse gas emissions; (9) create a regional emissions registry and explore a trading mechanism.

3. This section draws from Hoffmann 2011, chapter 6.

4. They are also not alone in setting standards—this has become a major tool of environmental activism, especially in the forestry sector with the Forest Stewardship Council. See Bernstein and Cashore (2007).

5. Carbon Fix and the Chicago Climate Exchange have also engaged in setting carbon offset standards but will not be explicitly addressed here.

6. Personal communication with Voluntary Carbon Standard representative at Point Carbon Conference, November 2009.

7. Relatively circumscribed transboundary environmental problems such as river pollution have been known for a much longer time but still tended to be dealt with through interstate negotiation, either multilaterally or bilaterally (Denmark and Hoffmann 2008).

8. These motivations are also discussed in Hoffmann 2011, chapter 3.

9. Personal observations at Toronto Mayors' Event and the conference of the parties to the UN Framework Convention on Climate Change in Bali 2007.

References

Agnew, John. 2005. Sovereignty Regimes: Territoriality and State Authority in Contemporary World Politics. *Annals of the Association of American Geographers* 95 (2):437–461.

Aulisi, Andrew, Alexander F. Farrell, Jonathan Pershing, and Stacy D. VanDeveer. 2005. *Greenhouse Gas Emissions Trading in U.S. States: Observations and Lessons from the OTC NOx Budget Program.* Washington, DC: World Resources Institute.

Ba, Alice D., and Matthew J. Hoffmann. 2005. *Contending Perspectives on Global Governance: Coherence, Contestation, and World Order.* London: Routledge.

Bäckstrand, Karin. 2008. Accountability of Networked Climate Governance: The Rise of Transnational Climate Partnerships. *Global Environmental Politics* 8 (3):74–102.

Bernstein, Steven. 2001. *The Compromise of Liberal Environmentalism.* New York: Columbia University Press.

Bernstein, Steven, and Benjamin Cashore. 2007. Can Non-state Global Governance Be Legitimate? An Analytical Framework. *Regulation and Governance* 1 (4):347–371.

Betsill, Michele M., and Harriet Bulkeley. 2004. Transnational Networks and Global Environmental Governance: The Cities for Climate Protection Program. *International Studies Quarterly* 48:471–493.

Biermann, Frank, Arthur P. J. Mol, and Pieter Glasbergen. 2007. Conclusion: Partnerships for Sustainability—Reflections on a Future Research Agenda. In *Partnerships, Governance and Sustainable Development: Reflections on Theory and Practice*, ed. Pieter Glasbergen, Frank Biermann, and Arthur P. J. Mol, 288–299. Cheltenham, UK: Edward Elgar.

Biermann, Frank, Philipp Pattberg, Harro van Asselt, and Fariborz Zelli. 2009. The Fragmentation of Global Governance Architectures: A Framework for Analysis. *Global Environmental Politics* 9 (4):14–40.

Bitzer, Verena, Mara Francken, and Pieter Glasbergen. 2008. Intersectoral Partnerships for a Sustainable Coffee Chain: Really Addressing Sustainability or Just Picking (Coffee) Cherries? *Global Environmental Change: Human and Policy Dimensions* 18 (2):271–284.

Bulkeley, Harriet. 2005. Reconfiguring Environmental Governance: Towards a Politics of Scales and Networks. *Political Geography* 24 (8):875–902.

Cashore, Benjamin, Graeme Auld, and Deanna Newsom. 2004. *Governing through Markets: Forest Certification and the Emergence of Non-state Authority.* New Haven, CT: Yale University Press.

Chicago Climate Exchange. 2009. Chicago Climate Exchange Offsets Report September–December 1(5). www.chicagoclimateex.com/content.jsf?id=1800.

Clapp, Jennifer, and Peter Dauvergne. 2005. *Pathways to a Green World: The Political Economy of the Global Environment*. Cambridge, MA: MIT Press.

David Suzuki Foundation. 2006. *All over the Map*. Vancouver, Canada: David Suzuki Foundation.

Denemark, Robert, and Matthew J. Hoffmann. 2008. Not Just Scraps of Paper: The Dynamics of Multilateral Treaty-Making. *Cooperation and Conflict* 43 (2):185–219.

Depledge, Joanna. 2006. The Opposite of Learning: Ossification in the Climate Change Regime. *Global Environmental Politics* 6 (1):1–22.

Duffy, Rosaleen. 2006. Non-governmental Organisations and Governance States: The Impact of Transnational Environmental Management Networks in Madagascar. *Environmental Politics* 15 (5):731–749.

Hajer, Maarten. 2003. Policy without Polity? Policy Analysis and the Institutional Void. *Policy Sciences* 36 (2):175–195.

Hall, Rodney Bruce, and Thomas J. Biersteker, eds. 2002. *The Emergence of Private Authority in Global Governance*. Cambridge, UK: Cambridge University Press.

Haufler, Virginia. 2001. *A Public Role for the Private Sector: Industry Self-Regulation in a Global Economy*. Washington, DC: Carnegie Endowment for International Peace.

Haufler, Virginia. 2003. Globalization and Industry Self-Regulation. In *Governance in a Global Economy: Political Authority in Transition*, ed. Miles Kahler and David Lake, 226–254. Princeton, NJ: Princeton University Press.

Hewson, Martin, and Timothy J. Sinclair, eds. 1997. *Approaches to Global Governance Theory*. Albany: SUNY Press.

Hoffmann, Matthew J. 2005. *Ozone Depletion and Climate Change: Constructing a Global Response*. Albany: SUNY Press.

Hoffmann, Matthew J. 2007. The Global Regime: Current Status of and Quo Vadis for Kyoto. In *A Globally Integrated Climate Policy for Canada*, ed. Steven Bernstein, Jutta Brunnée, David G. Duff, and Andrew J. Greene, 137–157. Toronto: University of Toronto Press.

Hoffmann, Matthew J. 2011. *Climate Governance at the Crossroads: Experimenting with a Global Response*. New York: Oxford University Press.

Kolk, Ans, and Jonathan Pinkse. 2008. A Perspective on Multinational Enterprises and Climate Change: Learning from "an Inconvenient Truth"? *Journal of International Business Studies* 39:1359–1378.

Lemos, Maria Carmen, and Arun Agrawal. 2006. Environmental Governance. *Annual Review of Environment and Resources* 31:297–395.

Lindseth, Gard. 2004. The Cities for Climate Protection Campaign (CCPC) and the Framing of Local Climate Policy. *Local Environment* 9 (4):325–336.

Lindseth, Gard. 2006. Scalar Strategies in Climate-Change Politics: Debating the Environmental Consequences of a Natural Gas Project. *Environment and Planning C: Government and Policy* 24 (5):739–754.

Moser, Susanne. 2007. In the Long Shadows of Inaction: The Quiet Building of a Climate Protection Movement in the United States. *Global Environmental Politics* 7 (2):124–144.

New England Climate Coalition. 2006. Report Card on Climate Change Action: Third Annual Assessment of the Region's Progress towards Meeting the Goals of the New England Governors/Eastern Canadian Premiers Climate Change Action Plan of 2001. Boston: New England Climate Coalition.

New England Climate Coalition. 2008. *Falling Behind: New England Must Act Now to Reduce Global Warming Pollution*. Boston: New England Climate Coalition.

NEG-ECP (New England Governors and Eastern Canadian Premiers). 2006. Climate Change Action Plan 2006 Discussion Paper. Boston: New England Climate Coalition.

Newell, Peter, and Matthew Paterson. 2010. *Climate Capitalism: Global Warming and the Transformation of the Global Economy*. Cambridge, UK: Cambridge University Press.

O'Neill, Kate, Jörg Balsiger, and Stacy D. VanDeveer. 2004. Actors, Norms, and Impact: Recent International Cooperation Theory and the Influence of the Agent-Structure Debate. *Annual Review of Political Science* 7:149–175.

Paterson, Matthew. 2001. Risky Business: Insurance Companies in Global Warming Politics. *Global Environmental Politics* 1 (4):18–42.

Pattberg, Philipp, and Johannes Stripple. 2008. Beyond the Public and Private Divide: Remapping Transnational Climate Governance in the 21st Century. *International Environmental Agreement: Politics, Law and Economics* 8 (4):367–388.

Prakash, Aseem, and Matthew Potoski. 2006. *The Voluntary Environmentalist? Green Clubs and Voluntary Environmental Regulations*. Cambridge, UK: Cambridge University Press.

Rabe, Barry. 2004. *Statehouse and Greenhouse: The Evolving Politics of American Climate Change Policy*. Washington, DC: Brookings Institution Press.

Rabe, Barry. 2008. States on Steroids: The Intergovernmental Odyssey of American Climate Policy. *Review of Policy Research* 25:105–128.

Rosenau, James N. 1990. *Turbulence in World Politics: A Theory of Change and Continuity*. Princeton, NJ: Princeton University Press.

Rosenau, James N. 1997. *Along the Domestic-Foreign Frontier*. Cambridge, UK: Cambridge University Press.

Rosenau, James N. 2005. Global Governance as Disaggregated Complexity. In *Contending Perspectives on Global Governance*, ed. Alice D. Ba and Matthew J. Hoffmann, 131–153. London: Routledge.

Schreurs, Miranda, Henrik Selin, and Stacy D. VanDeveer. 2009. Conflict and Cooperation in Transatlantic Climate Politics: Different Stories at Different

Levels. In *Transatlantic Environment and Energy Politics: Comparative and International Perspectives*, ed. Miranda Schreurs, Henrik Selin, and Stacy D. VanDeveer, 165–186. Aldershot, UK: Ashgate.

Selin, Henrik, and Stacy D. VanDeveer. 2005. Canadian-U.S. Environmental Cooperation: Climate Change Networks and Regional Action. *American Review of Canadian Studies* 35:353–378.

Selin, Henrik, and Stacy D. VanDeveer. 2006. Canadian-U.S. Cooperation: Regional Climate Change Action in the Northeast. In *Bilateral Ecopolitics: Continuity and Change in Canadian-American Environmental Relations*, ed. Philippe Le Prestre and Peter Stoett, 93–114. Aldershot, UK: Ashgate.

Selin, Henrik, and Stacy D. VanDeveer. 2007. Political Science and Prediction: What's Next for U.S. Climate Change Policy? *Review of Policy Research* 24 (1):1–27.

Selin, Henrik, and Stacy D. VanDeveer, eds. 2009a. *Changing Climates in North American Politics: Institutions, Policy Making, and Multilevel Governance.* Cambridge, MA: MIT Press.

Selin, Henrik, and Stacy D. VanDeveer. 2009b. Climate Leadership in Northeast North America. In *Changing Climates in North American Politics: Institutions, Policy Making, and Multilevel Governance*, ed. Henrik Selin and Stacy D. VanDeveer, 111–136. Cambridge, MA: MIT Press.

Shiva, Vandana. 2008. *Soil Not Oil.* Boston: South End Press.

Stoddard, Michael D., and Derek K. Murrow. 2006. *Climate Change Roadmap for New England and Eastern Canada.* Maine: Environment Northeast.

Visseren-Hamakers, Ingrid J., and Pieter Glasbergen. 2007. Partnerships in Forest Governance. *Global Environmental Change: Human and Policy Dimensions* 17 (3–4):408–419.

III

The New Interlinkages and Fragmentations

8

Horizontal Institutional Interlinkages

Fariborz Zelli, Aarti Gupta, and Harro van Asselt

In this chapter, we analyze the increasingly important phenomenon of institutional interlinkages in global environmental governance. Institutional interlinkages are connections among policy processes, rules, norms, and principles of two or more institutions. We focus on the international level and hence on horizontal interlinkages between one or more international (environmental) institutions.

From the mid-1990s onward, the global governance literature has put greater emphasis on analyzing such interlinkages (Herr and Chia 1995; Young 1996). In addition to initial conceptual approaches and single case studies (Rosendal 2001; Stokke 2001a; Young 2002, 2008), major research projects have analyzed conflictive and synergistic interlinkages across international institutions. These include the Inter-Linkages Initiative of UN University (Chambers 2008), the Institutional Interaction Project (Oberthür and Gehring 2006b), and the Institutional Dimensions of Global Environmental Change project (Young 2002; Young, King, and Schroeder 2008). In the Global Governance Project, we have examined horizontal institutional interlinkages from legal and political perspectives (e.g., van Asselt, Gupta, and Biermann 2005; van Asselt, Sindico, and Mehling 2008; van Asselt 2011a; Biermann et al. 2009, 2010; Falkner and Gupta 2009; Gupta 2008; Zelli 2007, 2011b; Zelli et al. 2010).

In the following, we build on this growing body of work by adopting a norm-based approach to the study of horizontal institutional interlinkages. Specifically, we place institutional interlinkages in an overarching context of global normative developments and consider whether and how this broader normative context is shaping the nature and evolution of a specific set of horizontal institutional interactions.

We take as our point of departure that a regime and its provisions and procedures cannot be understood in isolation from the broader normative context within which it is embedded. The normative structures that shape individual regimes also affect interactions between regimes. If specific regimes are (at least partial) articulations of broader governance norms, then it follows that interlinkages between them are sites for collusion or contestation over these broader norms.

To elaborate and test the validity of this claim, we proceed as follows. In the next section, we conceptualize in more detail the norm-based approach to horizontal institutional interlinkages adopted here. Following this, we apply our conceptual framework to the analysis of three dyadic institutional interlinkages in the global environmental and trade realms: between the UN climate regime and the World Trade Organization (WTO); between the UN climate regime and the Convention on Biological Diversity ("biodiversity convention"); and between the Cartagena Protocol on Biosafety under the biodiversity convention and the WTO.

In exploring the evolving institutional interactions in each of these cases, we argue that a dominant global norm of liberal environmentalism is shaping these interactions in important ways, even as the dominance of this global norm remains contested by key actors across all three cases. In concluding, we draw out the implications of our analysis for a future research agenda in the field of horizontal institutional interlinkages.

Conceptualization

In two decades of analysis of what has variously been termed *institutional interplay, interlinkage, interconnection,* or *interaction*—with, in our view, not much difference in meaning among these different terms—scholarly understanding of this phenomenon has advanced significantly. Leading scholars in this field still deplore, however, the "limited progress . . . on rooting the study of interplay theoretically" (Chambers, Kim, and ten Have 2008, 7) and the lack of "theoretical concerns that can help us to understand the origins and consequences of interplay" (Young 2008, 134). Others have criticized the proliferation of typologies of institutional interlinkages as a key scholarly focus. As Selin and VanDeveer (2003, 14) observe, "The literature on linkages remains littered with proposed taxonomies of linkages." Some scholars have sought to go beyond typological accounts and develop elaborate explanatory models (e.g., Oberthür and Gehring 2006a; Rosendal 2001; Stokke 2001b). Yet, as Underdal (2006, 9) notes, much focus has been "on interaction at the level of specific regimes and less on links to the kind of basic ordering principles or norms highlighted in realist and sociological analyses of institutions."

In this context, we explore in this chapter the promise of one particular analytical lens: examining institutional interactions within the broader normative context that shapes such interactions. We focus on how an overarching normative environment affects the prospects for conflict (or lack thereof) in such institutional interactions, paying attention to the conflictive and the possibly synergetic character of institutional interlinkages (Oberthür and Gehring 2006a). We examine whether conflicts across institutional arrangements might be precluded by the dominance of overarching norms of governance that privilege liberal or economic approaches to the issue. Thus, rather than conflict, institutional interactions in the global environmental domain might be characterized by a problematic collusion (that is, a homogeneity or similarity) of governance norms and approaches.

In line with the broader literature, we understand norms here as legitimate social purpose, akin to John Ruggie's definition of "intersubjective frameworks of understandings that include a shared narrative about the conditions that make regimes [or governance more broadly] necessary and . . . the objectives intended to [be] accomplish[ed]" (Ruggie 1998, 870). This understanding of norms extends beyond a focus on agreed standards of behavior or rules of conduct. This narrower understanding is often applied to the notion of regime-specific norms (Krasner 1983, 2). By contrast, our broader understanding also highlights that the generation and persistence of a global (set of) norms requires intersubjectively shared expectations and purposes, hence, that agency remains important and relevant.

Norms underpinning global environmental governance arrangements are the subject of renewed interest (see also Conca 2006), with Steven Bernstein's (2002) influential analysis positing the dominance of what he terms the "compromise of liberal environmentalism" in a global governance context. This compromise promotes an overarching set of norms of economic efficiency and environmental improvements through unfettered markets, deregulation, and privatization, with reliance on market-based regulatory mechanisms when necessary. Building on Bernstein's insights, we argue that liberal environmentalism not only shapes the provisions and practices of specific environmental institutions but also their interactions with each other.

For instance, by shaping agenda-setting and decision-making processes across regimes, a broad liberal normative bent in global environmental governance might prevent evolution of specific rules that conflict with such a normative bent. Or, more generally, it might support the prevalence of liberal institutions over more regulatory ones. One prominent example is the "shadow of the WTO" over development and evolution of global environmental regimes (Eckersley 2004; Zelli 2011b). Our take on this long-established claim is that if the WTO casts a shadow, it is because the overarching normative environment is conducive to such an outcome (see also Gupta 2002).

Experiences

To explore how our norm-based approach may provide added value, we turn now to examining a specific set of horizontal institutional interlinkages within the global trade, climate, biological diversity, and biosafety policy domains. The subsequent section analyzes whether and how the specific resolution of conflicts (or synergies) in each case of institutional interaction reflects the dominance of an overarching global set of norms of liberal environmentalism.

The UN Climate Regime and the WTO

Scholars from various disciplines have scrutinized the interlinkages between the UN climate regime and the world trade regime (e.g., Brewer 2003, 2004; Charnovitz 2003; Cottier, Nartova, and Bigdeli 2009; Zelli and van Asselt 2010). These authors have identified a range of overlapping issues that fall within the jurisdictional scope of both regimes, although disagreeing about the potentially synergetic or conflictive nature of these interlinkages.

One key issue of interaction concerns trade-related policies and measures by which industrialized countries are to achieve emission reductions under the Kyoto Protocol. The protocol does not specify concrete steps or targets to achieve such reductions, hence not ruling out that parties apply certain trade-distorting measures. These may include fiscal measures (subsidies, tariffs, or border taxes), regulatory measures (standards, technical regulations, and labeling), and government procurement practices. Industrialized countries might consider such steps to reduce emissions or protect domestic industries adversely affected by such reductions—in other words, to level the playing field between regulated domestic industries and unregulated foreign competitors (Frankel 2005, 15).

Yet these measures might be WTO incompatible. For example, taxes on energy-intensive goods from countries that are not party to the Kyoto Protocol or do not take comparable climate change action might violate the national treatment principle and the most-favored nation principle of the General Agreement on Tariffs and Trade. Offsetting measures at the border to complement an emissions trading system—most recently considered by the United States Congress, the French government and the European Commission—might also raise such concerns. Although some believe such measures can be defended under WTO law (Biermann and Brohm 2005; Ismer and Neuhoff 2007), others warn against their protectionist implications and possible violation of trade rules (Bhagwati and Mavroidis 2007).

How are these potential interlinkages evolving? Scholarly research suggests that in both arenas US-led coalitions were "highly influential in establishing a market approach to managing climate change" (Boyd, Corbera, and Estrada 2008, 106). Regarding debates and developments in the climate regime, it is striking to note that since the adoption of the Kyoto Protocol negotiators have avoided trade-restrictive modalities. The list of policies and measures has remained purely indicative and nonmandatory. An issue-specific actor coalition comprising the United States and several non-EU industrialized countries (the so-called Umbrella Group) tabled various successful initiatives for WTO-compliant elements. However, the same group rejected several proposals by the European Union for a binding list of policies and measures and their mandatory coordination or for quantitative limits to the use of trade-oriented flexibility mechanisms. Developing countries largely seconded the Umbrella Group's opposition to trade restrictions on these various occasions.

The institutional context to discuss such interlinkages within the trade regime is the WTO Committee on Trade and Environment (CTE), and the WTO Dispute Settlement Body remains the most likely arena where these overlaps might be settled (Stokke 2004, 339). By contrast, under the climate regime, the dispute settlement procedure remains weak. Although there is an elaborate compliance system, it does not include trade sanctions based on the greenhouse gas intensity of the product. Apart from deductions of emission allowances, noncompliance does not entail direct financial penalties, nor does it include any other trade sanctions, even though these were proposed by the European Union (Stokke 2004, 352).

In debates about interlinkage management within the CTE, a European Union–led coalition suggested granting further exceptions under WTO law in favor of environmental regimes, including the climate regime. These proposals were rejected, however, again by a United States–

led coalition and the majority of developing countries. In fact, the mandate of CTE discussions on exemptions was narrowed, so they are not even covering the climate regime's policies and measures. The rights of WTO members to challenge such measures hence remain intact (Eckersley 2004).

The UN Climate Regime and the Convention on Biological Diversity

Our second example concerns institutional interlinkages between the climate and biodiversity regimes. Several institutions have pointed to the complex interactions between the causes and consequences of climate change and conservation and sustainable use of biological diversity (CBD Secretariat 2003; IPCC 2002). Climate change has negative impacts on a range of ecosystems and species, even as ecosystems with high biological diversity are more resilient to climate variability and better able to adapt to climate change (CBD Secretariat 2003). Furthermore, certain ecosystems are either net carbon sinks or sources of emissions (CBD Secretariat 2003). Avoiding deforestation and forest degradation, as well as afforestation and reforestation, therefore have significant potential for climate change mitigation, although their effects on biodiversity may vary (CBD Secretariat 2003).

Institutional interlinkages between the climate regime and the biodiversity convention have emerged mainly in the implementation stages of the Kyoto Protocol. Particular attention has been paid to decisions on land use, land-use change, and forestry, and the use of so-called sinks in the protocol's Clean Development Mechanism (CDM) (Jacquemont and Caparrós 2002; Sagemüller 2006; Wolfrum and Matz 2003). More recently, interlinkages between the climate and biodiversity regimes have received renewed attention in discussions about reduced emissions from deforestation and degradation (REDD) as a climate change mitigation strategy (van Asselt 2011b).

Including sinks in emissions accounting, and especially in the CDM, has been a controversial issue since the 1990s. Although the inclusion of sinks lowers the cost of compliance with Kyoto targets, critics argue that the rules on CDM sinks do not sufficiently safeguard biodiversity and could frustrate the objectives of the biodiversity convention. The main concerns raised are that the rules allow for projects that result in destructive large-scale, monoculture plantations, a lack of protection for old-growth forests, and the use of invasive alien species and GMOs (Meinshausen and Hare 2003).

Whereas the European Union, supported by various developing countries, initially opposed the inclusion of forest carbon sinks in the CDM, the United States, supported by Latin American countries, pushed for their inclusion (Boyd, Corbera, and Estrada 2008, 106). A compromise reached in 2001 entails that, with some limitations, forestry projects can be eligible for credits under the CDM. One of the general principles governing forestry activities requires that "the implementation of land use, land-use change and forestry activities contributes to the conservation of biodiversity and sustainable use of natural resources" (UNFCCC 2006, annex, paragraph 1.e). This principle has been elaborated at the ninth conference of the parties to the climate convention in 2003 for forestry projects under the CDM. In these negotiations, the European Union, together with the Alliance of Small Island States, sought to accommodate biodiversity concerns by including sustainable development criteria. Yet the European Union found itself opposed by many developing countries as well as by Canada (Boyd, Corbera, and Estrada 2008). The United States was by then no longer involved in formal negotiations because it had withdrawn from the Kyoto process in 2001. The resulting rules require analysis of socioeconomic and environmental impacts of forestry projects but do not go as far as the European Union originally proposed (Sagemüller 2006).

In recent years, discussions on the role of forests in the climate regime have taken place mainly under the heading of REDD. Through a REDD mechanism, countries with tropical forests could be compensated for efforts to reduce deforestation and forest degradation. The idea of creating incentives for reducing deforestation is hardly contested but there is disagreement about the design of a REDD mechanism, with a key question being whether such a mechanism should be market based or fund based or a combination thereof (Stockwell, Hare, and Macey 2009). Although REDD provides an opportunity to cost-effectively reduce emissions through tackling deforestation, its specific design may lead to either positive or negative effects on biodiversity (Harvey, Dickson, and Kormos 2010). In particular, there are concerns that REDD might be concentrated on forested areas that are cheapest to protect rather than biodiversity "hotspots" (Grainger et al. 2009).

Governments have frequently sought to manage interlinkages between the two regimes. First, a number of decisions have been adopted by the conferences of the parties to the conventions on biodiversity and climate change, which have been considered instrumental in highlighting biodiversity concerns in decisions under the climate convention (Yamin and Depledge 2004). Second, at the request of the parties to the biodiversity convention, a joint liaison group has been established to share information and coordinate activities between the secretariats of the climate and biodiversity conventions, yet its mandate precludes it from becoming involved in rule development on overlapping issues (van Asselt 2011a). Third, parties to the biodiversity convention have established several ad hoc technical expert groups to provide scientific and technical advice on climate change and biodiversity interlinkages. Although these initiatives have created awareness of such interlinkages and fostered cooperation between actors involved in both regimes, they have failed so far to reduce tensions about the role of forests in climate mitigation activities.

The Cartagena Protocol on Biosafety and the WTO
The relationship between the global environmental regime of the Cartagena Protocol on Biosafety under the biodiversity convention and the WTO's Agreement on Application on Sanitary and Phytosanitary Measures (SPS agreement) has been much scrutinized (Isaac and Kerr 2003; Gupta 2002, 2008; Oberthür and Gehring 2006c; Safrin 2002; Young 2008). The protocol seeks to ensure safe transboundary transfers of GMOs by calling for the "advance informed agreement" of an importing country prior to trade in certain GMOs. Thus, it offers the prospects for trade in GMOs to be restricted under certain conditions. The notion of advance informed agreement of an importer encapsulates two important areas of potential trade-environment interlinkages. The first is the criteria that should underpin decisions about GMO imports, in particular, whether importing country trade restrictions can invoke the precautionary principle as justification. The second is the information to be disclosed by prospective exporters about GMOs in the agricultural commodity trade because such disclosure can have trade-restrictive effects.

With regard to these two elements, the European Union and most developing countries long demanded, first, that precautionary restrictions on GMO trade should be permitted under the Cartagena Protocol, given scientific uncertainties over harm, and second, that detailed information needs to be made available to potential importers about specific genetically modified varieties entering the global agricultural commodity trade. These demands were strongly opposed by an influential coalition of GMO-producing and -exporting countries, including the United States, Canada, Australia, Argentina, and Uruguay, most of whom have not ratified the Cartagena Protocol. These countries have long argued that trade restrictions are only justifiable when "sound" scientific evidence of harm caused by GMOs is available, and hence they oppose restrictions based on the precautionary principle. They also oppose demands for disclosure of comprehensive information about specific GMOs in the commodity trade to minimize disruption to such trade. These differences are articulated not only in negotiating Cartagena Protocol rules, but also within the context of the SPS regime and its dispute settlement mechanism (for detailed analysis, see Gupta 2002, 2008, and the references therein).

How have these conflicts been resolved in the two regimes (and in the interlinkages between them)? Views strongly differ about the path-breaking nature of the compromise language on precaution finally included in the Cartagena Protocol. These range from a view that its inclusion has broken new ground in institutionalizing the precautionary principle in global environmental governance (Isaac and Kerr 2003) to arguments that its scope is not fundamentally different from precautionary action already permitted under the SPS agreement (Gupta 2002; Safrin 2002). If so, it is in how reliance on precaution is interpreted and institutionalized within specific regulatory contexts that a conflict (or lack thereof) between these regimes can be ascertained (see also Millstone and van Zwanenberg 2003). It can also be illustrative to see if protocol interpretations are challenged as WTO incompatible, by whom, and if such challenges are being upheld. Many observers expected that a recent United States–led WTO challenge to the European Union's precautionary GMO regulatory regime would shed light on the issue of compatibility of the Cartagena Protocol with WTO rules. The WTO Dispute Settlement Body, however, avoided taking a position on this, holding that because not all parties to the WTO dispute were parties to the protocol (the United States has neither ratified the protocol nor the biodiversity convention), the protocol's provisions had no bearing on the dispute (Lieberman and Grey 2008).

Nonetheless, the United States, even as a nonparty to the protocol, continues to have influence on the development of its rules, partly because it is the largest transgenic crop producer globally, hence, its concerns have to be addressed, and partly because countries who are parties, such as Mexico, often articulate positions similar to those of the United States in this global forum (see Gupta 2010b for details).

With regard to information disclosure about GMO trade, the protocol's evolving obligations currently require only a minimal statement: that bulk agricultural commodity shipments declare that they "may contain" GMOs (Cartagena Protocol 2000, article 18.2.a). Most GMO exporters, such as the United States, Canada, or Australia, have strenuously opposed strengthening these disclosure requirements. As a result, current obligations are market following rather than market forcing.

They are neither detailed enough to force changes to the ways in which the commodity trade is currently organized, nor do they require GMO-exporting country practices to change (see Gupta 2010b for a detailed elaboration of this claim).

The protocol also calls for various categories of biosafety information to be disclosed by all parties to an online Biosafety Clearing-House. This includes information such as which GMO varieties are approved in producer countries and domestic biosafety laws and contact persons responsible for import decisions (CBD 2008a, 2008b, 2008c). The original intent of such disclosure was to further a right to know of potential GMO-importing countries. Because these countries are, however, the main parties to the protocol, the burden of disclosure has ironically fallen on them rather than on GMO producers. Most of these producers have not ratified the agreement and are not bound by its information disclosure obligations. As a result, paradoxically, it is now mainly importing countries that are systematically compiling and disclosing information about domestic biosafety laws and contact persons to the Biosafety Clearing-House. Yet disclosure of such information can have trade-facilitating rather than trade-restrictive effects because it shifts the burden of ferreting out such information (which is essential for trade to occur) away from GMO exporters (this argument is developed in detail in Gupta 2010a).

As this discussion implies, it is far from clear that protocol norms and rules, as now evolving and being institutionalized, are in conflict with global trade obligations. We turn in the next section to why this may be the case.

Explanations

In this section, we argue that the regime-specific developments we discussed above can be explained by the dominance of liberal environmentalism in a broader governance context. This dominance reflects a certain degree of normative collusion across overlapping regimes, yet it is becoming contested to a greater or lesser extent across the cases we examine—a trend that is partly mirrored in recent regime changes.

The UN Climate Regime and the WTO

Our explanation of the nature and resolution of institutional interactions in this case is related to underlying norm complexes in global governance. Bernstein (2001, 2002) and Eckersley (2008, 2009) argue that the compromise of liberal environmentalism has dominated debates on over-laps between trade and environment from the early 1990s onwards. It has replaced the dominance of slightly more trade-skeptical discourses on the environment-economy nexus, for instance, the sustainable development debate of the 1980s over the extent to which economic growth could be decoupled from environmental degradation (Eckersley 2009). Liberal environmentalism implies a focus "on efficiency gains from technological innovation" (Eckersley 2008, 2), claiming synergy among trade and environment while sidelining detrimental aspects.

With regard to climate change, this norm translates into the formula that trade liberalization promotes climate protection, for example, by enabling the diffusion of climate-friendly goods and the efficient allocation of resources. This strongly market-friendly norm embraces the promotion of market policy tools, such as emissions trading, over "command-and-control" regulation, that is, top-down domestic policies and measures (Eckersley 2009). The reluctance of the United States and developing countries to embrace trade-restrictive policies and measures can thus be seen as embedded in liberal environmentalism. Developing countries have repeatedly held that such policies represent a form of "green protectionism" (Thomas 2004, 17). From the inception of the climate convention, US negotiators have tried to feed market-friendly elements into the climate regime, often characterizing regulatory approaches as interventionist (Schreurs 2004). The European Union has eventually adopted aspects of this market-friendly stance, most visible in the 2005 launch of its own emissions trading system.

The dominance of liberal environmentalism reveals itself not only in rejections of certain regulatory proposals in the climate regime, but also in "self-censorship" (Eckersley 2008, 2). Ever since the Kyoto summit, negotiators have refrained from tabling ambitious proposals for trade-restrictive climate protection measures such as mandatory coordination of policies. The establishment of the WTO dispute settlement mechanism further intensified this "chill effect" (Stilwell and Tuerk 1999; Eckersley 2004), as parties to the UN climate regime try to avoid legal challenges and potential sanctions against them.

However, recent developments suggest that the dominance of liberal environmentalism is increasingly challenged in the climate-trade arena. Eckersley (2009, 15) discerns a "generic counter-discourse" in statements from environmental NGOs or green think tanks. Moreover, recent years have witnessed a shift of interests in US domestic politics toward more trade-restrictive approaches—but in order to safeguard domestic industries rather than for environmental reasons. For instance, in June 2009, the House of Representatives adopted a provision obliging the president to impose tariffs or offsetting requirements on goods from countries that do not take comparable action to limit greenhouse gas emissions. The European Union has also begun considering similar measures (van Asselt and Brewer 2010). The debate on border carbon adjustments in both regimes hints at a possible questioning of the dominance of liberal environmentalism in this area. This development, however, might also simply reflect that safeguarding industries and jobs has become a primary concern rather than implying a shift away from a broader liberal norm.

The UN Climate Regime and the Convention on Biological Diversity

The inclusion of sinks in the CDM is inextricably intertwined with the emergence of market-based flexibility mechanisms in the climate regime in general. In the early 1990s, primarily the United States proposed using emissions trading in international climate policy. As mentioned in the section on the climate regime and the WTO, the European Union was then still heavily opposed to the use of market mechanisms (van Asselt and Gupta 2009). The United States has also been influential in the CDM sinks discussion, despite its withdrawal from engagement in the Kyoto Protocol by 2003 (Boyd, Corbera, and Estrada 2008,). Referring to the United States and the other countries in the Umbrella Group, Bäckstrand and Lövbrand (2006, 61) identify flexibility, cost effectiveness, and a "seductive narrative of 'maximized synergies'" as the key elements of the "legitimizing discourse" for the inclusion of sinks in the CDM. Northern countries favoring the inclusion of sinks in the CDM have emphasized the cost-saving potential of expanding the scope of the mechanism, and countries in the South have highlighted the various (economic and noneconomic) co-benefits, including financial and technology transfers.

These legitimizing discourses reflect again a norm of liberal environmentalism that favors market-based approaches to environmental governance (Bernstein 2002). Nonetheless, these discourses remain contested. This is evident from ongoing efforts by different actors, such as the European Union and the Alliance of Small Island States (Boyd, Corbera, and Estrada 2008), to push for consideration of biodiversity concerns in the climate regime and efforts by parties to the biodiversity convention to manage interlinkages with the climate regime in various ways.

Bäckstrand and Lövbrand (2006, 64) argue that persisting concerns expressed about sinks in the CDM are part of a "critical discourse" that contests a dominant market-oriented liberal environmentalist perspective. This critical discourse not only emphasizes the potentially negative effects on biodiversity and ecosystem protection, but also draws attention to the social and equity aspects of including sinks in the CDM—as well as the use of market-based mechanisms more generally. The discourse, which found support among NGOs as well as some developing countries, provides an explanation for the requirement to conduct a socioeconomic and environmental analysis of CDM forestry projects (Bäckstrand and Lövbrand 2006). It also provides an explanation for the push to include biodiversity considerations in a REDD mechanism by NGOs, scientists, and a number of parties to the climate convention (e.g., Grainger et al. 2009), and the efforts of parties to the biodiversity convention to engage with the climate regime in drawing attention to complex climate-biodiversity interlinkages.

Nonetheless, interlinkage management efforts by parties to the biodiversity convention have yielded little effect to date. This is related, first, to the fact that any effort by actors in one regime to influence rule development in another is limited by the extent to which memberships and mandates of the two are congruent. An important barrier is that the United States is a party to the climate convention but not to the biodiversity convention. A broad mandate for the climate convention secretariat to cooperate with the biodiversity convention secretariat could give the impression that national sovereignty is eroded by "importing" concepts or rules from the biodiversity convention (Wolfrum and Matz 2003). Second, efforts to incorporate biodiversity concerns in the CDM in essence seek to alter the mechanism's market-based nature, and indirectly challenge the dominance of the norm of neoliberal environmentalism. Although it is clear that biodiversity concerns are not completely ignored in the climate regime, parties have yet to give biodiversity protection a more prominent place.

The Cartagena Protocol on Biosafety and the WTO

Evolving interlinkages between the Cartagena Protocol and the WTO reflect clear interest differences among major coalitions of actors on trade-restrictive GMO policies, more so than in the other two cases. Advance informed agreement as a way to govern GMO trade derives from the longer established notion of prior informed consent, relied on in a global context to govern trade in hazardous wastes and restricted chemicals. Prior informed consent is intended to be a compromise between an outright ban on risky trade and the opposite extreme of caveat emptor, or "let the buyer beware" (Mehri 1988, see also Gupta 2010b).

Yet, in the GMO case, the overarching normative context within which this compromise is interpreted and institutionalized remains contested (also Wolf 2000). On the one hand, informed consent can be interpreted as a way to ensure freedom from harm by providing the basis for trade restrictions (through comprehensive information disclosure and institutionalizing precaution as a justification for restrictions). On the other hand, it can be interpreted as a vehicle to ensure efficiency in decision making and thus to facilitate trade (through minimal information disclosure and institutionalizing sound science as a basis for trade decisions).

As seen earlier, the first interpretation is promoted globally by the European Union and many developing countries, and the second by those advocating unrestricted trade in GMOs, including the United States and other GMO-producing countries (Gupta 2010b). In an important way, this normative conflict is not merely between the WTO and the Cartagena Protocol but transcends both institutions. Thus, the norms and rules of each regime—how far-reaching they are and how far the shadow of the WTO extends in shaping those of the protocol—cannot be analyzed in isolation from the overall contested global normative context that shapes developments in both regimes.

Notwithstanding this, the manner in which institutional interlinkages are interpreted and institutionalized suggests a dominance of a liberal environmentalist approach to global risk governance. Even though the potential for the Cartagena Protocol to institutionalize a more trade-restrictive interpretation of a precautionary approach to GMO transfers (vis-à-vis the SPS agreement) remains alive, to date the protocol's institutionalization of precaution appears not to have directly influenced transatlantic disputes about GMO trade in a manner detrimental to trade.

This is partly because the specific use of the protocol as a bulwark against the WTO has been rendered difficult due to diverse memberships across the two regimes. In essence, the fact that key GMO exporters, such as the United States, are missing from the protocol has ensured that the protocol's normative contribution to global risk governance (or its potential to question dominant global governance norms) is weakened. This is also palpable in how information disclosure relating to the GMO trade is being institutionalized. As noted previously, these obligations, a raison d'être to negotiate the protocol, remain minimally trade disruptive and may even have trade-facilitating effects (Gupta 2010a, 2010b).

As a result, there is arguably a prioritization of market access over biosafety considerations in the existing global risk governance architecture for GMO trade, an outcome aligned with an overarching market-liberal bias in global environmental governance. Even the notion of advance informed agreement as the central global risk governance mechanism for GMOs can be seen as aligned with such a liberal perspective, one that elevates (individual or collective) choice about whether to import potentially risky substances over regulatory approaches such as outright bans.

Even so, the dominance of a market-liberal approach to global environmental and risk governance does not go wholly unchallenged in this area. In comparison to the other two cases, in the GMO case, a market-liberal approach faces the strongest challenge *and* asserts the strongest counter pressure. The transatlantic GMO trade conflict reflects fundamentally diverging views in the European Union and the United States about appropriate aims of GMO governance, as well as the means needed to fulfill them. In contrast to its self-censorship in the climate-trade case, the European Union has consistently pushed for trade-restrictive policies in all fora in the biosafety policy domain, even as the United States has consistently opposed these (see also Levidow 2007; Lieberman and Grey 2008). This normative tension endures partly because the very existence of a governance problem remains fundamentally contested. The United States position is that there is no need for GMO governance because GMOs are not intrinsically hazardous (again in contrast to acknowledgment by all of the need for at least some action on climate change). Given the United States' view in the GMO case, it is harder to push back against privileging open markets and trade facilitation, even though the European Union, supported by many developing countries, continually demands the flexibility to do so.

Conclusions and Outlook

This chapter has analyzed horizontal institutional interlinkages by stressing their embeddedness in overarching global norms. It has sought to explain the nature of institutional interlinkages in various policy domains and their consequences for the development of specific global regimes. We explored, in particular, how certain dominant global norms shape the nature and resolution of institutional interlinkages and conflicts. Our aim was to add to the evolving scholarly literature on interlinkages by offering a norm-based explanation of this much-studied phenomenon.

By highlighting how institutional interlinkages reflect or are, at the very least, sites for contestation over overarching global norms, we combined behavioral and structural elements in our analysis. We illustrated the benefit of this approach through analyzing institutional interlinkages across global environmental and trade domains, finding that all of them are characterized, to greater or lesser extent, by a dominance of liberal environmentalism, even as this dominance is incomplete and remains contested in important ways by key actors.

Our findings illustrate a number of interesting (comparative) claims. First, in the case of the climate-trade interaction, we postulate a dominance of a liberal environmental perspective that privileges market approaches through the influence of the United States and through self-censorship of the European Union. By contrast, we see that in the case of climate-biodiversity institutional interlinkages, there is no inherent conflict between the global institutions designed to address each subject matter. Yet it is in the processes of rule making and rule implementation, particularly within the climate regime, that inter-institutional conflict may manifest itself. Thus, the question whether climate-induced incentives to reduce deforestation will be synergetic or conflictive with biodiversity objectives will reveal itself in the design of the still new REDD mechanism. The most overt global normative conflict persists in the case of biosafety-trade interlinkages. It is in this issue area that market-liberal approaches to risk governance are open to the most serious challenge (given the European Union's desire for stringent regulation). It is also here, however, that any challenge to market liberalism is fiercely resisted (given the United States' view that GMOs do not merit stringent global regulation).

Our analysis also raises two important questions calling for further inquiry: first, if regime-specific developments (and respective institutional interlinkages) are related to certain dominant global norms, to what extent does this relation cut both ways? More concretely: can the persistence of inter-regime conflicts or the specific nature of their resolution contribute to global normative evolution? This might be the case, for example, if norms that question a dominant market liberal approach succeed in becoming institutionalized within the climate, biodiversity, or biosafety regimes.

Second, can one posit a dominance of liberal environmentalism when the "coalitions of the willing" vary considerably across issue areas, in particular, when developing countries end up on different ends of a normative spectrum promoting or resisting liberal approaches? For example, in the climate case, different interests and a push back against a market-liberal approach tend to line up the European Union against the United States *and* developing countries. This is similar regarding climate-biodiversity interlinkages. Yet in the GMO case, developing countries tend to ally themselves with the European Union's calls for precaution and stringent information disclosure in potentially restricting GMO trade. What do such varying (North-South) issue-specific interests suggest about our overarching claim that liberal environmentalism tends to dominate in global environmental governance?

Our claims thus require further theoretical and empirical consolidation. Such inquiry could be informed, for example, by recent insights into "discursive institutionalism" (Schmidt 2008; Arts and Buizer 2009) as well as identification of causal mechanisms that lead from norm collusion to conflicts among actors. Apart from the explanatory elements we emphasize here, additional theoretical approaches to the study of regime interlinkages may adopt different causal variables from theories of international relations and other disciplines, such as power constellations, institutional dynamics, and problem structures (Hasenclever, Mayer, and Rittberger. 1997). Furthermore, such approaches could scrutinize domestic drivers that shape country positions in regime interlinkages. Such analytical frameworks might for example draw on theories of multilevel governance (Putnam 1988; Scharpf 2002).

Scholars could further explore the extent to which horizontal interlinkages alter regime compliance rates and practices in diverse national contexts (see, e.g., Falkner and Gupta 2009) or how they shape the ultimate problem-solving effectiveness of regimes (Sprinz 2005). New approaches could also help explain the emergence of interlinkages or they could concentrate on options for and barriers to "interplay management" (Oberthür and Stokke 2011). In addition, given the proliferation of transnational institutions in global environmental governance (Pattberg, this book, chapter 5; Bäckstrand et al., this book, chapter 6), interlinkages involving such new mechanisms and actors may soon become a promising research object.

Finally, more work is necessary that goes beyond dyadic relations between distinct regimes and adopts an overarching or metaperspective on institutional interlinkages. Only recently have scholars of international relations identified regime complexes (Alter and Meunier 2009; Keohane and Victor 2011; Raustiala and Victor 2004) and the fragmentation of global environmental governance as timely research objects (Zelli 2011a). Biermann et al. (2009, 2010) introduced a first typology of different degrees of fragmentation and explored the pros and cons of advanced fragmentation in global climate governance. Similar to the aforementioned open questions on dyadic interlinkages, future research can address theoretical gaps relating to explanations for fragmentation or its variation across domains, or scrutinize management of fragmentation in a given issue area. In doing so, it may also shed light on an underlying question that motivated our analysis here: to what extent is fragmentation shaped by overarching normative collusion. And, conversely, future studies could scrutinize how fragmentation may induce normative changes in global governance.

References

Alter, Karen J., and Sophie Meunier. 2009. The Politics of International Regime Complexity. *Perspectives on Politics* 7 (1):13–24.

Arts, Bas, and Marleen Buizer. 2009. Forests, Discourses, Institutions: A Discursive-Institutional Analysis of Global Forest Governance. *Forest Policy and Economics* 11 (5–6):340–347.

Bäckstrand, Karin, and Eva Lövbrand. 2006. Planting Trees to Mitigate Climate Change: Contested Discourses of Ecological Modernization, Green Governmentality, and Civic Environmentalism. *Global Environmental Politics* 6 (1):50–75.

Bernstein, Steven. 2001. *The Compromise of Liberal Environmentalism.* New York: Columbia University Press.

Bernstein, Steven. 2002. Liberal Environmentalism and Global Environmental Governance. *Global Environmental Politics* 2 (3):1–16.

Bhagwati, Jagdish, and Petros C. Mavroidis. 2007. Is Action against US Exports for Failure to Sign Kyoto Protocol WTO-Legal? *World Trade Review* 6 (2):299–310.

Biermann, Frank, and Rainer Brohm. 2005. Implementing the Kyoto Protocol without the United States: The Strategic Role of Energy Tax Adjustments at the Border. *Climate Policy* 4 (3):289–302.

Biermann, Frank, Philipp Pattberg, Harro van Asselt, and Fariborz Zelli. 2009. The Fragmentation of Global Governance Architectures: A Framework for Analysis. *Global Environmental Politics* 9 (4):14–40.

Biermann, Frank, Fariborz Zelli, Philipp Pattberg, and Harro van Asselt. 2010. The Architecture of Global Climate Governance: Setting the Stage. In *Global Climate Governance beyond 2012: Architecture, Agency and Adaptation*, ed. Frank Biermann, Philipp Pattberg, and Fariborz Zelli, 15–24. Cambridge, UK: Cambridge University Press.

Boyd, Emily, Esteve Corbera, and Manuel Estrada. 2008. UNFCCC Negotiations (pre-Kyoto to COP-9): What the Process Says about the Politics of CDM-Sinks. *International Environmental Agreement: Politics, Law and Economics* 8 (2): 95–112.

Brewer, Thomas L. 2003. The Trade Regime and the Climate Regime: Institutional Evolution and Adaptation. *Climate Policy* 3 (4):329–341.

Brewer, Thomas L. 2004. The WTO and the Kyoto Protocol: Interaction Issues. *Climate Policy* 4 (1):3–12.

Cartagena Protocol. 2000. *Cartagena Protocol on Biosafety to the Convention on Biological Diversity: Text and Annexes.* Montreal: Secretariat of the Convention on Biological Diversity.

CBD (Convention on Biological Diversity). 2008a. *Monitoring and Reporting under the Protocol (Article 33): Analysis of Information Contained in the First National Reports.* Note by the Executive Secretary. UNEP/CBD/BS/COP-MOP/4/13, 4 February.

CBD. 2008b. *Operation and Activities of the Biosafety Clearing-House.* Note by the Executive Secretary. UNEP/CBD/BS/COP-MOP/4/3, 29 February.

CBD. 2008c. *Report of the 2007 Survey of Biosafety Clearing-House Users.* Note by the Executive Secretary. UNEP/CBD/BS/COP-MOP/4/INF/20, 3 March.

CBD Secretariat. 2003. *Interlinkages between Biological Diversity and Climate Change: Advice on the Integration of Biodiversity Considerations into the Implementation of the United Nations Framework Convention on Climate Change and Its Kyoto Protocol.* Montreal: Secretariat of the CBD.

Chambers, W. Bradnee. 2008. *Interlinkages and the Effectiveness of Multilateral Environmental Agreements.* Tokyo: United Nations University Press.

Chambers, W. Bradnee, Joy A. Kim, and Claudia ten Have. 2008. Institutional Interplay and the Governance of Biosafety. In Institutional Interplay: Biosafety and Trade, ed. Oran R. Young, W. Bradnee Chambers, Joy A. Kim, and Claudia ten Have, 3–18. Tokyo: United Nations University Press.

Charnovitz, Steve. 2003. Trade and Climate: Potential Conflicts and Synergies. In Beyond Kyoto: Advancing the International Effort against Climate Change, ed. Pew Center on Global Climate Change, 141–170. Arlington, VA: Pew Center on Global Climate Change.

Conca, Ken. 2006. *Governing Water: Contentious Transnational Politics and Global Institution Building.* Cambridge, MA: MIT Press.

Cottier, Thomas, Olga Nartova, and Sadeq Z. Bigdeli, eds. 2009. *International Trade Regulation and the Mitigation of Climate Change.* Cambridge, UK: Cambridge University Press.

Eckersley, Robyn. 2004. The Big Chill: The WTO and Multilateral Environmental Agreements. *Global Environmental Politics* 4 (2):24–40.

Eckersley, Robyn. 2008. A Critical Constructivist Theory of Regime Interplay: The Kyoto Protocol and the World Trade Organization. Paper Presented at the

Annual Convention of the International Studies Association. San Francisco, 26–29 March.

Eckersley, Robyn. 2009. Understanding the Interplay between the Climate and Trade Regimes. In Climate and Trade Policies in a post-2012 World, ed. United Nations Environment Programme (Benjamin Simmons) and the ADAM Project (Harro van Asselt and Fariborz Zelli), 11–18. Geneva: UNEP.

Falkner, Robert, and Aarti Gupta. 2009. Limits of Regulatory Convergence: Globalization and GMO Politics in the South. *International Environmental Agreement: Politics, Law and Economics* 9 (2):113–133.

Frankel, Jeffrey. 2005. Climate and Trade: Links between the Kyoto Protocol and WTO. *Environment* 47 (7):8–19.

Grainger, Alan, Douglas H. Boucher, Peter C. Frumhoff, William F. Laurance, Thomas Lovejoy, Jeffrey McNeely, Manfred Niekisch, et al. 2009. Biodiversity and REDD at Copenhagen. *Current Biology* 19 (21):R974–R976.

Gupta, Aarti. 2002. Advance Informed Agreement: A Shared Basis to Govern Trade in Genetically Modified Organisms? *Indiana Journal of Global Legal Studies* 9 (1):265–281.

Gupta, Aarti. 2008. Global Biosafety Governance: Emergence and Evolution. In Institutional Interplay: Biosafety and Trade, ed. Oran R. Young, W. Bradnee Chambers, Joy A. Kim and Claudia ten Have, 19–46. Tokyo: United Nations University Press.

Gupta, Aarti. 2010a. Transparency to What End? Governing by Disclosure through the Biosafety Clearing-House. *Environment and Planning C: Government and Policy* 28 (2):128–144.

Gupta, Aarti. 2010b. Transparency as Contested Political Terrain: Who Knows What about the Global GMO Trade and Why Does It Matter? *Global Environmental Politics* 10 (3):32–52.

Harvey, Celia A., Barney Dickson, and Cyril Kormos. 2010. Opportunities for Achieving Biodiversity Conservation through REDD. *Conservation Letters* 3 (1):53–61.

Hasenclever, Andreas, Peter Mayer, and Volker Rittberger. 1997. *Theories of International Regimes*. Cambridge, UK: Cambridge University Press.

Herr, Richard A., and Edmund Chia. 1995. The Concept of Regime Overlap: Toward Identification and Assessment. In *Overlapping Maritime Regimes: An Initial Reconnaissance*, ed. Bruce Davis, 11–26. Hobart, Australia: Antarctic Climate and Ecosystems Cooperative Research Centre and Institute of Antarctic and Southern Ocean Studies.

Intergovernmental Panel on Climate Change (IPCC). 2002. *Climate Change and Biodiversity*. Geneva: IPCC.

Isaac, Grant E., and William A. Kerr. 2003. Genetically Modified Organisms at the World Trade Organisation: A Harvest of Trouble. *Journal of World Trade* 37 (6):1083–1095.

Ismer, Roland, and Karsten Neuhoff. 2007. Border Tax Adjustment: A Feasible Way to Support Stringent Emission Trading. *European Journal of Law and Economics* 24 (2):137–164.

Jacquemont, Frédéric, and Alejandro Caparrós. 2002. The Convention on Biological Diversity and the Climate Change Convention 10 Years after Rio: Towards a Synergy of the Two Regimes? *Review of European Community & International Environmental Law* 11 (2):139–180.

Keohane, Robert O., and David G. Victor. 2011. The Regime Complex for Climate Change. *Perspectives on Politics* 9 (1):7–23.

Krasner, Stephen D. 1983. *International Regimes*. Ithaca, NY: Cornell University Press.

Levidow, Les. 2007. The Transatlantic Agbiotech Conflict as a Problem and Opportunity for EU Regulatory Policies. In *The International Politics of Genetically Modified Food: Diplomacy, Trade, and Law*, ed. Robert Falkner, 118–137. Basingstoke, UK: Palgrave Macmillan.

Lieberman, Sarah, and Tim Grey. 2008. The World Trade Organization's Report on the EU's Moratorium on Biotech Products: The Wisdom of the US Challenge to the EU in the WTO. *Global Environmental Politics* 8 (1):33–52.

Mehri, Cyrus. 1988. Prior Informed Consent: An Emerging Compromise for Hazardous Exports. *Cornell International Law Journal* 21:365–389.

Meinshausen, Malte, and Bill Hare. 2003. Sinks in the CDM: After the Climate, Biodiversity Goes Down the Drain. An Analysis of the CDM Sinks Agreement at CoP-9. Retrieved from http://www.greenpeace.org/international/Global/international/planet-2/report/2006/3/sinks-in-the-cdm-after-the-cl-2.pdf.

Millstone, Eric, and Patrick van Zwanenberg. 2003. Food and Agricultural Biotechnology Policy: How Much Autonomy Can Developing Countries Exercise? *Development Policy Review* 21 (5):655–667.

Oberthür, Sebastian, and Thomas Gehring. 2006a. Conceptual Foundations and Institutional Interaction. In *Institutional Interaction in Global Environmental Governance: Synergy and Conflict among International and EU Policies*, ed. Sebastian Oberthür and Thomas Gehring, 19–52. Cambridge, MA: MIT Press.

Oberthür, Sebastian, and Thomas Gehring, eds. 2006b. *Institutional Interaction in Global Environmental Governance: Synergy and Conflict among International and EU Policies*. Cambridge, MA: MIT Press.

Oberthür, Sebastian, and Thomas Gehring. 2006c. Institutional Interaction in Global Environmental Governance: The Case of the Cartagena Protocol and the World Trade Organization. *Global Environmental Politics* 6 (2):1–31.

Oberthür, Sebastian, and Olav Schram Stokke, eds. 2011. *Managing Institutional Complexity: Regime Interplay and Global Environmental Change*. Cambridge, MA: MIT Press.

Putnam, Robert D. 1988. Diplomacy and Domestic Politics: The Logic of Two-Level Games. *International Organization* 42 (3):427–460.

Raustiala, Kal, and David G. Victor. 2004. The Regime Complex for Plant Genetic Resources. *International Organization* 58 (2):277–309.

Rosendal, G. Kristin. 2001. Impacts of Overlapping International Regimes: The Case of Biodiversity. *Global Governance* 7 (1):95–117.

Ruggie, John Gerard. 1998. What Makes the World Hang Together? Neo-utilitarianism and the Social Constructivist Challenge. *International Organization* 52 (4):855–885.

Safrin, Sabrina. 2002. Treaties in Collision? The Biosafety Protocol and the World Trade Organization Agreements. *American Journal of International Law* 96 (3):606–628.

Sagemüller, Imke. 2006. Forest Sinks under the United Nations Framework Convention on Climate Change and the Kyoto Protocol: Opportunity or Risk for Biodiversity? *Columbia Journal of Environmental Law* 31 (2): 189–242.

Scharpf, Fritz W. 2002. Regieren im europäischen Mehrebenensystem. Ansätze zu einer Theorie. *Leviathan* 30 (1):65–93.

Schmidt, Vivien A. 2008. Discursive Institutionalism: The Explanatory Power of Ideas and Discourse. *Annual Review of Political Science* 11 (1):303–326.

Schreurs, Miranda A. 2004. The Climate Change Divide: The European Union, the United States, and the Future of the Kyoto Protocol. In *Green Giants? Environmental Policies of the United States and the European Union*, ed. Norman J. Vig and Michael G. Faure, 207–230. Cambridge, MA: MIT Press.

Selin, Henrik, and Stacy D. VanDeveer. 2003. Mapping Institutional Linkages in European Air Pollution Politics. *Global Environmental Politics* 3 (3):14–46.

Sprinz, Detlef F. 2005. Regime Effectiveness. The Next Wave of Research. Paper Prepared for the 2005 Berlin Conference on the Human Dimensions of Global Environmental Change, 2–3 December.

Stilwell, Matthew T., and Elisabeth Tuerk. 1999. Trade Measures and Multilateral Agreements: Resolving Uncertainty and Removing the WTO Chill Factor. WWF International Discussion Paper, November.

Stockwell, Claire, Bill Hare, and Kirsten Macey. 2009. Designing a REDD Mechanism: The TDERM Triptych. In *Climate Law and Developing Countries: Legal and Policy Challenges for the World Economy*, ed. Benjamin J. Richardson, Yves Le Bouthillier, Heather McLeod-Kilmurray, and Stepan Wood, 151–177. Cheltenham, UK: Edward Elgar.

Stokke, Olav Schram, ed. 2001a. *Governing High Seas Fisheries: The Interplay of Global and Regional Regimes*. Oxford: Oxford University Press.

Stokke, Olav Schram. 2001b. *The Interplay of International Regimes. Putting Effectiveness Theory to Work*. FNI Report No. 14/2001. Lysaker, Norway: Fridtjof Nansen Institute.

Stokke, Olav Schram. 2004. Trade Measures and Climate Compliance: Institutional Interplay between WTO and the Marrakesh Accords. *International Environmental Agreement: Politics, Law and Economics* 4 (4):339–357.

Thomas, Urs P. 2004. Trade and the Environment: Stuck in a Political Impasse at the WTO after the Doha and Cancún Ministerial Conferences. *Global Environmental Politics* 4 (3):9–21.

Underdal, Arild. 2006. Determining the Causal Significance of Institutions. Accomplishments and challenges paper prepared for the Institutional Dimensions of Global Environmental Change Project Synthesis Conference, Nusa Dua, Bali, Indonesia, 6–9 December.

United Nations Framework Convention on Climate Change (UNFCCC). 2006. *Decision 16/CMP.1, Land Use, Land-Use Change, and Forestry* (30 March 2006). UN Doc. FCCC/KP/CMP/2005/8/Add.3.

van Asselt, Harro. 2011a. Dealing with the Fragmentation of Global Climate Governance: Legal and Political Approaches in Interplay Management. In *Managing Institutional Complexity: Regime Interplay and Global Environmental Change*, ed. Sebastian Oberthür and Olav Schram Stokke, 59–85. Cambridge, MA: MIT Press.

van Asselt, Harro. 2011b. Integrating Biodiversity in the Climate Regime's Forest Rules: Options and Tradeoffs in Greening REDD Design. *Review of European Community & International Environmental Law* 11 (2):139–149.

van Asselt, Harro, and Thomas Brewer. 2010. Addressing Competitiveness and Leakage Concerns in Climate Policy: An Analysis of Border Adjustment Measures in the US and the EU. *Energy Policy* 38 (1):42–51.

van Asselt, Harro, and Joyeeta Gupta. 2009. Stretching Too Far? Developing Countries and the Role of Flexibility Mechanisms beyond Kyoto. *Stanford Environmental Law Journal* 28 (2):311–379.

van Asselt, Harro, Joyeeta Gupta, and Frank Biermann. 2005. Advancing the Climate Agenda: Exploiting Material and Institutional Linkages to Develop a Menu of Policy Options. *Review of European Community & International Environmental Law* 14 (3):255–264.

van Asselt, Harro, Francesco Sindico, and Michael A. Mehling. 2008. Global Climate Change and the Fragmentation of International Law. *Law & Policy* 30 (4):423–449.

Wolf, Amanda. 2000. Informed Consent: A Negotiated Formula for Trade in Risky Organisms and Chemicals. *International Negotiation* 5 (3):485–521.

Wolfrum, Rüdiger, and Nele Matz. 2003. *Conflicts in International Environmental Law*. Berlin: Springer.

Yamin, Farhana, and Joanna Depledge. 2004. *The International Climate Change Regime: A Guide to Rules, Institutions, and Procedures*. Cambridge, UK: Cambridge University Press.

Young, Oran R. 1996. Institutional Linkages in International Society: Polar Perspectives. *Global Governance* 2 (1):1–24.

Young, Oran R. 2002. *The Institutional Dimensions of Environmental Change: Fit, Interplay, and Scale*. Cambridge, MA: MIT Press.

Young, Oran R. 2008. Deriving Insights from the Case of the WTO and the Cartagena Protocol. In Institutional Interplay: Biosafety and Trade, ed. Oran R. Young, W. Bradnee Chambers, Joy A. Kim, and Claudia ten Have, 131–158. Tokyo: United Nations University Press.

Young, Oran R., Leslie A. King, and Heike Schroeder. 2008. Institutions and Environmental Change: Principal Findings, Applications, and Research Frontiers. Cambridge, MA: MIT Press.

Zelli, Fariborz. 2007. The World Trade Organization: Free Trade and Its Environmental Impacts. In Handbook of Globalization and the Environment, ed. Khi V. Thai, Dianne Rahm, and Jerrell D. Coggburn, 177–216. London: Taylor and Francis.

Zelli, Fariborz. 2011a. The Fragmentation of the Global Climate Governance Architecture. Wiley Interdisciplinary Reviews: Climate Change 2 (2):255–270.

Zelli, Fariborz. 2011b. Regime Conflicts and Their Management in Global Environmental Governance. In Managing Institutional Complexity: Regime Interplay and Global Environmental Change, ed. Sebastian Oberthür and Olav Schram Stokke, 199–226. Cambridge, MA: MIT Press.

Zelli, Fariborz, Frank Biermann, Philipp Pattberg, and Harro van Asselt. 2010. The Consequences of a Fragmented Climate Governance Architecture: A Policy Appraisal. In Global Climate Governance beyond 2012: Architecture, Agency and Adaptation, ed. Frank Biermann, Philipp Pattberg, and Fariborz Zelli, 25–34. Cambridge, UK: Cambridge University Press.

Zelli, Fariborz, and Harro van Asselt. 2010. The Overlap between the UN Climate Regime and the World Trade Organization: Lessons for post-2012 Climate Governance. In Global Climate Governance beyond 2012: Architecture, Agency and Adaptation, ed. Frank Biermann, Philipp Pattberg, and Fariborz Zelli, 79–96. Cambridge, UK: Cambridge University Press.

9

International-Domestic Linkages and Policy Convergence

Per-Olof Busch, Aarti Gupta, and Robert Falkner

Links between international and domestic policy choices are now a mainstay of global environmental governance research. A common analytical concern is the question of whether multilevel policy linkages fuel convergence of national policies. Most debates about convergence have taken place within a broader literature on globalization and its effects on domestic policies. In this chapter, we draw on this broader literature to consider whether and how linkages between international and domestic levels result in convergence or divergence of domestic policies across different countries. Drawing on two policy areas—governance of genetically modified organisms (GMOs) in developing countries and renewable electricity policies in the European Union—we analyze dynamics of environmental policy convergence across multiple jurisdictions, thereby focusing on linkages between policy decisions at the international and domestic levels.

Debates about such multilevel policy linkages have to date been predominantly concerned with whether convergence is occurring and in what direction. Thus, much theoretical and empirical attention has focused on documenting convergence toward more stringent ("race to the top") or less stringent ("race to the bottom") levels of domestic regulation. We argue here that this prevailing dichotomy in much of the literature is overly simplistic and fails to capture the messiness of international-domestic linkages. Through analysis of our cases, we highlight how and why convergence pressures from globalization are being counteracted in specific instances, resulting in persistent policy diversity. This holds even when strong economic and political pressures exist for convergence at the domestic level (as in the GMO case) and when a relatively advanced level of regulatory convergence may have already been achieved (as in the renewable energy case).

The analysis proceeds in three steps. In the next section, we review recent literature on global environmental governance, globalization, and comparative environmental politics that engages with multilevel policy linkages and the prospects for convergence versus divergence. The subsequent sections explore and explain convergence versus divergence in the two areas of global environmental governance analyzed here: GMO governance and renewable energy. In concluding, we draw out broader implications of our analysis for the study of policy linkages in multilevel environmental governance and identify elements of a future research agenda.

Conceptualization

The concept of convergence is apt to provoke confusion among researchers because of differences in its empirical and normative use (Holzinger, Jörgens, and Knill 2008). It is important, therefore, to clarify at the outset how we use it in this chapter. Since the early 1980s, convergence has been seen as "the tendency of societies to grow more alike, to develop similarities in structures, processes, and performances" (Kerr 1983, 3; see also Drezner 2001, 53). Thus, we understand convergence as a process (Bennett 1991). Our focus here is on convergence in regulatory policies, or simply, regulatory convergence. By this, we mean the growing similarity of institutional frameworks and regulatory approaches in a substantive policy area.

Much of the literature on the convergence effects of globalization on national policies has focused on whether globalization fuels cultural, social, political, or economic homogeneity (for an excellent and comprehensive overview, see Guillén 2001). In particular, a key concern is whether economic globalization, that is, horizontal economic interlinkages between countries relating to trade, investment, and financial flows, are making national policies more similar across the world.

Convergence effects of economic globalization have been studied in different geographical settings and for diverse issue areas. Scholars have, for example, examined domestic responses to economic globalization in the field of macroeconomic policies (e.g., Keohane and Milner 1996), environmental policies (e.g., Holzinger, Knill, and Arts 2008), regulatory policies (e.g., Vogel and Kagan 2004), and the broader development of political-economic institutions in capitalist systems (e.g., Hall and Soskice 2001). Most empirical studies have been conducted on convergence effects in the developed world, particularly in a European or transatlantic setting, with only a few studies exploring convergence in developing countries (e.g., Jordana and Levi-Faur 2005; Simmons and Elkins 2004;

Biersteker 1992; for overviews see Heichel, Pape, and Sommerer 2005; Drezner 2001).

Newer convergence studies have sought to extend this predominantly economic perspective to include analysis of interaction between political globalization and domestic policies as well. Their main analytical focus is multilevel or vertical policy linkages between international and domestic policy making and the effects of such vertical linkages on policy convergence across different jurisdictions. More precisely, they explore whether and to what extent international and transnational public and private actors and institutions contribute to crossnational policy convergence (e.g., Holzinger, Knill, and Arts 2008).

So far, the findings on convergence, whether resulting from economic or political globalization, are generally mixed. Of those studies that have observed policy convergence, some have noted convergence toward the lowest level of regulatory stringency, whereas others find convergence toward the most ambitious policies (for overviews see Guillén 2001; Heichel, Pape, and Sommerer 2005). Other studies reveal limited policy convergence, persisting policy divergence, and regulatory diversity.

This latter finding is in line with a longstanding alternative interpretation of how globalization affects domestic politics. In this view, globalization does not necessarily fuel convergence but can coexist with, or even enhance, regulatory diversity (for an overview see Guillén 2001). As some globalization analysts have long emphasized, globalization is not necessarily a straightforward story of homogenization (Appadurai 1996; Rosenau 1995; Garrett 1998) nor is convergence always attainable or desirable (Sykes 1999). Global economic integration can coexist with a significant degree of diversity in national policies (Wade 1996; Hirst and Thomas 1999), with convergence occurring only under restrictive conditions (Hay 2000; Hall and Soskice 2001). Furthermore, the mediating force of domestic institutions and domestic politics can result in a persisting diversity in national responses to globalization (e.g., Weiss 1998).

In the remainder of the chapter, we build on this latter tradition in the globalization-convergence literature to further two aims. First, we analyze how convergence or divergence evolves, thereby focusing on the mechanisms that translate globalization pressures into domestic policy choices. Second, we show how international and domestic factors work together, overlap, or compete with each other in shaping national policy responses, including convergence or lack thereof.

Experiences

Our detailed analysis of convergence dynamics within the two issue areas that we examine reveals that policy diversity, rather than convergence, is the norm so far. This section describes this persisting policy diversity and the next explains why this is the case.

With regard to global GMO governance, an early expectation in the literature followed a similar trajectory to that of broader globalization and convergence discussions. Early analyses suggested that globalization of agricultural biotechnology might fuel policy convergence in diverse national contexts, with the debate centering on whether such convergence would be toward the more restrictive precautionary approach of the European Union or the more permissive sound-science regulatory approach of the United States. Some scholars originally hypothesized that a nascent "trading-up" effect between the European Union and the United States was at work, which would lead to greater convergence between the two main contenders in international norm creation on GMO trade, in the direction of the more stringent EU approach (Prakash and Kollman 2003; Young 2003). Others pointed to corporate interest in convergence between global regulatory approaches and the global pressures on states to create "common means by which to identify and manage risks associated with genetically modified products" (Newell 2003, 63).

This expectation, however, has now given way to a more widespread recognition that such trading up is not taking place. Instead, the diverse US and European regulatory approaches continue to coexist in an international context (Falkner 2007; Gupta 2008; Murphy and Levidow 2006). Analysts have thus noted a trend toward regulatory "polarization" in global GMO governance (Bernauer 2003; Drezner 2007). As a result, the United States and the European Union have sought to export their competing regulatory models to the South (Bernauer and Aerni 2007). This has resulted in a shift in the research focus toward the question of whether and how international regulatory polarization is influencing domestic GMO policy choices in developing countries. Again, however, there has been an expectation that countries of the South might be forced to choose between one and the other of these two approaches, hence, that binary convergence toward one or the other approach is likely.

In analyzing these dynamics here, we focus on GMO policy processes and outcomes in three key players in the emerging field of agricultural biotechnology in the developing world: Mexico, China, and South Africa. The three countries all participate in the GMO trade as importers of genetically modified crops (with varying trade relationships with the United States and the European Union), requiring them to mediate competing global influences, including transatlantic regulatory polarization, in determining domestic policy directions. Each of the three countries has embraced biotechnology at the highest levels as part of an overall thrust toward technology promotion, trade liberalization, and a desire for greater integration into world markets. All three countries can also be considered early adopters and developers of genetically modified crops in the South, with China the most advanced in its biotechnology capacity. Furthermore, all three countries were among the first to develop domestic biosafety regulations, given their trajectory of GMO research and development dating back to the late 1980s. Even so, putting into place a domestic biosafety governance system remains an ongoing process in all three countries. Different laws and regulations have come into existence but domestic struggles over their implementation and legal revision continue. It is significant that these laws do not suggest either a sweeping policy convergence trend or a clear political commitment to either the permissive US or restrictive EU regulatory approach to GMOs. In other words, they do not result in a race to the top or a race to the bottom in policy choices across these three contexts.

Our field research and extensive interviews with various stakeholders on recent policy choices in all three countries reveal, instead, a combination of restrictive and permissive policies relating to GMO adoption and use (Falkner and Gupta 2009; Gupta and Falkner 2006). Key instances of restrictive policy measures include, for example, Mexico's blanket moratorium on the introduction of genetically modified maize into the environment, South Africa's on-off moratorium on approvals of genetically modified commodity imports into the country until their impact on domestic production and non-GMO export markets could be assessed, and China's consistently stricter labeling laws (and correspondingly stringent threshold standards for presence of genetically modified ingredients in food and feed). All of these are more aligned with a restrictive EU approach.

However, each of the three countries has also adopted a permissive approach in certain areas of GMO policy, particularly related to genetically modified cotton, but also to important food crops such as maize in Mexico and South Africa and soybean and rice in China. Despite its moratorium on deliberate release of genetically modified maize into the environment, Mexico permits increasing amounts of GMO-based maize imports from the United States. China gave permission to genetically modified soybean imports that did not meet stringent certification and documentation requirements after a protracted dispute with the United States over its demands for such documentation. And South Africa has resisted calls for broad-based GMO labeling requirements, pushing ahead with a broader research and development strategy for commercializing an ever-growing number of genetically modified crops.

Given this mix of permissive and restrictive policy choices in each of these three countries, we find that, contrary to expectations of broad policy convergence, policy choices in each case exhibit a significant degree of diversity. As a result, we argue that GMO policies in the South do not simply follow the binary logic of United States–European Union regulatory divergence. Instead, the countries examined here have adopted elements from both regulatory approaches and are steering a course that suggests substantial regulatory diversity in the South.

Just as GMO policies diverge across national contexts, so do national renewable energy policies differ in Europe. This divergence is striking insofar as convergence could be reasonably expected here, given that the European Commission began attempts to harmonize national renewable energy policies in EU member countries as early as 1998. The diversity is evident from the fact that two distinct approaches characterize national policies to promote renewable electricity in Europe. The first approach are feed-in tariffs, which oblige electricity producers, suppliers, or consumers to buy renewable electricity that operators of renewable energy plants feed into the grid, and to pay a fixed price for this electricity. Usually, the fixed price is set for a period of several or up to twenty years and is paid by electricity suppliers to domestic operators of renewable energy plants. The second approach are green certificate systems, which typically oblige electricity producers, suppliers, or consumers to acquire a minimum quantity of green certificates that are issued for the production, supply, or consumption of a specified amount of renewable electricity. The minimum quantity is defined as a share of the electricity production or consumption in percent or as amount in absolute units. Compliance is usually monitored and noncompliance sanctioned, for example, by fines or denial of access to the electricity grid. Most green certificates are tradable at least in domestic trading schemes. Hence, the minimum quantity of certificates can be acquired by producing or consuming renewable electricity or by buying surplus green certificates on the green certificate market. These approaches differ insofar as the latter privileges market mechanisms and incentives as a way to promote renewable energy use.

In 2008, twenty European governments supported renewable electricity through feed-in tariffs, whereas ten European governments used green certificate systems as the main policy instrument (Coenraads et al. 2008). This division of European renewable energy policy approaches into two blocs is a relatively recent phenomenon. Until the late 1990s, a strong convergence process toward feed-in tariffs could be observed. Between 1989 and 1998, feed-in tariffs were introduced in fourteen European countries, and green certificate systems—apart from some smaller pilot projects—were largely absent. This situation changed in 1999, when the Dutch government introduced a green certificate system for the promotion of renewable electricity generation (Busch 2003; Busch and Jörgens 2009). Since then, green certificate systems are more commonly introduced by European governments than feed-in tariffs.

Between 1999 and 2003, feed-in tariffs were abolished altogether in four European countries, namely Italy, Denmark, Sweden, and Belgium. As a result, the international proliferation of feed-in tariffs has slowed down since 1998 (Busch 2003; Busch and Jörgens 2009). The net increase in the number of countries in which feed-in tariffs were implemented was only six between 1999 and 2008 or less than half the number that came into being in the ten years before (fourteen). At the same time, the international proliferation of green certificate systems had started and the number of adoptions rose to ten in 2008.

The slowdown in convergence toward feed-in tariffs and the simultaneous increase in adoption of green certificate systems imply a relationship between these processes. An analysis of the decisions to abolish feed-in tariffs supports this interpretation. In fact, feed-in tariffs were not only abolished but also replaced by green certificate systems. In 1999, the Italian government decided against the renewal of the 1992 regulations that laid down the prescriptions for its feed-in tariff and instead introduced a green certificate system. In 2001, eight years after its adoption, the feed-in tariff in Poland was replaced by a green certificate system. In 2003, the Swedish government eventually followed through on its announcement from 2000 to put an end to the feed-in tariff and introduced a green certificate system. In 2001, the government of Belgium reviewed the feed-in tariff, which was adopted in 1993, and eventually shifted to a green certificate system, too. The Spanish government also considered replacing the feed-in tariff by a green certificate system but eventually refrained from doing so.

How can these dynamics be explained? What forces shape the outcomes in each of the two areas of multilevel environmental policy discussed previously? In particular, what prevents straightforward policy convergence toward single (or binary) regulatory approaches, that is, what explains the persisting policy diversity? We turn to these questions next.

Explanations

The dynamics of policy linkages in the two environmental issue areas examined previously suggest that alleged convergence pressures from globalization are not as clear-cut and unidirectional as is often assumed.

In the case of GMO policies in the South, a dominant assumption in the literature is that developing countries are likely to follow either the permissive US or restrictive EU model in their domestic policy choices (that is, that policy convergence to one of these two nodes is inevitable for developing countries). Such accounts largely privilege international influences in explaining domestic policy choices, suggesting that the transatlantic conflict shapes and limits Southern policy options (Drezner 2005; Bernauer 2003; Paarlberg 2001). Drezner (2005, 856) suggests, for example, "Divergent preferences among large states . . . lead these actors to attract as many allies as possible. In a bipolar distribution of power [that is, between the United States and the European Union], the result is a bifurcation of policies, but strong policy convergence at two different nodes."

Yet policy choices in key developing countries—Mexico, China, and South Africa—reveal that GMO policies in the South do not simply follow this binary logic of US-EU regulatory polarization. Instead, elements from both regulatory approaches have been adopted in ways that allow the three countries to steer a course between both ends of a contested international regulatory spectrum. We explain this persisting regulatory diversity by the complex mix of international and domestic imperatives that shape policy choices, and argue that the transatlantic conflict between US and EU regulatory approaches to GMOs has in fact created room to maneuver in key developing countries, rather than serving to restrict their policy choices (Falkner and Gupta 2009).

Restrictive elements of GMO policy in each of these three countries can be explained, partly, by domestic imperatives fueled by a combination of concerns relating to biosafety, domestic price stabilization, access to export markets, and overall economic effects of genetically modified crops on agricultural production and practices in each country. Such diverse concerns have given rise to a variety of actor coalitions that have sought to either promote or slow down commercialization of such crops. Environmental campaigners and some state officials have been strengthened by the creation of an international biosafety regime. When the introduction of genetically modified crops poses a threat to agricultural exports or domestic producers, these actors have been able to bolster their efforts to enforce stricter biosafety oversight with economic arguments, often against a broadly promotional stance by key state institutions (see in more detail Falkner and Gupta 2009).

This has been helped by the fact that all three countries have participated in negotiating, and have subsequently ratified, a global biosafety agreement, the Cartagena Protocol on Biosafety under the Convention on Biological Diversity, which allows for precautionary restrictions on GMO trade. Mexico ratified the protocol in 2003, although its North American Free Trade Agreement (NAFTA) partners, the United States and Canada, were vocal opponents of the protocol during its negotiation, and neither has since ratified it. One reason for Mexican ratification was to give domestic policy makers the option to withstand NAFTA and global trade imperatives through reference to their global biosafety rights and obligations, should it become necessary to do so (Gupta and Falkner 2006). China's decision to accede to the biosafety protocol reflects the growing strength of domestic elite support for a strengthened national biosafety agenda, but also to China's broader desire to achieve full integration into international society (Falkner 2006). South African ratification of the protocol came just before the World Summit on Sustainable Development in 2002. Despite an ambivalent attitude toward the protocol among elements of the country's political elite, its ratification was seen as an important signal of South Africa's support for multilateral environmental processes as it played host to the key sustainability event of the decade.

In addition to domestic biosafety obligations acquired as a result of protocol ratification, trade imperatives in each country pull in different directions as well, ensuring that GMO policies in the South do not simply reflect either a restrictive or a permissive GMO regulatory approach. In the case of China, a concern with traditional commodity exports to European and other Asian markets calls for a restrictive approach to GMO trade and production, whereas growing reliance on US imports has simultaneously created incentives for a more permissive approach. The opening of China's farm markets has led to a sharp rise in agricultural imports, including of genetically modified soybeans (mainly from the United States) for domestic food processing and animal feed. It has also, however, increased exports (to the European Union and Japan) in areas where China maintains a leading position, such as rice. Neither of these two external influences has come to dominate GMO policy. Instead, the gradual enmeshment of China's agricultural system with world markets has led to a complex web of dependencies, with mixed effects on domestic regulatory choices. For example, rice export markets in the European Union or Japan have been threatened by the domestic testing of genetically modified rice varieties in China, and dependence on genetically modified soybean imports from the United States has boosted domestic support for genetically modified soybean production.

Over time, China's regulatory approach has evolved from being largely permissive and product based in the 1990s to a more comprehensive, precautionary, and process-based model that is closer to that of the European Union than the United States. At the same time, however, support for basic and applied research in agricultural biotechnology has increased dramatically and new genetically modified crop developments are still expected to enter the market in the near future. Conflicting international influences are employed by domestic interest groups— within and outside the core state—to shape GMO policy, without either side gaining control over the regulatory process. China's biotechnology policy has thus come to include elements of both US-style and EU-style regulation, and the political leadership is intent on maintaining a finely balanced approach that secures a significant degree of political choice within competing external constraints.

For Mexico and South Africa, trade with the United States and other GMO producer countries is, again, an important influence on regulatory directions. Furthermore, unlike with China, a concern with losing EU markets for nongenetically modified agricultural commodity exports is not as strong a countervailing force in these two countries. One could assume then that the neoliberal thrust of economic and agricultural policy in each case would push both countries more unambiguously in the direction of openness in GMO research and trade, aligned with the US approach. This is, however, not entirely the case. In Mexico, the key counterforce to an overall permissive GMO policy is to be found in cultural attitudes to biodiversity, and particularly the perception of a unique relationship between Mexico and maize. Imports of genetically modified maize from the United States (for the animal feed and food-processing industry) continue to fuel domestic controversy and conflict, given that maize is at the center of the national diet and is of enormous cultural, political, and social significance. Concerns over ecological, social, and health consequences of importing or planting genetically modified maize thus force Mexico, too, to balance openness and caution in its domestic policy.

A similar dynamic is observable in South Africa. Its main trading partners for genetically modified crops such as maize and soybean are the United States and Argentina. As a result, various varieties of genetically modified maize and soybean approved in these two producer countries have also received rapid approval in South Africa to be imported for use in the food, feed, and processing sector. Although Europe is South Africa's most important agricultural trading partner, this is not yet the case for crops subject to genetic modification. These trade dynamics have resulted, therefore, in a largely permissive and open policy toward GMO imports in South Africa. Competing trade and market access considerations arise, however, vis-à-vis other African countries that push toward a more restrictive approach. South Africa is an important agricultural exporter of white and yellow maize to countries in the region, many of whom are opposed to transgenic crop imports. This is an important countervailing influence to an otherwise permissive approach to production and commercialization of these crops.

Given such diverse domestic and international trade and biosafety imperatives, greater regulatory diversity thus exists in the developing world than the binary logic of policy polarization around the EU versus US approaches implies. Our explanations for this persisting regulatory diversity are thus in line with analysts who question a convergence trend because of globalization, also in the field of GMO politics. In a relatively early and prescient analysis of how the global regulatory landscape was shaping GMO policy choices in the South, Millstone and van Zwanenberg (2003, 655) suggested that "the tendency towards convergence is severely attenuated." They also suggested that persisting scientific conflicts with regard to GMO safety provide leeway to countries, including in the South, to pursue divergent choices (on this point, see also Gupta 2004). Others who have emphasized divergent rather than convergent responses in the South have attributed this diversity almost wholly to global trade imperatives (Clapp 2006) rather than to scientific conflicts, international treaty obligations, or domestic politics more generally.

Our detailed empirical scrutiny of GMO policies in these countries reveals, however, that regulatory diversity in the South is related not only, as Millstone and van Zwanenberg (2003) posit, to interpretive flexibility of international obligations or persisting scientific uncertainties and conflicts over biosafety that allow differing local interpretations and policy choices. It also reflects the fact that globalization produces potentially conflicting dynamics and competing trade imperatives within each country. These dynamics interact with domestic politics and priorities in a way that allows multiple domestic nodes of power and actor coalitions to negotiate policy directions that combine restrictive and permissive regulatory directions. What we see, then, is not convergence of one of the two regulatory nodes but rather a "sustainable diversity" (Millstone and van Zwanenberg 2003, 664) in GMO policies in the South. Our explanation highlights that international factors such as trade links and bilateral relations pose constraints but also enable domestic interests within and outside a state to pursue competing policy objectives. There is no straightforward transmission of international imperatives into domestic ones. Their relevance in a domestic context depends on the mobilization of domestic interests, the creation of actor coalitions, and the alliances formed with key representatives of state institutions. The net result of this complex international-domestic interaction is a more diverse field of regulatory policies and outcomes than is commonly acknowledged in debates on environmental policy convergence.

Contestation between two regulatory approaches at the international level also plays a crucial role in explaining evolution of renewable electricity support policies in Europe. The disruption of an already advanced convergence process toward feed-in tariffs and the emergence of two blocs of countries with different regulatory approaches in the promotion of renewable electricity can be traced back to a dismissive attitude of major European institutions toward feed-in tariffs (Busch 2003; Busch and Jörgens 2009). For instance, the European Commission emphasized in several official policy documents, reports, and public statements that it perceived green certificate systems as the only suitable model for promoting renewable electricity in a liberalized European energy market and that feed-in tariffs were not a viable policy alternative (see Lauber 2001 for a similar assessment; Hinsch 1999; European Commission 1998a, 1998b). Its dismissive attitude toward feed-in tariffs culminated in an explicit rejection of this instrument during the preparation of a draft directive for the harmonization of renewable electricity policies in Europe.

Due to concerns about possible undesirable effects on trade and competition within the liberalized European electricity market, the European Commission concluded in 1998, "The move from a fixed tariff approach towards one based on trade and competition is at some stage inevitable" (European Commission 1998a, 17). In the very same document, the

European Commission made clear that green certificate systems qualify as such an approach (European Commission 1998a). The final directive on the harmonization of renewable electricity support schemes in Europe, which was adopted in 2001, did not explicitly prefer one policy approach to the other and postponed the final decision about a harmonization that, as of November 2011, was not yet made (European Parliament and European Council 2001). This decision should be based, however, on evaluation criteria that in the view of the European Commission evidently favor green certificate systems, namely, the compatibility of the support scheme with European market, competition, and trade rules. The efforts of the European Commission mattered in the decisions to adopt green certificate systems in the United Kingdom (Mitchell and Anderson 2000), Denmark (Meyer 2003; Ruby 2001), and the Netherlands (Junginger et al. 2004; van Beek and Benner 1998), as well as the considerations about introducing this instrument in Ireland (Ireland 2000), which was ultimately not executed.

Overall, these examples support the conclusion by Lauber that parallel to the discussions of green certificate systems in preparation of the European directive, "several states prepared such systems at the domestic level, on the assumption that this was the best market approach and with the expectation that a European market for RECs [green certificates] would develop in the near future" (Lauber 2001, 8). Together with the finding that four countries replaced feed-in tariffs by green certificate systems, these observations support the interpretation that international contestation of feed-in tariffs through the European Commission contributed to the disruption of convergence toward feed-in tariffs.

In addition, decisions and activities of other actors at the European level supported the introduction of green certificate systems to the disadvantage of feed-in tariffs. More precisely, in 1998 the European Parliament rejected the proposal for harmonizing renewable electricity support policies by introducing a Europeanwide feed-in tariff that was put forward by the Social Democrats and Greens. In the same year, the German energy company Preussen Elektra brought action against the German feed-in tariff at a German court that forwarded this case to the European Court of Justice. Preussen Elektra argued that the German feed-in tariff constitutes a state subsidy that violates European competition laws and contravenes the principles of the internal European electricity market. In March 2001, the European Court of Justice dismissed the action but pointed out possible implications for international trade by warning that the German feed-in tariffs "were capable, at least potentially, of hindering intra-Community trade" (Court of Justice of the European Communities 2001, 2). In sum, these decisions and the related developments created political and legal uncertainty about the future of feed-in tariffs by signaling to European countries that feed-in tariffs were being dismissed as an appropriate instrument for the promotion of renewable electricity in Europe and that important and influential European institutions favored green certificate systems. As a result, the convergence process toward feed-in tariffs has slowed down.

At a more general level, the advancing economic and political integration within Europe in the area of energy policy contributed to the influence of the European Commission and other European institutions. The concerns about the compatibility of renewable energy support policies with the rules of free market economies, competition, and trade, which ultimately contributed to the favorable attitude toward green certificate systems and the dismissive attitude toward feed-in tariffs, only gained importance after the liberalization of the internal European electricity market in 1996. The liberalization led to an economic integration of hitherto isolated domestic electricity markets and introduced the principles of free trade and international competition in European energy policies (Lauber 2001). In other words, the liberalization and thus the progressing economic integration within Europe introduced criteria for the assessment of renewable electricity support policies that favored the adoption of green certificate systems, given that they were perceived to be more compatible with the rules of the internal electricity market than feed-in tariffs. At the same time, the liberalization largely shifted regulatory competencies in the regulation of electricity markets from the national to the supranational level. This shift increased the influence of the European Commission on domestic policy decisions even without actually making use of its regulatory competencies but only by announcing and promoting its preferred approach.

Previous convergence studies have also identified such forces as shaping convergence. Nonetheless, the case of renewable electricity support policies suggests that the predominant perspective on political and economic integration in the convergence literature must be revised. In general, political and economic integration are conceptualized as drivers for policy convergence. Although the convergence of green certificate systems supports this conceptualization, the obvious interference of this process with the convergence of feed-in tariffs calls for a more differentiated conceptualization. The analysis here shows that in the case of feed-in tariffs the increasing political and economic integration in fact impaired a further convergence process by providing favorable circumstances for an alternative, competing model. Hence, if two competing models (regulatory polarization) exist in a given policy area, economic and political integration may facilitate convergence toward one model and—as a side effect—impede the convergence of the other model, even if the convergence of the latter is already well advanced. This can result in persisting policy divergence rather than convergence toward any one approach. This also suggests that the conceptual and empirical discussion in the convergence literature about whether a race to the bottom or race to the top is to be expected falls short of acknowledging other potential outcomes.

Finally, the analysis also indicates that the perceived compatibility of feed-in tariffs and green certificate systems with rules of free trade and competitiveness is a critical factor shaping the dynamics of policy convergence. As such, it suggests that compatibility of policies with prevailing global and supranational norms deserves more attention in developing propositions about the direction of policy convergence (see also Zelli, Gupta and van Asselt, this book, chapter 8, on norms in horizontal institutional interactions). This is highlighted in the GMO case as well, where dominant norm complexes relating to market liberalization and trade have been a crucial factor in shaping global governance regimes but have, so far, failed to produce outright policy convergence in directions supportive of such norms (see also Gupta 2010).

Conclusions and Outlook

Numerous studies of globalization have suggested that greater global economic and political integration is pushing countries toward policy convergence. This chapter has sought to shed light on the nature and limits of this convergence trend and to investigate the ways in which international and supranational forces are transmitted into the domestic context of regulatory policies in a multilevel environmental governance context.

As we find here, the dichotomous perspective on policy consequences of globalization that prevails in the convergence literature and mainly distinguishes between a race to the top and a race to the bottom is oversimplified and does not adequately capture empirical realities. The specific experiences examined here suggest, instead, that contestation of regulatory approaches at the international level either counteract convergence pressures from globalization or provide room for policy diversity.

More precisely, international contestation over appropriate regulatory approaches, or "regulatory polarization" (Bernauer 2003), can interact with domestic priorities to prevent policy convergence toward one or the other international approach, despite various economic and political pressures promoting convergence. In the case of GMOs, the competition at the global level between a more permissive regulatory approach in the United States and a more restrictive approach in the European Union has, we argued, created room for maneuver that key developing countries have exploited in defining their policy choices. Consequently, greater regulatory diversity exists in GMO regulation in developing countries than is typically assumed.

In this case, despite overarching pressures to facilitate trade and enhance competitiveness in international markets—in line with the dominance of what Bernstein (2002) has referred to as the "compromise of liberal environmentalism"—GMO policy choices are not all moving in this direction. This is not even the case in countries such as China, South Africa, and Mexico, where technology policies are closely aligned with global norms of trade facilitation and market liberalization. Furthermore, international norm contestation may create circumstances in which a trend toward policy convergence is impeded, as with the example of renewable energy support policies where the perceived incompatibility of feed-in tariffs with prevailing norms of free trade and international competition slowed down the convergence toward that regulatory approach. Hence, convergence studies need to pay closer attention to consensual or polarized policy models toward which convergence is expected and to domestic mechanisms and policy processes that mitigate or counteract external convergence pressures. As such, the analysis here indicates a need for further scrutiny of the specific policy choices that countries make under the influence of globalizing forces and the role played by domestic dynamics as a mediating force.

Our analysis gives rise to at least three questions that are worth investigating in future research. First, it suggests that more conceptual and empirical scrutiny needs to be devoted to international regulatory polarization within a policy area, its causes, and its effects on the evolution of domestic policies. Second, it suggests that more conceptual and empirical attention has to be directed to the interactions between convergence pressures resulting from globalization and—possibly counteracting—linkages between international and domestic policy processes. Third, it indicates a need for further empirical scrutiny of our claim here that, instead of fueling convergence, dominant global norms of trade liberalization and greater integration of markets coexist with domestic policy diversity.

References

Appadurai, Arjun. 1996. *Modernity at Large: Cultural Dimensions of Globalization*. Minneapolis: University of Minnesota Press.

Bennett, Colin J. 1991. What Is Policy Convergence and What Causes It? *British Journal of Political Science* 21 (2):215–233.

Bernauer, Thomas. 2003. *Genes, Trade, and Regulation: The Seeds of Conflict in Biotechnology*. Princeton, NJ: Princeton University Press.

Bernauer, Thomas, and Philipp Aerni. 2007. Competition for Public Trust: Causes and Consequences of Extending the Transatlantic Biotech Conflict to Developing Countries. In *The International Politics of Genetically Modified Food: Diplomacy, Trade, and Law*, ed. Robert Falkner, 138–154. Basingstoke, UK: Palgrave Macmillan.

Bernstein, Steven. 2002. Liberal Environmentalism and Global Environmental Governance. *Global Environmental Politics* 2 (3):1–16.

Biersteker, Thomas J. 1992. The Triumph of Neo-classical Economics in the Developing World: Policy Convergence and the Basis of Governance in the International Economic Order. In *Governance without Government: Order and Change in World Politics*, ed. James N. Rosenau and Ernst-Otto Czempiel, 102–131. Cambridge, UK: Cambridge University Press.

Busch, Per-Olof. 2003. *Die Diffusion von Einspeisevergütungen und Quotenmodellen: Konkurrenz der Modelle in Europa*. [The Diffusion of Fixed Feed-in Tariffs and Quotas: Competition of Models in Europe] Berlin: Environmental Policy Research Centre.

Busch, Per-Olof, and Helge Jörgens. 2009. *Governance by Diffusion. International Policy Coordination in the Era of Globalization*. Doctoral dissertation. Berlin: Freie Universität Berlin.

Clapp, Jennifer. 2006. Unplanned Exposure to Genetically Modified Organisms: Divergent Responses in the Global South. *Journal of Environment & Development* 15 (1):3–21.

Coenraads, Rogier J. A. C., Mario Ragwitz, Gustav Resch, Inga Konstantiniaviciute, and Tomás Chadim. 2008. *Renewable Energy Country Profiles*. Utrecht: Ecofys Netherlands.

Court of Justice of the European Communities. 2001. An Obligation to Purchase at Minimum Prices Does not Constitute State Aid Merely Because It Is Imposed by Statute. Press release No 10/2001, 13 March.

Drezner, Daniel W. 2001. Globalization and Policy Convergence. *International Studies Review* 3 (1):53–78.

Drezner, Daniel W. 2005. Globalization, Harmonization, and Competition: The Different Pathways to Policy Convergence. *Journal of European Public Policy* 12 (5):841–859.

Drezner, Daniel W. 2007. *All Politics Is Global: Explaining International Regulatory Regimes*. Princeton, NJ: Princeton University Press.

European Commission. 1998a. *Electricity from Renewable Energy Sources and the Internal Electricity Market.* Brussels: European Commission.

European Commission. 1998b. *Report to the Council and the European Parliament on Harmonisation Eequirements Directive 96/92/EC Concerning Common Rules for the Internal Market in Electricity.* Brussels: European Commission.

European Parliament and European Council. 2001. Directive 2001/77/EC of the European Parliament and of the Council of 27 September 2001 on the Promotion of Electricity Produced from Renewable Energy Sources in the Internal Electricity Market.

Falkner, Robert. 2006. International Sources of Environmental Policy Change in China: The Case of Genetically Modified Food. *Pacific Review* 19 (4): 473–494.

Falkner, Robert. 2007. The Political Economy of "Normative Power" Europe: EU Environmental Leadership in International Biotechnology Regulation. *Journal of European Public Policy* 14 (4):507–526.

Falkner, Robert, and Aarti Gupta. 2009. The Limits of Regulatory Convergence: Globalization and GMO Politics in the South. *International Environmental Agreement: Politics, Law and Economics* 9 (2):113–133.

Garrett, Geoffrey. 1998. *Partisan Politics in the Global Economy.* Cambridge, UK: Cambridge University Press.

Guillén, Mauro F. 2001. Is Globalization Civilizing, Destructive, or Feeble? A Critique of Five Key Debates in the Social Science Literature. *Annual Review of Sociology* 27:235–260.

Gupta, Aarti. 2004. When Global Is Local: Negotiating Safe Use of Biotechnology. In *Earthly Politics: Local and Global in Environmental Governance,* ed. Sheila Jasanoff and Marybeth Long-Martello, 127–148. Cambridge, MA: MIT Press.

Gupta, Aarti. 2008. Global Biosafety Governance: Emergence and Evolution. In *Institutional Interplay: Biosafety and Trade,* ed. Oran R. Young, W. Bradnee Chambers, Joy A. Kim and Claudia ten Have, 19–46. Tokyo: United Nations University Press.

Gupta, Aarti. 2010. Transparency as Contested Political Terrain: Who Knows What about the Global GMO Trade and Why Does It Matter? *Global Environmental Politics* 10 (3):32–52.

Gupta, Aarti, and Robert Falkner. 2006. The Influence of the Cartagena Protocol on Biosafety: Comparing Mexico, China, and South Africa. *Global Environmental Politics* 6 (4):23–55.

Hall, Peter A., and David Soskice, eds. 2001. *Varieties of Capitalism: The Institutional Foundations of Comparative Advantage.* Oxford: Oxford University Press.

Hay, Colin. 2000. Contemporary Capitalism, Globalization, Regionalization and the Persistence of National Variation. *Review of International Studies* 26 (4): 509–531.

Heichel, Stephan, Jessica Pape, and Thomas Sommerer. 2005. Is There Convergence in the Convergence Literature? An Overview of Empirical Literature in the Field of Policy Convergence. *Journal of European Public Policy* 12 (5): 817–840.

Hinsch, Christian. 1999. Aufgeschoben ist nicht aufgehoben. Europäische Einspeiserichtlinie wird hinter den Kulissen weiter diskutiert. *Neue Energie* 3:56–58.

Hirst, Paul, and Grahame Thomas. 1999. *Globalization in Question: The International Economy and the Possibilities of Governance*. 2nd ed. Cambridge, UK: Polity Press.

Holzinger, Katharina, Helge Jörgens, and Christoph Knill. 2008. State of the Art: Conceptualising Environmental Policy Convergence. In *Environmental Policy Convergence in Europe: The Impact of International Institutions and Trade*, ed. Katharina Holzinger, Christoph Knill, and Bas Arts, 7–30. Cambridge, UK: Cambridge University Press.

Holzinger, Katharina, Christoph Knill, and Bas Arts, eds. 2008. *Environmental Policy Convergence in Europe? The Impact of International Institutions and Trade*. Cambridge, UK: Cambridge University Press.

Ireland. 2000. *Strategy for Intensifying Wind Energy Deployment*. Dublin: Renewable Energy Strategy Group.

Jordana, Jacint, and David Levi-Faur. 2005. The Diffusion of Regulatory Capitalism in Latin America: Sectoral and National Channels in the Making of a New Order. *Annals of the American Academy of Political and Social Science* 598 (1):102–124.

Junginger, Martin, Susanne Agterbosch, Andre Faaij, and Wim C. Turkenburg. 2004. Renewable Electricity in the Netherlands. *Energy Policy* 32 (9):1053–1073.

Keohane, Robert O., and Helen V. Milner, eds. 1996. *Internationalization and Domestic Politics*. Cambridge, UK: Cambridge University Press.

Kerr, Clark. 1983. *The Future of Industrial Societies: Convergence or Continuing Diversity?* Cambridge, MA: Harvard University Press.

Lauber, Volkmar. 2001. The Different Concepts of Promoting RES-Electricity and their Political Careers. Paper read at 2001 Berlin Conference on the Human Dimensions of Global Environmental Change, "Global Environmental Change and the Nation State," Berlin, 7–8 December.

Meyer, Niels I. 2003. European Schemes for Promoting Renewables in Liberalised Markets. *Energy Policy* 31 (7):665–676.

Millstone, Erik, and Patrick van Zwanenberg. 2003. Food and Agricultural Biotechnology Policy: How Much Autonomy Can Developing Countries Exercise? *Development Policy Review* 21 (5–6):655–667.

Mitchell, Catherine, and Teresa Anderson. 2000. The Implications of Tradable Green Certificates for the UK. Science and Technology Policy Research: London Science and Technology Policy Research.

Murphy, Joseph E., and Les Levidow. 2006. *Governing the Transatlantic Conflict over Agricultural Biotechnology: Contending Coalitions, Trade Liberalisation, and Standard Setting.* London: Routledge.

Newell, Peter. 2003. Globalization and the Governance of Biotechnology. *Global Environmental Politics* 3 (2):56–71.

Paarlberg, Robert L. 2001. *The Politics of Precaution: Genetically Modified Crops in Developing Countries.* Baltimore: The Johns Hopkins University Press.

Prakash, Aseem, and Kelly L. Kollman. 2003. Biopolitics in the EU and the US: A Race to the Bottom or Convergence to the Top? *International Studies Quarterly* 47 (4):617–641.

Rosenau, James N. 1995. Distant Proximities: The Dynamics and Dialectics of Globalization. In *International Political Economy: Understanding Global Order*, ed. Björn Hettne, 46–65. London: Zed Books.

Ruby, Jorn. 2001. Zweifelhafte Zertifikate. Nach heftigen Kontroversen warten die Dänen weiter auf ihr neues Ökostrom-Gesetz. *Neue Energie* 8:74–76.

Simmons, Beth, and Zachary S. Elkins. 2004. The Globalization of Liberalization: Policy Diffusion in the International Political Economy. *American Political Science Review* 98 (1):171–189.

Sykes, Alan O. 1999. The (Limited) Role of Regulatory Harmonization in International Goods and Services Markets. *Journal of International Economic Law* 2 (1):49–70.

van Beek, A., and J. H. B. Benner. 1998. *International Benchmark Study on Renewable Energy: Final Report to the Dutch Ministry of Economic Affairs.* Rotterdam: Consultants on Energy and Environment.

Vogel, David, and Robert A. Kagan, eds. 2004. *Dynamics of Regulatory Change: How Globalization Affects National Regulatory Policies.* Berkeley: University of California Press.

Wade, Robert. 1996. Globalization and Its Limits: Reports of the Death of the National Economy Are Greatly Exaggerated. In *National Diversity and Global Capitalism*, ed. Suzanne Berger and Ronald P. Dore, 60–88. Ithaca, NY: Cornell University Press.

Weiss, Linda. 1998. *The Myth of the Powerless State: Governing the Economy in a Global Era.* Cambridge, UK: Polity Press.

Young, Alasdair R. 2003. Political Transfer and "Trading Up"? Transatlantic Trade in Genetically Modified Food and U.S. Politics. *World Politics* 55 (4):457–484.

10

Regional Governance Arrangements

Tatiana Kluvánková-Oravská and Veronika Chobotová

Recent decades have witnessed in many parts of the world a shift of authority away from states up to regional levels. Where regions have become stronger, regional governance has often transformed the coordination of social relations, including informal and formal institutions, the role of different actors, and the nature of decision-making processes (Rosenau 1992, 1997; Rhodes 1996; Stoker 1998; Hooghe and Marks 2003; Bache and Flinders 2004; Jordan 2008). This process is particularly relevant in European regional integration, which is thus the focus of this chapter. In particular, we study the influence of regional governance arrangements on the new member states of the European Union in Central and Eastern Europe. These countries had been characterized, before they joined the Union, by hierarchical modes of governance and the absence of strong markets, along with the exclusion of business community and civic actors from policy making (Kluvánková-Oravská et al. 2009).

Our primary concern is how interactions between national and EU institutions result in convergence or divergence of environmental policies in the new Central and Eastern European member states. Massive institutional changes in these countries since the late 1980s reflect a political, economic, and social transformation from socialist political and economic institutions to democratic and market-oriented institutions. Yet the ability of the new democratic governments to develop appropriate institutions for multilevel governance has been affected by institutional rebuilding, particularly the interaction of new, mainly European Union, and postsocialist institutions.

The dispersion of competencies from the European Union to national and subnational levels as well as respective bottom-up processes back to the regional level was also transposed into the environmental directives on the governance of natural resources (Bache and Flinders 2004). The involvement of nonstate actors in EU governance aims at a deliberative approach to implementation rather than a linear model of dispersing action from the supranational to lower levels and an intention to support bottom-up decision making (Baker 2006). The conditions for multiactor collaboration and network approaches to public policy making have been enhanced by the adoption of the Aarhus Convention on Access to Information, Public Participation in Decision Making, and Access to Justice in Environmental Matters from 1998, along with a number of EU directives. Civil society actors are also considered an important source of information and novel ideas (Kluvánková-Oravská et al. 2009). Yet the Aarhus Convention grants participatory rights primarily for representative participation at the local level, and it is thus subject to limitations (Baker 2006).

In this chapter, we analyze factors that may explain the convergence or divergence between EU policies and domestic biodiversity policies in three Central and Eastern European countries: Poland, the Czech Republic, and Slovakia. We are interested especially in the links and interactions between domestic institutions and EU environmental policies and institutions. In particular, we analyze the role of informal institutions, such as institutional maturity, leadership, or organizational culture. The analysis covers the period from 1990 to 2009. We discuss first the theoretical concept of institutional change, particularly institutional coevolution in Central and Eastern Europe. We then give examples of interactions between the European Union and domestic policies in Central and Eastern Europe. We finally explain the convergence or divergence between the biodiversity policies in Central and Eastern Europe and the EU standards, and then conclude our analysis.

Conceptualization

Our theoretical notion of institutional change draws on research on Central and Eastern Europe in the broader context of multilevel regional environmental governance (Bromley 2000; Gatzweiler and Hagedorn 2002; Kornai, Matyas, and Roland 2008; Roland 2008).

The evolution of governance in Central and Eastern Europe is characterized by institutional change, notably from state-led, command-and-control systems to democratic governance and market economy. In socialism, the property rights to means of production were predominantly held by state agencies. To facilitate top-down control, many internal institutions of civil society in Central and Eastern Europe were replaced with externally designed, predominantly prescriptive institutions, and central planning substituted for the spontaneous coordination of markets (Kasper and Streit 1998). Yet because Central and Eastern European countries were politically and economically diverse (e.g., with regard to the level of industrialization and centralization, the existence of small-scale market operations, socialist control, and ideological isolation), these countries started the transformation from very different points of development (Kluvánková-Oravská et al. 2009). This has largely determined the capacity of individual countries to reconstruct and rebuild their political and economic institutions as well as their civil society after 1989.

In the early transition process, the Western model of privatization was planned to be implemented quickly, ignoring the interaction of old and new institutions, based on the belief that capitalism would appear magically from the morning mist if only the heavy hand of government would get out of the way (Bromley 2000). Yet transition involves not the imposition of a blueprint on a blank social and economic space but a reworking of the institutions of central planning (Gatzweiler and Hagedorn 2002; Williams and Baláž 2002; Bromley 2000). Transition in Central and Eastern Europe is thus less a simple replacement than a recombination: actors in the postsocialist context rebuilt institutions not *on* the ruins but *with* the ruins of communism (Stark 1996). The interaction between existing and newly imposed institutions thus explains why the transplantation of "best-practice" institutions does not work (Roland 2008) and why reforms in the region must take into account existing institutions. Successful institutional change in Central and Eastern Europe requires coexistence and co-adaptation of institutions and learning rather than a "shock therapy" (Chobotová 2007).

The European Union plays a key role in the recombination of institutions by inducing a shift in decision making from government to governance (Kluvánková-Oravská 2010). Governance implies the involvement of various actors that are independent of a central power and operate at different levels of decision making (Rhodes 1996; Stoker 1998), often described as multilevel governance (Bache and Flinders 2004), multitiered governance or multiperspective governance (Marks and Hooghe 2004), condominio (Schmitter 1996), or polycentric governance (Ostrom, Tiebout, and Warren 1961).

A key issue in European politics is the growing dissociation between territorial constituencies and functional competencies (Schmitter 2000). Mechanisms for the involvement and participation of nonstate actors are thus often seen as necessary. Nongovernmental organizations are gaining importance in most European political systems. This affects also the role of the state in multilevel governance, notably in the rescaling of state power as a response to subnational and supranational pressures in order to increase state capacity (Bache and Flinders 2004). As a consequence, reconciling top-down and bottom-up decision making in the European environmental governance remains a challenge.

Multilevel governance in Central and Eastern Europe is also marked by increased participation of nonstate actors, yet often without proper institutions for their involvement in decision making. States lack capacity to change from regulators to strategic planners and to co-coordinators of interests. There are also few mechanisms for the coordination of governance styles (Kluvánková-Oravská and Chobotová 2010). Environmental governance is thus prone to create tensions in this context.

The concept of convergence and divergence becomes important here. The concept has been used in different contexts focusing largely on public policies such as health, education, social welfare, and transport (Greer 2003; Jeffery 2007; Shaw, MacKinnon, and Docherty 2009; also Busch, Gupta, and Falkner, this book, chapter 9). Policy divergence exists where policy can be made according to local needs and preferences. The governance processes support the development of EU policies that are better tailored to the national economic and social conditions, encouraging policy divergence through the introduction of local solutions to local problems (Jeffery 2002). Conversely, EU multilevel governance and "policy learning" between the EU member states is likely to reinforce tendencies toward policy convergence. Local institutions have previously been found as key variables of policy convergence (Marsden and May 2006; Shaw, MacKinnon, and Docherty 2009). In particular, institutional maturity and other informal factors such as leadership or organizational culture are seen to promote policy convergence.

In this context, the ability of existing institutions of biodiversity governance to coevolve with the new EU institutions also depends on the ecosystems to be governed. Human dependence on the capacity of ecosystems to generate essential services and the vast importance of ecological feedbacks for societal development suggest socioecological interconnections (Berkes and Folke 1998; Galaz et al. 2008). The connectivity within and between social systems and ecosystems plays an important role in designing effective institutions for environmental multilevel governance and understanding dynamics across the scales where global institutions influence local agendas (Gatzweiler and Hagedorn 2002). The quality of the relation between institutions and the ecosystem is an important factor for the convergence of national and regional governance.

The decentralization of previously hierarchical and centralized governance in Central and Eastern Europe occurred predominantly in a top-down fashion, heavily influenced by external political factors such as EU policies. This chapter demonstrates that the coevolution of new EU economic and political institutions with existing subnational institutions of biodiversity governance is a precondition for successful policy convergence in a multilevel context. In particular, institutional maturity, the long-enduring institutions, organizational culture, trust, and other informal factors are promoting effective synchronization of policies.

Experiences

We now give concrete examples of the interaction between European and national governance mechanisms in Central and Eastern Europe. For all countries, overexploitation of protected areas and lack of environmental awareness among state officials were the most serious problems for biodiversity governance under socialist rule. In most Central and Eastern European countries, land was nationalized shortly after the introduction of socialist regimes. Protected areas were owned and regulated by the state with limited resource use for citizens. Environmental objectives were supported only in legal regulations, and environmental protection was primarily shaped by an ideological legacy. Very often, institutions for environmental protection existed only on paper, and the absence of a functioning market allowed the state to be the only regulatory body, often resulting in open-access resource regimes (Kluvánková-Oravská et al. 2009; Pavel, Slavikova, and Jilkova 2009). Consequently, intensive economic activities such as tourism, timber harvesting, and agriculture expanded in protected areas under state management (Kasprzak and Skoczylas 1993; Mirek 1996; Kluvánková-Oravská and Chobotová 2006).

The countries of Central and Eastern Europe started their integration into the European Union from very different points of development, including different degrees of decentralization and differences in property rights. Such a situation had a diversifying effect on their biodiversity governance. In Poland, for example, small-scale private ownership enabled the development of compensation programs for landowners in the early stage of transformation. Biodiversity governance and land ownership in national parks remains in public hands in the Czech Republic but under the reconstructed institutions. In the Slovak Republic, land was fully privatized, yet without appropriate institutions for market operation. Biodiversity governance here has been subordinated to regional administrations and centralized decision making. This is in contrast to the Czech Republic and Poland, where decision making on nature conservation lies with the respective park administration (Kluvánková-Oravská et al. 2009). The effect of the regional EU institutions and governance practices is critical for the adaptation of domestic biodiversity policies in the new EU member states. In the next section, we give four examples of institutional interaction in biodiversity governance in new EU member states. Two illustrate policy convergence and two show policy divergence.

The first example is the involvement of nonstate actors in decision making. The Habitats and Birds Directives are the primary legal framework for the present regional biodiversity policy, providing for the creation of a European network of special conservation areas for priority habitat types and species, known as *Natura 2000* network. Yet the implementation of this regional policy has encountered various problems and conflicts in old and new member states (e.g., Krott et al. 2000; Alphandery and Fortier 2001; Stoll-Kleemann 2001; Hiedanpää 2002; Paavola 2004; Gibbs, While, and Jonas 2007; Paavola, Gouldson, and Kluvánková-Oravská 2009; Rauschmayer et al. 2009). In the new member states of Central and Eastern Europe, the Habitats Directive is an example of an entirely new institution placed within postsocialist governance structures. Its implementation has increased the importance of nonstate owners in negotiations. It failed, however, to provide a formal framework to protect native Central and Eastern European species, which are underrepresented in the annexes to Natura 2000 (Baker 2006), given that these were originally compiled for Western Europe. The involvement of new actors in decision making also remains a problem because the Habitats Directive leaves public consultation to member states (article 6). This allows country-specific solutions that rely on local practices and institutions. In most new member states, the critical factors in influencing implementation are a weak history of participatory governance, including the absence of collective choice and conflict-resolution mechanisms, and a lack of responsibility for the coordination of resources under the common regime. Also in most new member states, not only NGOs but also local governments and nonstate landowners are excluded from consultations on the designation of Natura 2000 sites (Kluvánková-Oravská et al. 2009).

The Habitats Directive was designed to integrate economic, social, and environmental dimensions but the European Union delegated procedures for designating sites for the Natura 2000 network to member states. Member states followed mainly the environmental orientation of the directive and designated sites based on scientific criteria, ignoring NGO preferences. The designation of Natura 2000 sites based on scientific criteria increased the overall frustration of private landowners in the new member states because their aversion to follow biodiversity protection stemmed from the absence of market incentives to do so. Compensation schemes and their monitoring have required cooperation among many governmental units and interest groups, which have not yet evolved in the new member states. Consequently, the Natura 2000 program was often understood as a restrictive policy for nature conservation. The designation of sites was thus contentious (Young et al. 2007) and resulted in the preparation of shadow lists by NGOs in most new member states. (Shadow lists are usually independently created by NGOs, providing specific and additional information and evidence to help evaluate the government list.)

The second example is the institutional mismatch between the European Habitats Directive and the subnational forest management regimes, which led to a conflict between forest and biodiversity state agencies over the division of competencies and intensity of forest use. Forestry represents a historically dominant economic activity in central Europe. The establishment of territorial administrations with competencies for the long-term management of forests dates back to the late nineteenth century. Yet the biodiversity protection authority in most Central and Eastern European countries has existed only since the beginning of the 1990s. Thus, for a long period, forest authorities took most of the conservation responsibilities (Kozová and Vološčuk 2008). They followed mainly forest management objectives and gave priority to large-scale professional management and technological approaches (Kluvánková-Oravská 2010).

Today, forest and nature conservation authorities in Slovakia, Hungary, and the Czech Republic are competing for competencies (Kluvánková-Oravská et al. 2009; Kohlheb and Balász 2010). Because the division of competencies has never been clearly decided, there is a tension between these authorities, which has a significant effect on policy convergence and coordination of responsibilities. In particular, forest authorities benefit from well-established governing practices and their elite position in domestic dialogs and decision making, which helps them to promote technological practices, large-scale management, and centralized decision making (Kluvánková-Oravská et al. 2009). New biodiversity protection measures are often ignored or only formally implemented (Betak et al. 2005). Such technocratic forest management then increases pressures to implement intensive forestry practices also in Natura 2000 sites, which contradicts the regional EU biodiversity policies. A growing number of investigations for the potential violation of EU law (infringement) from the new EU member states document this trend. The number of environmental infringements initiated in 2009 stands at twenty-three in Poland, twenty-six in the Czech Republic, and nineteen in Slovakia (http:// ec.europa.eu/environment/legal/law/statistics.htm).

The third example relates to the consolidation of biodiversity governance due to the implementation of the Habitats Directive, which has created tension in implementation at subnational levels. Yet at the same time, it increased the importance of private owners in negotiations. In particular, it created rules for their participation by integrating the directive's consultations with private actors. Similarly, the monitoring of compliance by the European Union provides incentives for the evolution of internal monitoring and sanctioning mechanisms. Moreover, the Natura 2000 program has improved access to information and encouraged public participation, particularly at the local level. Such trends can be supported by experience from several protected areas, where the regional EU rules evolved in line with existing domestic institutional elements, for example, the historically determined civic movements in the Czech Republic and the long tradition of small-scale green markets in Polish parks (Kluvánková-Oravská et al. 2009). Thus, consultations of nonstate actors have increased the understanding of participation. The lesson learned from the conflictive implementation of Natura 2000 without public participation is the need to create room for the evolution of domestic institutional structures for public participation. These are effective drivers of institutional consolidation and the convergence with EU governance.

The fourth example is the new network mechanisms at the subnational level. Mechanisms for effective communication and interaction between actors at various decision-making levels do not fully exist in the region because democratization and decentralization are new. A new institution for coordination, however, has appeared recently in Polish, Czech, and Slovak biodiversity governance.

A primary example is the institution of national park councils in Poland and the Czech Republic. (In Poland, national park councils also existed before the transformation.) Councils advise park administrations on all important management processes (especially zoning, management planning, visiting rules, forest management, land-use plans, and so forth). The members of the national park councils include nonstate actors, such as scientists, environmental organizations, and local government representatives (Kluvánková-Oravská et al. 2009). These structures accelerate cross-scale interactions because they enable economic and civil society actors to engage in new forms of activities related to biodiversity (Birner and Wittmer 2004). The effect of EU enlargement, in particular the overall increase in democracy and subsidiarity, are the main triggers of change toward network-style governance.

New mechanisms to involve nonstate actors in multilevel biodiversity governance are emerging in Central and Eastern Europe, notably in partnerships among governments, NGOs, and corporations. In Slovakia for example, the Associations of Municipalities operates in protected areas. In the Slovensky Raj National Park, this association includes the voluntary membership of surrounding municipalities, the park administration, and others. The association supports nature conservation and cultural activities, and it cooperates on providing tourist services. It can interact with other nonstate actors, particularly at the EU level, and create local partnerships for EU funding. This ensures at least informal cooperation and legitimacy of new actors in multilevel biodiversity governance (Kluvánková-Oravská et al. 2009).

Examples can be found in several national parks within the Czech Republic, where the national park administration initiated the foundation of a nonprofit organization intended for cooperation and communication with municipalities, NGOs, and other nonstate actors. The existence of such partnerships is largely determined by the joined interest to apply for EU funds. In the Czech Republic, however, it is also supported by a tradition of civic movements. Such partnerships try to integrate the interests of the state administration, municipalities, and NGOs, including joint projects, information centers, websites, local eco-labels, and programs to improve multilevel communication and cooperation (Správa NP a CHKO Šumava 2006; Kluvánková-Oravská et al. 2009).

In Poland, elements of multiactor interaction are derived from a long tradition of market structures that, on a small scale, persisted even during the socialist period. For instance, in the Barycz Valley network, inhabitants recognized and used benefits from the Natura 2000 network, such as wide-scale free promotion of the region, development of environmentally friendly tourism, development of agro-tourism, and development of a label for local products (Kluvánková-Oravská et al. 2009).

Explanations

These four examples of vertical interlinkages between the European Union and subnational biodiversity governance in Central and Eastern Europe demonstrate policy convergence as well as divergence. In this section, we argue that whether the coevolution of institutions or regimes results in policy convergence or divergence depends largely on the robustness of existing institutions, which create trust among actors, offer flexibility of the transforming institutions or regimes, and are able to fit with relevant ecosystems. Such institutions are characterized by self-organization, transfer of knowledge, resources, and institutions across the scales. They may form a set of independent self-governed systems with multiple centers of power and can more effectively blend local, indigenous knowledge with scientific knowledge, which is often available at a higher (national) level (Ostrom 1998; Berkes and Folke 1998; Poteete, Janssen, and Ostrom 2010).

In the first example, the EU Habitat Directive was implemented within the new EU member states with the exclusion of the majority of the nonstate actors. The designation, however, resulted in an alternative proposal from NGOs submitted to the European Commission. Top-down designation and ignorance of local knowledge are thus the main reasons for the failure to reach an agreement on Natura 2000 sites.

In the second example, forest and nature conservation bureaucracies failed to coordinate economic interests and the division of power within multilevel environmental governance of the European Union. As a result, several legal provisions of forest and biodiversity management contradict each another and EU biodiversity policy principles are regularly violated.

In both examples, the prevailing institutional structures—in particular authoritative, centralized decision making and low capacity of state agencies to accept new coordinating roles—resulted in a divergence between regional EU requirements for participation and market coordination and the existing practice at the domestic level of the new EU members. Authoritative decision making is historically determined in Central and Eastern Europe (Kluvánková-Oravská and Chobotová 2006), where formal institutions as well as informal institutions of civil society were replaced under socialism with external, predominantly prescriptive institutions of central planning. This is in line with the development in postcolonial states in Africa or Asia, where formal institutions were often used by political elites to control power. That combination of centralization and bureaucratic authoritarianism may also result in the ignorance of local knowledge (Compagnon, Chan, and Mert, this book, chapter 11).

In the first two examples, transforming institutions have not succeeded in fitting with ecosystems. In the first example, ecological criteria dominated the Natura 2000 site designation, ignoring the social and economic dimensions. In the second case, technocratic forestry management failed to respect ecosystem needs. This ecosystem-institution misfit contributed to the evolution of conflicts that affected the regional level by requiring an intervention from the European Union.

On the contrary, the two other cases of institutional consolidation and new multilevel mechanisms demonstrated the successful convergence of the regional European Union and domestic policies and governance styles. Rules for biodiversity management in the EU Natura 2000 sites, such as monitoring, sanctioning, access to information, and public participation, were successfully transformed into domestic biodiversity protection regimes in areas where informal institutions such as markets or public funds enhanced coevolution. Environmental infringements created learning experience for authoritative leaders and the acceptance of wider participation in multilevel decision making. Europeanization thus improved collective choice and consolidation of existing biodiversity policies.

The emergence of novel mechanisms for involving nonstate actors in multilevel governance, such as advisory national park councils, partnerships, or markets, are also an effect of the successful coevolution of EU institutions with existing institutions. New mechanisms for voluntary cooperation on biodiversity protection at the domestic level became an incentive in the competition for EU structural funds, and they have resulted in the convergence of local economic development interests with the objectives of national and EU policies.

In the two successful examples of convergence, learning experiences created room for evolution of institutions for multilevel governance. Creation of management and collective choice rules and mechanisms for involving nonstate actors also demonstrate the ability to fit with local circumstances and ecosystems. Furthermore, compliance with EU rules requires real implementation and long-term monitoring, which provided another incentive for new member states whose primary interest is to comply with the practice of the group of countries they joined. New institutions or networks of actors did not appear in a vacuum but could evolve due to existing institutions, such as small-scale markets in protected areas in Poland operating during socialist times, or the traditional civic movement in the Czech Republic with an extended network of organizations and individuals acting at local and regional levels. Trust among individuals at the community level, together with democratization of new political systems, enabled coevolution and policy convergence across subnational levels but also to the national level. These findings support Elinor Ostrom's arguments that flexibility and local experience create conditions for renewal of long-lasting institutions that have demonstrated their ability to adapt to external factors such as ecological conditions or regime change (Ostrom, Gardner, and Walker 1994).

These arguments are supported by the contradicting experience in non-EU countries such as Belarus or Serbia (Kluvánková-Oravská et al. 2009; Falaleeva and Rauschmayer 2010). In these countries, even large environmental investments through EU funds were unable to induce the Europeanization of national environmental policies. Consequently, the European Union has little influence on institutional changes in the countries' jurisdictions and informal institutions. These are seen external to existing governance structures, and thus cannot trigger changes in behavior and jurisdictions of prevailing hierarchical governance systems.

Conclusions and Outlook

Environmental governance in Central and Eastern Europe is characterized by a prevailing hierarchical structure arising from a limited tradition of decentralization and self-government, rapidly affected by transformation and EU integration. The situation varies from country to country, depending on historical determinants. These aspects determine the overall effectiveness of institutional changes to transform postsocialist governance structures into multilevel systems of the European Union.

Overall, our research indicates that the EU integration is an important driving force behind changes of biodiversity policies in the new EU member states. The successful coevolution of new political and economic institutions at the regional level with existing domestic institutions for biodiversity protection is a primary condition for institutional consolidation. In addition, we found that linkage between ecosystems and their institutions contribute to policy convergence. However, mismatches between the old hierarchical institutions developed under socialism and the new regional EU institutions often also led to the divergence of policies, for example, by the designation of some Natura 2000 sites that led to the preparation of alternative lists by NGOs. One area of future research is the role of the state in multilevel governance, in particular regarding the transitional states in Central and European Europe. Another area of future research is the study of self-governing systems with respect to their adaptive capacity to maintain vertical interlinkages. This may enable institutions to cope with external system disturbances such as changes in the global economy or global environmental change.

Acknowledgment

The research reported in this chapter has been conducted within the context of the European Marie Curie Research Training Network "Multilevel Governance of Natural Resources: Tools and Processes for Water and Biodiversity Governance in Europe" (GOVERNAT).

References

Alphandery, Pierre, and Agnes Fortier. 2001. Can Territorial Policy Be Based on Science Alone: The System for Creating the NATURA 2000 Network in France. *Sociologia Ruralis* 41:311–328.

Bache, Ian, and Matthew Flinders. 2004. Multi-level Governance: Conclusions and Implications. In *Multi-level Governance*, ed. Ian Bache and Matthew Flinders, 195–206. New York: Oxford University Press.

Baker, Susan. 2006. *Sustainable Development: Introduction into the Environmental Series*. Abingdon, UK: Routledge.

Berkes, Frikret, and Carl Folke, eds. 1998. *Linking Social Ecological Systems: Management Practices and Social Mechanisms for Building Resilience*. Cambridge, UK: Cambridge University Press.

Betak, Juraj, Livia Bizikova, Jan Hanusin, Mikulas Huba, Vladimir Ira, Jan Lacika, and Tatiana Kluvánková-Oravská. 2005. *Smerom k trvalo udrzatelnému tatranskému regiónu*. [Towards Sustainable Development of Tatra Region] Bratislava: REC Slovakia and STUŽ/SR.

Birner, Regina, and Heidi Wittmer. 2004. On the "Efficient Boundaries of the State": The Contribution of Transaction-Costs Economics to the Analysis of Decentralization and Devolution in Natural Resource Management. *Environment and Planning C: Government and Policy* 22:667–685.

Bromley, Daniel W. 2000. A Most Difficult Passage: The Economic Transition in Central and Eastern Europe and the Former Soviet Union. Paper presented at the KATO Symposium, Berlin.

Chobotová, Veronika. 2007. Evolution of Institution for Sustainable Tourism in the Context of Transition Process of Slovakia. Working Paper 1. Bratislava: Institute for Forecasting, SAS.

Falaleeva, Maria, and Felix Rauschmayer. 2010. Positive Assessment May Be Short-Lived: On Outcomes and Processes of a World Bank Biodiversity Project in Belarus. In *From Government to Governance? New Governance for Water and Biodiversity in an Enlarged Europe*, ed. Tatiana Kluvánková-Oravská, 178–200. Prague: Alfa Printing.

Galaz, Victor, Per Olsson, Thomas Hahn, and Uno Svedin. 2008. The Problem of Fit among Biophysical Systems, Environmental and Resource Regimes, and Broader Governance Systems: Insights and Emerging Challenges. In *Institutions and Environmental Change: Principal Findings, Applications, and Research Frontiers*, ed. Oran R. Young, Leslie A. King, and Heike Schroeder, 147–186. Cambridge, MA: MIT Press.

Gatzweiler, Franz, and Konrad Hagedorn. 2002. The Evolution of Institutions in Transition. *International Journal of Agricultural Resources, Governance, and Ecology* 2:37–58.

Gibbs, David, Aidan While, and Andrew E.G. Jonas. 2007. Governing Nature Conservation: The European Union Habitats Directive and Conflict around Estuary Management. *Environment and Planning A* 39:339–358.

Greer, Scott. 2003. Policy Divergence: Will It Change Something in Greenock? In *The State of the Nations: The Third Year of Devolution in the United Kingdom*, ed. Robert Hazell, 195–214. Exeter, UK: Imprint Academic.

Hiedanpää, Juha. 2002. European-wide Conservation versus Local Well-Being: The Reception of the NATURA 2000 Reserve Network in Karvia, SW-Finland. *Landscape and Urban Planning* 61:113–123.

Hooghe, Liesbet, and Gary Marks. 2003. Unraveling the Central State, but How? Types of Multi-level Governance. *American Political Science Review* 97:233–234.

Jeffery, Charles. 2002. Uniformity and Diversity in Policy Provision: Insights from the US, Germany, and Canada. In *Devolution in Practice: Public Policy Differences within the UK*, ed. John Adams and Peter Robinson, 176–197. London: Institute for Public Policy Research and the Economic Social Research Council.

Jeffery, Charles. 2007. The Unfinished Business of Devolution: Seven Open Questions. *Public Policy and Administration* 22:92–108.

Jordan, Andrew. 2008. The Governance of Sustainable Development: Taking Stock and Looking Forwards. *Environment and Planning C: Government and Policy* 26:17–33.

Kasper, Wofgang, and Manfred E. Streit. 1998. *Institutional Economics: Social Order and Public Policy*. Cheltenham, UK: Edgar Elgar.

Kasprzak, Krzysztof, and Janusz Skoczylas. 1993. *Rozwój Ochrony Przyrody Nieozywionej i Ozywionej, Historia i Współczesnosc.* [Development of Nature Protection, History and Modernity] Poznan: Foundacion "Warta."

Kluvánková-Oravská, Tatiana. 2010. New Environmental Governance. In *From Government to Governance? New Governance for Water and Biodiversity in an Enlarged Europe,* ed. Tatiana Kluvánková-Oravská, 14–28. Prague: Alfa Printing.

Kluvánková-Oravská, Tatiana, and Veronika Chobotová. 2006. Shifting Governance. Managing the Commons: The Case of Slovensky Raj National Park. *Sociologia* 38:221–244.

Kluvánková-Oravská, Tatiana, and Veronika Chobotová. 2010. The Emergence of Multilevel Governance: The Case of the Biodiversity in the Enlarged European Union. *Journal of Economics* 58 (4):407–422.

Kluvánková-Oravská, Tatiana, Veronika Chobotová, Ilona Banaszak, Lenka Slavíková, and Sonja Trifunovová. 2009. From Government to Governance for Biodiversity: The Perspective of Central and Eastern European Transition Countries. *Environmental Policy and Governance* 19:186–196.

Kohlheb, Norbert, and Bálint Balász. 2010. Human-Nature Interplay of Forest Governance: Institutional Mapping of Hungarian Forestry. In *From Government to Governance? New Governance for Water and Biodiversity in an Enlarged Europe,* ed. Tatiana Kluvánková-Oravská, 178–200. Prague: Alfa Printing.

Kornai, János, László Matyas, and Gérard Roland. 2008. *Institutional Change and Economic Behavior.* Basingstoke, UK: Palgrave Macmillan with the International Economic Association.

Kozová, Maria, and Ivan Vološčuk. 2008. Zásadné problémové konfliktné oblasti v manažmente územia. [Mayor Problematic Conflict Areas in Landscape Management] In *Krajinno ekologicky optimálne priestorové a funkcne vyuzitie: Územia biosférickej rezervácie Tatry* [Landscape Planning and Functional Use], ed. Jan Drdoš and Eduard Bublinec, 150–158. Bratislava: VEDA.

Krott, Max, Bruno Julien, Michael Lammertz, Jean-Marie Barbier, Sandra Jen, Marta Ballestreros, and Caroline de Bovis. 2000. Voicing Interests and Concerns. NATURA 2000: An Ecological Network in Conflict with People. *Forest Policy and Economics* 1:357–366.

Marks, Gary, and Liesbet Hooghe. 2004. Contrasting Visions of Multilevel Governance. In *Multi-level Governance,* ed. Ian Bache and Matthew Flinders, 15–31. New York: Oxford University Press.

Marsden, Greg, and Anthony D. May. 2006. Do Institutional Arrangements Make a Difference to Transport Policy and Implementation? Lessons for Britain. *Environment and Planning C: Government and Policy* 24:771–789.

Mirek, Z. 1996. Tatry i Tatrzanski Park Narodowy—wiadomosci ogolne. [Tatras and Tatra National Park—General Information]. In *Przyroda Tatrzanskiego Parku Narodowego: Tatry i Podtatrze 3* [The Nature of Tatra National Park.

Tatras and the Tatra Region], ed. Z. Mirek, Z. Glowacinski, K. Klimek, and H. Piekos-Mirkowa. Zakopane-Krakow: Tatrzanski Park Narodowy.

Ostrom, Elinor. 1998. Scales, Polycentricity, and Incentives: Designing Complexity to Govern Complexity. In *Protection of Biodiversity. Converging Strategies*, ed. Lakshman Guruswamy and Jeffrey McNeely, 149–167. Durham, NC: Duke University Press.

Ostrom, Elinor, Roy Gardner, and James Walker. 1994. *Rules, Games, and Common-Pool Resources*. Ann Arbor: The University of Michigan Press.

Ostrom, Vincent, Charles M. Tiebout, and Robert Warren. 1961. The Organization of Government in Metropolitan Areas. *American Political Science Review* 55:831–842.

Paavola, Jouni. 2004. Protected Areas Governance and Justice: Theory and the European Union's Habitats Directive. *Environmental Sciences* 1:59–77.

Paavola, Jouni, Andrew Gouldson, and Tatiana Kluvánková-Oravská. 2009. The Institutions, Ecosystems, and the Interplay of Actors, Scales, Frameworks, and Regimes in the Governance of Biodiversity. *Environmental Policy and Governance* 19:148–158.

Pavel, Jan, Lenka Sláviková, and Jiřina Jílková. 2009. Ekonomické nástroje v politice zivotního prostredí: drahé dane a nízká úcinnost. [Economic Instruments in Environmental Policy: Expensive Taxes and Low Effectiveness] *Journal of Economics* 57 (2):132–144.

Poteete, Amy R., Marco A. Janssen, and Elinor Ostrom. 2010. *Working Together: Collective Actions, the Commons, and Multiple Methods in Practice*. Princeton, NJ: Princeton University Press.

Rauschmayer, Felix, Augustin Berghöfer, Ines Omann, and Dimitrios Zikos. 2009. Examining Processes or/and Outcomes? Evaluation Concepts in European Governance of Natural Resources. *Environmental Policy and Governance* 19:141–147.

Rhodes, R. A. W. 1996. The New Governance: Governing without Government. *Political Studies* 44:652–667.

Roland, Gérard. 2008. Fast Moving and Slow Moving Institutions. In *Institutional Change and Economic Behavior*, ed. János Kornai, László Matyas, and Gérard Roland, 134–158. Basingstoke, UK: Palgrave Macmillan with the International Economic Association.

Rosenau, James N. 1992. Governance, Order, and Change in World Politics. In *Governance without Government*, ed. James N. Rosenau and Ernst-Otto Czempiel, 1–29. Cambridge, UK: Cambridge University Press.

Rosenau, James N. 1997. *Along the Domestic-Foreign Frontier: Exploring Governance in a Turbulent World*. Cambridge, UK: Cambridge University Press.

Schmitter, Philippe C. 1996. Examining the Present Euro-polity with the Help of Past Theories. In *Governance in the European Union*, ed. Gary Marks, Fritz W. Scharpf, Philippe C. Schmitter, and Wolfgang Streeck, 121–150. London: Sage.

Schmitter, Philippe C. 2000. *How to Democratize the European Union: And Why Bother?* Boulder, CO: Rowman and Littlefield.

Shaw, Jon, Danny MacKinnon, and Iain Docherty. 2009. Divergence or Convergence? Devolution and Transport Policy in the United Kingdom. *Environment and Planning C: Government and Policy* 27 (3):546–567.

Správa NP a CHKO Šumava. 2006. *Rocenky Správy Národního parku a Chránené krajinné oblasti Šumava, 1997–2006.* [Yearbook of National Park Administration and Landscape Area Šumava] Vimperk: National Park Administration and Landscape Area Šumava.

Stark, David. 1996. Recombinant Property in East European Capitalism. *American Journal of Sociology* 101:993–1027.

Stoker, Gerry. 1998. Governance as Theory: Five Propositions. *International Social Science Journal* 50 (155):17–28.

Stoll-Kleemann, Susanne. 2001. Barriers to Nature Conservation in Germany: A Model of Explaining Opposition to Protected Areas. *Journal of Experimental Psychology* 21:369–385.

Williams, Allan M., and Vladimir Baláž. 2002. The Czech and Slovak Republics: Conceptual Issues in the Economic Analysis of Tourism in Transition. *Tourism Management* 23:37–45.

Young, Juliette, Caspian Richards, Anke Fischer, Lubos Halada, Tiiu Kull, Antoni Kuzniar, Urmas Tartes, Yordan Uzunov, and Allan Watt. 2007. Conflicts between Biodiversity Conservation and Human Activities in the Central and Eastern European Countries. *Ambio* 36 (7):545–550.

11

The Changing Role of the State

Daniel Compagnon, Sander Chan, and Ayşem Mert

Devoting a chapter to the role of the state in global governance in a book focusing mainly on nonstate actors and governance beyond the state might be unusual. Is it necessary once more to bring the state back in (Mol 2007), and for what purpose? The valid critique of the overstated centrality of the state in classical international relations theory—in the realist and the liberal traditions—should not lead us to support the opposite and perilous assumption that the state as a concept has lost relevance in governance theory. Private governance is not altogether a new reality if one thinks about the British and French royal-chartered companies of the colonial era, with their quasi-governmental authority over wide territories, or private regulatory institutions of the nineteenth century such as The Universal Postal Union. Yet, the state has been the sole unit of analysis in most studies on international relations until the late 1990s. Now that global governance studies have emphasized the role of nonstate or nonpublic authorities and platforms (Barnett and Sikkink 2008), it is time to explore the remaining role of the state.

There is a particularly strong case for reassessing the role of the state in the area of environmental governance. On the one hand, the fast development of various private governance initiatives (Pattberg, this book, chapter 5) is a potential challenge to the power and legitimacy of the state as the main source of global environmental policies. On the other hand, private authority and transnational governance rely on the international state system for legal frameworks of operation and normative foundations. This does not suggest that the state contrives to its own demise but merely that the new forms of governance are intrinsically hybrid (Falkner 2003), enjoying some support from state actors to operate effectively. Moreover, the state is still perceived by nonstate actors as a prominent decision maker that they strive to influence, and a key broker between international regimes and between global and domestic policy domains. Thus, taking stock of the role of the state in the midst of the transformation of global environmental governance seems justified and important.

Although the role of the state remains central (Lake 2008), it has largely been transformed. The functions that states perform and their influence in environmental policy making have been altered by a multidimensional globalization process and the multiple initiatives and demands from nonstate actors. The role of the state is not necessarily less important because of these processes (Vogler 2005). It is on face value an increasingly popular form of collective governance: from only seventy internationally recognized states in 1949, we have now reached two hundred states, 192 of them with UN membership. Why would political actors favor the state if it were devoid of power in today's world affairs? Simultaneously, this number suggests various types of statehood, a fact that receives little attention in governance studies because of the sustained legacy of realist theorizing. In fact, governance studies neglected the implications of the growing differentiation between empirical expressions of statehood, taking the largely mythical Westphalian ideal type for granted.

This chapter aims to fill this lacuna by focusing on the relationship between increasingly private-led governance and the changing roles of states. To do this, the next two sections focus on the two paradigmatic changes, one internal and one external to the discipline of international relations: first, we focus on deviations from the fictitious Westphalian model derived from the OECD countries' historical trajectory and explore the so-called emerging economies and areas of limited statehood in the South. The latter are as much overlooked in the governance literature as they are in international relations research. Then, we explore the most dramatic change in global governance that transformed the role of the state: globalization. We do not propose here a Weberian typology of states but we point at different forms of statehood, which are present to some extent in the various contemporary states. The differentiation in state models and the impact of globalization are then illustrated in the following section. The main lessons on the changing role of the state will be drawn in a third section, keeping in mind the various forms of statehood, before a succinct concluding section.

Conceptualization

Regime theory with its sophisticated but somewhat decontextualized debates on conditions of interstate cooperation and the definition of national interest originally downplayed the importance of private actors in regime making and regime implementation (Cutler, Haufler, and Porter 1999; Haufler 2002). In addition, if regime theory emphasized the pivotal role of states in international negotiations, it paid limited attention to the implementation of international agreements through national policies. In this respect, the debate narrowed around disputed measurements of regime effectiveness (Young 1999, 2002; Miles et al. 2001), where in-built regime features played a prominent role (Mitchell 2006) and local social dynamics were largely ignored. Both neo-Gramscian accounts of global environmental governance (Newell 2000, Levy and Newell 2005) and recent analyses of private governance (Pattberg 2007; Dingwerth 2007), on the contrary, tend to downplay the role of state actors. As the literature moved away in the early 2000s from state-centric, static, and problem-solving regime theory (and the outdated hegemonic stability hypothesis) toward a more sociological account of decision making, in the form of multilayered, multiactor, and change-prone environmental governance (Stokke 1997; Biermann and Pattberg 2008), the relationship between the state and its socioeconomic environment gained renewed attention. Reassessing the changing role of state actors in governance systems, however, first requires a better understanding of the nature of the contemporary state by focusing on the variety of forms of statehood and the effect of globalization on them.

Deviating Models of Statehood

Most theories of international relations (including functional regime theory) take for granted the alleged stability and universality of the Westphalian state (Brown 2006), which in fact is the Western model of statehood (Neuman 1998). This state is "a figment of the nineteenth-century imagination stylized still further, and reified by the discipline of IR [international relations]" (Osiander 2001, 284). Similarly, the global governance discourse is based largely on the experiences and models of OECD countries. The term *developing countries* (or *the South*) is used as a general category to signify all other models of statehood, without paying much attention to their specificities. The growing importance of these states in global environmental governance warrants exploring the diversity and variability of forms of statehood in today's world (Sørensen 2001).

In spite of the fiction that all sovereign states enjoy equal rights and prerogatives in the international arena, many states that emerged from decolonization do not meet the major criteria of "effective" statehood.

These deviant cases have been described as *quasi-states* (Jackson 1990) or *postcolonial* states (Sørensen 2001) to denote a limited capacity of autonomous action in the international system and their dependence on the United Nations and the great powers to maintain their independence and integrity. Such was the basis of France's relations with its retinue of client states in Western and Central Africa, a complex often labeled *Françafrique*. Not fully enjoying the attributes of "positive" sovereignty— that is military and financial capacities to protect themselves and control their territory—they rely only on "negative" sovereignty, provided primarily by international recognition by other states and membership in the UN system. Their governments display a ritualistic and largely symbolic diplomatic activity, which is fairly ineffective and quite beyond their financial means (Clapham 1996).

The eagerness of quasi-states to sign environmental treaties results from an outside pressure that they are badly equipped to deter, but also from their need to foster their existence on the international scene and from their expectations of attracting more Western funding through a kind of permanent if implicit bargaining. Often, predatory elites rely on the international system to complement a weak national resource base: many of these states became independent without a viable economy or squandered the little revenue base they had and have survived on multilateral and bilateral development aid and external borrowing ever since (Englebert 2009). An extreme illustration is the nearly bankrupt ministate of Nauru that recently recognized the independence of the secessionist regions of Abkhazia and South Ossetia in exchange for a substantial financial aid package from the Russian government (Harding 2009). Cases of small African and Pacific states supporting Japan's demands at the International Whaling Commission in exchange for development aid illustrate the issue in the domain of environmental governance (The Times 2010a, 2010b).

The lack of implementation of environmental agreements, however, is not just a question of insufficient financial means to do so. It is also linked to the internal structure of the postcolonial state (Blaikie and Simo 1998). The internal institutional arrangements of many postcolonial states have been characterized in political sociology often as *weak* (Migdal 1988), *neo-patrimonial* (Médard 1991; Bratton and Van de Walle 1994), *fragile* (Moreno Torres and Anderson 2004; Châtaigner and Magro 2007), if not *failed* (Herbst 1996) or *shadow* (Reno 1998). Thomas Risse (2005, 64) proposed the notion of *limited statehood* to encompass these external (quasi-state) and internal (weak state) dimensions of the postcolonial state:

"Limited statehood" refers to countries whose governments are only partially, if at all, in control of the legitimate means of force, those inside the country as well those which could be employed beyond its borders. Moreover, they are either not in the position, or only partially so, to implement political decisions of the central government and to enforce the law. In other words, areas of limited statehood lack full "effective authority" over their territory, a minimal characteristic of modern statehood.

By no means are all "developing" countries on equal footing. Worst cases of limited statehood are more likely to be found among the least-developed countries as opposed to the emerging economies. There are also striking differences within emerging countries between regions or social segments enjoying effective policing and others affected by the same evils as the weakest states, including corruption and ineffective governance. In many countries, environmental policy is usually the lowest-ranking priority, and agencies in charge of the environment are the least influential of all bureaucracies. Development agencies have tried to overcome policy consequences of this situation by dealing with subnational actors such as NGOs and local communities. Bypassing the state was a matter of efficiency. Yet these attempts (especially the policy prescriptions imposed by donors, international organizations, and Western NGOs) were regarded as infringements of national sovereignty—the founding pillar of the international system and still a powerful ideology (Krasner 1999; Osiander 2001)—thus further impeding effective policy implementation.

The Uneven Impact of Globalization
Another important factor in understanding the current role of the state is the uneven effects of globalization. The growing influence of private actors and unregulated global markets prompted the prognosis of state decline in a globalized economy (Strange 1996). More than the material forces of globalization as such, the rise of neoliberal orthodoxy in European and US policy-making circles in the late 1970s and early 1980s promoted the so-called Washington Consensus and undermined the state's status as a prominent policy actor. The state was deemed too large to manage local environmental problems or too small to address global environmental risks. Yet nation-state ideology endures and is sometimes fostered by trends such as the new surge of identity politics. Thus, the state is transformed rather than obliterated (Mann 1997).

It has become a "globalized state" (Clark 1999), one penetrated by transnational networks, such as multinational corporations, advocacy networks, or illegal networks (Williams and Baudin-O'Hayon 2002), and influenced, promoted, and punished by global standards and jurisdictions (Mert 2012). The national policy process is fragmented horizontally and vertically. Agents of the state in different policy areas act sometimes autonomously from the government, but in close connection with transnational policy networks from which they draw expertise and legitimacy. Increasingly, national governments must share public authority with regional intergovernmental organizations like the European Union, where a complex system of multilevel environmental governance has a strong coordination effect on national policies (McCormick 2001; Hooghe and Marks 2001). Even when regional organizations are less institutionalized and effective, they shape state policies at the national level (Compagnon, Florémont, and Lamaud 2011). The national interest is more than ever a contested notion, as contending social groups, NGOs and private firms lobby decision makers to influence the outcomes of international negotiations (Putnam 1988; Moravcsik 1997).

The globalized state is also subjected to "market discipline" (Gill 1995), which is largely a self-imposed discipline rooted in elites' "imagined globalization" (Cameron and Palan 2004). Influenced by neoliberal ideology and business lobbies, the state acts primarily as a "competition state" (Cerny 2005), where the national interest is constructed as economic growth and private companies' interests, and state policies follow suit. Thus, the constraints of free trade competition and deregulated financial markets are internalized by political elites, particularly in industrialized and emergent economies. In this process, states assume new functions, internalize globalization, and become the key actors in its implementation (Sassen 1996). The question is not whether corporate interests supplement the retreating state but how the accommodation of these interests affects the capacity of the state to address environmental governance challenges at different scales.

Globalization also entrenches existing inequalities between countries, some of which are rooted in the colonial era. The voices of developing countries are often marginalized (Miller 1998), especially in environmental treaty making. The weakest states such as the least-developed countries, penetrated by the complex forces of globalization, cannot match corporate influence in private and hybrid regimes such as the ISO 14000 series (Clapp 1998). Industrialized countries are better equipped with norms and institutions (as well as technologies) to adjust to globalized statehood. They enjoy greater capacity and legitimacy to counter the worst effects of globalization and foster ecologically sustainable policies, if they choose. Postcolonial states, on the contrary, regard development as a priority over everything else (Najam 2005) to compensate for past exploitation, taking advantage of globalization even when it implies lowering environmental standards. The growing heterogeneity between emergent economies and least-developed countries does not translate yet into the demise of the Group of 77 in international negotiations (Kasa, Gullberg, and Heggelund 2008). Emergent powers still claim to voice the concerns of the "Global South." Yet, emerging economies benefit far more from globalization than least-developed countries. The divergence of interest between these two groups is likely to widen, with a substantial impact on global environmental governance.

In sum, contemporary statehood is more diverse than ever. Different states are influenced by the effects of globalization to varying degrees and will adopt diverging political strategies in global environmental governance. This diversity of state profiles, especially when assessed with two criteria—the degree of statehood effectiveness and the exposure to the effects of globalization—defeats simplistic typologies. Rather, it reveals a kaleidoscope of state behavior that suggests a variety of roles for the state in global environmental governance.

Experiences

The resilience of the state as a site of resistance against the demands of globalization forces and, somehow paradoxically, as cog and wheel in policy implementation and norm transfer could be addressed from many angles. We focus on cases derived from recent research within the Global Governance Project to reflect the diversity of contexts where the state plays a crucial albeit contrasted role in global environmental governance. First, we look at China's contribution to global environmental governance shaped by an authoritarian version of ecological modernization, cast in an attempt to maximize the economic benefits of globalization. We then explore "limited statehood" as a factor in biodiversity conservation policies in Africa. Finally, we scrutinize discourses on public-private partnerships as the product of the globalized state and an epitome of a major shift in global environmental governance.

China's Authoritarian Modernizing State

China combines today a fast-growing market economy fueled by globalization and an entrenched authoritarian regime. The political system is characterized by the monopoly of the ruling communist party and its successful obliteration of all significant spaces of democratic expression since the Tiananmen demonstrations in 1989. This tension raises interesting questions on the role of the Chinese state in environmental governance. China is increasingly brokering globalization and globalization is increasingly changing the state (Zhang 2005), but not necessarily in the same way as in Europe or North America. At first look, many contemporary governance trends can also be observed in China: a move from state to society through the expansion of the nongovernmental sector or a shift toward nonterritorial politics, networks, and global platforms of governance as a source of public authority. China could also be seen to have embarked on a path of ecological modernization "colored by specific local conditions and positions in the world-system" (Mol 2006, 31). Yet, the Chinese state remains firmly in control of all major governance practices.

From the perspective of the Chinese state, global governance and its institutions are shaped by Western ideas. As China has gained power in international relations, the Chinese government increasingly seeks to reformulate these institutions and rules according to its own interests. For instance, the current climate regime is regarded as unfair because it prioritizes Western interests and values. A post-Kyoto regime hinges on the consent of the Chinese delegation, giving China more leeway to influence its design with a major role for the state actors. If China can lead the Group of 77 toward a more equitable climate regime, the North-South polarization that plagues most environmental regimes can be overcome and the role of the state in global governance can be redrawn. Failure to address these equity issues within a consolidated Kyoto process may move climate negotiations to arenas outside the United Nations, such as the Group of 20. Either way, China's involvement in climate governance aims to transform these platforms into a power-based variant of global governance, less intrusive for national sovereignty and more intergovernmental in nature (Zhang 2000).

Although China has increasing influence on global environmental governance, the impact of globalization on its domestic environmental governance may be even stronger. The development of environmental policies and institutions in China is closely related to progress in international environmental regimes (Heggelund and Backer 2007). From the 1972 Stockholm Conference onwards, international environmental negotiations were a means for China to position itself as a legitimate and independent state (Heggelund 2003). Active high-level participation in a series of global environmental conferences paralleled domestic institutionalization of environmental concerns. Yet although institutions, laws, and policies are in place, effective implementation is problematic, particularly in relation to observance of the rule of law. This difficulty is partly explained by the specific structure of the Chinese state.

China's (environmental) governance has traditionally been marked by centralization and vertical and horizontal fragmentation. Central planning in a one-size-fits-all manner has often created conflicts between local and central authorities in areas ranging from coastal management (Chen and Uitto 2003) to land-use policies (Jia 2009). These tensions are also inherent in the relations between local environmental protection bureaus and the Ministry of Environmental Protection. Moreover, central environmental protection agencies lack supervisory authority and capacity to enforce the law.

Horizontal and vertical fragmentation of governance suggests that the role of this multifaceted state is elusive. On the one hand, environmental policy generated a new type of relations between the state and private actors. Environmental NGOs multiplied; in 2005, as many as 2,768 environmental NGOs were registered with the state (Xinhua News Agency 2006). On the other hand, the sharp increase in numbers does not directly translate into a stronger influence of these actors over policy making. As Schroeder (2009) notes, many CDM projects have been implemented without civil society participation. The registration of NGOs is strictly controlled by the Ministry for Civil Affairs, and registration requirements are stringent. Every new NGO needs a government agency to endorse its application. There are restrictions on foreign funding and crossregional organization, inhibiting the development of a truly autonomous civil society. This organized dependence on the government and the blurred boundary between government and nongovernment is especially visible with the phenomenon of governmentally organized NGOs, some of which are little more than just another branch of the state (Wu 2002). Civil society hence operates in the shadow of the state. NGOs become "embedded" (Ho and Edmonds 2008) and, paradoxically, they are tasked by the government to fill the gaps in the provision of public goods (Wang and Liu 2009).

As a staunch advocate of national sovereignty and intergovernmental negotiations, China voices a positive perspective on the role of the state as a central actor in global governance. Other players such as international financing institutions are viewed with suspicion for their intrusiveness and their imposition of policy norms and radical economic restructuring on sovereign states. This view rejects "civilian rule, elections and multiparty democracy" as prerequisites to legitimate rule and conditions for development funding (Weiss 2000, 799).

Does this state-centrist version constitute a credible alternative model of global governance? According to Joshua Cooper Ramo (2004), a "Beijing consensus" indeed seeks to replace the Washington consensus. Its characteristics are gradualism instead of imposed shock therapy, development through innovation, and self-determination. It assumes state control to prevent destabilizing changes, and it protects against external interferences and policy prescriptions. Although the Chinese government does not present the Beijing consensus as a model of global governance (as it is modeled on Chinese development), it has become an alternative doctrine at the global level for developing countries, from the political elites of Iran to the governments of resource-rich Angola and Nigeria. China's own development aid efforts make its development model even more alluring for the least-developed countries: China offers "no-strings investment finance," which preserves the political structure and institutions, and most important, the centrality of political elites in the recipient countries. This model is a direct challenge to international finance institutions guided mostly by Western values and led by powerful countries. The Beijing consensus might facilitate the participation of developing countries in global governance while fostering China's new international role. The gradualism, the dithering, and the pro-growth bias, however, raise questions about the adequacy and effectiveness of such governance for environmental protection.

Limited Statehood and Conservation Policies in Africa

Africa has a record number of least-developed countries, many of which are often seen as fragile or even "failed" states. From its inception the postcolonial state was perceived as alien (Badie 2000) and a source of nuisance or threat for local people. The relationship between the state and the communities has been a one-way, top-down flow, with little sensitivity to the needs of local communities and a lack of responsiveness to their demands—even in formally democratic countries (Hitchcock and Holm 1993; Twyman 1998). Centralization is a common feature in postcolonial states but does not deliver policy effectiveness. The combination of centralization and bureaucratic authoritarianism means that not only the needs but also the conservation practices and empirical knowledge of local communities are ignored or despised. When policy decentralization occurs, it does not always benefit representative and accountable local institutions (Ribot 2002). It often leads to localized systems of domination by patrimonial regional barons whose impact on local communities can be worse than that of the central state (Oyono 2004, 2005), for instance, when some Kenyan politicians-turned-businessmen wanted to appropriate and log a Masaï sacred forest (Péron 2000). Although a source of patronage through its access to donor money, the neopatrimonial state, with its abundant legislation seldom or arbitrarily enforced and narrow-minded elites seeking self-aggrandizement, fails to deliver public goods and implement minimal state functions. Thus, limited statehood undermines policy making in the environment as well as in other issue areas.

Since independence, African conservation policies have been authoritarian in essence and largely ineffective. Local people perceived national parks and other protected areas against a historical legacy of European colonialism and, more recently, Western green imperialism (Duffy 2000). In the eyes of those dispossessed of their land, conservation was the continuation of colonial oppression. The state imposed standards alien to the local culture and banned the use of resources, thus threatening the survival of the communities. Repressive antipoaching policies have been a case in point (Gibson 1999). Not only do top-down conservation policies always lack popular legitimacy, but they are also usually undermined by neopatrimonial behaviors: corrupt political entrepreneurs and bureaucrats turn a blind eye on organized poaching, when they are not fully involved in it, and the full wrath of the state falls on survival hunters.

Community-based natural resources management projects, such as the well-publicized Communal Areas Management Program for Indigenous Resources (CAMPFIRE) in Zimbabwe or the Administrative Management Design for Game Areas (ADMADE) in Zambia, aiming at the sustainable use of wildlife, became the favorite alternative for donors willing to support conservation in Africa. It seemed to provide a formula to overcome the conservation impasse (Hulme and Murphree 1999). Community-based natural resources management, however, relies on an idealized vision of local communities (Compagnon 2000), whereas discriminations based on gender, age, ethnicity (Dzingirai 2003), or social status led to the exclusion of specific groups from accessing resources (Blaikie 2006). It is also questionable whether community-based natural resources management is viable in a context of limited statehood or authoritarian neopatrimonial state: even when policy focuses on local communities, there is an encapsulation effect of the state with all its perverse tendencies. In Zimbabwe, in the 1990s, there was a fundamental contradiction between the CAMPFIRE philosophy (decentralization, wide popular participation, rational management of wildlife stocks, and accountability) on the one hand, and the nature of the ruling party's domination of the polity and elite behavior on the other (Duffy 1997; Mofson 1997).

After the politically motivated "land crisis" began in February 2000 and Robert Mugabe's regime went amok, the hitherto seemingly rational conservation policy was derailed. Private wildlife conservancies—which play a pivotal role in the conservation of black rhino and other threatened species—were invaded and vandalized like agricultural commercial farms. Scores of wildlife were killed on private land, communal areas, and more recently within the limits of the national parks with the complicity of some park rangers. A local NGO, formed in April 2001 to document the impact of government's policies on the environment, roughly estimated "that games ranches have lost between 80 percent and 90 percent of wildlife to poachers, and the larger conservancies have lost around 60 percent" (Zimbabwe Conservation Task Force 2006; Reuters 2007). The poaching of elephants and rhinos and the illicit trade in ivory and rhino horn resumed on a wider scale than ever with the prevailing climate of anarchy, thus depleting the resource base (Swain 2008; Economic Times 2009; The Times 2009; Washington Examiner 2009). The collapse of the Zimbabwean state institutions and the rule of law, the ensuing economic free fall, and the severed relation with donor countries (Compagnon 2011) completed the ruin of CAMPFIRE (Mapedza and Bond 2006; Balint and Mashinya 2006).

The Zimbabwean state, which has been originally the facilitator of this acclaimed conservation policy, became its major liability. In other parts of Africa, the nature of the postcolonial state is a major factor in the relative success or the total failure of projects on community-based natural resources management (Blaikie 2006). Therefore, the attempt by Western donors to circumvent the state by dealing directly with local communities—often through NGOs—is doomed to fail. Alternate strategies of regionalizing conservation include, for instance, the promotion of transboundary, protected areas and the concept Parks for Peace promoted by the World Conversation Union since 1997 in order to enhance regional cooperation for biodiversity conservation and regional peace (Sandwith, Hamilton, and Sheppard 2001). One example of such protected areas in Southern Africa is the Great Limpopo Transfrontier Park (Wolmer 2003; Duffy 2006). However, these initiatives are likely to stumble once again on the shortcomings of member states (especially

Mozambique and Zimbabwe in this particular case) in terms of policy effectiveness and public accountability.

Globalizing States in Environmental Governance Platforms

A third example for the new role of the state can be found in the nego-tiations at the 2002 World Summit on Sustainable Development. Here, one can explore in detail how the globalized competition state (as described previously) behaves under market discipline and makes deci-sions on global environmental governance. Moreover, this example allows us to look into the different ways states pose themselves in rela-tion to their outside rather than toward their populace.

The summit was a symbolic turning point because of the record number of participating states and government heads: state actors either could not afford not to participate or did not want to miss the opportu-nity to be on an international platform. More important for environmen-tal governance, the summit did not result in any international agreements. The only tangible result was the endorsement of "type II outcomes," that is, transnational public-private partnerships that were intended to com-plement the binding agreements ("type I outcomes") in achieving the Millennium Development Goals (see Bäckstrand et al., this book, chapter 6). The summit was a turning point because it symbolized the consolida-tion of environmental governance practices of the decade leading up to it, characterized by deregulation in environmental issue areas, favoring of voluntary, market-based mechanisms as solutions to environmental problems, and a further inclusion of nonstate actors in decision making in the name of participation. These practices do not necessarily point at a withering of the state because they are strongly influenced by state agen-cies and national legislations or regulations or the lack of. Within the United Nations system, state actors closely monitor these gradual and ambivalent steps toward a privatization of governance.

The privatization practices in the United Nations have been manifest in the establishment of the United Nations Fund for International Part-nerships, the Global Compact, the proposal for the establishment of carbon markets as a solution to climate change, and the many texts and documents that have been produced in the platforms of these organiza-tions. Some of these developments have generated severe internal and external criticism (Zammit 2003). Yet, the discursive ground for this transformation has been in place since the United Nations Conference on Environment and Development in Rio de Janeiro in 1992. When the Stockholm Declaration was signed in 1972 (UN 1972, paragraph 2), the

sovereign rights of states coincided with environmental responsibilities
and the rights of the populace and future generations. This has been a
careful arrangement that neither dismisses the developmental demands
of the South nor the environmental demands of the North. The resulting
texts of the Rio Summit highlighted instead development as a right and
responsibility of every state. The second principle of the Rio Declaration
(UN 1992a) evokes the "sovereign right [of states] to exploit their own
resources," and "the right to development" is defined in the third principle. Simultaneously, chapter II of Agenda 21 (UN 1992b, paragraphs
2.3–2.7) is titled and devoted to "international cooperation to accelerate
sustainable development in developing countries" and points at a requirement for all countries to remove:

Tariff and non-tariff impediments, [together with a] substantial and progressive
reduction in the support and protection of agriculture. . . . Trade liberalization
should therefore be pursued on a global basis across economic sectors so as to
contribute to sustainable development, [as well as] enhancing the role of enterprises and promoting competitive markets through adoption of competitive
policies.

It was no surprise then that the documents of the World Summit on
Sustainable Development started to make direct references to globalization as if it is a force of nature: an objective, irreversible feature of the
world that can neither be disputed nor influenced or overcome. The
Johannesburg Plan of Implementation (UN 2002, para. 47) devotes its
chapter V to "sustainable development in a globalizing world," and
paints a rather neoliberal picture of globalization:

Globalization offers opportunities and challenges for sustainable development.
We recognize that globalization and interdependence are offering new opportunities for trade, investment and capital flows and advances in technology, including
information technology, for the growth of the world economy, development and
the improvement of living standards around the world. At the same time, there
remain serious challenges, including serious financial crises, insecurity, poverty,
exclusion, and inequality within and among societies.

Although the opportunities are narrated as a direct consequence of
globalization, the challenges are the remainder, as if these are problems
that globalization is yet to solve, rather than it caused or deepened. More
important, the opportunities it represents are directly linked to the
growth of a world economy and advancing of technology. In this context,
the ways in which state actors are expected to implement international
decisions are described at the introduction of the Johannesburg Plan of
Implementation (UN 2002, paragraph 3):

The implementation should involve all relevant actors through partnerships, especially between Governments of the North and South, on the one hand, and between Governments and major groups, on the other, to achieve the widely shared goals of sustainable development. As reflected in the Monterrey Consensus, such partnerships are key to pursuing sustainable development in a globalizing world.

The negotiations on sustainability partnerships were an actualization of these principles. During the negotiations, state delegations had diverse and rather crucial reasons for supporting or opposing these new mechanisms of governance (Mert 2009): although the United States was unwilling to commit more public funds and opposed binding commitments, the European Union claimed sustainability partnerships to be complementary to an agreement. The least-developed countries were wary of the potential eviction effect of classic development aid being redirected toward the partnerships and the dominance of powerful nonstate actors. For developing countries, partnerships could serve to circumvent their governments and channel donor money through chosen NGOs and corporations, being the new framework for previously existing development aid programs (Stewart and Gray 2006; Biermann et al. 2007). Some authoritarian regimes such as China and Russia saw the inclusion of multiple stakeholders and the participatory approach contained in these partnerships as a political threat. The linking of foreign agencies, transnational NGOs, and businesses with domestic actors was perceived as undue interference in internal affairs likely to erode government control over society.

Immediately after the summit, states supportive of these partnerships launched the majority of registered partnerships, and in these arrangements they are often the leading partners instead. A database on these partnerships and those later registered with the UN Commission on Sustainable Development (UNCSD) compiled and analyzed within the Global Governance Project (Biermann et al. 2007) shows that lead partner governments are predominantly from donor countries, that more than a quarter of all partnerships involve only industrialized countries, and that more than half of partnerships have no state partners from the developing world. Therefore, what is often portrayed as the embodiment of private governance is more likely a new modality of action of the (OECD) state (albeit more indirect and subtler) in a world of financial and political constraints: the need to attract additional funds from the private sector has influenced the way Southern and Northern governments acted, but in the end it was governmental negotiations and the strategies of governments that determined the character of these governance instruments.

To conclude, state involvement determines the success or failure of a voluntary, hybrid regime of environmental governance mechanisms such as sustainability partnerships. Our results support the argument that partnerships can tackle environmental problems properly only when coupled with command-and-control regulation or a coordinating body (Gunningham 2007) or when implemented in issue areas that are premature for direct regulation. In the globalization context, state actors can use the fuzzy boundaries between public and private to their own benefit and reconfigure their role through hybrid governance mechanisms. They make use of the market logic to transfer some of their erstwhile authority to private actors, in ways and issue areas they find agreeable. However, global private-led governance mechanisms are offered as obvious remedies to the "inevitable" consequences of globalization, a move that transmutes market failures into state failures. Such an image is put forth by the partnerships under the UN Commission on Sustainable Development, as mechanisms "to implement what states failed to implement," or in the creation of standards by corporations "to regulate where states fail to regulate" (Mert 2012).

Explanations

Overall, it seems that at the beginning of the twenty-first century the state as agency is seriously undermined, circumvented, and bounded by the intervention of supranational and subnational actors, including NGOs and private companies, and by globalization forces that change most public institutions. Sometimes the state delegates policy formulation and implementation to other levels of authority (e.g., EU institutions) or empowers private actors to produce public goods and other functional equivalents to public policies (e.g., CSD partnerships).

Nevertheless, our empirical illustrations show that the state remains pivotal in global environmental governance. Powerful states use private and hybrid mechanisms to further their national interests in international arenas. Others use them to justify inaction. Even when state capacities are residual or declining—such as in many areas of limited statehood—governments use the conservation of the environment as a bargaining chip with donor countries to obtain economic gains. All these, paradoxically, underline the importance of the state. Therefore, stressing the role of private actors taking over governance functions does not mean neglecting the role of the state in shaping international regime complexes (Keohane and Victor 2011) and in providing regulatory frameworks for implementation at national level. The reliance on hybrid governance mechanisms, therefore, does not signify a retreat of the state. It is rather a new functional mode of a globalized state.

We should also take into account the variability of statehood, each form creating a range of strategies in the context of globalization. For the emerging economies as well as the least-developed countries, state-led global governance is still a preferred option, although donor countries and organizations try to evade it. Even in areas of limited statehood, the state matters. In these areas, there is a need to reengage state actors because political decay and the absence of basic state functions can derail all efforts toward sustainability. In sum, the state, however fragile, dysfunctional, or ineffective as it might appear in many cases, fulfills several roles in global environmental governance (the following being not necessarily exhaustive).

First, as gatekeeper. Governments to some extent still control various flows: external funding, outside manpower, and expertise (through the potential ban of rival actors such as international NGOs and corporations) and sometimes even new ideas and information (e.g., China's control of its citizens' access to the Internet). Governments can influence or prevent the transfer of policy models if it suits them. Western interference in developing countries, for instance, can always be discounted as mere "imperialism," especially when donor countries and international organizations want to activate environmental conditionality clauses. In many countries, the participation of local civil society in global governance (such as UN conferences) depends on state approval and support. Gatekeeping can end up being either detrimental or beneficial to the local people and their environment.

Second, as regulator. The state is a norm producer when adapting its national legislation and regulations to international treaties (EU member states do it on a routine basis because a significant share of their environmental laws stem from European legislation). By doing so, the state also disseminates global norms within its own society. In this capacity, it is far from being a neutral vehicle or an innocuous translator. It always has leverage. Framed in the state elite's discourse, twisted to suit the government's agenda, global norms are altered and transformed. For instance, there are probably as many legal embodiments of the precautionary principle as independent states. Admittedly, this norm transfer power is more problematic in least-developed countries but many of these have a rather lax attitude toward international law anyway. The sovereignty myth is a powerful tool for state elites willing to deflect external criticisms or prescriptions.

Third, as facilitator. Even the weakest least-developed country's government can grant outsiders legitimate access to the local communities and specific territories for policy implementation or withdraw such privilege at will. Many Western environmental NGOs learned that lesson the hard way during the last decades. Similarly, international organizations such as UNEP or United Nations Development Programme (UNDP) operate in a country only with the consent of its government and must submit to its whim. By facilitating activities of external actors in the country, state authorities can keep them in check. For instance, in facilitating CDM projects run by corporations or NGOs, the Chinese government could use them for its own policy objectives (Schroeder 2009). In OECD countries, the state can facilitate the ecological modernization more effectively than most other actors and change into a "green state" promoting sustainability (Barry and Eckersley 2005).

Fourth, as international advocate. When relaying local views and demands at global level, or pretending to do so, the state bureaucracy can frame these "voices from grassroots" in a way to foster its own status in the international arena (something Zimbabwe achieved in 1997 with the promotion of community-based sustainable use of wildlife within in the Convention on International Trade in Endangered Species of Wild Fauna and Flora (CITES)). By "speaking for the people," the state can draw much legitimacy that can be used then to resist encroachments from larger states, global markets, and corporations. This is exactly the kind of pressure exerted by coalesced least-developed countries in international negotiations toward a more protective access-and-benefit-sharing regime within the Convention on Biological Diversity (CBD). They put forward the fate of marginalized indigenous communities to advance their strategic objectives.

Finally, as protector. The state still can, to a certain extent, shield its population from the most adverse effects of globalization—for example, through the enforcement of labor laws, sanitary regulations, environmental management standards, or social welfare policies. For example, a carbon tax at the border on imported goods is currently being discussed as a policy option within the European Union to safeguard ambitious climate mitigation efforts. State regulations—when complied with—are still more efficient to secure environmental protection, and EU governance is largely based on this regulatory power (Jordan, Wurzel, and Zito 2005).

By performing some of these—and sometimes all—five roles, the state retains a prominent status in global environmental governance. Its claim to exclusive political authority over a territory—even when challenged in practice—gives it unmatched leeway, including the potential capacity to hinder or block operations by external actors and to slow down policy change.

In addition, private governance when effective promotes less stringent standards and only for specific domains. Besides, it relies on a whole set of legal and institutional frameworks provided by various branches of government. For example, eco-certification would not work without international trade rules, custom services, and labeling regulations in consumer markets.

Therefore, expecting the private sector alone to provide governance by default because of state inaction could prove misleading. It is certainly not a viable option in areas of limited statehood. A greener or responsible corporate sector can be expected only in countries with a strong regulatory environment. One example is the behavior of oil corporations in the Niger Delta, which is characterized in Nigeria by what Amnesty International calls "absentee government" (Human Rights Watch 1999; Frynas 2001; Hallowes and Butler 2005; Amnesty International 2009), and in the Guinea Gulf at large (Wood 2004). Nonpolitical authority, which is one not based on political legitimacy, often leads to worse environmental governance—or nongovernance (Overbeek et al. 2010)—than any bad government.

Conclusions and Outlook

The state remains of paramount importance in global and national environmental governance, if only because the world society is still partly based on state units and international negotiations are largely conducted and concluded by state representatives in spite of dreams of a postsovereign world order (Karkkainen 2004). The state is also an important cog in the complex multilevel governance that links the local to the global. Although policy making and, more important, policy implementation are scale dependent, the nation state is well positioned as a broker between local governments and indigenous communities on the one end, and transnational companies and international arenas on the other. Yet the role of the state is constantly changing under the forces of economic globalization and global environmental change.

This said, however, it becomes increasingly difficult in today's global environmental governance to disentangle the state's singular contribution from the roles of other actors. In the future, state bureaucracies are likely to work more and more in symbiosis with NGOs and private companies for the sake of efficiency and self-perpetuation. The neoliberal discourse provides the ideological rationale for such accommodation but this trend has deeper roots. Most affected are the areas of weak or limited statehood but this process has relevance for emerging economies as well, including China where the state remains the dominant actor, and for Western democracies where participatory policy making is increasingly in fashion. Therefore, further research needs to focus more precisely on these accommodation strategies and the ensuing forms of hybrid governance. As also stated by others (Mol 2007), we need to further theorize the role of the state in these new modes of governance.

From a policy perspective, it is crucial to take into account the different models of states with their significant variations in power resources and in the legitimacy of internal institutions because they have an unequal capacity to influence global governance and increase effectiveness. Undermining the state in the North and South is not a recipe for success. On the contrary, in two thirds of the world, strengthening state structures is as necessary as supporting civil society to make governments more responsive and accountable. Reforming the often weak or authoritarian state in parts of the South and acknowledging the true role of legitimate public authority in the industrialized countries remain preconditions for enhanced environmental governance.

References

Amnesty International. 2009. *Nigeria: Petroleum Pollution and Poverty in the Niger Delta*. London: AI Publications.

Badie, Bertrand. 2000. *The Imported State: The Westernalization of the Political Order*. Palo Alto, CA: Stanford University Press.

Balint, Peter J., and Judith Mashinya. 2006. The Decline of a Model Community-based Conservation Project: Governance, Capacity, and Devolution in Mahenye, Zimbabwe. *Geoforum* 37:805–815.

Barnett, Michael, and Kathryn Sikkink. 2008. From International Relations to Global Society. In *Oxford Handbook of International Relations*, ed. Christian Reus-Smit and Ducan Snidal, 62–83. Oxford: Oxford University Press.

Barry, John, and Robyn Eckersley. 2005. W(h)ither the Green State? In *The State and the Global Ecological Crisis*, ed. John Barry and Robyn Eckersley, 255–272. Cambridge, MA: MIT Press.

Biermann, Frank, Chan Man-san, Ayşem Mert, and Philipp Pattberg. 2007. Multi-stakeholder Partnerships for Sustainable Development: Does the Promise Hold? In *Partnerships, Governance and Sustainable Development: Reflections on Theory and Practice*, ed. Pieter Glasbergen, Frank Biermann, and Arthur P. J. Mol, 239–260. Cheltenham, UK: Edward Elgar.

Biermann, Frank, and Philipp Pattberg. 2008. Global Environmental Governance: Taking Stock, Moving Forward. *Annual Review of Environment and Resources* 33:277–294.

Blaikie, Piers. 2006. Is Small Really Beautiful? Community-based Natural Resource Management in Malawi and Botswana. *World Development* 34 (11): 1942–1957.

Blaikie, Piers, and John Mope Simo. 1998. Cameroon's Environmental Accords: Signed, Sealed, but Undelivered. In *Engaging Countries: Strengthening Compliance with International Environmental Accords*, ed. Edith Brown Weiss and Harold K. Jacobson, 437–474. Cambridge, MA: MIT Press.

Bratton, Michael, and Nicholas Van de Walle. 1994. Neo-patrimonial Regimes and Political Transition in Africa. *World Politics* 47:453–489.

Brown, William. 2006. Africa and International Relations: A Comment on IR Theory, Anarchy and Statehood. *Review of International Studies* 32:119–143.

Cameron, Angus, and Ronen Palan. 2004. *The Imagined Economies of Globalization*. London: Sage.

Cerny, Philip G. 2005. Political Globalization and the Competition State. In *The Political Economy of the Changing Global Order*, ed. Richard Stubbs and Geoffrey R.D. Underhill, 376–386. Oxford: Oxford University Press.

Châtaigner, Jean-Marc, and Hervé Magro. 2007. *Etats et sociétés fragiles: Entre conflits, reconstruction et développement*. Paris: Karthala.

Chen, Sulan, and Juha I. Uitto. 2003. Governing Marine and Coastal Environment in China: Building Local Government Capacity through International Cooperation. *China Environment Series* 1 (6):67–80.

Clapham, Christopher. 1996. *Africa and the International System: The Politics of State Survival*. Cambridge, UK: Cambridge University Press.

Clapp, Jennifer. 1998. The Privatization of Global Environmental Governance: ISO 14000 and the Developing World. *Global Governance* 4 (3):295–316.

Clark, Ian. 1999. *Globalization and International Relations Theory*. Oxford: Oxford University Press.

Compagnon, Daniel. 2000. Impératifs et contraintes de la gestion communautaire. In *Administrer l'environnement en Afrique: Gestion communautaire, conservation et développement durable*, ed. Daniel Compagnon and François Constantin, 13–35. Paris: Karthala.

Compagnon, Daniel. 2011. *A Predictable Tragedy: Robert Mugabe and the Collapse of Zimbabwe*. Philadelphia: University of Pennsylvania Press.

Compagnon, Daniel, Fanny Florémont, and Isabelle Lamaud. 2011. Sub-Saharan Africa: Fragmented Environmental Governance without Regional Integration. In

The Regionalisation of Environmental Governance, ed. Lorraine Elliott and Shaun Breslin, 92–112. London: Routledge.

Cutler, Claire A., Virginia Haufler, and Tony Porter. 1999. *Private Authority and International Affairs*. Albany: SUNY Press.

Dingwerth, Klaus. 2007. *The New Transnationalism: Transnational Governance and Democratic Legitimacy*. Houndsmill, UK: Palgrave Macmillan.

Duffy, Rosaleen. 1997. The Environmental Challenge to the Nation-State: Super-parks and National Parks Policy in Zimbabwe. *Journal of Southern African Studies* 23 (3):448–449.

Duffy, Rosaleen. 2000. *Killing for Conservation: Wildlife Policy in Zimbabwe*. London: James Currey.

Duffy, Rosaleen. 2006. The Potential and Pitfalls of Global Environmental Governance: The Politics of Transfrontier Conservation Areas in Southern Africa. *Political Geography* 25 (1):89–112.

Dzingirai, Vupenyu. 2003. "CAMPFIRE is not for Ndebele Migrants": The Impact of Excluding Outsiders from CAMPFIRE in the Zambezi Valley, Zimbabwe. *Journal of Southern African Studies* 29 (2):445–459.

Economic Times. 3 November 2009. Quarter of Zimbabwe's Rhinos Killed by Poachers. Retrieved from http://economictimes.indiatimes.com/Quarter-of -Zimbabwes-rhinos-killed-by-poachers/articleshow/5192716.cms.

Englebert, Pierre. 2009. *Africa: Unity, Sovereignty, and Sorrow*. Boulder, CO: Lynne Rienner.

Falkner, Robert. 2003. Private Environmental Governance and International Relations: Exploring the Links. *Global Environmental Politics* 3 (2):72–87.

Frynas, Jedrzej George. 2001. Corporate and State Responses to Anti-oil Protests in the Niger Delta. *African Affairs* 100:27–54.

Gibson, Clark C. 1999. *Politicians and Poachers: The Political Economy of Wildlife Policy in Africa*. Cambridge, UK: Cambridge University Press.

Gill, Stephen. 1995. Globalization, Market Civilization, and Disciplinary Neo-liberalism. *Millennium: Journal of International Studies* 24 (3):399–423.

Gunningham, Neil. 2007. Environmental Partnerships in Agriculture: Reflections on the Australian Experience. In *Partnerships, Governance and Sustainable Development: Reflections on Theory and Practice*, ed. Pieter Glasbergen, Frank Biermann, and Arthur P. J. Mol, 115–137. Cheltenham, UK: Edward Elgar.

Hallowes, David, and Mark Butler. 2005. Whose Energy Future? Big Oil against People in Africa The Ground Work Report 2005, Pietermaritzburg, South Africa: Ground Work.

Harding, Luke. 2009. Tiny Nauru Struts World Stage by Recognising Breakaway Republics. *The Guardian*. Retrieved from http://www.guardian.co.uk/world/2009/ dec/14/nauro-recognises-abkhazia-south-ossetia.

Haufler, Virginia. 2002. Crossing the Boundary between Public and Private: International Regimes and Non-state Actors. In *Regime Theory and International*

Relations, ed. Volker Rittberger and Peter Mayer, 94–111. Oxford: Oxford University Press.

Heggelund, Gørild. 2003. *The Significance of the UN Global Conferences on China's Domestic Environmental Policymaking. FNI Report, 11/2003.* Lysaker, Norway: Fridtjof Nansen Institute. 23p.

Heggelund, Gørild, and Ellen Bruzelius Backer. 2007. China and UN Environmental Policy: Institutional Growth, Learning, and Implementation. *International Environmental Agreement: Politics, Law and Economics* 7 (4):415–438.

Herbst, Jeffrey. 1996. Responding to State Failure in Africa. *International Security* 21 (3):120–144.

Hitchcock, Robert K., and John D. Holm. 1993. Bureaucratic Domination of Hunter-Gatherer Societies: A Study of the San in Botswana. *Development and Change* 24 (2):305–338.

Ho, Peter, and Richard Louis Edmonds, eds. 2008. *China's Embedded Activism.* Abingdon, UK: Routledge.

Hooghe, Liesbet, and Gary Marks. 2001. *Multi-level Governance and European Integration.* Lanham, MD: Rowman and Littlefield.

Hulme, David, and Marshall Murphree. 1999. Communities, Wildlife, and the "New Conservation" in Africa. *Journal of International Development* 11 (2):277–286.

Human Rights Watch. 1999. The Price of Oil: Corporate Responsibility and Human Rights Violations in Nigeria's Oil Producing Communities. New York: Human Rights Watch Report. Retrieved from http://www.hrw.org/reports/1999/02/23/price-oil.

Jackson, Robert H. 1990. *Quasi-states: Sovereignty, International Relations, and the Third World.* Cambridge, UK: Cambridge University Press.

Jia, Wenhua. 2009. Desertification in Ordos. Presentation at the EU-Earth System Governance Roundtable on the Future of Environmental Governance in China, EC Delegation, Beijing, 22 October.

Jordan, Andrew, Rüdiger Wurzel, and Anthony Zito. 2005. Environmental Governance . . . or Government? The International Politics of the Environmental Instruments. In *Handbook of Global Environmental Politics*, ed. Peter Dauvergne, 202–217. Cheltenham, UK: Edward Elgar.

Karkkainen, Bradley C. 2004. Post-sovereign Environmental Governance. *Global Environmental Politics* 4 (1):72–96.

Kasa, Sjur, Anne T. Gullberg, and Gørild Heggelund. 2008. The Group of 77 in the International Climate Negotiations: Recent Developments and Future Directions. *International Environmental Agreement: Politics, Law and Economics* 8:113–127.

Keohane, Robert O., and David G. Victor. 2011. The Regime Complex for Climate Change. *Perspectives on Politics* 9 (1):7–23.

Krasner, Stephen. 1999. *Sovereignty: Organized Hypocrisy.* Princeton, NJ: Princeton University Press.

Lake, David A. 2008. The State and International Relations. In *The Oxford Handbook of International Relations*, ed. Christian Reus-Smit and Duncan Snidal, 41–61. Oxford: Oxford University Press.

Levy, David, and Peter Newell, eds. 2005. *The Business of Global Environmental Governance*. Cambridge, MA: MIT Press.

Mann, Michael. 1997. Has Globalization Ended the Rise and Rise of the Nation-State? *Review of International Political Economy* 4 (3):472–496.

Mapedza, Everisto, and Ivan Bond. 2006. Political Deadlock and Devolved Wildlife Management in Zimbabwe. The Case of Nenyunga Ward. *Journal of Environment & Development* 15 (4):407–427.

McCormick, John. 2001. *Environmental Policy in the European Union:* Houndsmill, UK: Palgrave.

Médard, Jean-François. 1991. L'Etat néo-patrimonial en Afrique noire. In *Etats d'Afrique Noire: Formations, mécanismes et crise*, ed. Jean-François Médard, 323–353. Paris: Karthala.

Mert, Ayşem. 2009. Partnerships for Sustainable Development as Discursive Practice: Shifts in Discourses of Environment and Democracy. *Forest Policy and Economics* 11:109–122.

Mert, Ayşem. 2012. Partnerships and the Privatisation of Environmental Governance: On Myths, Forces of Nature and Other Inevitabilities. *Environmental Values* 21 (4).

Migdal, Joel S. 1988. *Strong Societies and Weak States: State-Society Relations and State Capabilities in the Third World*. Princeton, NJ: Princeton University Press.

Miles, Edward L., Arild Underdal, Steinar Andresen, Jørgen Wettestad, Jon Birger Skjærseth, and Elaine M. Carlin, eds. 2001. *Environmental Regime Effectiveness: Confronting Theory with Evidence*. Cambridge, MA: MIT Press.

Miller, Marian A. L. 1998. Sovereignty Reconfigured: Environmental Regimes and Third World States. In *The Greening of Sovereignty in World Politics*, ed. Karen Liftin, 173–192. Cambridge, MA: MIT Press.

Mitchell, Ronald B. 2006. Problem Structure, Institutional Design, and the Relative Effectiveness of International Environmental Agreements. *Global Environmental Politics* 6 (3):72–89.

Mofson, Phyllis. 1997. Zimbabwe and CITES: Illustrating the Reciprocal Relationship between the State and the International Regime. In *The Internationalization of Environmental Protection*, ed. Miranda A. Schreurs and Elizabeth Economy, 162–187. Cambridge, UK: Cambridge University Press.

Mol, Arthur P. J. 2006. Environment and Modernity in Transitional China: Frontiers of Ecological Modernization. *Development and Change* 37 (1):29–56.

Mol, Arthur P. J. 2007. Bringing the Environmental State Back In: Partnerships in Perspective. In *Partnerships, Governance and Sustainable Development: Reflections on Theory and Practice*, ed. Pieter Glasbergen, Frank Biermann, and Arthur P. J. Mol, 214–236. Cheltenham, UK: Edward Elgar.

Moravcsik, Andrew. 1997. Taking Preferences Seriously: A Liberal Theory of International Politics. *International Organization* 51 (4):513–553.

Moreno Torres, Magüi, and Michael Anderson. 2004. Fragile States: Defining Difficult Environments for Poverty Reduction. PRDE Working Paper 1, London: UK Department for International Development (DFID), August.

Najam, Adil. 2005. Why Global Environmental Politics Looks Different from the South. In *Handbook of Global Environmental Politics*, ed. Peter Dauvergne, 111–126. Cheltenham, UK: Edward Elgar.

Neuman, Stephanie G., ed. 1998. *International Relations Theory and the Third World*. London: Macmillan.

Newell, Peter. 2000. *Climate for Change, Non-state Actors and the Global Politics of the Greenhouse*. Cambridge, UK: Cambridge University Press.

Osiander, Andreas. 2001. Sovereignty, International Relations, and the Westphalian Myth. *International Organization* 55 (2):251–287.

Overbeek, Henk, Klaus Dingwerth, Philipp Pattberg, and Daniel Compagnon. 2010. Global Governance: Decline or Maturation of an Academic Concept? *International Studies Review* 12 (4):619–642.

Oyono, Phil René. 2004. One Step Forward, Two Steps Back? Paradoxes of Natural Resources Management's Decentralization in Cameroon. *Journal of Modern African Studies* 42 (1):91–111.

Oyono, Phil René. 2005. Profiling Local-Level Outcomes of Environmental Decentralizations: The Case of Cameroon's Forests in the Congo Basin. *Journal of Environment & Development* 14 (3):317–337.

Pattberg, Philipp. 2007. *Private Institutions and Global Governance: The New Politics of Environmental Sustainability*. Cheltenham, UK: Edward Elgar.

Péron, Xavier. 2000. Communauté locale contre collectivité locale (Maasaï-Loïta, Kenya). In *Administrer l'environnement en Afrique: Gestion communautaire, conservation et développement durable*, ed. Daniel Compagnon and François Constantin, 383–404. Paris: Karthala.

Putnam, Robert D. 1988. Diplomacy and Domestic Politics: The Logic of Two-Level Games. *International Organization* 42:427–460.

Ramo, Joshua C. 2004. *The Beijing Consensus*. London: The Foreign Policy Centre.

Reno, William. 1998. *Warlord Politics and African States*. Boulder, CO: Lynne Rienner.

Reuters. 7 May 2007. Poaching Rises in Zimbabwe's Game Parks Report.

Ribot, Jesse C. 2002. *Democratic Decentralization of Natural Resources: Institutionalizing Popular Participation*. Washington, DC: World Resources Institute. Available at http://www.wri.org/publication/democratic-decentralization-natural -resources-institutionalizing-popular-participat.

Risse, Thomas. 2005. Two-Thirds of the World: Governance in Areas of Limited Statehood Is a Global Problem. [Transatlantic edition] *Transnationale Politik* 6 (4):64–69.

Sandwith, T., C. Shine, L. Hamilton, and D. Sheppard. 2001. *Transboundary Protected Areas for Peace and Co-operation*. Gland, Switzerland: IUCN.

Sassen, Saskia. 1996. *Losing Control? Sovereignty in an Age of Globalization*. New York: Columbia University Press.

Schroeder, Miriam. 2009. Varieties of Carbon Governance: Utilizing the Clean Development Mechanism for Chinese Priorities. *Journal of Environment & Development* 18 (4):371–394.

Sørensen, Georg. 2001. *Changes in Statehood: The Transformation of International Relations*. Houndmills, UK: Palgrave.

Stewart, Amy, and Tim Gray. 2006. The Authenticity of "Type Two" Multistakeholder Partnerships for Water and Sanitation in Africa: When Is a Stakeholder a Partner? *Environmental Politics* 15 (3):362–378.

Stokke, Olav Schram. 1997. Regimes as Governance Systems. In *Global Governance: Drawing Insights from the Environmental Experience*, ed. Oran R. Young, 27–63. Cambridge, MA: MIT Press.

Strange, Susan. 1996. *The Retreat of the State: The Diffusion of Power in the World Economy*. Cambridge, UK: Cambridge University Press.

Swain, John. 2008. Poachers Terrorize Zimbabwe's Rhinos. The Times, July 20. Retrieved from http://www.timesonline.co.uk/tol/news/world/africa/article4364116.ece.

The Times. 2009. Zambian Villagers at War with Elephants Fleeing Zimbabwean Poachers. June 22. Retrieved from http://www.thetimes.co.uk/tto/news/.

The Times. 2010a. Flights, Girls, and Cash Buy Japan Whaling Votes. June 13. Retrieved from http://www.timesonline.co.uk/tol/news/environment/article 7149091.ece.

The Times. 2010b. Revealed: Japan's Bribe on Whaling. June 13. Retrieved from http://www.timesonline.co.uk/tol/news/environment/article7149091.ece.

Twyman, Chasca. 1998. Rethinking Community Resource Management: Managing Resources or Managing People in Western Botswana? *Third World Quarterly* 19 (4):745–770.

UN (United Nations). 1972. Report of the United Nations Conference on the Human Environment. Stockholm: United Nations Publications.

UN. 1992a. Report of the United Nations Conference on Environment and Development. Document No. A/CONF.151/26 (Vol. I). New York: United Nations General Assembly.

UN. 1992b. Agenda 21. United Nations Conference on Environment and Development, Rio de Janeiro. Retrieved from http://www.un.org/esa/sustdev/documents/agenda21/english/agenda21toc.

UN. 2002. Johannesburg Plan of Implementation. World Summit on Sustainable Development, Johannesburg. Retrieved from http://www.un.org/esa/sustdev/documents/WSSD_POI_PD/English/WSSD_PlanImpl.pdf.

Vogler, John. 2005. *Defense of International Environmental Cooperation: In the State and the Global Ecological Crisis*. ed. John Barry and Robyn Eckersley, 229–253. Cambridge, MA: MIT Press.

Wang, Ming, and Qiushi Liu. 2009. Analyzing China's NGO Development System. *China Nonprofit Review* 1 (1):5–35.

Washington Examiner. 2009. Conservationists Say Poaching of Zimbabwe Rhino Doubles; Blame Law Enforcement Breakdown. June 20. http://washingtonexaminer.com.

Weiss, Thomas. 2000. Governance, Good Governance, and Global Governance: Conceptual and Actual Challenges. *Third World Quarterly* 21 (4):795–814.

Williams, Phil, and Gregory Baudin-O'Hayon. 2002. Global Governance, Transnational Organized Crime and Money Laundering. In *Governing Globalization: Power, Authority and Global Governance*, ed. David Held and Anthony McGrew, 127–144. Cambridge, UK: Polity Press.

Wolmer, William. 2003. Transboundary Conservation: the Politics of Ecological Integrity in the Great Limpopo Transfrontier Park. *Journal of Southern African Studies* 29 (1):261–278.

Wood, Geoffrey. 2004. Business and Politics in a Criminal State: The Case of Equatorial Guinea. *African Affairs* 103 (413):547–567.

Wu, Fengshi. 2002. Old Brothers or New Partners: GONGOs in Transnational Environmental Advocacy in China. *China Environment Series* 5:45–58.

Xinhua News Agency. 2006. Chinese Environmental NGOs Called on to Play a Bigger Role. 30 October. Retrieved from www.china.org.cn/english/environment/186754.htm.

Young, Oran R., ed. 1999. *The Effectiveness of International Environmental Regimes: Causal Connections and Behavioral Mechanisms*. Cambridge, MA: MIT Press.

Young, Oran R. 2002. Evaluating the Success of International Environmental Regimes: Where Are We Now? *Global Environmental Change: Human and Policy Dimensions* 12:73–77.

Zammit, Ann. 2003. *Development at Risk: Rethinking UN-Business Partnerships*. Geneva: UNRISD and South Centre.

Zhang, Yongjin. 2005. *China Goes Global.* London: The Foreign Policy Centre.

Zhang, ZhongXiang. 2000. Can China Afford to Commit Itself to an Emission Cap? An Economic and Political Analysis. *Energy Economics* 22:587–614.

Zimbabwe Conservation Task Force. 2006. Retrieved from http://www.zctf.mweb.co.zw/page2.html.

12

Conclusions

Frank Biermann and Philipp Pattberg

Among the many insights presented in this book, one thread runs through all studies: there is hardly any coherent, systematic, structured system of global environmental governance. Instead, global environmental governance presents itself as a complex web of multiple and interacting actors, networks, and institutions. For one, the number and type of actors in global environmental governance has multiplied in the last decades. Particularly striking is the strengthened role of international bureaucracies (Bauer, Andresen, and Biermann, this book, chapter 2), multinational corporations (Tienhaara, Orsini, and Falkner, this book, chapter 3), and scientists (Gupta et al., this book, chapter 4). As a result, the sites of authority in global environmental governance also have become more diverse. Several new mechanisms of global governance have emerged in addition to, and at times competing with, the traditional institutions of the intergovernmental system (see part II, this book). Given these developments, global environmental governance in itself has become more fragmented. Interactions horizontally (among international and transnational institutions) and vertically (among international and national institutions) have gained in importance and at the same time in complexity.

Often, these processes are related to a stronger role of actors beyond the state, from NGOs and corporations to novel nonstate governance arrangements such as transnational certification and labeling institutions. This development of nonstate agency, however, does not need to signal the demise of state authority in international politics. The state remains important (even though this importance differs for different types of states; see Compagnon, Chan, and Mert, this book, chapter 11). Moreover, the state itself remains a powerful agent in many alternative sites of governance, for example, as the final principal of intergovernmental bureaucracies (Bauer, Andresen, and Biermann, this book, chapter 2) or as a regulator and guarantee of some private governance mechanisms (Bäckstrand et al., this book, chapter 6).

This complex system of global environmental governance presents a tremendous research challenge for the social sciences. This book presents in ten analytical chapters the core approaches and findings of the Global Governance Project, a long-term research program of a dozen European institutions in close collaboration with colleagues in North America and other regions. In this concluding chapter, we address several overarching questions flowing from this analysis. We also highlight some of our policy-relevant findings and suggest future research directions.

Crosscutting Findings

From the breadth of theoretical and analytical work summarized in this book, we can discern a few common research threads that run through the chapters.

One is the particular perspective on the consequences of new mechanisms of global governance and of the behavior of its new actors. Whereas traditional regime theory in the 1990s focused on the effectiveness of intergovernmental regimes as social institutions, most work presented in this book deployed a more complex understanding of the effectiveness of governance. In general, most studies have looked at the wider effects of governance mechanisms rather than effectiveness in the narrow sense of goal attainment or problem solving. This has included broader cognitive, discursive, normative, and material influences of governance as well as high attention to potentially unintended effects of governance. In many studies in this book, the concept of *effectiveness* has thus been replaced by the broader notion of the *influence* of governance (e.g., Bauer, Andresen, and Biermann, this book, chapter 2; Gupta et al., this book, chapter 4; Pattberg, this book, chapter 5; Bäckstrand et al., this book, chapter 6).

A second recurrent theme in this book is the relevance of power and power relationships. In much policy writing on global governance, power relationships are often neglected, if not ignored, by an implicit assumption of joint action for common goods in the common interest. Most contributions to this book implicitly or explicitly contest this claim and provide detailed analysis of what power means in systems of global governance. For instance, how can the power of the new actors of global governance such as corporations be conceptualized (Tienhaara, Orsini, and Falkner, this book, chapter 3)? What does power mean in the context of scientific networks (Gupta et al., this book, chapter 4)? And to what extent is power a meaningful variable when it comes to new types of transnational governance arrangements beyond traditional intergovernmental collaboration (Bulkeley et al., this book, chapter 7)? Power resources and relationships of power matter in domestic politics and global governance. Yet in global governance, power is generally more diffused. It rests with more actors and it is less easily translated from one issue or political context to another. It is in this context that this book has also investigated the remaining or reemerging relevance of the state, as an actor and as a site, in global environmental governance (Compagnon, Chan, and Mert, this book, chapter 11).

Third, many contributions to this book emphasize the relevance of new types of legitimization in the diffuse and partially private systems of global governance. When non-nation state actors such as international bureaucracies, global corporations, or scientific advisory bodies gain influence in shaping global governance, questions of their accountability and legitimacy arise. When transnational environmental regimes such as the Forest Stewardship Council—which excludes states as participants— set standards that widely influence outcomes, issues of the democratic quality of these new types of governance emerge (Pattberg, this book, chapter 5). Also, the growing reliance on transnational public-private partnerships in global environmental governance increases scholarly interest in questions of legitimacy (in particular regarding participation, accountability, and deliberation; see Bäckstrand et al., this book, chapter 6; also Pattberg et al. 2012). Moreover, diffuse settings of vertical and horizontal interlinkages in global governance—as studied in part III of this book—blur issues of accountability and legitimacy. Once governance occurs at multiple levels and in multiple arenas, it becomes difficult to locate sources of legitimate authority (Kluvánková-Oravská and Chobotová, this book, chapter 10).

In sum, the world that this book describes is a world that is more complex, diffuse, and at first sight more chaotic. Yet it is also a world that is still comprehensible, with new governance mechanisms and actors that can contribute to steering societies toward more sustainable development paths. However, these new actors and new mechanisms of governance, which often interact and overlap in complex ways, also are contested, as evidenced by many contributions to this book. What global environmental governance is and how it can be shaped in the future remains a political struggle, characterized by diverging interests and identities.

It is important to note that the overall findings presented in this book cast doubt on alternative research programs that build on the assumption of the state as a rational unitary actor with a preeminent role in global affairs. Given the plethora of new actors, mechanisms, and interlinkages in this domain, traditional rationalist-institutionalist research programs that focus on state actors and state interests appear to be of diminishing value. Game-theoretic reasoning on collective-action problems among state actors, for instance, hardly reflects the various types and locations of nonstate authority or the diffuse types of cognitive or discursive institutional influences, which have been emphasized by much of the research reported in this book.

Yet the role of the state—as one actor among many and an actor with multiple identities, interests, and interactions—remains crucial. Chapter 11 of this book (Compagnon, Chan, and Mert) has been especially designed to "bring the state back in" in global governance debates that have emerged and are sustained by the idea of authority and action "beyond the state." But what exactly the remaining role of the state is in complex systems of global governance that are populated by myriad actors is still not conclusively answered. It may well be one of the most exciting questions of the new phase of research on global governance to come.

Policy Reform

The numerous studies reported in this book and in the wider context of the Global Governance Project have also resulted in a broad array of policy proposals.

First, the increasing role of nonstate actors has not been without friction and has become the center of major political reform debates. Developing countries, in particular, often object to increases in the influence of nongovernmental organizations in international fora because they view these groups as being more favorable to Northern agendas, perspectives, and interests. Developing countries argue that most nongovernmental organizations are headquartered in industrialized countries, that most funds, public and private, donated to their cause come from the North, and that this situation influences the agenda of these groups to be more accountable to Northern audiences (e.g., South Centre 1996). This critique is often justified. Much research reported in this book, however, suggests that this should not necessarily lead to a decrease in the participation of civil society, but rather to the establishment of mechanisms that ensure a balance of opinions and perspectives.

An example of such mechanisms is the recent institutionalization and formalization of the advice of scientists on climate change (Gupta et al., this book, chapter 4). The key institution here is the Intergovernmental Panel on Climate Change (IPCC). The evolution of the IPCC is typical for the institutionalization of nonstate participation in global environmental governance: the panel has been initiated not by governments but by international bureaucracies—the World Meteorological Organization and the UN Environment Programme. It comprises private actors—experts, scientists, and their autonomous professional organizations—who are nonetheless engaged in a constant dialogue with representatives from governments. The history of this institution has been marked by a continual political struggle for influence, especially between industrialized and developing countries (Gupta et al., this book, chapter 4, with further references). When the IPCC was set up in 1988, only a few experts and scientists from developing countries were actively involved. This has led, as many observers from developing countries argued, to a substantial lack of credibility, legitimacy, and saliency of these reports in the South (Biermann 2006). Continual complaints from delegates from developing countries resulted in a number of reforms, which brought about an increasing institutionalization of the involvement of private actors of the North and South in this subsystem of global governance. IPCC's governance structure now has a quota system that resembles some purely public political bodies that are governed by North-South parity procedures, such as the meetings of parties to the Montreal Protocol, the executive committee of the ozone fund (Multilateral Fund for the Implementation of the Montreal Protocol), or the Global Environment Facility. Our research suggests that such politicization and institutionalization of nonstate involvement in global environmental governance might be regrettable to some (for example, for some involved scientists who long for a return to "pure science"), but it is nonetheless an important element to further the overall effectiveness of the governance system (Gupta et al., this book, chapter 4).

This holds as well for the many transnational environmental regimes, such as the Forest Stewardship Council, that have institutionalized detailed decision-making procedures to ensure balance in the consideration of social, environmental, and economic interests in their programs (Pattberg, this book, chapter 5; Pattberg 2006).

Likewise, the increasing fragmentation and segmentation of global environmental governance have led to important debates on political and institutional reform, notably to the proposal of a world environment organization. One rationale for such proposals—many of which have been published by our project in Biermann and Bauer (2005)—is that strong and powerful international bodies oriented toward economic growth such as the World Trade Organization, the World Bank, or the International Monetary Fund are hardly matched by UNEP, the modest UN program for environmental issues. The debate about creating such a world environment organization therefore has been going on for some time. Views were divided also within the Global Governance Project, with some members arguing in favor of institutional reform and the establishment of a world environment organization (Biermann 2000, 2005; Biermann, Davies, and van der Grijp 2009) and others cautioning against this idea (Oberthür and Gehring 2005).

Current policy research suggests that the best way forward here would be to initially maintain the current system of decentralized, issue-specific international environmental regimes along with existing specialized organizations, yet to strengthen this structure by upgrading UNEP from a mere UN program to a full-fledged international organization. This organization would have its own budget and legal personality, increased financial and staff resources, and enhanced legal powers. In this model, a UN environment organization would function among the other international institutions and organizations but governments would likely shift some competencies related to the environment to the new agency. The creation of a UN environment organization could be modeled on the World Health Organization and the International Labor Organization, that is, independent international organizations with their own membership. Such a reform has recently been advanced—based on earlier proposals—by the French government, and now enjoys the support of more than fifty nations, including all member states of the European Union.

A third line of policy reform proposals emanating from the Global Governance Project relates to the area of transnational institutions and mechanisms (see part II of this book). At present, numerous transnational regimes, public-private partnerships, and governance experiments compete for regulatory influence, normative power, and public attention. In this context, some studies reported in this book have proposed a gradual approach to further streamline and integrate existing transnational governance mechanisms (e.g., Pattberg 2010; Pattberg et al. 2012).

Similar to the case of the world environment organization, an argument for increased cooperation can be made in the case of transnational environmental governance. Increased coordination among, for example, the climate convention and the many related transnational partnerships that emerged from the 2002 Johannesburg Summit could be mutually beneficial (Bäckstrand et al., this book, chapter 6). However, similar to the discourse about a world environment organization, the possibility of administrative congestion and overburdening of already burdened bureaucracies presents an important caveat to such an idea. Therefore, a light coordination mechanism that would deliver real benefits yet thrive on limited resources could be an option. As a first step toward greater coordination between international and transnational governance mechanisms, a clearinghouse could be institutionalized that gathers information about existing nonstate environmental governance initiatives, evaluates their complementarity with international mechanisms, and makes recommendations toward improved integration. The Commission on Sustainable Development could host such a clearinghouse that would essentially provide an authoritative overview of the current landscape of transnational environmental governance. As an observer to various conferences of the parties, the commission could serve as the missing link between the international negotiations and the burgeoning arena of transnational environmental governance.

A European Perspective?

Despite close collaboration with colleagues all over the world, most research in the Global Governance Project was done by researchers based in Europe. This raises the question whether, and to what extent, the regional concentration of this research program has left its mark on the questions, approaches, and findings reported in this book.

Various hypotheses are conceivable. One could maintain that European political and historical experiences and subsequent national and regional cultures shape how global environmental governance is understood and analyzed. Today, many political decisions affecting the lives of Europeans are taken in multilevel governance systems in which the individual role of the nation state is diminishing (for an argument about the complex interrelation between old and new institutions in regional environmental governance, see Kluvánková-Oravská and Chobotová, this book, chapter 10). This longstanding experience with multilevel governance systems may foster more openness toward multilateralism among

Europeans—including European researchers—and hence influence research agendas and generate a more affirmative understanding of effective systems of global governance. A more positive attitude toward multilateralism might also stem from centuries of violent conflict among European nations, which might make cooperation a much more principled approach. Many European countries also evince a stronger role of the state as compared with, for instance, North America. This might foster a more positive attitude toward international organizations and their bureaucracies. Last but not least, some European countries have shown in the last decades a relatively strong commitment toward development cooperation, with transfer rates of sometimes well above the 0.7 percent target for official development assistance as prescribed by international documents. Again, this might give rise to a particular "European" approach toward global environmental governance.

However, although the many researchers involved in this project engaged in long but stimulating discussions on the similarities and dissimilarities of our research and on whether there is such a thing as a "European approach," we concluded that statements to this effect would be certainly exaggerated—and most likely wrong. Not the least it would do injustice to the many researchers and collaborators outside Europe who share the perspectives, approaches, and findings of the Global Governance Project. All researchers in this project have come over the years to a common understanding of global environmental governance that is reflected in the high degree of collaboration and coauthorship in the many chapters of this book and its underlying research. This builds on long-term cooperation within our region, supported by the particular funding policies of the European Union that stimulate intra-European collaboration. It is not, however, necessarily a reflection of a "European perspective" on global environmental governance.

Toward a New Research Agenda

This book does not only point to the relevance of core trends of global environmental governance that make it different from traditional interstate cooperation. It also points to many new areas of academic inquiry that are not at present sufficiently analyzed and understood. We therefore turn now to the question of a future research agenda in the area of global governance and global environmental governance in particular. We believe that this agenda should include five additional categories of considerations that have been studied only insufficiently so far: institutional dynamics and change, overarching institutional architectures, legitimacy and accountability, equity and allocative outcomes, and the appropriate methods for integrating governance research into the more formalized streams of earth system science.

Institutional Dynamics and Change

First, we see an important research need in developing a better understanding of processes of change in global environmental governance and the institutional dynamics that play an important role in the emergence, evolution, and eventual effectiveness of institutions (Young 2010). In more general terms, this is the challenge of analyzing at the global level the adaptiveness and resilience of social-ecological systems (Janssen and Ostrom 2006; Folke et al. 2005) as well as learning processes in governance (e.g., Siebenhüner 2004; Haas 2000; Parson and Clark 1995). This line of research should also pay attention to the larger discursive struggles about what constitutes effective and legitimate global environmental governance.

In addition, it is important to focus research more sharply on the governance of adaptation to widespread environmental change, notably, global warming and climate change. Most existing work has focused on institutions to mitigate environmentally harmful activities, such as emission of pollutants, trade in harmful substances or endangered species, or destruction of habitats. Only at the national and local levels have scholars seriously begun to study how institutions and governance mechanisms can adapt to the impacts of global environmental change and foster societal adaptation. This research will eventually need to expand from local adaptation research into a research program on the core functions of global public policy. Given that natural scientists predict widespread harm if current trends of earth system transformation continue (e.g., Rockström et al. 2009), scholars of global governance need to better understand what mechanisms can best assist in effective "global adaptation governance" (Biermann and Boas 2010).

Much research in these areas will require particular attention to research methodology. When it comes to adaptation, global environmental governance is called on to analyze and design governance systems that respond to emergencies that are merely predicted for the future but are likely to exceed in scope and quality most of what is known today. Adaptive governance systems that take account of changes in monsoon patterns, large-scale breakdowns of ecosystems, or modifications in the thermohaline circulation will need to deal with scales of change that are unprecedented. Whereas traditional social science builds on the development and testing of theories and hypotheses through historical experience, global environmental governance, which is inherently future oriented, has thus increasingly to rely on new forms of evidence and new forms of validity and reliability of empirical knowledge.

From Institutional Analysis to the Study of Governance Architectures

A second overarching conclusion from this book is that we need to understand better the overarching systems of principles, rules, and norms that go beyond single institutions. Most research since the 1990s has focused on the creation and effectiveness of single institutions. This line of research began with the many studies in the 1990s on the effectiveness of intergovernmental regimes (e.g., Brown Weiss and Jacobson 1998; Haas, Keohane, and Levy 1993; Helm and Sprinz 2000; Keohane and Levy 1996; Miles et al. 2001; Underdal 2001; Young 2001; Young, King, and Schroeder 2008; Young, Levy, and Osherenko 1999; Victor, Raustiala, and Skolnikoff 1998). Most of these studies have focused on the effectiveness of single institutions. Only recently has the increasing number and scope of international environmental institutions led to new research on their interaction, for example, in studies on regime interlinkages, regime clusters, or regime complexes (see Zelli, Gupta, and van Asselt, this book, chapter 8; as well as, for instance, Chambers 2001; Keohane and Victor 2011; Oberthür and Gehring 2005; Raustiala and Victor 2004; Stokke 2000; van Asselt, Gupta, and Biermann 2005; Zelli 2011). In other words, increasingly the debate turns toward what we describe as the overarching "architecture" of global environmental governance, that is, the entire interlocking web of widely shared principles, institutions, and practices that shape decisions by stakeholders at all levels in this field (see in more detail a conceptualization and new research questions in Biermann et al. 2009).

Legitimacy and Accountability

Third, the research reported in this book reinforces the call for a better understanding of the legitimacy and accountability of systems of global environmental governance. This understanding is important in its own right but also with a view to the effectiveness of institutions (Mason 2005; Newell and Wheeler 2006; Gupta 2010). The contributions to this book show, for example, the importance of legitimacy and accountability in the study of international bureaucracies (Bauer, Andresen, and Biermann, this book, chapter 2), science networks (Gupta et al., this book, chapter 4), and public-private partnerships (Bäckstrand et al., this book, chapter 6).

A stronger focus on questions of accountability and legitimacy is especially important given the focus of many studies in this book on nonstate actors and governance mechanisms. In purely intergovernmental norm-setting processes, legitimacy can flow from the accountability of governments to their citizens. Also, international bureaucracies can derive legitimacy through their principals, the governments, who are accountable to their citizens. Such long lines of accountability, however, have been questioned (overview in Biermann and Gupta 2011). Many authors see a solution in the stronger participation of various stakeholders in global governance. Securing the accountability and legitimacy of these nonstate actors remains problematic, however. Private organizations may derive legitimacy through their members or donors or from the environmental good that they seek to protect. Yet few citizens have the means to donate time and money to philanthropic organizations. Given the financial requirements of participation, more rights and responsibilities for nonstate actors in global environmental governance could thus privilege representatives of industry and business at the cost of other groups, especially in the international context with its high disparities in wealth and power. More research in this area is needed, including on policy-relevant dimensions (see for a conceptualization and more detailed discussion Biermann and Gupta 2011).

Equity and Allocative Outcomes
Fourth, we argue that with the increasing relevance of global environmental governance, allocation mechanisms and criteria—and thus more broadly questions of equity and justice—will become central questions to be addressed by social scientists. At stake are not only the costs of mitigating global problems. Given the large-scale and potentially disastrous consequences of global environmental change, questions of fairness in adaptation will also gain prominence. Compensation and support through the global community of the most affected and most vulnerable regions, such as small island states, will not only be a moral responsibility but also politically and economically prudent. This situation calls for allocation modes that all stakeholders in the North and South perceive as fair (Adger et al. 2006). Questions of allocation among nations are especially contested in global environmental governance (Adger, Brown, and Hulme 2005; Tóth 1999). In particular, the causes and consequences of different allocation mechanisms in global environmental governance

are still not sufficiently understood. Little systematic analysis has been devoted to studying allocation as an independent variable and to analyzing allocation mechanisms in relation to variant effectiveness of the core institutions of global environmental governance. Hence, given the growing relevance of global environmental change, allocation is certain to become a major concern for researchers and practitioners of global environmental governance alike.

Integrating Governance Research with Earth System Science

Fifth, we see an urgent need for improved methodologies and approaches to integrate social science knowledge on environmental governance and institutions into more formal approaches in earth system science, such as modeling and scenario development (de Vos et al. 2010). For the more quantitatively oriented modeling and scenarios research programs, it becomes increasingly important to include data on international regimes and organizations or transnational governance mechanisms. Numerous approaches exist in international relations and global environmental governance research to understand and measure the effectiveness of institutions and organizations to steer societies toward sustainability. Yet what is lacking so far is a concerted effort to bring this social science knowledge into formal modeling and scenario approaches.

Finally, and yet more important, the very concept of global environmental governance remains an issue for debate and discussion. Notably, a new long-term crosscutting global research program under the International Human Dimensions Programme on Global Environmental Change builds on another, more recent concept: earth system governance (Biermann 2007). The Earth System Governance Project was formally launched in 2009 and will last until 2018. Its Science and Implementation Plan (Biermann et al. 2009) adds to the concept of global environmental governance a new connotation that links institutional research to the eventual core concern of environmental politics: the ongoing transformation of the entire earth system, from global warming, large-scale changes in biogeochemical cycles to unprecedented rates of species loss. Earth system governance bridges levels from global to local as well as academic communities from natural science–oriented modeling and scenario building to political science and philosophy. Although the concept of earth system governance is still recent and requires more substantiation in research, it might well evolve into a powerful new paradigm that describes the core governance challenge that lies ahead: the long-term transformation of the entire earth system driven by humankind.

References

Adger, W. Neil, Katrina Brown, and Mike Hulme. 2005. Redefining Global Environmental Change. *Global Environmental Change: Human and Policy Dimensions* 15:1–4.

Adger, W. Neil, Jouni Paavola, Saleemul Huq, and M. J. Mace, eds. 2006. *Fairness in Adaptation to Climate Change.* Cambridge, MA: MIT Press.

Biermann, Frank. 2000. The Case for a World Environment Organization. *Environment* 42 (9):22–31.

Biermann, Frank. 2005. The Rationale for a World Environment Organization. In *A World Environment Organization: Solution of Threat for Effective International Environmental Governance?* ed. Frank Biermann and Steffen Bauer, 117–144. Aldershot, UK: Ashgate.

Biermann, Frank. 2006. Whose Experts? The Role of Geographic Representation in Global Environmental Assessments. In *Global Environmental Assessments: Information and Influence,* ed. Ronald B. Mitchell, William C. Clark, David W. Cash, and Nancy M. Dickson, 87–112. Cambridge, MA: MIT Press.

Biermann, Frank. 2007. "Earth System Governance" as a Crosscutting Theme of Global Change Research. *Global Environmental Change: Human and Policy Dimensions* 17:326–337.

Biermann, Frank, and Steffen Bauer, eds. 2005. *A World Environment Organization: Solution or Threat for Effective International Environmental Governance?* Aldershot, UK: Ashgate.

Biermann, Frank, Michele M. Betsill, Joyeeta Gupta, Norichika Kanie, Louis Lebel, Diana Liverman, Heike Schroeder, and Bernd Siebenhüner. with contributions from Ken Conca, Leila da Costa Ferreira, Bharat Desai, Simon Tay, and Ruben Zondervan. 2009. Earth System Governance: People, Places, and the Planet. Science and Implementation Plan of the Earth System Governance Project. *Earth System Governance Project 1, IHDP Report 20.* Bonn: The Earth System Governance Project.

Biermann, Frank, and Ingrid Boas. 2010. Global Adaptation Governance: Setting the Stage. In *Global Climate Governance beyond 2012: Architecture, Agency, and Adaptation,* ed. Frank Biermann, Philipp Pattberg, and Fariborz Zelli, 223–234. Cambridge, UK: Cambridge University Press.

Biermann, Frank, Olwen Davies, and Nicolien van der Grijp. 2009. Environmental Policy Integration and the Architecture of Global Environmental Governance. *International Environmental Agreements: Politics, Law and Economics* 9:351–369.

Biermann, Frank, and Aarti Gupta. 2011. Accountability and Legitimacy in Earth System Governance: A Research Framework. *Ecological Economics* 70: 1856–1864.

Biermann, Frank, Philipp Pattberg, Harro van Asselt, and Fariborz Zelli. 2009. The Fragmentation of Global Governance Architectures: A Framework for Analysis. *Global Environmental Politics* 9 (4):14–40.

Brown Weiss, Edith, and Harold K. Jacobson, eds. 1998. *Engaging Countries: Strengthening Compliance with International Environmental Accords.* Cambridge, MA: MIT Press.

Chambers, W. Bradnee, ed. 2001. *Inter-linkages: The Kyoto Protocol and the International Trade and Investment Regimes.* Tokyo: United Nations University Press.

de Vos, Martine, Peter Janssen, Sofia Frantzi, Philipp Pattberg, Arthur Petersen, Frank Biermann, and Marcel Kok. 2010. Formalizing Knowledge on International Environmental Regimes for Integrated Assessment Modeling. In *Proceedings of the iEMSs Fifth Biennial Meeting: International Congress on Environmental Modelling and Software* (iEMSs 2010), ed. David A. Swayne, Wanhong Yang, Alexey A. Voinov, Andrea Rizzoli, and Tatiana Filatova. International Environmental Modelling and Software Society: Ottawa, Canada.

Folke, Carl, Thomas Hahn, Per Olsson, and Jon Norberg. 2005. Adaptive Governance of Social-Ecological Systems. *Annual Review of Environment and Resources* 30:441–473.

Gupta, Aarti. 2010. Transparency in Global Environmental Governance: A Coming of Age? *Global Environmental Politics* 10 (3):1–9.

Haas, Peter M. 2000. International Institutions and Social Learning in the Management of Global Environmental Risks. *Policy Studies Journal: The Journal of the Policy Studies Organization* 28:558–575.

Haas, Peter M., Robert O. Keohane, and Marc A. Levy, eds. 1993. *Institutions for the Earth: Sources of Effective International Environmental Protection.* Cambridge, MA: MIT Press.

Helm, Carsten, and Detlef F. Sprinz. 2000. Measuring the Effectiveness of International Environmental Regimes. *Journal of Conflict Resolution* 44:630–652.

Janssen, Marco A., and Elinor Ostrom. 2006. Resilience, Vulnerability, and Adaptation: A Cross-cutting Theme of the International Human Dimensions Programme on Global Environmental Change (editorial). *Global Environmental Change: Human and Policy Dimensions* 16:237–239.

Keohane, Robert O., and Marc A. Levy, eds. 1996. *Institutions for Environmental Aid: Pitfalls and Promise.* Cambridge, MA: MIT Press.

Keohane, Robert O., and David G. Victor. 2011. The Regime Complex for Climate Change. *Perspectives on Politics* 9 (1):7–23.

Mason, Michael. 2005. *The New Accountability.* London: Earthscan.

Miles, Edward L., Arild Underdal, Steinar Andresen, Jørgen Wettestad, Jon Birger Skjærseth, and Elaine M. Carlin, eds. 2001. *Environmental Regime Effectiveness: Confronting Theory with Evidence.* Cambridge, MA: MIT Press.

Newell, Peter J., and Joanna Wheeler. 2006. *Rights, Resources, and the Politics of Accountability.* London: Zed Books.

Oberthür, Sebastian, and Thomas Gehring. 2005. Reforming International Environmental Governance: An Institutional Perspective on Proposals for a World Environment Organization. In *A World Environment Organization: Solution or Threat for Effective International Environmental Governance?* ed. Frank Biermann and Steffen Bauer, 205–234. Aldershot, UK: Ashgate.

Parson, Edward A., and William C. Clark. 1995. Sustainable Development as Social Learning: Theoretical Perspectives and Practical Challenges for the Design of a Research Program. In *Barriers and Bridges to the Renewal of Ecosystems and Institutions*, ed. Lance H. Gunderson, Charles S. Holling, and Stephen S. Light, 428–460. New York: Columbia University Press.

Pattberg, Philipp. 2006. Private Governance and the South: Lessons from Global Forest Politics. *Third World Quarterly* 27:579–593.

Pattberg, Philipp. 2010. The Role of Networked Climate Governance. In *Global Climate Governance beyond 2012: Architecture, Agency and Adaptation*, ed. Frank Biermann, Philipp Pattberg, and Fariborz Zelli, 146–164. Cambridge, UK: Cambridge University Press.

Pattberg, Philipp, Frank Biermann, Sander Chan, and Ayşem Mert, eds. 2012. *Public-Private Partnerships for Sustainable Development: Emergence, Impacts, and Legitimacy*. Cheltenham, UK: Edward Elgar.

Raustiala, Kal, and David G. Victor. 2004. The Regime Complex for Plant Genetic Resources. *International Organization* 58 (2):277–309.

Rockström, Johan, Will Steffen, Kevin Noone, Åsa Persson, F. Stuart Chapin, Eric F. Lambin, Timothy M. Lenton, et al. 2009. A Safe Operating Space for Humanity. *Nature* 461:472–475.

Siebenhüner, Bernd. 2004. Social Learning and Sustainability Science: Which Role Can Stakeholder Participation Play? *International Journal of Sustainable Development* 7:146–163.

South Centre. 1996. *For a Strong and Democratic United Nations: A South Perspective on UN Reform*. Geneva: South Centre.

Stokke, Olav S. 2000. Managing Straddling Stocks: The Interplay of Global and Regional Regimes. *Ocean and Coastal Management* 43:205–234.

Tóth, Ferenc L., ed. 1999. *Fair Weather? Equity Concerns in Climate Change*. London: Earthscan.

Underdal, Arild. 2001. One Question, Two Answers. In *Environmental Regime Effectiveness: Confronting Theory with Evidence*, ed. Edward L. Miles, Arild Underdal, Steinar Andresen, Jørgen Wettestad, Jon Birger Skjærseth, and Elaine M. Carlin, 3–45. Cambridge, MA: MIT Press.

van Asselt, Harro, Joyeeta Gupta, and Frank Biermann. 2005. Advancing the Climate Agenda: Exploiting Material and Institutional Linkages to Develop a Menu of Policy Options. *Review of European Community & International Environmental Law* 14:255–264.

Victor, David G., Kal Raustiala, and Eugene B. Skolnikoff, eds. 1998. *The Implementation and Effectiveness of International Environmental Commitments: Theory and Practice*. Cambridge, MA: MIT Press.

Young, Oran R. 2001. Inferences and Indices: Evaluating the Effectiveness of International Environmental Regimes. *Global Environmental Politics* 1:99–121.

Young, Oran R. 2010. *Institutional Dynamics: Emergent Patterns in International Environmental Governance*. Cambridge, MA: MIT Press.

Young, Oran R, Leslie A. King, and Heike Schroeder, eds. 2008. *Institutions and Environmental Change: Principal Findings, Applications, and Research Frontiers*. Cambridge, MA: MIT Press.

Young, Oran R., Marc A. Levy, and Gail Osherenko, eds. 1999. *Effectiveness of International Environmental Regimes: Causal Connections and Behavioral Mechanisms*. Cambridge, MA: MIT Press.

Zelli, Fariborz. 2011. The Fragmentation of the Global Climate Governance Architecture. *Wiley Interdisciplinary Reviews: Climate Change* 2 (2):255–270.

Glossary

This glossary of key terms is based on common usage of terminology in the Global Governance Project.

Accountability A relationship in which those who govern are subject to control and held accountable by their constituencies, for instance, through obligation to report on activities or the possibility to be rewarded or punished.

Carbon markets Emission trading venues in which specified quantities of carbon or carbon dioxide are bought and sold, often in the form of credits that represent the right to emit these gases.

Cognitive influence The influence of (transnational) actors to shape global agendas through synthesizing scientific findings and distributing knowledge and information to different stakeholders.

Earth system governance The interrelated system of formal and informal rules, rule-making mechanisms, and actor networks at all levels of human society (from local to global) that are set up to steer societies toward preventing, mitigating, and adapting to environmental change and earth system transformation.

Executive influence The influence of (transnational) actors to develop and maintain operational activities and capacities at the country level.

Governance The process of steering or guiding societies toward collective outcomes that are socially desirable and away from those that are socially undesirable. Global environmental governance describes this process at the transnational level in the domain of environmental protection.

Horizontal fragmentation The segmentation of governance into parallel, often overlapping, rule-making systems maintained by different groups of actors at the same level of decision making.

Horizontal institutional interlinkages Connections among policy processes, rules, norms, and principles of two or more institutions at the same level of decision making, for instance, between international regimes.

Implementation gap The perceived lack of implementation of international environmental agreements. Discussed especially during the 2002 Johannesburg Summit, where public-private partnerships were promoted as solution.

Input legitimacy   A type of legitimacy that focuses on procedures of governance, generally linked to criteria such as the transparency, fairness, inclusiveness, accountability, or deliberative quality of governance.

Institutions   Clusters of rights, rules, and decision-making procedures that give rise to a social practice, assign roles to participants in the practice, and guide interactions among occupants of these roles.

International bureaucracies   Hierarchically organized groups of civil servants that act to pursue a policy in the international area within the mandate of an international organization or regime and within the decisions of the assembly of its member states.

International organizations   Institutional arrangements that combine a normative framework, a group of member states, and a bureaucracy as administrative core.

International regimes   A set of implicit or explicit principles, norms, rules, and decision-making procedures generated by states, around which the expectations of actors converge in a specific issue area.

Multilevel governance   A type of governance that is fragmented vertically between different layers of rule making and rule implementation, ranging from supranational to international, national, and subnational layers of authority.

Nongovernmental organizations   Institutional actors that are not part of or predominantly funded by governments or states. They usually represent social, cultural, legal, and environmental advocacy groups with primarily noncommercial goals.

Normative influence   The influence of (transnational) actors to shape global cooperation through influencing outcomes of intergovernmental negotiations at various stages of international and transnational policy making.

Output legitimacy   A type of legitimacy that focuses on the outcomes of governance, generally linked to criteria such as effectiveness and problem-solving capacities of governance.

Participation   The involvement and representation of stakeholders (e.g., individuals or societal groups, NGOs, or businesses) in the negotiation and implementation of institutions and other policy-making processes.

Policy convergence   The process in which institutional frameworks and regulatory approaches in a policy area become more and more similar.

Policy divergence   The process by which policy making in different countries or constituencies (increasingly) differs according to local or national needs and preferences.

Regime conflict   A situation when two or more international regimes with (partially) contradictory rules or rule-related behavior interact and functionally overlap in the international arena, negatively affecting the effectiveness of at least one of the regimes.

Regime interplay   A situation when the operation of one institutional arrangement affects the outputs, outcomes, and impacts of another or others.

Regimes   *See* International regimes.

Specialized agencies Independent organizations of the United Nations established through intergovernmental agreement as legally autonomous bodies with their own governing bodies, budgets, and secretariats.

Sustainable development Commonly defined as development that meets the needs of the present without compromising the ability of future generations to meet their own needs.

Transnational business actors Private corporations or industry associations acting beyond national borders.

Transnational (environmental) regimes Sets of norms, rules, and decision-making procedures that are made and implemented across borders predominantly through the activities of nonstate actors (and that deal with environmental concerns). Mechanisms include certification schemes, reporting initiatives, or accounting standards.

Transnational public-private partnerships Multisectoral network governance instruments that usually bring together representatives of business, civil society, governments, international organizations, and other actors.

Transparency The provision of and access to information about the performance and effectiveness of, among others, political processes or institutional arrangements. It serves to enhance procedural legitimacy and accountability.

Treaty secretariats Bureaucracies within international treaties, conventions, or protocols, such as the secretariat of the Convention on Biological Diversity.

Vertical fragmentation The segmentation of governance into different layers and clusters of rule making and rule implementing among supranational, international, national, and subnational layers of authority.

Vertical institutional interlinkages Connections among policy processes, rules, norms, and principles of two or more institutions at different levels of policy making.

Contributors

Steinar Andresen is a research professor with the Fridtjof Nansen Institute, Norway, and a faculty member of the Global Governance Project. He was a visiting research fellow at the University of Washington, United States, from 1987 to 1988; a part-time senior research fellow at the International Institute for Applied Systems Analysis, Austria, from 1994 to 1996; a visiting research fellow at Princeton University, United States, from 1997 to 1998; and a professor with the Department of Political Science, University of Oslo, from 2002 to 2006. He was also research director of the Fridtjof Nansen Institute from 1992 to 1997. He has published extensively on international environmental politics.

Karin Bäckstrand is an associate professor (tenured) of political science, Lund University, Sweden, and a faculty member of the Global Governance Project. Her research interests are global environmental politics and the role of scientific expertise in environmental negotiations. Her dissertation explored the role of scientific advice and dominant framings of risk and scientific uncertainty in transboundary air pollution diplomacy. Her postdoctoral work examined the normative dimension of scientific expertise, encapsulated in calls for public participation in scientific decision making. Her research has been published in *Environmental Politics* and *Global Environmental Politics* as well as in chapters in international book volumes. She teaches at the Department of Political Science and at the Lund University Center for Sustainability Studies, where she has developed and taught a range of courses in environmental politics since 1997.

Steffen Bauer is a senior researcher with the German Development Institute in Bonn, Germany, a research analyst with the German Advisory Council on Global Change, and Germany's science and technology correspondent to the United Nations Convention to Combat Desertification. He is a founding member of the Global Governance Project, where he coordinated the research group Managers of Global Change (MANUS). He specializes in international organization and global environmental governance, with a focus on the United Nations, and has published widely on international bureaucracies, sustainable development, global environmental governance, and the security and development implications of global climate change. He is coeditor (with Frank Biermann) of *A World Environment Organization: Solution or Threat for Effective International Environmental Governance?* (Ashgate 2005) and (with Imme Scholz) *Adaptation to*

Climate Change in Southern Africa: New Boundaries for Development (Earthscan 2010). He holds a PhD magna cum laude in political science from the Freie Universität Berlin.

Frank Biermann   is the founder and director of the Global Governance Project. He is professor of political science and professor of environmental policy sciences at the VU University Amsterdam, the Netherlands, and visiting professor of earth system governance at Lund University, Sweden. He specializes in global environmental governance with an emphasis on climate negotiations, UN reform, global adaptation governance, public-private governance mechanisms, the role of science, and North-South relations. Biermann holds a number of research management positions, including head of the Department of Environmental Policy Analysis at the VU University Amsterdam and director-general of the Netherlands Research School for Socioeconomic and Natural Sciences of the Environment (SENSE), a national research network of nine research institutes with 150 scientists and four hundred PhD students. Biermann is also the founding chair of the annual series of Berlin Conferences on the Human Dimensions of Global Environmental Change and the chair of the Earth System Governance Project, a ten-year core project of the International Human Dimensions Programme on Global Environmental Change launched in 2009.

Harriet Bulkeley   is professor of geography, energy, and environment at the Department of Geography, and deputy director of the Durham Energy Institute, Durham University, United Kingdom. Her research interests are in the nature and politics of environmental governance, and she focuses on policy processes, climate change, and urban sustainability. She is coauthor (with Michele M. Betsill) of *Cities and Climate Change* (Routledge 2003) and (with Peter Newell) of *Governing Climate Change* (Routledge 2010), and coeditor (with Vanesa Castan-Broto, Mike Hodson, and Simon Marvin) of *Cities and Low Carbon Transitions* (Routledge 2011). She is an editor of *Environment and Planning C,* and from 2008 to 2011 was editor of *Policy and Governance* for WIREs Climate Change. She currently holds a Climate Change Leadership Fellowship, "Urban Transitions: Climate Change, Global Cities, and the Transformation of Socio-technical Systems," from the UK's Economic and Social Research Council. In 2007, Bulkeley was awarded a Philip Leverhulme Prize in recognition of her research in this field, under which she is currently examining the governing of climate change beyond the state in the United Kingdom.

Per-Olof Busch   is postdoctoral researcher and lecturer at the Chair of International Organizations and Public Policy at the Faculty of Economics and Social Sciences of the University of Potsdam, Germany. His current research focuses on international institutions and organizations; the role of communication, emulation, and learning in international policy coordination; the repercussions of political and economic globalization on national and international politics; and crossnational policy diffusion and policy convergence. Within this context, he specializes in the study of international environmental politics and the comparison of national environmental policies. He is a fellow of the Global Governance Project; member of the management committee of the European COST Action, "The Transformation of Global Environmental Governance: Risks and Opportunities"; and one of three speakers of the Environmental Policy and Global Change section of the German Political Science Association.

Sabine Campe is a senior consultant at SEEK Development, a global health and development consulting group, and a former fellow of the Global Governance Project. She is an adviser to the GAVI Alliance in Germany and leads the European Development Platform, an online resource about bilateral activities of major European donors. She has been research associate at Freie Universität Berlin and the Potsdam Institute for Climate Impact Research, Germany, and a visiting researcher at VU University Amsterdam, the Netherlands. She has published articles on development policy, public-private partnerships, and intergovernmental organizations. She studied at Columbia University, New School University, and Freie Universität Berlin, where she received an MA in international relations.

Sander Chan is a doctoral candidate in international environmental governance with the Department of Environmental Policy Analysis, Institute for Environmental Studies, VU University Amsterdam, the Netherlands. He is also a research fellow under the EU Science and Technology Fellowship Program in China, hosted by Renmin University of China's School of Environment and Natural Resources, and a fellow of the Global Governance Project. He specializes in the application of global environmental governance instruments in China. Currently, he is conducting research on the effectiveness and legitimacy of partnership governance in China's forestry and biodiversity policy. The research is part of a project on partnerships for sustainable development at VU University Amsterdam, funded by the Netherlands Organisation for Scientific Research, which included the development of the Global Sustainability Partnerships Database. He also organized a 2009 EU Roundtable on the Future of Environmental Governance in China and coordinates the China network of the Earth System Governance Project.

Veronika Chobotová is a researcher with the Centre for Transdisciplinary Study of Institutions, Evolutions, and Policies (CETIP) at the Institute of Forecasting of the Slovak Academy of Sciences in Bratislava, Slovak Republic, and a research fellow with the Global Governance Project. She specializes in ecological and institutional economics, with emphasis on biodiversity and rural development. She has a special interest in market-based instruments for biodiversity protection, multicriteria evaluation, and participatory techniques. She holds a PhD from the University of Sussex, United Kingdom.

Daniel Compagnon is a full professor of political science and international relations at Sciences Po, University of Bordeaux, a researcher at the Centre Emile Durkheim, and a faculty member of the Global Governance Project. He teaches about the environment in international relations and global environmental governance, with a special interest in Third World countries. With significant fieldwork expertise on Africa, his research currently focuses on the actual and potential contribution of "fragile" states and "areas of limited statehood" to global environmental governance. He holds a BA in political science, a master's degree in social sciences, and a PhD in political science, all from French universities. He previously served as director of the French Institute for Africa in Harare,

Zimbabwe, and as professor at the University of the French West Indies. His latest book is *A Predictable Tragedy: Robert Mugabe and the Collapse of Zimbabwe* (University of Pennsylvania Press 2010).

Robert Falkner is a senior lecturer in international relations at the London School of Economics, United Kingdom, and a faculty member of the Global Governance Project. His research interests are in international political economy, with special emphasis on global environmental politics, multinational corporations, risk regulation, and global governance. He is an associate of the Grantham Research Institute on Climate Change and the Environment at the London School of Economics and Political Science and an associate fellow of the Energy, Environment, and Development Programme at Chatham House. After reading politics and economics at Munich University, he gained a doctorate in international relations from the University of Oxford. Before joining the London School of Economics, Falkner held teaching positions at the universities of Munich, Oxford, Kent, and Essex. From 2006 to 2007, he was a visiting scholar at Harvard University. He is the author of *Business Power and Conflict in International Environmental Politics* (Palgrave Macmillan 2008).

Aarti Gupta is a senior lecturer (tenured) in the Environmental Policy Group of Wageningen University's Department of Social Sciences, the Netherlands. She is also a faculty member of the Global Governance Project; vice-chair of the European Union COST Action IS0802 "The Transformation of Global Environmental Governance"; and co-coordinator of the thematic cluster "Environmental Governance" within the Netherlands Research School for Socioeconomic and Natural Sciences of the Environment (SENSE). She holds a PhD from Yale University and has held post- and predoctoral positions at the universities of Columbia and Harvard. Her research focuses on global risk governance, interlinkages between trade and environment, and the role of science, knowledge, and transparency in global environmental governance. She has published extensively on these topics in edited volumes and journals, including in *Ecological Economics, Environment and Planning C: Government and Policy, Food Policy, Futures, Global Environmental Politics,* and *International Environmental Agreements,* among others.

Matthew J. Hoffmann is an associate professor of political science at the University of Toronto, Canada. His research interests include global environmental governance, the politics of climate change, innovation in governance, and international relations theory. He is author of *Climate Governance at the Crossroads: Experimenting with a Global Response after Kyoto* (Oxford University Press 2011) and *Ozone Depletion and Climate Change: Constructing a Global Response* (SUNY Press 2005); coeditor (with Alice Ba) of *Contending Perspectives on Global Governance: Coherence, Contestation and World Order* (Routledge 2005); and has published articles and book chapters on climate change, multilateral treaty making, complexity theory, and international relations theory. He is currently engaged in a collaborative research project (with Steven Bernstein, Michele Betsill, and Matthew Paterson) on the governance and legitimacy of carbon markets, which is funded by the Social Science and Humanities Research Council of Canada.

Tatiana Kluvánková-Oravská is an ecological institutional economist and director of the Centre for Transdisciplinary Study of Institutions, Evolutions, and Policies (CETIP) at the Institute of Forecasting at the Slovak Academy of Sciences in Bratislava, Slovak Republic. She is also a faculty member of the Global Governance Project and of the new Earth System Governance Project. She served on the scientific committee of the International Human Dimensions Programme on Global Environmental Change (2002–2007) and has been vice-president of the European Society for Ecological Economics since 2010. She specializes in interdisciplinary research of nature-society interrelations, such as the human dimensions of global environmental change and the coevolution of institutional change in central and Eastern Europe, with a focus on biodiversity.

Ayşem Mert is a postdoctoral researcher with the Amsterdam Global Change Institute (AGCI). She wrote her doctoral thesis on partnerships for sustainable development and the discourses of environment and democracy in global environmental governance at the Department of Environmental Policy Analysis, Institute for Environmental Studies, VU University Amsterdam, the Netherlands. She holds master's degrees in International Relations and Environmental Sciences. Among other things, she has been manager of the 2007 Amsterdam Conference on the Human Dimensions of Global Environmental Change and managing editor of the working paper series of the Global Governance and Earth System Governance Projects. Her research appeared in *Forest Policy and Analysis* and *Environmental Values,* as well as in the edited book *Partnerships for Sustainable Development* (Edward Elgar 2007). Her current research focuses on the democratization of transnational spaces in global environmental governance.

Victoria Milledge lives in Durham, United Kingdom. From 2008 to 2010, she was the research facilitator for the Leverhulme Network on Transnational Climate Governance based at the Department of Geography, Durham University. Her research focused on understanding issues of legitimacy, influence, and effectiveness for transnational climate change governance initiatives, with a particular focus on climate and clean energy.

Amandine Orsini (née Bled) is a postdoctoral researcher from the Belgium National Fund for Research hosted by the Université Libre de Bruxelles, Belgium, and a fellow with the Global Governance Project. Her research focuses on non-state actors in international negotiations and on regime interplay regarding access to genetic resources and forests. She holds a PhD from the Institute for Political Science in Bordeaux, France (published in French in 2010). She has been a visiting fellow at Keele University in 2006, at Warwick University in 2007, and at the Geneva Graduate Institute in 2011. Her work has appeared in *Business and Society, Global Society, International Environmental Agreements,* among other journals.

Philipp Pattberg is an associate professor (tenured) of transnational environmental governance with the Department of Environmental Policy Analysis, Institute for Environmental Studies, VU University Amsterdam, the Netherlands. He also serves as the deputy director of the Global Governance Project. Further, he is chair of the management committee of the European COST Action, "The Transformation of Global Environmental Governance: Risks and Opportunities," and one of three speakers of the Environmental Policy and Global Change section of the German Political Science Association. From 2006 to 2010, he acted as the academic director of a series of PhD-training schools on earth system governance, supported by the EU Marie Curie Program. He was a visiting full professor at the Technical University Darmstadt, Germany (2009); visiting professor at American University, Washington, DC (2009); and visiting professor at Sciences Po Bordeaux (2007). He is the author of *Private Institutions and Global Governance: The New Politics of Environmental Sustainability* (Edward Elgar 2007) and coeditor (with F. Biermann and F. Zelli) of *Global Climate Governance beyond 2012: Architecture, Agency and Adaptation* (Cambridge University Press 2010). In 2009, he was awarded the Science Prize of the German Political Science Association for his work on sustainability.

Marco Schäferhoff is a senior consultant at SEEK Development, a global development consulting group. Before joining SEEK Development, he was a research associate at the Freie Universität Berlin, Germany, where he worked in a project on transnational public-private partnerships. He has published numerous articles and book chapters on transnational cooperation, development financing institutions, and international health financing.

Bernd Siebenhüner is a professor of ecological economics at the Oldenburg Center for Sustainability Economics and Management at Carl von Ossietzky University of Oldenburg, Germany. He is also the vice-president of the University of Oldenburg and coordinator of the master's program "Sustainability Economics and Management." He has been a founding faculty member of the Global Governance Project and serves on the scientific steering committee of the Earth System Governance Project. He holds a PhD in economics and master's degrees in economics and political science. He has conducted numerous research projects on international organizations, global environmental governance, social learning, corporate sustainability strategies, climate and biodiversity governance, and the role of science in global environmental governance.

Kyla Tienhaara is a postdoctoral research fellow in the Climate and Environmental Governance Network, a part of the Regulatory Institutions Network at the Australian National University. She is also a member of the Global Governance Project. Her research focuses on the intersection between international economic law and policy and environmental regulation. She studied the scientific basis of contemporary environmental problems at the University of British Columbia, Canada, before moving on to study international environmental law at the University of Nottingham, United Kingdom. She completed her doctorate in international relations at the Institute for Environmental Studies of the VU University Amsterdam. She is the author of *The Expropriation of Environmental Governance: Protecting Foreign Investors at the Expense of Public Policy* (Cambridge University Press 2009).

Harro van Asselt is a Marie Curie Fellow with the Environmental Change Institute at University of Oxford, United Kingdom, and a PhD candidate with the Department of Environmental Policy Analysis, Institute for Environmental Studies, VU University Amsterdam, the Netherlands. He is also a research fellow with the Global Governance Project. He has been a visiting associate at the Tokyo

Institute of Technology, Japan, and a visiting research scholar at the University of Georgia School of Law, United States. He is coeditor (with Andrew Jordan, Dave Huitema, Tim Rayner, and Frans Berkhout) of *Climate Change Policy in the European Union* (Cambridge University Press 2010) and has published extensively on issues related to global climate governance in edited books and journals, including *Global Environmental Politics*, *Climate Policy*, and *Stanford Environmental Law Journal*.

Stacy D. VanDeveer is an associate professor of political science at the University of New Hampshire, United States. His research interests include international environmental policy making and its domestic effects, the connections between environmental and security issues, and the role of expertise in policy making. He has received fellowships from the Belfer Center for Science and International Affairs at Harvard University's John F. Kennedy School of Government and the Watson Institute for International Studies at Brown University. He has received research funding from the United States National Science Foundation, the European Union, and the Swedish Foundation for Strategic Environmental Research (MISTRA), among others. In addition to authoring and coauthoring more than fifty articles, book chapters, working papers, and reports, he coedited several books, including *Changing Climates in North American Politics* (Henrik Selin, MIT Press 2009), *Comparative Environmental Politics* (Paul Steinberg, MIT Press forthcoming), *Transatlantic Environment and Energy Politics* (Miranda Schreurs, Henrik Selin, Ashgate 2009), *EU Enlargement and the Environment* (Joann Carmin, Routledge 2005), and *Saving the Seas* (Anathea Brooks, Maryland Sea Grant Press 1997).

Fariborz Zelli is a research fellow with the German Development Institute in Bonn, Germany. He is also a visiting fellow at the Tyndall Centre for Climate Change Research, where he served as senior research associate from 2006 to 2009. Since 2004, he has been coordinating the Global Governance Project's research group on institutional interplay (MOSAIC). From 2001 to 2003, he was a research assistant at the Centre for International Relations at the University of Tübingen, Germany. His recent publications include *Global Climate Governance Beyond 2012* (coedited with Frank Biermann and Philipp Pattberg, Cambridge University Press 2010) and *Climate and Trade Policies in a Post-2012 World* (coedited with Benjamin Simmons and Harro van Asselt, UNEP 2009). Zelli is one of three speakers of the Environmental Policy and Global Change section of the German Political Science Association. He holds a PhD in international relations and received the University of Tübingen's outstanding doctoral thesis award.

Index